BRITAIN
1945-1970

BRITAIN
1945-1970

L. A. MONK
Head of History Department
Trinity School of John Whitgift

LONDON
G. BELL & SONS LTD
1976

First published in 1976 by
G. Bell & Sons Ltd
York House, 6 Portugal Street
London WC2A 2HL

Schl. Edn. ISBN 0 7135 1902 9
Gen. Edn. ISBN 0 7135 1897 9

Printed in Great Britain by
W. & J. Mackay Ltd., Chatham, Kent

Preface

The writing of very recent history involves clearly recognised hazards. The long-term consequences of policies and ideas remain uncertain, and an author cannot be confident that he has emphasised the issues which later centuries will see to have been significant. Some matters which seemed at the time to have been important may have been treated at disproportionate length, while great trees may grow from acorns which have been overlooked. Developments may not be those anticipated by the policy-makers. Was the Welfare State the blessing that it appeared to be in the middle decades of the twentieth century, for example, or did it in fact weaken the enterprising spirit of the British people? Did the European Economic Community and other international organisations encourage the political unity of Western Europe or merely exacerbate tensions? Was Economic Growth really the ultimate virtue or only a light that failed, exhausting irreplaceable resources and polluting an over-crowded world? Tendencies which in the 1950s and 1960s may have appeared inevitable and necessary may be proved by time to have been serious errors, and the historians who welcomed them may earn only condemnation for lack of judgment.

However, uncertainties of this kind should not prevent mortals from venturing along paths which angels might prefer to avoid. It can at least be claimed that, with Press, radio, television and statisticians more able than ever before to present information to the world, the main facts are generally discoverable. On only a very small number of important developments, such as the Suez war of 1956, has essential information been concealed for as long as a decade. The historian must be more troubled by a superabundance of published material than by an insufficiency. Furthermore, the B.B.C. and the compilers of week-by-week or annual summaries of events have striven conscientiously to make available their raw material in as unbiased a manner as possible. They may have selected for emphasis items which will later seem trivial; but they have not left the historian with an otherwise partisan record, and it is not, therefore,

v

inevitable that contemporary history should be less than objective history.

This book was written in the belief that a straightforward general survey was needed to occupy the gap between the necessarily rather brief final chapters of histories covering a considerably longer span and the detailed monographs on particular aspects of post-war Britain. It is primarily and intentionally a political history, bestowing greatest attention on issues in which governments have been involved. Problems of the economy and of foreign relations therefore dominate. Some stress has been laid on the conversion of Empire to Commonwealth, lest the importance to several generations of the British of overseas possessions and the problems that they created for British governments as they approached independence should be unjustifiably forgotten. Lastly, since governments play a part (which, should, perhaps, not be exaggerated) in moulding society, the changes in social life are also considered; and these entail some reference to the arts and to the effects on industry and agriculture of technological advances.

The book was begun with the needs of students of History in mind but it was finished in the hope that it might equally serve anyone who might wish to be reminded of the principal events and characteristics of a period which, if not often dramatic, at least brought rapid, extensive and lastingly significant changes in Britain's social, economic, imperial and cultural life.

The author would like to acknowledge the following sources which have proved so valuable in the preparation of this book.

For the later years of the period it was necessary to turn for material to the Press, to the weeklies and annuals, *The Times*, *The Listener*, *The Economist*. Many quotations from politicians and others have been reproduced by permission of Keesing's *Contemporary Archives* (Longman Group Limited). *Britain: an Official Handbook*, and *Whitaker's Almanack* become important sources of information for the historian when, for most others, they appear to be out of date. The *Annual Register of World Events* and *The Statesman's Year Book* are useful. Essential statistics are provided in the *Annual Abstract of Statistics*, in the publications of the London and Cambridge Economic Service, and in the Central Statistical Office's *Social Trends*. A. F. Sillitoe's *Britain in Figures* is interesting. Details of all kinds relating to the politics of the period are to be found in *British Political*

Facts by David Butler and Jennie Freeman.

On the earlier years of the period it was less necessary to resort to the daily Press and annual reviews. A number of valuable surveys of the economy were available: by Sidney Pollard, A. J. Younger, J. C. R. Dow, Andrew Shonfield, Samuel Brittan, G. D. N. Worswick and P. H. Ady (editors), Michael Stewart, J. and A.-M. Hackett. The Welfare State was examined in books by Pauline Gregg and Maurice Bruce. Studies of the social scene were written by Harry Hopkins, Anthony Sampson, Arthur Marwick and Bernard Levin; others were edited by Michael Sissons and Philip French, Vernon Bogdanor and Robert Skidelsky. C. M. Woodhouse considered British foreign policy in general; Uwe Kitzinger, Richard Mayne, Nora Beloff and Miriam Camps concentrated on the moves towards European unity and the Common Market negotiations, Anthony Nutting and Hugh Thomas on the Suez war. Elizabeth Monroe reviewed British policy in the Middle East, while books by Ian Stephens, Percival Spear, Nicholas Mansergh, Penderel Moon and Hugh Tinker were among those which were found valuable on India and Pakistan. John Hatch, Kenneth Kirkwood, Kenneth Ingham and Basil Davidson dealt with African issues, J. M. Gullick with Malaysia, Michael Balfour with Germany, Muriel Grindrod with Italy, Isaac Deutscher with Stalin's Russia and Edward Crankshaw with Khrushchev's.

Biographies of living politicians have tended to be polemical and therefore of restricted value. Anthony Sampson's account of Macmillan was helpful, though. Lord Attlee's newspaper articles on his contemporaries were illuminating. Autobiographies were written by Attlee, Morrison, Macmillan, Eden, Kilmuir and Butler. That by Hugh Dalton was the most revealing. Lord Slim's record of the war in Burma was a source of valuable information. So was Chester Wilmot's work on the war in Europe.

Among the volumes consulted on the arts those by Francis Routh on music, David Robinson on the cinema, Stuart Hall and Paddy Whannel on the popular arts and Peter Brinson on ballet contained useful facts of an up-to-date nature.

To these writers, among others, to a large number of unknown journalists, and to colleagues who gave advice on certain specialised sections of this History, the author is most grateful.

September 1975   L.M.

Contents

PART THREE: THE COMMONWEALTH

PART FOUR: 1964–1970

PART FIVE: SOCIETY, SCIENCE AND THE ARTS

Introduction

No generalisation that might be made about a period of twenty-five years in the mid-twentieth century could be immune from a charge of over-simplification. The history of Britain during those years was too complex for a summary in a single phrase. An Age of Austerity was followed by an Age of Affluence, and this in turn gave way to a period of doubt as it was realised that other countries were achieving more than Britain. An Age of the Common Man mercifully benefited from the work of uncommon men. Few trends could be observed operating in every sphere of national life throughout the entire period. While the graphs of inflation,[1] expenditure on such social services as health and education,[2] the number of cars on the roads[3] and the human population rose consistently, the very unsteady development of foreign trade revealed in the balance of payments graph[4] suggested the difficulty of describing a trend in all departments of the economy. The output of coal and cotton goods[5] and the number of trains that ran went progressively down. Trends among teenagers aroused interest, yet a high proportion of the young were clearly little affected by them. The more readers and listeners sought trends in literature and music, the more elusive did they seem to be. The main political parties failed, frequently, to follow the lines that tradition was believed to have laid down for them: at times between 1945 and 1970 the Conservative Party behaved in a remarkably radical manner, while the trade union supporters of Labour could appear to be one of the more conservative elements of society, strenuously resistant to change. As usual, the force of circumstances affected the pattern of events. Consequently the history of this quarter of a century is the history rather of a large number of different incidents and differing personalities than of a few easily summarised lines of progress.

However, the existence of hazards is no good reason for making no attempt at all to draw attention to some of the main features of the period surveyed by this book, and to compare the situation at its beginning and end. It is still possible to suggest various approaches to the period which might be helpful. In the first place, despite the impressions of deep-rooted party divisions conveyed by contenders for Parliament at the elections between 1945 and 1970, the areas of national agreement were in fact very much more extensive than areas of dispute.[6] If any single character symbolised the twenty-five years after 1945, it was 'Butskell', half Conservative, half Labour, both halves Liberal in spirit. Foreign and colonial policy and the essentials of the Welfare State produced no significant controversy. Economic crises and recoveries occurred regardless of the parties that chanced at the time to hold power. The period was indeed one of 'consensus' politics, during which extremists on either wing made little real impact. Britain experienced none of the problems created for other European powers in the twentieth century by large Fascist or Communist minorities. It suffered no *coup d'état* of the kind which affected every small East European country in the late 1940s. Governments lasted much longer than they did during much of the period in France or Italy. Only at the end of the 1960s did extremist doctrines lead to violence: in Northern Ireland. If Britain enjoyed any genuine, undoubted successes during the 1950s and 1960s it was in spheres like music and ballet, broadcasting and scholarship, agriculture and the creation of national parks, which were at no time the material of political controversy. One of the essential purposes of this book is to draw attention to historical facts of this sort.

The period began with the British striving to reconstruct after the war in the face of formidable financial difficulties and an ominous relationship with Communist ex-Allies.[7] Compared with developments after the First World War the policies which were adopted during the late 1940s and 1950s brought some substantial successes. Unemployment remained even lower than had been envisaged by the architects of the final stages of the the Welfare State, whereas at least 10 per cent of insured workers had been unemployed in every year but one from 1921 to 1939. Strikes involved the loss of far fewer working days than had been lost in nearly every year of the early 1920s.[8] Wartime technological inventions and medical advances were seen to be of lasting value.[9] The idealism expressed in a series of war-time White Papers and other proposals for reconstruction did not fade with the end of the fighting, and Britain was able to embark on a phase of social reforms as important as any in its history. Cynics may have attacked Harold Macmillan for claiming after a decade and a half of peace that Britons had never had it so good; but the statistical and statutory evidence in fact justified the comment.

Abroad Britain had neither the wealth, power nor inclination to assert its traditional authority in the Middle East and India in opposition to vigorous nationalism,[10] and it had to share with the United States much of the hostility of the Soviet Union.[11] But in the Western world it had during the war earned respect which was not immediately effaced by failures and misfortunes. In collaboration with an America which no longer sought to withdraw into isolation it played a part in restoring peace to the West, and the experience of the following decades suggested that the work had not been done ineffectively. It retained an Empire, most parts of which seemed in the late 1940s prepared still to accept their dependent status. In addition, it co-operated in the establishment of such international bodies as the United Nations Organisation, the Organisation for European Economic Co-operation, NATO and the Council of Europe.[12] Its people had been neither tainted by Nazi occupation during the war nor overwhelmed by the movement of millions of displaced persons immediately afterwards. In comparison with Central and Eastern Europe, where boundary changes and these population movements undid, in a couple of years, the history of centuries, Britain appeared uncommonly stable. Its institutions had neither broken down under the strain of war nor been revolutionised. The war had probably speeded up social changes, scientific advances and imperial independence, but it had not otherwise altered inescapable and predictable developments. The changes were helped by the presence in the government of men of experience who had, at least until 1950, a large parliamentary majority to back them.[13]

A quarter of a century later grounds existed for some disillusionment. Endeavours to create an economically stable country had met with only limited success. Serious balance of payments deficits had developed with increasing frequency.[14] Devaluation of the pound had twice been needed to rectify British disadvantages. Inflation had continued throughout the period, even during the 1950s and early 1960s, when prices of the imported raw materials and fuel of industry had fluctuated comparatively little.[15] By 1970 very substantial wage demands and an increase in the number of days lost through strikes threatened to counterbalance a triumphant turn for the better in the sphere of international trade. The Welfare State appeared to have generated greed, the Affluent Society to have become a Permissive Society.[16] Meanwhile, the social antagonisms stimulated by a rapidly rising number of coloured immigrants had forced governments of both parties to abandon traditional policies of asylum.[17] Antagonisms in Northern Ireland[18] were beginning to prove intractable, reminiscent on a small scale of the communal passions which had produced massacres on the frontiers of India and Pakistan after the grant of independence to these dominions. Within a decade all Britain's colonies in Africa and most of them elsewhere had been surrendered, and little now remained of an Empire which in 1939 had seemed so secure. Disharmony and the abandonment of democratic practices in countries which had formerly been British dependencies were inspiring doubts about the virtues of the Commonwealth[19] at the same time as British endeavours to form a new association, with the European Economic Community, were ending in rebuff.[20] Germany and Japan, both shattered in 1945, appeared to be enjoying the consequence brought by ever-mounting wealth while Britain was paying a very heavy price for victory. The British were increasingly conscious that they lived in a world in which the U.S.A. and the U.S.S.R. were now the super-powers and that the years in which they possessed almost half the world's merchant shipping and controlled a third of the world's trade had passed for ever.

Fortunately, the history of a people has many facets. Endeavours have been made in this book to emphasise the positive successes as well as the failures. Even in an atmosphere of economic Stop-Go the real wealth as well as the money incomes of the nation continued progressively to rise. Even when current trade balances were adverse, invisible exports were consistently to Britain's advantage after 1947. Expectation of life rose, and opportunities for its enjoyment by the entire community, not merely by a privileged minority, were constantly expanded. Chances of obtaining a higher education grew with a proliferation of universities, endowed with an unusually generous ratio of lecturers to students[21]. Leisure was enlivened by a great increase in the number of cars, overseas package holidays and television sets, and by more and more opportunities for enjoying sports of all kinds. Britain emerged as one of the leading centres of the world for music and ballet. Its drama and broadcasting were enterprising and original, its imaginative literature vigorous.[22] At the same time it experienced unobtrusive changes in the agricultural field which had an almost dramatic effect on its farm output.[23] British technological inventiveness remained significant.[24] As anxiety increased about the consequences of over-rapid exhaustion of the world's resources of minerals and fuels and the pollution which had accompanied this process, so concern for the conservation of natural scenery, flora and fauna was strengthened.

In the sphere of imperial and foreign relations successes balanced misfortunes. Lives were lost, it was true, during the final stages of Empire in Malaya and Kenya; more were lost during the withdrawal in the Punjab, in Cyprus and Aden. But a greater number of British dependencies celebrated their independence with rejoicing than with bloodshed, and at least no British army suffered a defeat on the scale of Dien Bien Phu.[25] Historians will probably find it difficult to exonerate the Suez adventure[26] of 1956, but they will perhaps look more kindly on the part played by the British in NATO and other defensive pacts, on the diplomacy which led to a ban on nuclear tests, even on the endeavours to reconcile the interests of the E.E.C., EFTA and Commonwealth during the Common Market negotiations.[27] It is to be hoped that they will appreciate the generous sums of money granted or loaned to under-developed countries and the consciences which stirred British organisations like Oxfam and Christian Aid to assist the less prosperous or disaster-stricken peoples of the world.[28] Perhaps they will also approve of the measures undertaken to maintain Britain's reputation (and language) abroad by the B.B.C., the British Council, and the publishers who exported books worth, in 1970, more than £68m.

This book is not an adventure story and it contains little of the cruel drama that a history of the decade before 1945 would have. It does, however, chronicle a period in which changes of all sorts were probably far more rapid than in any previous period of comparable length. If the term 'revolution' could be applied to the industrial and agricultural developments of the late eighteenth century or to a diplomatic exchange of partners, it can certainly be applied to the changes during the 1940s,

1950s and 1960s in the realms of transport and television, university expansion and the arts, the transition from Empire to Commonwealth and the initiation of bold projects for the integration of European defence and economy, quite apart from industry and agriculture. In many respects the mid-twentieth century was for Britain an age of valuable and memorable achievements.

---

[1] p. 124
[2] p. 57
[3] p. 343
[4] p. 32
[5] pp. 355 and 356
[6] Chapter 15
[7] Chapters 3 and 6
[8] p. 281
[9] Chapter 3
[10] Chapters 11 and 13
[11] Chapter 10
[12] Chapter 10
[13] Chapter 4
[14] Chapters 5, 16, 22, 25, 37 and 44

[15] Chapters 17 and 38
[16] Chapter 45
[17] Chapter 34
[18] Chapter 43
[19] Chapter 42
[20] Chapters 24 and 40
[21] Chapter 23
[22] Chapter 49
[23] Chapter 47
[24] Chapter 48
[25] Chapters 26–33 and 40
[26] Chapter 20
[27] Chapters 21 and 24
[28] Chapter 42

1

The end of the war in Europe

By February, 1945, the German State was clearly disintegrating. Much of the Ruhr lay in ruins. The Russians had taken Silesia. German coal and steel output had been reduced to one-fifth of the output of the previous summer, and rail and water transport were so dislocated that it was hard to move all the supplies that were needed by the factories in southern Germany. Only about a quarter of Hitler's secret flying bombs and rockets, known as V1s and V2s, were reaching London, their principal target. Meanwhile, American divisions, reaching Europe at the rate of about one a week, were able to break through the Siegfried Line with negligible casualties. On the second of March they reached the Rhine opposite Düsseldorf, on the fifth they entered Köln, on the seventh they managed to cross the river at Remagen. Within five days fifteen German divisions were caught on the west side of the Rhine and were taken prisoner along with thousands of demoralised defenders of the Siegfried Line. American forces could then drive on towards Koblenz, over the Mosel, and across the Rhine a few miles south of Mainz.

On the northern sector of the front, in the neighbourhood of Wesel, the first really large-scale crossing of the Rhine was effected by troops under Montgomery's command at the end of March. Montgomery's wish now was to sweep on to the Elbe and Berlin. The Allies had ample petrol and other supplies and the aircraft with which to deliver them. Whereas on the eastern front German armies were still holding the Russians on the Oder-Neisse Line and blocking the easiest approach to Vienna, in the west they were breaking to pieces. The Western Allies could have reached Berlin and Prague, before the Russians had they all desired to do so. Yet at this point ideas on the best strategy to be followed diverged, with consequences of profound

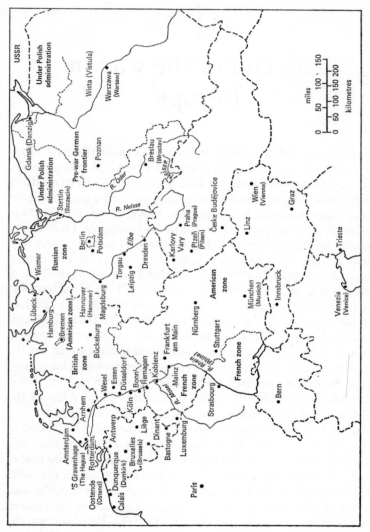

Germany 1944–48

importance for Eastern Europe and for relations between the war-time Allies. On 28 March Eisenhower, the Supreme Commander, without consulting the Combined Chiefs of Staff or Montgomery, sent a telegram to Stalin announcing that he proposed to concentrate on advances towards Dresden and the Bavarian Alps, where, it was believed, the Nazis intended to make a last stand. Other American military leaders supported Eisenhower.

Stalin cabled his approval of Eisenhower's decision not to advance on Berlin, claiming that the capital had 'lost its former strategic importance'.[1] The British, on the other hand, were dismayed. Alan Brooke (the Chief of the General Staff) and his colleagues felt no assurance that the Germans would in fact resist in the Bavarian or Austrian Alps. They feared that in advancing in the centre and south Eisenhower was failing to concentrate his forces adequately, and considered that the Supreme Commander's direct approach to Stalin had been a usurpation of powers which did not rightly lie with him alone. Churchill, who regarded the war as already won and was deeply concerned about the political future, was equally worried. His attitude was clearly expressed when he wrote to Eisenhower (2 April, 1945): 'I deem it highly important that we should shake hands with the Russians as far East as possible.'[2] Stalin might pretend that Berlin had lost its strategic value; but Churchill never pretended that it possessed no political significance.

TENSION BETWEEN RUSSIA AND THE WEST

These differences were of crucial importance. As symptoms of the growing estrangement between Communist Russia and the West, soon to develop into the Cold War, they need to be explained. Relations had, indeed, never been easy, and Churchill at least had had no illusions about the nature of Soviet Communism. The pact arranged by Molotov and Ribbentrop, the Russian and German Foreign Ministers, in August, 1939, the division of Poland between Germany and Russia a month later, Russia's war on Finland and its annexation of the Baltic States would have been grounds for suspicion even if the political philosophy of Communists and Western democrats had not been fundamentally divergent. Inevitably, the situation altered after the German attack on Russia in June, 1941, and for the time being Churchill was prepared to subordinate his feelings to the need to defeat and eliminate the Nazi menace. He endured Stalin's importunate insistence on a premature second front in north-west Europe and the apparent lack of Russian gratitude for equipment provided with great difficulty and at heavy cost. He revealed no anxiety during 1943 about Russian political designs for Eastern Europe. In May, 1944, he backed a proposal to allow the Russians a leading role in post-war Romania in return for non-interference with British influence in Greece. Even in October, 1944, he recognised that Soviet influence in Bulgaria and Yugoslavia, as well as in Romania, was bound to remain strong. And yet, all the time, his doubts were only temporarily dormant. By the middle of 1944 he was becoming increasingly concerned about Russian methods and intentions. In August Lord Moran, his doctor, recorded that 'Winston never talks of Hitler these days; he is always harping on the dangers of Communism. He dreams of the Red Army spreading like a cancer from one country to another. It has become an obsession and he seems to think of little else.'[3] He was not alone in his fears. Anthony Eden agreed that there were 'unhappily increasing signs of Russia's intentions to play her own hand in the Balkans regardless of our desires and interests'.[4]

In August, 1944, in response to Russian encouragement, the underground opposition to the Nazis in Warsaw rose in revolt against them. The Polish belief that the Russians were on the verge of crossing the Vistula and could give them military support may have been an illusion; but the Russian refusal to allow the Western Allies to use their airfields and to send supplies to the Poles was a cruel gesture that neither the Poles nor the Western Allies could pardon. The rising, crushed by the Germans after nine weeks, marked a turning-point in Anglo-Russian relations. A most profound distrust of Soviet Communism was re-awakened among men in positions of authority in Britain.

From this time onwards comparable causes of Western anxiety multiplied. Poland, particularly, remained a problem. Churchill was prepared to accept Russian annexation of its Eastern territory if only because the Russians had 'the right of reassurance against future attacks from the West',[5] and because the Poles could be compensated at German expense. But the

Polish government in exile in London refused to submit to this decision, and their premier, Mikolajczyk, resigned rather than accept the loss of the Carpathian oil fields and the city of Lwow. Churchill urged in vain a reconciliation between Poles and Russians. The Russians, with no obvious regard for the government in exile, established at Lublin a National Committee of Liberation which was in time to provide Poland's Communist government.

Meanwhile, a certain amount of tension began to develop between the British and American leaders over the political future. At a meeting in Malta between Churchill and President Roosevelt before their conference with Stalin in February, 1945, at Yalta, it became clear that the Americans were less worried about Russian post-war intentions than about British. Roosevelt suspected Britain's 'colonialism'. He told Stettinius, the American Secretary of State, that 'the British would take land anywhere in the world even if it were only a rock or a sandbar.'[6] He feared that Churchill's arrangement with Stalin about their countries' respective spheres of influence in south-east Europe was not without a sinister element of British imperialism. The despatch of British troops to Greece in December, 1944, to prevent the overthrow of the government by Communists, was regarded in America with suspicion. Churchill's claims that the British were in Greece at the request of a government of all parties except the Communists, in order that Athens should not be left 'to anarchy and misery',[7] did not impress such American leaders as Stettinius. British intentions in the Far East also aroused suspicions in the United States. Admiral Leahy, for instance, suspected that if once British forces gained control of Japanese or Dutch territory 'it might be difficult to pry them loose'.[8]

Doubts about Britain tended to be associated in America with an innocent faith in Russia. Roosevelt, his special envoy, Harry L. Hopkins, and Eisenhower could not envisage any fundamental conflict of interest between America and Russia. 'Of one thing I am certain,' Roosevelt wrote to Mikolajczyk. 'Stalin is not an imperialist.'[9] Since Roosevelt died on 12 April, 1945, he was spared the spectacle of Russian emergence from the war not only with the eastern half of Poland but also with Estonia, Latvia and Lithuania, and with territories annexed from Finland, Czechoslovakia and Romania. But Eisenhower and Hopkins, who had agreed with him on Russian intentions, were to live to see the extent to which British fears were justified. Even in 1970 Russians were still practising their neo-colonialism in eastern Europe, while a worldwide empire had been granted self-government by the British.

THE YALTA CONFERENCE

The existence of suspicions and disagreements could not easily be concealed when Stalin, Churchill and Roosevelt met at Yalta in February, 1945. When the Polish question was discussed Churchill contested Stalin's view that only the Lublin Committee should be regarded as the legitimate government of liberated Poland. He also contested the adoption of the Western Neisse as the new frontier of Poland. Roosevelt, determined that there should be no rift between America and Britain on the one hand and the Soviet Union on the other, tried mediation and only weakened the Western case. Further differences arose over the treatment of Germany. The Russians wished to see the country partitioned into a number of separate states, deprived of 80 per cent of its heavy industry, and obliged to pay reparations in kind amounting to about 20 billion dollars, half of which should go to Russia. Churchill, however, did not envisage the disappearance of Germany. He believed, moreover, that excessive reparations would make German economic recovery impossible and would impose insupportable burdens upon the occupying powers. Once again Roosevelt endeavoured to adopt an intermediate viewpoint, and three separate attitudes tended to develop. Russian and Western approaches to Germany were never to harmonise.

On the Far East decisions were reached at a meeting of Stalin and Roosevelt at which no British representatives were present. The allegedly non-imperialist Stalin not merely claimed all the territories that in the past Russia had acquired and lost (Dairen, Port Arthur and South Sakhalin); he wanted also the Kuriles (which had never been Russian) and the recognition of Russian influence in Outer Mongolia. Knowledge of these arrangements deeply worried the British, Eden in particular, since most of them would have compensated Russia not at Japanese but at Chinese expense.

Both Churchill and Roosevelt, reporting respectively after the

Yalta conference to the House of Commons and to a joint session of Congress, preserved the appearances. Churchill declared that he felt that the word of the Russian leaders was their bond. Roosevelt was sure that a more stable Europe than ever before would emerge as a result of the agreements that had been reached. In fact, though, the Cold War was developing even before the hot one had ended. On the very day that Churchill made his statement to the Commons the Russian Deputy Commissar for Foreign Affairs, Vishinsky, gave King Michael of Romania a two-hour ultimatum to dismiss General Radescu, the Prime Minister of an all-party government. On the day of Roosevelt's statement Vishinsky delivered a second ultimatum, demanding the appointment to the premiership of the Communist Petru Groza. In Poland the Americans found their activities strictly circumscribed by the Russians. The sole mission allowed to enter the country found itself prohibited from visiting any prisoner-of-war camps, from bringing in medical aid or food, from using American planes to evacuate the sick, even though at Yalta it had been agreed that Western missions should have the same rights as were granted to Russian missions in the West. The Americans were not permitted to use certain Hungarian airfields, despite agreement at Yalta. When negotiations with the German armies in north Italy were first hinted at, the Americans were virtually accused in notes from Stalin and Molotov of treacherously planning a separate peace. Stalin was reluctant to allow Molotov to attend a preliminary United Nations Organisation conference at San Francisco in April.

Indeed, the high expectations aroused by the evident approach of the end of military operations in Europe were plainly doomed to be frustrated by the new political antagonisms.

GERMANY DEFEATED

While the politicians argued the war went on. At the beginning of April Field-Marshal Model's entire army group was surrounded in the Ruhr. It resisted for eighteen days, but then 325000 troops surrendered, and Model committed suicide. On 11 April the Americans reached the Elbe near Magdeburg, and yet again Churchill and the British chiefs of staff urged that the importance of Berlin should be recognised. Most of Eisenhower's forces, however, were to the south of the Harz Mountains, heading instead for Dresden and the imagined National German Redoubt in south Germany. Eisenhower continued to believe that the taking of Berlin would be a mere show, and, backed in America by General Marshall, he left the Russians to be first in the capital's outskirts, on 21 April. At Russian request he also checked the advance of Patton's forces towards Prague. They stopped instead at a line through Karlovy Vary, Plzen and Budějovice. In the north, though, British forces were permitted to advance through Schleswig-Holstein, taking Hamburg, Lübeck and Wismar, and perhaps preventing Denmark from being absorbed into the Communist empire, even if they were unable to preserve eastern Germany and Czechoslovakia.

Russian troops reached the Elbe and made contact with the Americans at Torgau on 25 April. Hitler's suicide occurred on 30 April. The German forces remaining in Holland, Denmark and north west Germany surrendered on 4 May, and on 7 May General Jodl surrendered on behalf of Grand Admiral Doenitz and the Supreme Command. The war had ended with British or Americans in Rome and Athens as well as in Western Europe, but with Russians in Berlin and Prague and all the East European capitals. That Germany had lost the war was evident to everybody. What was less clear was who had won it.

---

[1] Sir Arthur Bryant (Ed.), *Triumph in the West: the Alanbrooke War Diaries*, p. 348, William Collins, Sons & Co. Ltd (London 1959)

[2] Ibid., p. 349, Churchill to Eisenhower, 2.4.45

[3] Lord Moran, *Winston Churchill: the Struggle for Survival, 1940–65*, p. 173, Constable & Co. Ltd (London 1966)

[4] Lord Avon, *The Reckoning*, p. 459, Cassel & Co. Ltd (London 1965)

[5] Chester Wilmot, *Struggle for Europe*, p. 629, Collins, Sons & Co. Ltd (London 1952). Churchill in House of Commons, 15.12.44

[6] E. R. Stettinius, *Roosevelt and the Russians*, p. 212, Jonathan Cape Ltd (London 1950)

[7] Wilmot, p. 637, Churchill in the House of Commons.

[8] Admiral W. D. Leahy, *I was There*, p. 300, Victor Gollancz Ltd (London 1950)

[9] S. Mikolajczyk, *The Pattern of Soviet Domination*, p. 65, Sampson Low (London 1948)

2
Victory over Japan

The sense of relief in Britain as German resistance disintegrated was, of course, enormous. The rejoicing was modified, however, by the fact that the Japanese war had still not finished, and nobody could predict, in May, 1945, that it would come to an apparently abrupt halt only three months later. For the British forces involved, the task of clearing surviving Japanese soldiers out of the more remote parts of Burma remained, even after the capture of Rangoon on 3 May; and Malaya, Singapore, Hong Kong and the British possessions in Borneo were still in Japanese hands.

Ultimately, however, victory would have been inevitable even if no atomic bomb had been employed. The survivors of the Japanese army in Burma were in a desperate position once they had lost their means of escape through the ports in the south of the country. Many groups endeavouring to escape eastwards were cut to pieces by British and Indian forces or drowned in the flooded Sittang, and by 4 August the campaign in Burma was over.

One essential factor in the victory had been the overwhelming British superiority in the air. Troops were transported by air and casualties were flown back. The forces were supplied entirely by air from bases built up in India after the calamitous British retreat from Burma in 1942. The Japanese, meanwhile, were unable, because of shipping losses, to transport oil from the southern regions of their Great East Asia Co-Prosperity Sphere, were unable to keep their remaining aircraft supplied with fuel and could therefore make no response to the British planes. During the later stages of the war the British and Indians benefited from the support given by the hill peoples of Assam and Burma, particularly the Nagas, the Kachins and the Karens, whose assistance did something to compensate for the apathy or disloyalty of other Burmese. The reorganisation of the forces

9

under Admiral Lord Louis Mountbatten had helped to overcome the immensely complicated problems of supplying an army serving in abominably hot and unhealthy conditions. Malaria, the principal complaint that had made it necessary in 1943 to withdraw 120 men from the battle zone for health reasons for every one who was evacuated with wounds, had been largely mastered by 1945 as a result of the use of mepacrine. And throughout the campaign of reconquest General Sir William Slim had proved a commander of exceptional ability. Quiet but resolute, he was prepared to admit mistakes, to accept advice and to give praise to his subordinates of all ranks and services.

While the British had been advancing through Burma, American forces had been progressively depriving the Japanese of one island conquest after another in the Pacific. By the summer of 1945 not only had the Co-Prosperity Sphere almost disappeared but the loss of about three-quarters of the Japanese shipping had virtually ended links between the remaining outposts and the mainland. The conviction had grown in Japan, even in 1944, that peace must be made, and during 1945 it was strengthened. It was true that the Army High Command and the War Minister resolutely opposed the idea, and that the Potsdam Declaration (26 July, 1945) calling for the unconditional surrender of Japan, military occupation, disarmament and a loss of territory produced a temporary hardening of the opposition to any dishonourable conclusion to the war. But on 6 August the first atomic bomb was dropped and much of Hiroshima was obliterated; on 8 August the Russians declared war; on 9 August the second atomic bomb was dropped, on Nagasaki. At this stage the Emperor ruled in favour of the peacemakers, and although officers of the War Ministry and the General Staff endeavoured to prevent the acceptance of peace without conditions, the decision was not reversed. The War Minister and some others committed *hara-kiri*, several doing so opposite the gates of the royal palace; but their gesture was futile. The cease-fire took place on 16 August, a new government with an imperial prince at its head was established, and an American army of occupation moved in.

Japan became now largely an American problem. The British were left with the difficulties of restoring order in Burma. They were also left (as were the Americans) with the far more lasting anxiety arising from the knowledge of the catastrophes inherent in the possession of atomic weapons. More immediately they were concerned with the repatriation of their troops, many of whom had suffered the heat and discomfort of the Far East, and separation from families, for more than four years. A British government decision that three years and four months should be the maximum period away from England was clearly just; but at the time when it was decreed it threatened to deprive the commanders in the East of many essential members of their forces at a period when it still appeared that another campaign would be necessary for the recovery of Malaya. As it happened, the atomic bombs and the Japanese surrender made the campaign in Malaya needless. The problem turned out to be not the loss of experienced men but the profitable employment of those who were not eligible for early repatriation or demobilisation. Some found themselves in the Dutch East Indies, others in India, where their presence was allegedly justified by fear of disorder as the White Raj approached its end. Few of these could feel convinced of the value of their service.

3

The cost of the war and plans for the future

The lists of names on the memorials to those who had been killed during the war were normally not nearly so long as those commemorating the dead of the previous generation, nor were they as long as many of the German lists. Yet they still had to record the loss of more than 397 000 members of the British and Commonwealth forces. Few of the pilots of the Battle of Britain or of the Fleet Air Arm had lived to serve throughout the war. R.A.F. bomber crews suffered heavy losses. So did those army units on which fell the full force of the fighting during Allied offensive operations. 35 000 merchant seamen and 62 000 civilians had lost their lives, the latter generally as victims of bombs, rockets and shells. At the same time about 200 000 houses in Britain had been totally destroyed; two out of every seven had been damaged in one way or another; and only about 200 000 new houses had been built during the war. Illegitimate births, juvenile delinquency and venereal diseases had increased. The government was absorbing three-fifths of the Gross National Product, and taxation was taking more than a third of the national income. A third of an ordinary consumer's expenditure was on rationed commodities.

Britain's balance of payments position had become critical despite government control of imports and the reduction of imports to 62 per cent of their pre-war volume. During the middle years of the war British exports had been reduced to only a third of their pre-war volume, and although the situation improved, the country was still exporting only 46 per cent of its pre-war total in 1945. Overseas markets had been lost. Much of the British trade with South American countries, for example, had been taken over by United States merchants. Invisible receipts had been badly affected by the sale during the war of a

12

quarter of British overseas investments, including investments in the United States which produced dollar assets. Furthermore, the war-time coalition had been obliged to borrow extensively, mainly by crediting the sterling accounts of the lenders. A total of £2879 m of new external debts had been incurred, largely as a result of the need to pay for the troops and services provided by India and the other less affluent British dependencies. Two-thirds of the 1939 gold reserve had been used up.

WHITE PAPERS AND REPORTS

Yet even in the most anxious years endeavours were made to ensure that the disillusionment which had followed the First World War did not also follow the Second. The Conservative party set up a Post-War Problems Committee as early as 1941. Another committee, concerned with social reconstruction, was founded by a large number of well-known figures of the moderate Left. Many of the ideas that were current were embodied in a series of White Papers.

The most celebrated of the White Papers was the report produced in November, 1942, by a committee presided over by Sir William Beveridge. This recommended all the essentials of a social security system to cover all ages and conditions: maternity benefits and family allowances; unemployment, sickness and disability benefits and workmen's compensation; benefits for widows and orphans; and pensions. It showed the need for a national health service which would enable everyone to obtain free medical treatment. Its recommendations were by no means revolutionary. They were, for the most part, not even new. Its novelty lay instead in its advocacy of a co-ordinated administration of all the various services by a single ministry instead of by nine different government departments, three different sets of local authorities, and a multitude of Friendly Societies and similar organisations. A single weekly contribution by each individual would entitle him, when need arose, to any of the benefits. Those who wished to pay for even better provisions, such as supplementary pension schemes, were to remain at liberty to do so; but the state was to provide the same basic advantages for everybody. All this, with its accompanying attacks on the 'five Giant Evils'—Want, Disease, Ignorance, Squalor and Idleness—had a remarkably popular appeal.

Within a few months 250000 copies of the report had been sold, and 350000 copies of an abridged version. Forty-two thousand copies were sold in the United States.

The Beveridge Committee, and the authors of a government White Paper published in 1944, all assumed that there would be no return to the conditions of widespread and demoralising unemployment which were remembered as the worst of all the pre-war social evils. Full employment was a *sine qua non* of a social security system, to take precedence over any other economic consideration. In a second report Beveridge and a group of economists who had been influenced by the writings of J. M. Keynes unofficially recommended measures which would reduce the post-war unemployment rate to 3 per cent, a proportion which was in the event to be regarded as alarmingly high.

Both before and after the appearance of Beveridge's bestseller a number of official reports were published with recommendations on town planning and the use of land. The *Montague-Barlow Report* (1940) indicated the dangers of the continuing growth of London, advocated the dispersal of one and a quarter million of its inhabitants, and urged the redevelopment of slum areas and the maintenance of the green belt round the capital. The *Scott Report* (1942) considered the planned use of land for efficient agriculture and forestry and recommended improvements in rural housing and in supplies of gas, electricity and water for the countryside. The *Uthwatt Report* (1944) sought to give planning authorities power to purchase compulsorily areas needing redevelopment. Also in 1944 Professor Patrick Abercrombie's Greater London plan recommended that the excess population of the capital should be housed in 'New Towns'. Meanwhile, a Ministry of Town and Country Planning had been created in 1943, and a Housing Act of 1944 provided for the expenditure of £150m on pre-fabricated bungalows which could be rapidly erected and occupied until permanent homes were available. Plans were laid for the building of 300000 new permanent houses within two years of the end of the war in Europe.

The last of the outstanding war-time productions which contributed significantly to the post-war Welfare State was R. A. Butler's Education Act of 1944. This was based on a White Paper published the year before, in which was envisaged the reorganisation of schools so that everybody should have the kind of education to which he was most suited. 'After 11 secondary education, of diversified types but of equal standing, will be provided for all children.'[1] 'This ideal, the essential feature of the 1944 Act, was at the time generally welcomed. Only later, when hope had given way to cynicism and disillusionment, was it to be doubted whether diversity and equality of opportunity could really be achieved simultaneously.

STIMULUS TO TECHNOLOGY AND MEDICINE

Few could believe while the war lasted that any lasting gain could arise out of it. Since its outcome depended largely on technological developments, however, the post-war world was, after all, able to make use of discoveries and developments which may have been made anyway in due time but would probably have been made less rapidly. The acceptance of flying as a normal method of transport, the phenomenal increase in the speed of air travel and the development of night flying owed something to war-time research. Jet engines had been patented in 1929, and the elements of radar had been developed by R. A. Watson-Watt before the war had broken out; but both received an incalculable impetus from war requirements. So did that branch of science known as solid state physics, which was stimulated by the need to produce miniature gadgets and led on later to the creation of transistor radios. Electronics was advanced by research into guided missiles. Acute though doubts about the morality of the atomic bombs may have been, the value of atomic research for peaceful purposes was not denied.

Medical research made essential by the war proved invaluable. Anti-malarial mepacrin, for example, had been produced as early as 1929 in Germany, but it was only when the harm done by malaria to troops in the Far East threatened seriously to affect the campaigns there that it was manufactured and used on a large scale. Another anti-malarial drug, paludrine, was developed by Imperial Chemical Industries towards the end of the war. Meanwhile, penicillin, discovered originally by Sir Alexander Fleming, was developed by Professor Howard Florey and manufactured in great quantities in America after 1941. The development of the synthetic anti-bacterial sulphonamide drugs (already discovered during the 1930s) and research into blood transfusion and skin grafting were also encouraged by the war.

---

[1] *White Paper on Educational Reconstruction*, H.M.S.O. (1943)

4

The revival of party politics: the General Election of 1945

The Parliament elected in November 1935 had continued to sit throughout the war. Its character had been almost frozen by a party truce: it was understood that if a seat fell vacant, the candidate of the party which had previously held it would not be opposed by candidates of the other major parties. This arrangement, however, had not been universally popular. It had provoked the emergence of a Common Wealth party and the candidacy of Independents who had not felt obliged to accept the truce; and in a number of cases they had been successful at by-elections. Clearly, a general election could not be delayed. Although the Japanese war was still not at an end, Parliament was dissolved on 15 June, 1945, and the election of its successor took place in July.

Inevitably, the party programmes contained much in common. The restoration of peacetime social and economic conditions featured in all the manifestos. So did the demobilisation of the forces after the end of the war against Japan, implementation of the recommendations of the Beveridge Committee on social security, the introduction of family allowances and a National Health Service, the educational changes foreshadowed in the 1944 Act, and the elimination of unemployment. Labour added the nationalisation of the country's principal industries and services. Conservatism added the leadership of Churchill and depended largely on posters portraying him. Most political observers during the election campaign assumed that the Conservatives would emerge victorious and that the Prime Minister of the wartime coalition would, as he hoped, be given the chance of winning the peace. Clement Attlee later admitted that he had believed that Labour would lose; and even more sanguine

17

members of his party, like Herbert Morrison, did not anticipate
a great Labour majority.

However, public opinion had moved further towards a change
of government than they realised. The Conservatives were associated with the distress of the 1930s and with attempts to appease
the dictators between 1935 and 1938. Labour presented its
programme more effectively than the Conservatives presented
their four year Plan. And for many of the electors, Churchill,
by himself, was not enough. Anthony Eden confessed that his
party had 'fought the campaign badly. It was foolish to try
to win on [Winston's] personality alone instead of on a programme. Modern electorate is too intelligent for that, and they
didn't like being talked down to.'[1] They had probably suspected
particularly Churchill's claim that 'socialism is in its essence an
attack not only upon British enterprise, but upon the right of
an ordinary man or woman to breathe freely without having a
harsh, clumsy, tyrannical hand clapped across their mouths
and nostrils.'[2] They did not believe, as Churchill did, 'that
the attempt to turn Great Britain into a Socialist State', would
'produce widespread political strife, misery and ruin at home.'[3]
Their voting certainly did not suggest that they anticipated the
introduction into Britain of a Gestapo, a secret police of a Nazi
type, if men like Attlee, Morrison and Bevin were returned to
office. When the armed forces' postal votes had been added to
those of the civilian population, Labour was found to have won
a landslide victory, with 11 995 152 votes (47·8 per cent of those
cast) and 393 seats out of 640. The Conservatives and their
National Liberal allies had received only 9 988 306 votes (39·8
per cent) and 213 seats. The Liberals, despite their 9 per cent
of the poll, won no more than 12 seats. The Communists gained
2 seats, the Irish Nationalists 2, the Common Wealth party 1.
There were 17 others, many of them Independents who had
been returned by the universities or had retained the seats they
had won during the war.

Predictably, Labour's greatest following was found in the
boroughs. No Conservatives were returned by Bradford, Hull,
Stoke, Wolverhampton, Leicester, Plymouth or Cardiff. Labour
won 79 seats which had never previously returned a Labour
M.P. Five Cabinet ministers and twenty-six junior office holders
in the government lost their seats, including Harold Macmillan.
Leo Amery and Brendan Bracken, Leslie Hore-Belisha, Walter

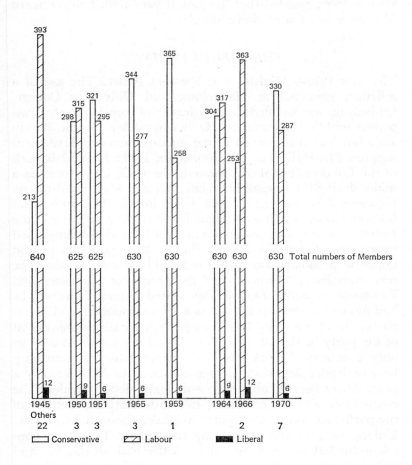

Party representation in the House of Commons

Elliot and Peter Thorneycroft. It was evident that Labour had won the support of about a third of the suburban middle class, the office workers and less affluent professional voters, in addition to their traditional adherents among the manual workers. They could not otherwise have gained so striking a triumph.

Eden found Churchill feeling 'pretty wretched'.[4] Harold Macmillan, commenting on the defeat during a television interview in 1969, asserted that 'he took it very well. I never heard him say a word of recrimination.'[5]

THE LABOUR CABINET

The new Prime Minister was Clement Attlee. The son of a solicitor, educated at Haileybury and University College, Oxford, he was the first Labour leader of comparatively prosperous middle-class origins. He had qualified for the Bar in 1906 but had then turned to the management of a settlement supported by Haileybury, in Limehouse. He had joined the staff of the London School of Economics in 1913, had served as a major during the war, and had later become Mayor of Stepney. He entered Parliament in 1922, when he was 39, and in 1924 became Under-Secretary of State for War. As a member of the Indian Statutory Commission between 1927 and 1930 he gained experience of a world beyond that of local government and domestic problems. During MacDonald's second ministry he was successively Chancellor of the Duchy of Lancaster and Postmaster-General. Despite this varied career, however, he had not so far been considered as a future leader of the Labour party. The opportunity was presented by the catastrophic defeat of the party in the 1931 election. Of all the Labour ministers only Lansbury, Cripps and Attlee were returned. Lansbury became leader, and since Cripps had been an M.P. for only a year, Attlee became almost automatically deputy leader. The competition was limited. Thirty-two of the forty-six members of the parliamentary Labour party had been sponsored by Trade Unions, twenty-three of them by the miners. They were conscientious but not very articulate. Attlee had his chance, and although other ex-ministers were returned at by elections during 1932 and 1933, it was he who became acting leader when Lansbury fell off a platform and was taken to hospital in December, 1933. On Lansbury's resignation in 1935 he was elected to the leadership. 'I have been a very happy and fortunate man . . . ,' he wrote in his autobiography, 'in having been given the opportunity of serving in a state of life to which I had never expected to be called.'[6]

To Herbert Morrison, Attlee seemed remote and difficult to know. Courteous and considerate to members of his Cabinet, he could be 'schoolmasterly and rather contemptuous'[7] to junior ministers and parliamentary secretaries. Harold Macmillan was later to describe him as 'a good butcher',[8] ruthless at times in his relations with his colleagues. Perhaps, though, without such qualities he would have been less effective as Prime Minister. Reticence might have lent authority to an ostensibly unassuming man on whom was imposed the task of controlling a Cabinet the members of which sometimes felt strong personal antipathies towards each other. And Morrison, who came to believe that Attlee had deliberately retained the leadership of the Labour party until it was too late for him to succeed to it, agreed that the Prime Minister was a good chairman of Cabinet committees. Meetings over which he presided 'were not so entertaining as those with Churchill in the chair but they were more business-like and ended sooner.'[9] Macmillan agreed. 'He listened to other people's arguments and put forward very few opinions himself. . . . He would sum up shortly, succinctly and decisively'.[10] Not even Churchill could stand up effectively to his brief and simple speeches in the Commons, as Macmillan conceded. Beneath Attlee's 'curiously matter-of-fact and pedestrian replies the whole great Churchillian fabric began to waver and collapse. Before his sarcastic and down-to-earth approach, imagination, romance, grandeur seemed to wither away.'[11] The approach was remarkably successful. He remained head of the ministry for six exceptionally difficult years and was ultimately responsible for legislation of real importance.

The Labour Cabinet was more heterogeneous than most twentieth century Conservative Cabinets. On one hand were men like Bevin and Bevan, who had experienced early poverty and had climbed to office with trade-union backing or through local government. On the other were university teachers and graduates, like Attlee, Cripps, Dalton, and a little later Gaitskell and Wilson, whose background was in some cases prosperous and comfortable. These differences of upbringing did not them-selves divide the ministry: Bevin and Cripps, according to Attlee, 'hit it off very well'[12] after 1945. But other factors must have made the Cabinet at times out of harmony: for example, Bevin had little in common with Morrison, whom he distrusted and disliked.

Herbert Morrison was Lord President of the Council and Leader of the Commons. He had begun his career as an errand boy and shop assistant, had become Mayor of Hackney, leader of the London County Council, and M.P. successively for South Hackney and East Lewisham. Patient and moderate, he sought to compromise rather than ruthlessly to override opposition. Macmillan regarded him as 'the greatest party manager in political history'[13] after Lord Woolton and was to praise his unpretentious yet gay and effective extempore speeches and the tact and good humour which gained the appreciation of both sides of the House. Morrison was to hope in 1955 to succeed Attlee as leader of the Labour party, though it was in fact to be the younger Hugh Gaitskell who was to be elected by his parliamentary colleagues to the office.

Labour's Foreign Secretary was Ernest Bevin, whose life before entering the government in 1940 as Minister of Labour and National Service had been spent as organiser of the Dockers' Union and General Secretary of the Transport and General Workers' Union. Experience of bitter industrial conflict before 1914 had left him with a hatred of exploitation and of the inequality and injustice of the social and economic system of the time. To this he had added in the 1920s and 1930s a wide knowledge of the industrial and social conditions of many foreign countries, and experience of negotiation for the improvement of working conditions. In a conventional sense he had enjoyed little education. As Attlee was to observe, his grammar was improvised. 'Life and the men he met were Ernest's book.'[14] Macmillan claimed that 'he did not affect the delicacies of diplomacy.'[15] But it was generally felt that he was a success as Foreign Secretary. 'Everyone speaks well of him, from the ambassador to the cleaners,' Attlee was to write. 'He inspired loyalty because he understood people and showed it. He treated people as human beings regardless of rank.'[16]

Aneurin Bevan, the Minister of Health, had suffered a background of the mines of Monmouth and South Wales. He had left school at thirteen, yet despite this had made himself one of the principal orators of his party. Tempestuous, sometimes arrogant and an element of discord in the ministry, he none the less gained an enthusiastic following, particularly among the constituency Labour parties. He had represented Ebbw Vale in Parliament since 1929.

The Chancellor of the Exchequer, Hugh Dalton, and the President of the Board of Trade, Sir Stafford Cripps, had known very different early environments to those in which Bevin and

Bevan had grown up. Dalton had been educated at Eton and King's College, Cambridge, Cripps at Winchester and University College, London. Dalton had become a barrister and a lecturer at the London School of Economics, Cripps a barrister and, between 1940 and 1942, British ambassador in Russia. According to Macmillan, Dalton, before the war, had been a 'robust patriot'[17] seeking to discourage Labour's pacifist attitude to rearmament, while Cripps, an eccentric but intellectually able 'parlour Bolshevist',[18] had 'urged the workers of Britain to refuse to make munitions to defend a capitalist society'.[19] To the jovial, indiscreet Dalton politics and life appeared to be great fun. To the fervent, ascetic, Christian Cripps policies that he was constrained to impose as Chancellor after Dalton rested not only on 'sound material arguments' but on moral truths to be pursued 'with an extraordinary white heat of devotion, even fanaticism.'[20]

Arthur Greenwood, at one time a lecturer at Leeds University, became Lord Privy Seal. Ellen Wilkinson, the champion of the unemployed of Jarrow, was appointed to the Ministry of Education. Chuter Ede, an ex-schoolmaster with local government experience, became Home Secretary. Emanuel Shinwell took responsibility for some of the more important of the government's measures of nationalisation as Minister for Fuel and Power. Lord Pethick-Lawrence was the new Secretary of State for India and Burma. At the Colonial Office Arthur Creech Jones became Secretary of State in 1946.

Few of the achievements of this Labour government were really revolutionary. Nearly all had been heralded during earlier decades by measures introduced by governments of varied party character or advocated during the war by independent committees and commissions. Problems of post-war revival had already been experienced after 1918. Yet Labour's positive contribution to the evolution of Britain was, for all the precedents, very considerable. A philosophy which had its origin in sympathy with the under-privileged and poverty-stricken guaranteed the completion of the Welfare State. The public ownership of basic industries and services was taken as far as seemed desirable to the more moderate members of the victorious party. Self-government for India, Ceylon and Burma brought to a culmination the series of Acts passed by pre-war ministries. Earnest endeavours to solve international problems by discussion in various United Nations agencies represented a revival of the hopes once placed in the League of Nations. In short, progress within a clearly recognisable framework, advance and continuity in equal measure: these were the essential features of the years of Labour government whose achievements have now to be considered.

---

[1] Lord Avon, *The Reckoning*, p. 551
[2] Churchill's Broadcast, *The Listener*, 7.6.45
[3] W. S. Churchill, *The Sinews of Peace* (1948)
[4] Lord Avon, p. 551
[5] Harold Macmillan, *The Listener*, TV interview (1969)
[6] Earl Attlee, *As it Happened*, p. 217, William Heinemann Ltd (London 1954)
[7] Lord Morrison of Lambeth, *An Autobiography*, p. 249, Odhams Press (London 1960)
[8] Harold Macmillan, *Tides of Fortune*, p. 51, Macmillan International Ltd (London 1969)
[9] Lord Morrison, p. 209
[10] Macmillan, p. 50
[11] Ibid., p. 42
[12] Lord Attlee, *The Observer*, 20.3.60
[13] Macmillan, p. 54
[14] Lord Attlee, *The Observer*, 13.3.60
[15] Macmillan, p. 56
[16] Lord Attlee, *The Observer*, 13.3.60
[17] Macmillan, p. 57
[18] Ibid.
[19] Ibid., p. 60
[20] Ibid., p. 63

5
The economy 1945–51

To those who had survived the sense of relief brought by the end of the war was profound. After the years of destruction, when life was cheap and resources were squandered on armaments, reconstruction could at last begin in a world free from the anxieties of the previous decade. The immediate concerns were a return to civilian existence, demobilisation and the restoration of a peace-time economic structure. The problems of the future could not possibly be so urgent or so calamitous as those of the recent past. Experience of the rapid disillusionment which had followed the First World War would, it was hoped, enable those on whom power had been bestowed to avoid a repetition of the mistakes and misfortunes of the early 1920s.

Popular expectations were to some extent justified. The end of the war had not found the country ill-prepared for peace, and the new government contained men of recognised ability who had held positions of heavy responsibility during the war. Some relaxation of the burdens could be anticipated. And indeed, despite the novel expenditure which the proposed new welfare measures would necessarily involve, Hugh Dalton, the Chancellor of the Exchequer, was at least able to reduce income tax: by £292m in 1945, by £82m in 1946, and by £87m in 1947. During the first two of these years taxes on consumers' expenditure also fell. The percentage of the Gross National Product absorbed by taxation declined by 3·4 in 1945 and by a further 1·1 in 1946. It was true that National Insurance contributions were raised in 1946 and at intervals thereafter; but these increases were, after all, designed to produce increased benefits. The overall reduction of taxation, leaving ordinary citizens with a greater proportion of their incomes at a time of unavoidable scarcity of purchasable goods, might have been expected to produce inflation, and this certainly occurred; but the retention of war-time price regulations at least prevented it from soaring out of control. Some anxiety was felt about the danger of serious unemployment as three million men were demobilised during the first year of peace; yet this did not in fact develop.

CRITICAL PROBLEMS: THE AMERICAN LOAN

Unfortunately, these favourable symptoms could not disguise the fact that from the vital point of view of international trade trade and finance the British position was critical. In a sense the problem was not a new one created by war. The financial yield of Britain's exports had almost always, since quite early in the nineteenth century, been less than the cost of its imports. In 1938, when imports had cost £835m, exports had brought in only £533m, enough to cover only 64 per cent of the cost of imports. Some of the deficit, however, had been covered by income from overseas investments. Before 1939 income from British property abroad had amounted to nearly £250m a year while payment to foreign owners of property in Britain had amounted to only £60m. The favourable balance of some £190m paid for 20 per cent of goods imported into Britain. Money was also earned by British merchant ships used by foreigners, and by British insurance facilities. Money spent in Britain by tourists contributed to the national wealth. Regrettably, by the 1930s these invisible earnings had been no longer bridging the whole of the trade gap, and this situation was enormously exacerbated by the sale during the war of a quarter of the overseas invest- ments and by the extensive borrowing necessary to finance the war effort. Mutual Aid arrangements with Canada, credits negotiated with countries of the sterling area and a few South American countries, and, above all, the Lend-Lease provisions made between Britain and the United States had been indis- pensable factors behind the victory. However, by 1945 they had left Britain with external debts of £3355m; and when, within a week of the end of the Japanese war, the Americans abruptly terminated the Lend-Lease arrangements, Britain was faced with a probable overseas deficit of at least £1250m by the end of the year, and comparable deficits for, perhaps, the three years to come. For Dalton the situation was almost desperate. British overseas expenditure could not suddenly stop. The armed forces in Germany and the Far East could not all be brought home immediately. Despite the expansion of agricultural output during the war, Britain could not exist without imported food. Without a dollar loan, as Dalton wrote, 'we would go deeper into the dark valley of austerity than at any time during the war',[1] and this would occur at the very moment when people were anticipating recovery and some relaxation of the stringent conditions of the previous six years.

For three months Lord Keynes and Lionel Robbins (professor of Economics at the London School of Economics, and Director during the war of the Economic Section of the Offices of the Cabinet) negotiated in Washington for the necessary loan. In the end Britain gained a credit of $3750m from the United States and a further $1250m from Canada; but the conditions were regarded in London as harsh. The loans were made dependent on the British acceptance of the proposals put forward at Bretton Woods, U.S.A., for the creation of an International Monetary Fund and an International Bank; and although these would no doubt have been accepted in any case, the circumstances of the time allowed the members of the Commons only five days in which to examine the complicated documents relating to the new organisations. The interest on the loan was to be 2 per cent, the capital was to be repaid over a period of fifty years, and Britain was to settle its debts to its sterling creditors. Finally, the point on which the British representatives came close to breaking off negotiations was the demand that within the demand that within a year sterling should be made freely convertible for all current transactions. This would mean that any other country which enjoyed a favourable balance of payments position as a result of its business deals with Britain could call upon Britain to supply it with dollars to an amount equivalent to its favourable balance. Only six of the Conservative members of the Commons voted for acceptance of these terms. The Conservative Front French abstained, and about a third of the party in the House opposed acceptance. The Labour Party felt obliged to surrender, but Attlee's explanation did not conceal the embarrassment which the government felt in making the agreement. Without the loan, he admitted, it would have been impossible to avoid hardships which no one had the right to impose on the British people at such a time. The government saw no alternative to acceptance.

Even more unfortunate than the terms of the loan was the rapidity with which it drained away. It soon seemed likely that the entire sum would be spent by the middle of 1948. This was the result not of unrestrained British extravagance but of a number of factors which were really not amenable to control by a British government. In the first place, the value of the dollar depreciated so rapidly during the fifteen months which followed the negotiation of the loan that the price of goods bought from America rose by about 40 per cent. Secondly, the responsibility for preserving the population of the British zone of Germany from starvation fell upon Britain; and when the American and British zones were merged in July, 1946, Britain had for some time to pay the costs of feeding both zones. Thirdly, after July, 1947, Britain became the victim of the predictable disadvantages of the convertibility of sterling. Many countries still suffering the effects of the war were in need of supplies; the United States was in the best position to provide them; dollars were required, and for those countries which had favourable trade balances with Britain, Britain was under an obligation to make them available. The results were reflected in the rates at which the government was forced to draw upon its American loan: whereas during the second quarter of 1947 the average weekly drawing rate had been $75m, in July it was $115m, and in the four weeks before 23 August, $150m. As Dalton explained, in a broadcast, 'sterling, alone of all the other currencies of the European belligerents, was freely convertible,' and 'the burden of the desperate dollar shortage of so many other countries was simply shifted to our shoulders.'[2] Convertibility was then, necessarily, suspended, and was not restored until 1958.

ENDEAVOURS TO KEEP OUT OF DEBT: MARSHALL AID

Nor, unfortunately, was the problem of the American loan the only economic difficulty of 1947. In February a fuel crisis deprived the country of heat and power, and while ordinary citizens suffered the effects of an exceptionally cold winter, unemployment rose temporarily from $2\frac{1}{2}$ per cent of insured workers to 15 per cent and industry lost an estimated £200m worth of exports. This was all the more serious since Britain had reached the end of 1946 with a balance of payments deficit of £295m and the prospects for 1947 were discouraging. British industry was, it was true, obtaining 2·2 times as much as in 1938 for its exports; but imports were costing 2·6 times as much. Furthermore, it was not easy in 1947 for exporting industries to expand. Even before the fuel crisis a 'manpower gap' of 630 000 had existed which could be filled only by men released from the forces and the armaments industries. Dalton, who had already managed to cut defence costs in his first budget of 1947 from £1653m to £899m, continued to seek a reduction of 10 per cent in expenditure on the forces and a limitation of such overseas commitments as the provision of aid for the Greek army against Communist rebels. Aid for Greece, in fact, was brought to an end; but A. V. Alexander, the Minister of Defence, would offer only a 5 per cent cut in expenditure on the forces and persisted in opposing what his ministry regarded as the excessively rapid contraction of Britain's military strength. Attlee and other cabinet colleagues also appeared at first to be unimpressed by Dalton's arguments.

In the end, however, to prevent foreign currency from draining out of the country and the balance of payments deficit from reaching catastrophic proportions, crisis measures had to be introduced. Food imports, especially those from dollar countries, were cut by £12m a month. Imports of American tobacco were stopped, on which the British were spending almost as much as they earned from their total exports to the United States. The petrol ration for ordinary drivers was reduced by a third. A half hour daily increase of work for miners was introduced. Programmes of capital investment were to be cut by £200m. In August 1947 (the month in which the convertibility of sterling was ended), the meat ration was cut, foreign travel suspended, the basic petrol ration abolished altogether. Dalton's emergency budget, in November, was designed to reduce spending even more, and, by taking money out of the pockets of the masses, not only to limit imports but in addition to check the inflation which was showing no signs of coming to an end by itself. Expectations that further taxes would bring in an extra £208m a year were more than fulfilled. Unfortunately, the problem of inflation remained, apparently interminably, to bedevil the economy; and, despite the crisis measures of the summer, the total deficit on balance of payments for 1947 could not be kept below £442m.

Unfortunately, too, for Hugh Dalton, the use made by a journalist of a slightly premature comment on the contents of the November budget brought an obligation to resign. The new Chancellor of the Exchequer was Sir Stafford Cripps. Harold Wilson succeeded Cripps at the Board of Trade.

Cripps inherited a predicament which was by no means peculiar to Britain. Other European countries were in a similar position, facing bankruptcy and the exhaustion of their gold reserves as they endeavoured to finance their recovery schemes after the war. Many were being forced to impose such restrictions on their imports of raw materials and fuel that industry seemed bound to come to a halt; and insufficient currency was available for food imports to maintain the strength of the labour force. An essential factor in the emergence of Europe from these conditions was the Marshall Aid generously granted by the United States. General Marshall, now American Secretary of State, offered support for a European recovery programme if the countries accepting it would first agree on their requirements and co-ordinate their projects. The Plan stressed the value of 'a large domestic market with no internal trade barriers' (in other words, the elimination of tariffs between the participating countries). Ernest Bevin, the British Foreign Secretary, normally distrusted 'continental entanglements' but he nonetheless took the initiative in giving substance to the Plan. Ultimately sixteen nations prepared a four-year programme, and in 1948 the Organisation for European Economic Co-operation (O.E.E.C.) came into being to put the programme into practice. From the point of view of the economic integration and recovery of non-Communist Europe the Marshall Plan was to be a milestone of great significance. Britain benefited substantially. Its aid from America amounted to £144m in 1948, to £244m in 1949, to £239m in 1950, and to £54m in 1951, after which the grants were suspended, their purpose achieved.

AUSTERITY

American generosity would not, of course, have succeeded had the British government not also made strenuous efforts to develop its own remedies for its economic problems. Sir Stafford Cripps maintained Dalton's austere policy, and, with his reputation for frugal living and for working fourteen hours a day, seemed indeed to symbolise it. As President of the Board of Trade he had encouraged industries to work towards pre-arranged targets, which may well have acted as stimuli to the production of goods for export. He had encouraged a voluntary dividend restraint, and from February, 1948, as Chancellor, he inspired a restraint of demands for wage increases which operated for two and a half years: during this period wages rose by only 5 per cent even though retail prices went up by 8 per cent. He refused to countenance any premature relaxation of endeavour. 'Our own consumption requirements,' he told a meeting at Workington in January, 1949, 'have to be the last in the list of priorities. First are exports, . . . second is capital investment; and last are the needs, comforts and amenities of the family.'

Such austerity did not have an immediately dramatic effect, but from 1948 to 1950, in important respects, conditions gradually improved. In 1948 a labour force which had expanded by only 2 per cent increased industrial production by 12 per cent. Output of steel, coal, textiles and agricultural produce especially improved. Investment in industry grew at a greater rate than had been anticipated, and 300 new or enlarged factories were completed in the areas which had experienced the greatest distress in the 1930s. Imports in 1948 rose only 4 per cent above their 1947 level, and a smaller proportion came from dollar countries. Exports meanwhile rose by 25 per cent in 1948, and there was a substantial improvement in the balance of invisible payments. The result was that in 1948 an overall balance of payments of £1m in Britain's favour was recorded. The trend continued. In 1949 the favourable balance was raised to £31m, and in 1950 it continued to rise, even more steeply.

One problem, however, remained intractable. The more encouraging trade figures could not disguise the fact that Britain still, in 1948 and 1949, suffered a deficit in its trade with the dollar countries. This became so serious in the second quarter of 1949 that a drastic restriction of dollar imports became necessary, both for Britain and for other countries of the sterling area. The restrictions were not immediately effective; nor was it possible to prevent an alarming withdrawal of gold and dollars from Britain by overseas creditors who suspected that sterling would be devalued and that the money owed to them would, in terms of the dollar, be worth less. In the end the devaluation which Cripps had striven to prevent appeared to be unavoidable. In September, therefore, it was announced that sterling would be devalued by 30·5 per cent and that £1, previously equivalent to $4·03, would henceforth be worth only $2·80. It was realised that this move would increase the price of goods sold to Britain by America (and by any other country which had not devalued its currency at the same time) and that it would indirectly send up the British cost of living; but it was hoped that before this occurred, British sales to the United States and Canada would increase sufficiently (fewer dollars having to be paid for each £'s worth of British goods) to bring the dollar deficit to an end. To some extent the hopes of improvement were justified. Between September, 1949, and the middle of the next year British gold and dollar reserves rose from $1425m to $2422m. All the reserves lost during the summer of 1949 had been recovered within eight months.

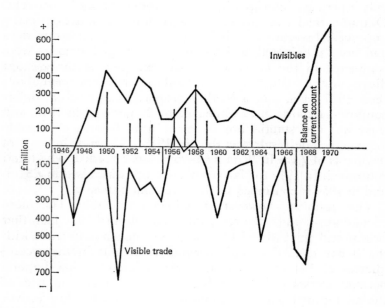

Balance of payments trends 1946–70. Upper graph shows balance of invisible trade. Lower graph shows balance of visible trade. Vertical lines show balance on current account (i.e. visibles and invisibles combined). *Source*: based on figures provided in the *Annual Abstract of Statistics*. Defence aid payments from 1951 omitted. Basis of calculation from 1966 changed to allow for net under-recording of exports.

The extent to which devaluation had contributed to the changes in Britain's fortunes remained a subject of debate. The American recovery from a transitory recession, and purchases in the United States of a greater quantity of wool, cocoa and other commodities from countries of the sterling area were factors which played an important part; and the earlier British cuts in dollar imports also contributed. The precise parts played by each of these factors could not be calculated. Devaluation, no doubt, had some ultimate effects on the cost of living in Britain, but since many other countries with which Britain had trading relations devalued to the same or a lesser extent at the same time, the exact impact was equally incalculable. What was clear was that at last, in the first half of 1950, the economic difficulties left behind by the war had been overcome. National output of industrial goods was increasing by about 4 per cent a year, and since domestic consumption was rising less rapidly, a 60 per cent rise in exports could be recorded during the three years of Cripps's Chancellorship. Imports rose during this period by only 14 per cent. Inflation had at least been prevented from getting out of control.

EFFECTS OF WAR IN KOREA

Unfortunately, when the situation appeared to be so promising, further difficulties developed. Overseas devaluations and domestic inflation, which had the effect of increasing the price of British exports once more, began to nullify the advantages of the British devaluation, and by the early 1950s the competition of German and Japanese products began to be felt. More serious was the impact of the war in Korea. The war resulted in an urgent demand, particularly in the United States, for raw materials. World-wide rivalry for the limited supply of such materials, which had developed even before the war broke out, was now exaggerated, and it brought about a rapid increase in prices. Between March, 1950, and March, 1951, wool and cotton prices doubled, while rubber prices more than trebled. Within five months (June to November 1950) tin prices soared from £300 per ton to £1280 per ton. Initially, Britain benefited. Gold and dollar reserves rose, and the balance of payments on current account for 1950 amounted, in British favour, to £297m. Some of the Commonwealth countries of the sterling area also benefited in 1950: the rise in prices of essential raw materials brought substantial dollar earnings to Australia, Malaya, Ceylon and some of the African colonies. However, symptoms of a deterioration in the terms of trade could be discerned, and the gains of 1950 rapidly turned to serious losses in 1951. Already, by February, 1951, the price of imports into Britain was 25 per cent above their 1950 average and nearly 50 per cent above their 1949 average. Higher prices were responsible for about two-thirds of an increase of £1100m in the British import bill in 1951. Such expenditure was difficult to avoid, since, in order to build up gold and dollar reserves and to reduce dependence on Marshall Aid from America, imports had deliberately been kept down the previous year, and further postponement of their purchase was not possible. Furthermore, the European Payments Union, established in 1950, called for the abandonment of quota restrictions on imports from countries participating in the Organisation for European Economic Co-operation, and consequently a sharp rise in the money spent on imports from Europe added to the problems of price increases attributable to the war in Korea. Altogether, the volume of British imports in 1951 was 16 per cent higher than in 1950. The rise in import prices between April 1950, and May 1951, amounted to 41 per cent, while the value of exports rose by only 17 per cent. Exports, moreover, were hampered by a steel shortage created by the government's defence programme and by a world recession in the demand for British textiles and clothing.

After May, 1951, import prices began to fall again, but the change did not come soon enough to preserve Britain from having an adverse trade balance of over £400m in 1951 or from suffering a fall in reserves which came to £110m in October 1951, and continued, at a less alarming rate, for the next four months. Britain also had to contend with the Persian seizure in 1951 of the Abadan oil installations, which obliged the government to spend more than £100m during the next year on oil from dollar sources.

The Chancellor during most of this troubled year was Hugh Gaitskell. From Winchester and New College, Oxford, Gaitskell had gone in 1928 to University College, London, as a lecturer in Economics. He had entered Parliament in 1945 and had risen rapidly to become successively Minister of Fuel and Power and Minister of State for Economic Affairs and to play an increasing part in the shaping of economic policy. He succeeded to the Chancellorship in October, 1950, when ill health obliged Cripps to resign. Faced by the soaring prices of imports and his government's enormous rearmament programme, he aimed in his 1951 budget to reduce consumer expenditure by doubling purchase tax on cars, radios and other goods using metal which was now required for armaments or was competing in other ways with defence needs. He also added 6d to income tax and imposed ceilings on the money to be spent on food subsidies and the health service. The last proposal, which involved the imposition of a charge for dentures and spectacles, produced a political crisis within the Labour ministry. Aneurin Bevan, the Minister of Health, argued that while the U.S.A. was stockpiling the raw materials of war, Britain could not possibly be supplied with the machine tools, sulphur and other essentials of its own defence arrangements, and it might as well restrict its expenditure on arms and leave the health service intact. Rather than surrender, Bevan resigned from the government. So did Harold Wilson, the President of the Board of Trade. In the event they proved to have been right. Many of the required imports were in fact unprocurable, and the Conservatives, once in office, were obliged to scale down the defence programme.

---

[1] Hugh Dalton, *High Tide and After*, pp. 84–5, Frederick Muller Ltd (London 1962)
[2] Hugh Dalton, broadcast, 20.8.47

6

Planning the new society

Notwithstanding the embarrassments caused by the recurrent economic crises, Labour could not abandon its obligations to restore the features of a peace-time Britain nor shelve its policies for a new society. It had received a plain mandate from the electorate such as the two previous Labour governments had not obtained from the elections of 1923 and 1929. It had a long-considered philosophy to put into practice and, at least during the early years of its ministry, an earnest faith in the justification for its programme.

Planning and a state-controlled economy during the war had been indispensable to victory. An inadequately planned society had suffered two decades of unemployment, a general strike and the repercussions of a world-wide slump. The moral was clear. Post-war Britain could escape the misfortunes and un-happiness of these years only if its governments could achieve a compromise between the freedom of the individual and a greater degree of regulation of the economic environment by the state. The Labour Party manifesto of 1945 recognised this in promising 'a firm constructive hand on our whole productive machinery' and in assuring the electorate that it would 'plan from the ground up, giving an appropriate place to constructive enterprise and private endeavour in the national plan.' Herbert Morrison, Leader of the House of Commons and Lord President of the Council, was given responsibility for implementing these ideals. The new President of the Board of Trade, also increasingly concerned with economic planning, was Sir Stafford Cripps, who believed that without government control of a war-time character full employment would not be maintained, and that a Central Economic Planning Staff should be created to exercise this control. From the left wing of the Labour Party came even more far-reaching proposals. For example, a pamphlet published in 1947 by R. H. S. Crossman, Michael

Foot and Ian Mikardo sought a still greater amount of centralised planning, the direction of labour to essential industries by
means of such concessions as lower taxes, and the nationalisation
of 'every industry which has a hold over the economy or which
cannot be made efficient in private hands.'[1] Barbara Wootton
had written in 1945 that planned production implied 'either
compulsory industrial direction or a planned wage structure'.[2]

GOVERNMENT CONTROL OVER INDUSTRY AND TRADE

To some extent these ideas were put into effect. A number of
councils, boards and committees established during the war to
serve as links between government and industry were retained.
Cripps's proposed Central Economic Planning Staff, consisting
of senior civil servants and economists, was established after the
fuel crisis in the early weeks of 1947 with Sir Edwin Plowden at
its head. Cripps himself became the first Minister for Economic
Affairs in September, 1947, combining the office with the
Chancellorship of the Exchequer six weeks later. Meanwhile,
the coal mines, railways, gas and electricity, the most important
sections of civil aviation, many of the road transport concerns
and the iron and steel industries were being brought under
public control or threatened with it. Ninety-six per cent of the
goods imported into Britain in 1946 were subject to government
control, and the figure did not fall below 90 per cent until 1950,
when it declined to 73 per cent. In 1946, 64 per cent of imports,
food, coal and cotton in particular, were acquired by the
government itself; and the government continued to be responsible for the purchase of 46 per cent of imports as late as 1950.
Control over goods bought from dollar countries remained
especially stringent and was inherited by the Conservatives in
1951. It was only slowly relaxed after 1953. It was true that the
Labour government had no more intention than its Conservative successor of establishing this pattern of state purchase as a
permanent policy; but in conditions of post-war scarcity both of
goods and of foreign exchange, the ministries appeared to be in a
better position than private merchants to obtain the country's
requirements, and their long-term contracts were thought to
guarantee cheaper imports. At the same time the government
used its influence to ensure that vital export markets should be

retained or built up after the war. The supply of cars on the
home market remained very limited for a decade in order that
overseas purchasers should not be deprived of their vehicles.
The export of engineering goods was similarly encouraged.
Such control was helped by the fact that the great degree of
power exercised during the war by the government over the
allocation to various industries and firms of essential raw
materials was only gradually relinquished after 1945. It remained significant, indeed, until 1953. The control of coal
allocation did not end until 1958.

The post-war scarcity of supplies from which manufacturing
industry suffered also affected building. Justice demanded that
the supplies should be distributed in such a way that the most
pressing needs should be met first. Accordingly, it was enacted
in 1945 that licences should be obtained for any sort of building
costing more than £20. The regulations were relaxed in 1948 to
allow the construction of industrial and agricultural buildings,
warehouses, schools and some offices without licence if the cost
were less than £1000, while other buildings costing less than
£100 required no licence. Controls of this sort could not always
be rigorously applied; and as long as the effects of the war were
still felt, they were not always very necessary, since shortages of
materials and manpower by themselves limited new building
schemes. However, they were not entirely ended until 1955.

Some control was exercised until 1950 over the prices of
rationed commodities, and this, together with a voluntary
endeavour by traders and shopkeepers to maintain a certain
amount of price stability, probably helped to prevent runaway
inflation. It did not result in static prices, though. The government was obliged to negotiate increases in charges when increasing raw material costs and higher wages were inevitably
passed on to goods of all kinds.

The budget was now generally accepted as another means of
regulating the economy, and successive Chancellors used it for
this purpose. Higher taxes were supposed to reduce citizens'
spending power and thereby to leave more manufactures for
export and to limit inflationary trends at home. A reduction of
taxation would serve as a stimulus to purchasing and would
consequently encourage industrial production and help to
maintain a high level of employment. Budgets had become,
more than ever before, a means of redistributing wealth and of

creating a more egalitarian society. Direct taxes on income and indirect ones on consumers' expenditure could be adjusted to achieve social purposes as well as to bring in revenue; and all Chancellors, Labour and Conservative alike, used their financial powers to attain, with varying degrees of success, a variety of ends. Bank Rate could also be manipulated, for similar reasons. Low interest rates of the sort prescribed by Dalton (2 per cent) would allow cheap borrowing and, consequently, industrial expansion. Financial planning of this sort had, it was true, its limitations, partly because it was dealing with the not always predictable reactions of human beings, and partly because a measure that was in one way advantageous might in another have less desirable results. However, it may well have played a part in enabling the country to avoid a repetition of the economic calamities of the inter-war years.

THE LIMITS OF GOVERNMENT CONTROL

Quite evidently, however, Labour's approach to planning was not that of a totalitarian government employing a Gestapo to lay a tyrannical hand on British enterprise, as Churchill had feared. Much of its planning and many of the controls that it exercised over the economy were unavoidable survivals of the war or responses to the difficult conditions of the post-war world. The responses would no doubt have been similar whichever party had occupied the ministries in 1945. Controls which were never intended to be permanent were those imposed during the war on ordinary citizens' purchases of food, clothes and durable household goods, and maintained until world trade had once again resumed a normal pattern. Twenty-eight per cent of consumers' expenditure was absorbed by these controlled wares in 1946, and during the next two years the proportion actually increased, reaching 31 per cent in 1948. Bread, freely available throughout the war, was rationed for two years from July, 1946. Potato rationing was imposed in November, 1947. In 1949, though, the situation very rapidly improved. Only 12 per cent of consumer expenditure was on controlled goods during that year, and thereafter the proportion steadily declined until, after 1954, only coal remained rationed. Similarly, when the government could reasonably get rid of import controls it did not hesitate to do so. The restrictions on imports from the sterling area were the first to disappear. In view of the persistent adverse balance of British trade with the dollar countries, imports from North America were controlled longer than those from other regions, but before 1951 trade in such raw materials from the dollar area as wool and iron ore, rubber, flax, hides and timber had been handed over to individual merchants. Control of the import of iron, steel and tin manufactures from dollar countries had been ended in 1949, and in the same year most of the controls over imports from Europe, apart from the Communist bloc, had been swept away under arrangements made by the Organisation for European Economic Co-operation. Meanwhile, a large number of Board of Trade controls over home manufactures and the distribution of various raw materials had been given up in 1948 and 1949. It was true that in 1950 and 1951 the restoration of the freedom of the importers and manufacturers was interrupted by the Korean war, which even impelled the government to bring back control of the import of such commodities as metals, sulphur and nylon, but these measures were clearly only temporary.

What was less clear was the government's determination to pursue its long-term planning of industry in all its aspects, with quite the same zest that some of its members had manifested when they had first assumed office. The state-owned industries were, indeed, subjected to a substantial measure of planning; but the more moderate members of the Labour party had no great enthusiasm for unlimited nationalisation. In spheres where it might have been thought twenty years later that planning would have been beneficial, nothing significant was done. Rail and road transport had been brought under state control; but long-term arrangements to integrate the various transport systems were still being called for in the 1960s. No national plan compelled the Coal, Electricity and Gas Boards to evolve a long-term fuel policy, so that in the 1960s coal was still struggling to survive in the face of competition from other fuels. A National Economic Development Council was not established until 1962, when it was introduced by Conservatives. A national incomes policy experiment also had to wait until the 1960s. Labour did, indeed, in 1947, pass the Industrial Organisation and Development Act, permitting the appointment of councils to increase industrial efficiency and to promote research and exports; but only four bodies emerged from this Act, and of these the Cotton

Board was not really new, the clothing and jewellery boards were unsuccessful and were disbanded in 1953, and only the Furniture Development Council survived and was useful. Not for nearly two more decades after 1947 did comparable councils for various industries proliferate and function effectively.

The limitations of Labour's apparent success in the sphere of industrial planning was not discreditable. It arose from a much greater respect for British democratic traditions than Churchill, in 1945, had given it credit for. The government's Economic Survey for 1947 stated the problem of reconciling planning and individual freedom quite plainly when it declared that 'the execution of the economic plan must be much more a matter for co-operation between the government, industry and the people than of rigid application by the state of controls and compulsions.' The issue of a government incomes policy drew an equally clear *Statement on Personal Income, Cost and Prices* (1947): 'It is not desirable for the government to interfere directly with the income of individuals otherwise than by taxation.' Regulation of wages and salaries 'would be an incursion by the government into what has hitherto been regarded as a field of free contract between individuals and organisations.'

These were the characteristic attitudes of a liberal society. They were reinforced by the attitudes of the trade unions, which resisted particularly any attempt by the government to impose a planned policy for the wages of their members. Two months of negotiation in 1947 on this issue brought no concessions from the General Council of the T.U.C., and at the Labour Party conference in the same year the case of the unions was once again emphasised: 'Under no circumstances,' declared Arthur Deakin, Secretary of the Transport and General Workers Union, 'will we accept the position that the responsibility for the fixation of wages and the regulation of conditions of employment is one for the government.'[3] The unions did, in fact, accept Cripps's appeals for a voluntary wage freeze in 1948. Whereas in 1946 incomes had, on an average, risen 8 per cent, in 1949 they rose less than 2 per cent, and between January and September, 1950, not at all. Yet even during this period the unions insisted on retaining the right to demand increases necessary to preserve traditional differentials between various classes of worker or to improve the wages of the lowest paid. In the later months of 1950 the T.U.C. passed another resolution opposing restraint, wages began to rise again, and throughout the next two decades demands for frequent increases became habitual. During the late 1960s, when another Labour government was in office, union leaders were still refusing to accept government control over their accustomed right to bargain for the improved remuneration of their members. Socialists could at times be remarkably conservative.

---

[1] Keep Left, a *New Statesman* pamphlet
[2] Barbara Wootton, *Freedom under Planning*, Chapel Hill (1945)
[3] *Labour Party Conference Report* 1947, p. 144

7

Nationalisation

From its beginnings Labour had sought the transference to public ownership of the means of production, distribution and exchange. Its supporters had always believed that such basic industries as coal mining, iron and steel, electricity and gas, the railways and the banking system were of such essential importance to the nation as a whole that it was wrong that private individuals should be making out of them the profits that ought to be left instead in the hands of salaried boards and used for the good of the industry concerned. Some of the Labour party statements had gone so far as to promise the public ownership of land, insurance, shipping, ship-building, engineering, textiles and chemicals, cement and water supply. Not all members of the party accepted such a programme, but that certain measures of nationalisation would figure prominently in the legislation after 1945 was inevitable. To some of these measures opposition was unlikely to be strong. The railways had long been subject to public control, especially during the wars. Predominantly Conservative governments had passed Acts at intervals in the 1930s increasing government control of coal mining. A third of the gas supply was already in public hands. As long ago as 1889 a Conservative government had bound private electricity companies to hand over to local authorities after forty-two years, and it had been a Conservative government which had created the Central Electricity Board in 1926. Furthermore, a number of public boards of the type to be introduced for nationalised concerns by the Labour government had existed for decades: apart from the Electricity Board, there were the Post Office, the Port of London Authority, the London Passenger Transport Board, the B.B.C. and British Overseas Airways. Conservatives and Liberals had never regarded these as socialistic. They were merely administratively convenient.

The nationalisation of the Bank of England in 1946 made

negligible difference. Relations between the Bank and the Treasury had for long been so close that the Act merely legalised an existing situation. Churchill agreed that no matter of principle was raised and that important examples of central banking institutions could already be found in the Dominions and in the United States. Strong emotions were not aroused. Nor did they develop when the Civil Aviation Act (1946) brought British European Airways and British South American Airways (merged in 1949 with British Overseas Airways Corporation) into line with B.O.A.C. by making them into a publicly owned corporation.

COAL MINING, RAILWAYS, ELECTRICITY AND GAS

A far more significant step was the nationalisation of coal mining. Already Acts had been passed affecting safety, hours of work and minimum wages in the coal industry. However, these were not enough for the miners, whose dissatisfaction had lain behind a high proportion of the industrial upheavals of the inter-war years. Even before 1914 the slogan 'The Mines for the Miners' had suggested that a syndicalist solution, control of the industry by the workers themselves, was contemplated. During the 1920s control by the state became the aim. In 1945 a committee of mining engineers, all colliery directors or former directors, under Sir Charles Reid, reported that the industry was grossly inefficient and, after analysing the reasons for its low productivity, recommended a radical reorganisation. The statistics of coal production in 1946 emphasised the validity of the Reid Committee's condemnation: total output was less than 190m tons, only about two-thirds of production in 1913. Output per manshift was 1·03 tons, compared with 1·17 tons in 1938. Relations between owners and men were embittered, and the number of miners was declining. Curiously, as Emanuel Shinwell, the Minister of Fuel and Power, admitted, no detailed plan for nationalisation had already been drawn up, despite the decades during which state ownership had been regarded as a fundamental aim of Labour party policy. 'I found that nothing practical and tangible existed,'[1] he revealed. However, in other respects the government's difficulties were not particularly serious. Opposition objections to nationalisation were more concerned with compensation for owners and methods of checking the decline of the mines than with questions of principle. The debate in the Commons was not acrimonious, and the features of state control on which the government had ultimately decided were widely regarded as desirable. A National Coal Board was set up to undertake the necessary reorganisation from the beginning of 1947. The country was divided into eight regions for mining purposes, £150m were granted for the re-equipment of the mines, and the original owners received compensation.

The immediate effects of the nationalisation of the mines, however, were discouraging. Within a few weeks of nationalisation a fuel crisis coincided with a period of exceptionally prolonged snow (January to March, 1947). Power stations and industry ran out of fuel supplies, and the weather hindered their replenishment. Equally unfortunate was the persistence, in the period immediately following nationalisation, of strikes on the coalfield. In the year before the introduction of state control there had been 1329 unofficial strikes. In 1947 there were 1635, including a serious one in Yorkshire, involving 50000 men. The large quantities of machinery put into the pits had little noticeable effect on production for several years.

In 1950 the National Coal Board announced plans to invest £520m in the industry in the next fifteen years and to raise 18 per cent more coal despite a reduction by 80000 of the number of miners. By this time the new machinery was winning acceptance in the pits, and the miners were becoming increasingly anxious to earn more money with which to improve their living standards. However, nationalisation could not possibly have saved coal from the competition of oil and, to a lesser extent, of hydro-electricity, nuclear power and natural gas. Exports fell and home consumption of coal declined; and in 1956 it became necessary to revise the long-term plans. The later stages of these developments are dealt with on page 354.

The Act for state control of the mines was followed in 1947 by one for the nationalisation of the railways, the canals, Port Authorities and London Transport. The changes were of limited scope since the railways had already been largely subject to government control, while the London Passenger Transport Board had existed since 1933. Criticism had been levelled for years against the wastefulness of competition in this sphere; and the need for an 'integrated' or 'rationalised' transport system, in which buses and trains would be linked and more remote districts be adequately served, had been strongly emphasised. The war had had a damaging effect on stock and had made substantial capital expenditure necessary. Public control could ensure that criticisms, recommendations and expenses would be met. Existing owners received very generous compensation, amounting to more than £1000 million. This was about seven times the price paid for the coal mines. It guaranteed that there should be no great resentment at the measure.

The nationalisation of electricity had been advocated in a report issued in 1942. It was not a very revolutionary development. Five hundred and fifty independent undertakings had to be reorganised under fourteen Area Boards. The generating stations had to be taken over by the state. But the Central Electricity Board had already owned the Grid, and the industry had been sufficiently controlled previously for little serious opposition to the measure to arise. The Act was passed in February, 1947. The nationalisation of the gas industry (1948) was accepted with similar readiness, public ownership having been advised by the Heyworth Committee in 1945.

DISPUTES OVER ROAD TRANSPORT, IRON AND STEEL

So far Labour had experienced few difficulties. Its philosophy of public ownership, however, came into serious collision with the Conservative view of private industry when the nationalisation of road transport and of iron and steel were at stake.

The British Transport Commission was empowered in 1947 to take over vehicles which had been licensed for public haulage (as opposed to being licensed for the carriage by traders of only their own goods). These nationalised vehicles were to be predominantly engaged on long-distance haulage. By 1951 the Commission had acquired 3266 undertakings with 44283 vehicles and trailers. The Conservatives strongly opposed the measure and made clear their intention to restore the vehicles to private ownership when they returned to office.

The fiercest resentment also developed over the nationalisation of iron and steel. The Opposition claimed that the industry was too successful in private hands to deserve public ownership. Since its foundation in 1934 the Iron and Steel Federation had co-operated effectively with the government in planning the industry on a national scale so as to avoid both cut-throat competition and the evils of monopoly. It had passed on the fruits of research and had co-ordinated long-term development schemes. The Labour government had already ensured that sight should not be lost of these aims when it set up in 1946 the Iron and Steel Board to supervise costly plans for expansion, to regulate imports and exports and to fix prices at a level which would not give easy profits to inefficient plants. The results, declared both the industry and the Conservatives, were good. Whereas total production immediately before the war had been about 10m tons a year, by 1948 it was almost 15m tons. A very successful drive for scrap supplies after the war had surpassed expectations, and twice as much steel was exported in 1949 in the form of finished products like cars and machinery as had been exported before the war. British prices had risen by only 69 per cent since 1938, though wages had gone up by more than 100 per cent and the costs of industrial materials and manufactures in general had risen by 136 per cent. These prices were lower than those of continental countries and in almost every respect lower than American prices. Productivity per man was nearly 30 per cent greater than it had been before the war. At the same time, labour relations were exceptionally good. Successful arbitration methods had been practised for half a century. No major strike had started in steel in the twentieth century. Workers and management had always co-operated well. The steel workers' leaders were indifferent or even opposed to nationalisation. Furthermore, the Conservatives indicated, it would be difficult to know where to draw the line between steel and the various branches of the engineering industry which used steel; the nationalisation of one might ultimately involve the nationalisation of the rest or, at least, might produce a complex situation in which some industries would find themselves partly under public and partly under private control. Altogether, it was doubted whether nationalisation would increase efficiency, reduce costs, or accelerate plans for expansion. Opponents believed that privately owned industry would in all respects be more effective.

On the other side, supporters regarded the capitalist system as so essentially evil in its effects that it should, on doctrinaire grounds, be replaced by public ownership. This was a traditional socialist viewpoint which may have appealed more to the extremists than to the moderates of the movement but was, for the former, important. Others believed that since steel was already so closely connected with the state it might as well become a state monopoly. It was doubted whether the industry could really carry out under private ownership all the modernisation that was essential. State ownership, it was thought, would bring greater stability. During the years of depression in the 1930s unemployment amongst steel workers had risen to 46 per cent and had never fallen below 18 per cent. If such conditions recurred, the government would be in a stronger position than the private owners to keep the plant running, even at a loss, until times improved.

Not all members of the Labour party were convinced by these arguments. Nationalisation of steel had not been specifically mentioned in the party's 'Home Policy' statement of 1940. Some of its leaders, Herbert Morrison especially, had doubts about the wisdom and feasibility of nationalising; and, according to Dalton, who had always insisted on the public ownership of the industry, even George Strauss, the minister with primary responsibility for the parliamentary bill, did not seem 'very ardent'.[2] The government, nonetheless, went ahead. An Iron and Steel Corporation was created, which took over the shares, at Stock Exchange valuation, of 107 major steel companies along with some of their engineering interests, and assumed the task of running the industry. In fact, though, the companies never had time to lose their separate identities. The House of Lords held up the bill for a year; in the end its full operation was delayed until after the 1951 election; and when this was won by the Conservatives, the firms, with one exception, were sold back into private ownership. The Labour party promised renationalisation when once again they had the opportunity.

By 1951 about 20 per cent of British industry had been nationalised. The extent to which the rest should be taken over by the state remained throughout the 1950s and early 1960s a subject of debate within the Labour movement. Among the majority interest declined. Conservatives and Liberals opposed any extension of a policy which, even if there had been no other arguments against it, had left the government with two major concerns, coal mining and the railways, which consistently lost ground during the next two decades and required massive financial support to survive. Apart from this, governments, of whichever party, found themselves faced by two particular difficulties which deserve consideration. One was the degree to which ministers should be responsible for running the industries which had been nationalised. Could ministers be held chargeable for the difficulties which beset mining and the railways? Under the Conservatives, from 1952, a parliamentary select committee on the nationalised industries existed, but no precise definition of ministerial accountability received statutory form; only the general conclusion evolved that governments could lay down basic principles and be answerable for these but that the day-to-day management of the industries must be left in the hands of the boards or commission which had been set up by the nationalising Acts. The problem, in so far as it affected mining, was still a disputed issue in 1970. The other problem was that of wages in the publicly owned industries. Demands for increased incomes did not cease with nationalisation, and in fact the annual agitation frequently began in nationalised industries. When the demands were conceded, as generally happened, it was not easy for the owners of private concerns to impose restraint on their own employees when they, in their turn, formulated new wage claims.

---

[1] Emanuel Shinwell, *Conflict without Malice*, p. 172 (Odhams Press 1955)
[2] Hugh Dalton, *High Tide and After*, p. 309

8

Labour and the Welfare State

The Welfare State was not, of course, an invention of the post-war world. Factory and Mines Acts and the introduction of grants for education had symbolised as early as the 1830s the readiness of the state to interfere on behalf of the well-being of the masses and to invade spheres which had previously depended on private charity. No government after the 1830s had failed to add something to the welfare structure. Some, like Disraeli's Conservative ministry 1874–80 and the Liberal ministry after 1905, had added a great deal. Yet experience of unemployment, slump and poverty during the 1920s and 1930s had made clear that large numbers of the less affluent still required protection from the worse features of an industrial society. The authors of the war-time White Papers, the economists who adopted the recommendations of John Maynard Keynes and the leaders of all the political parties, had accepted the need for radical changes and the inevitability of electoral defeat if they did not do so. No post-war government could have evaded legislation of a far-reaching character. A Labour government, whose very *raison d'être* was the improvement of the conditions of life and work of the under-privileged, would welcome whole-heartedly the opportunity to put into practice the ideals of reformers. Some of the hope, in the new dawn, was expressed in the speeches and writings of Hugh Dalton, the Labour Chancellor of the Exchequer: 'this lively new government,' he declared in an address to the Fabian Society in November 1945, 'this great Labour majority in Parliament is determined to advance along the road towards economic and social equality.'[1] In his autobiography Dalton referred to unabated interest in Parliamentary proceedings throughout the country during 1945 and 1946, the soaring sales of Hansard reports of these proceedings, the queues for seats in the public gallery of the House of Commons, the 'living and dramatic

50

spectacle'[2] presented by Parliament. From the other side of the house Lord Kilmuir (Sir David Maxwell Fyfe) confirmed this interest. Clearly, a Parliament the main preoccupation of which was the development of the Welfare State was a matter of popular concern.

The *Beveridge Report* was the source of inspiration for much of the welfare legislation. Family allowances were the first of its recommendations to be implemented. These were inspired not only by Beveridge but by the *Memorandum* produced by the government in 1942 at the request of M.P.s, and by the disturbing revelations in the survey, *Our Towns* (1943),[3] of the squalid backgrounds of many slum children evacuated during the war to safer environments. The measure was readily accepted. It gave parents an allowance of five shillings per week for each child except the first.

THE NATIONAL HEALTH SERVICE

Family allowances were followed the next year (1946) by the National Insurance and National Health Service Acts. The first of these, in accordance with Beveridge's suggestions, was more concerned with the unified administration of unemployment, sickness and maternity benefits, retirement and widows' pensions than with any revolutionary new principle. The benefits and pensions had all existed previously, even though they may have been administered by different bodies; and a Ministry of National Insurance had already been created, in 1944, by the Coalition Government. So the measure was not controversial. On the other hand, to certain of the Labour proposals for the Health Service the Conservatives in Parliament raised objections: that the right of patients to retain their own family doctors would be prejudiced, that the termination of local ownership of hospitals would retard the development of the service, that the power of the 138 English and Welsh executive councils of the Service to dissuade doctors from settling in an already adequately served South-east England and the government ban on the sale of practices, threatened the liberty of the medical profession. However, to the general principle of a National Health Service the Conservatives raised no opposition; and amendments embodying their objections to the Labour bill did not pass. Opposition from the doctors themselves was more serious. In February, 1948, a British Medical Association plebiscite suggested that about 90 per cent were hostile to the Act. Such opposition weakened, though. From their conflict with the Minister of Health, Aneurin Bevan, the doctors gained a number of concessions: a generous superannuation scheme, the creation by the government of a £66m fund to compensate them for the loss of the right to sell their practices on retirement, and acceptance of the right of a doctor who had joined the Health Service also to practise privately. By April, 1948, a second B.M.A. plebiscite showed that only 65 per cent of the profession opposed the scheme. By 1950 88 per cent of the doctors had joined it.

The Health Service came into operation in 1948. It quickly became clear that, whatever critics may have claimed, a real need had been met. Widespread poverty and war had created problems which could have been solved only with difficulty had the pre-war system remained unaltered. Many hospitals, dependent on voluntary contributions, had been almost bankrupt by 1939 and had been saved only by big government subsidies during the war. They faced even more serious difficulties after 1945 when subsidies were withdrawn at the same time as the costs of medical care were rapidly rising and new discoveries were demanding the expenditure of greater and greater sums of money. No new hospitals had been built since 1939. The position of general practitioners in many areas had also been less satisfactory than most people realised. A Committee (1946-8) under the chairmanship of Sir Will Spens had no doubt that low incomes had, 'in fact, been a source of grave worry to many general practitioners and must have prejudiced their efficiency.' Many uninsured patients in regions of serious unemployment had fallen into debt. Many of these were thereafter reluctant to see their doctors when they needed to do so. Such problems could be swept away by the National Health Service. Doctors were no longer obliged, in a period of rapid medical advances, to ask themselves whether a patient could afford a particular course of treatment. And that there existed a very great pent-up demand among people who had previously needed but had not sought treatment was suggested by dramatically increased expenditure, particularly on spectacles, false teeth, hearing aids and other appliances. The original estimates for 1948-9 were £150m, but supplementary estimates added

£58m; and expenditure on the service during the next year soared to £460m. The costs were, indeed, so high that in 1949 the Labour government passed a measure permitting, though not imposing, charges for medicines and medical appliances.

Pensions were raised again in 1946, so that single people who had been receiving 10s (50p) a week now received 26s (£1·30), while married couples were given 42s (£2·10). Additional benefits were granted to those who continued their work beyond a normal retirement age. Unfortunately, in a period of constantly rising prices, the benefits were not sufficient for large numbers of old people. Nor were normal insurance payments for the sick and unemployed. Accordingly, a National Assistance scheme, originally (in 1948) expected to apply only to a small minority, became an indispensable source of income, serving 1 350 000 people by the end of 1950.

A most revealing indication of the effects of these welfare provisions and of full employment after 1945 was the last of B. S. Rowntree's three surveys of social conditions in York. Published in 1951, this showed that the proportion of working-class people living in poverty was no more than 2·8 per cent. The survey that Rowntree had completed in 1936 had shown 31·1 per cent to have been living in poverty. In 1936 nearly one-third of the poor had attributed their condition to unemployment. Not one did so in 1951. In addition, it was clear that children were taller and heavier than they had been in 1936. Rowntree concluded that the new benefits had done even more than increased wages to eliminate the poverty of the 1930s, and that, had it not been for them, the proportion of the population suffering real hardship would have been not 2·8 per cent but 22·2 per cent.

Infant mortality figures confirmed the evidence of York about the value of the post-war reforms. In 1939 the mortality rate had been 47·4 for every 1000 births. In 1949–50, although the families of unskilled workers still lost more than twice as many of their newly born children as did professional families, the national average had declined to 29·3 per thousand.

HOUSING AND TOWN AND COUNTRY PLANNING

Associated with health was housing. The minister responsible for both was Aneurin Bevan. A series of Acts since 1875, including those associated in the early 1920s with successive Ministers of Health, Christopher Addison, Neville Chamberlain and John Wheatley, had established the authority of governments to direct developments, and in the late 1940s, with only a limited supply of essential materials available and a labour force disrupted by the war, the government's role was inevitably important. Only 158000 of the new houses built between 1945 and 1950 were put up for private owners; private builders were responsible for only about a tenth of the houses they had constructed in 1938. The others were built by local authorities, subsidised along pre-war lines by state grants. It was not easy to meet the requirements of an ever-increasing number of families, and Bevan was not prepared to allow dwellings of a poor standard. Whereas in 1939 a house built by a local authority had cost, on an average, only £380, by 1947 the cost had risen to £1242. As a result of the difficulties facing the industry no more than 55000 permanent houses could be completed in 1946, and only 140000 in 1947. However, the situation improved. During the later years of the Labour government the annual total did not fall below 200000, and, in addition, 157000 small, prefabricated temporary houses were financed by the Exchequer. The government resisted pressure from the extreme left of the Labour Party for the nationalisation of all house-building, and in 1949 met Conservative criticisms of their earlier policy by making subsidies available for owners who wished to renovate their properties or to convert them into flats. Rents of older houses were kept at their pre-war level, and an Act of 1946 extended this provision to about a million furnished houses. Tribunals were established which were, in 1949, empowered also to limit the rents of unfurnished properties.

The war-time reports advocating improved planning of urban and rural development were followed in the late 1940s by several others which also emphasised the error of allowing the larger centres of population to expand without control. The *Abercrombie Reports* (1943 and 1944), like the *Montague-Barlow Report* of 1940, indicated the dangers of the unrestrained growth of suburban London, recommended the dispersal of one and a quarter million of its inhabitants and urged the redevelopment of slum areas and the preservation of the Green Belt round the capital. The *Clement Davies Report* advocated similar measures in 1946. Inspired by these documents, and by the earlier *Scott* and *Uthwatt Reports*, the government introduced several significant Acts. A Redistribution of Industry Act, passed by the coalition government in 1945, empowered the ministry to encourage new industrial development in the distressed areas of the 1930s. According to a White Paper published in 1948, 443 new factories had been built in these regions within three years of the end of the war, and a similar number had been planned. Meanwhile, the New Towns Act of 1946 had provided for the creation of 15 towns to absorb the excess populations of London and Glasgow and to serve industrial development in the counties of Durham, Northampton, Monmouth and Fife. In 1947 the first of a post-war series of Town and Country Planning Acts transferred planning functions from small local authorities to the larger ones, imposed on these an obligation to plan the development of their areas, increased their powers of compulsory purchase of property and provided for government grants to assist them. This Act also allowed the government to levy a development charge on the increased value of newly exploited land; but the measure was unpopular and difficult to administer and was later to be virtually abandoned by the Conservatives. On the other hand, no controversy could be aroused by the National Parks and Access to the Countryside Act of 1949, which aimed to preserve the more splendid scenery of the British Isles. Hugh Dalton, particularly, was interested in the conservation of open spaces. As Chancellor he encouraged the Forestry Commission with financial assistance and expressed his willingness to accept land or property (to be administered normally by the National Trust) in place of more normal death duties.

EDUCATION

In the sphere of education Labour had only to put into practice the 1944 Act introduced by R. A. Butler, and, at the time, generally accepted in all its essentials by members of all parties. The independent Public Schools continued as before, often admitting the need to widen their clientele by accepting pupils from less privileged strata of society but finding it far less simple to implement such a policy. The direct grant grammar schools also retained a large degree of independence, receiving financial assistance directly from the government and not from local authorities, on condition that at least 25 per cent of their pupils held free places paid for by local authorities. They claimed, with variable justification, that this enabled them to make available their facilities to pupils from all social classes, and they earned, collectively, a high reputation for their academic successes. Anglican and Roman Catholic schools (described henceforth as 'voluntary aided') preserved a certain amount of independence as long as they could find 50 per cent of the costs of the modernisation and repair of their buildings; they were assisted financially by the local authorities, but at least they could control their staff appointments and maintain their own types of religious instruction.

The other secondary schools were now grouped in three categories: grammar, secondary modern and technical. Responsibility for them rested with the local authorities, who paid all their expenses (fees being abolished) and distributed boys and girls to them at the age of eleven after an examination designed to suggest which type of school was most suitable for each individual. It was never intended that one type of school should be considered superior to another. 'Parity of esteem' was the prevailing doctrine, and at least during the 1940s endeavours were made to pretend that such parity could be achieved. In the end, though, disillusionment was bound to follow. The grammar schools, taking about 20 per cent of the children (though the proportion varied considerably in different parts of Britain), too evidently attracted the academically more highly qualified teachers and offered to the more intelligent pupils the greater opportunities, the university places and ultimately the most successful careers. Furthermore, it was clearly impossible, at eleven, to be sure that each boy and girl had been fairly allocated to a particular school, and fears began to find expression that latent talents were being submerged in secondary modern environments and were never finding opportunities for full development. From an early stage the Labour-controlled London County Council, in search of an answer to these causes of anxiety, experimented with the idea of all-purpose, multilateral schools of 2000 pupils or more, which could educate children of all abilities on the same precincts and, if necessary, transfer them with ease from one class to another after the age of eleven. As the next two decades passed, the creation of such 'comprehensive' schools became a most crucial subject of educational and, to some extent, unfortunately, of political debate.

The 1944 Act provided that the school-leaving age should be raised to fifteen from April, 1945, and to sixteen at some later date. In fact the more modest aim had to be postponed, and a decision on a date for keeping pupils at school until they were sixteen had to wait until 1969. Provision was made, however, for the part-time instruction of young people from the time when

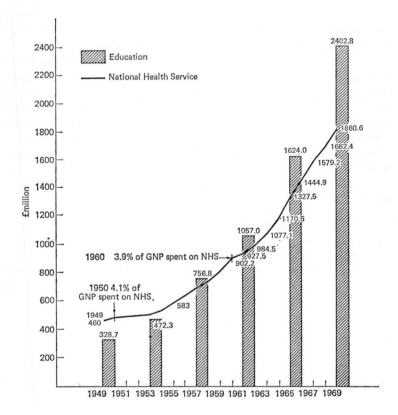

Rising costs of the Welfare State. Consolidated current and capital expenditure by public sector (central and local). Statistics of expenditure on education include 'loan charges' until 1958 and 'imputed rents' thereafter. Statistics of expenditure on N.H.S. include 'imputed rents' of hospitals from 1958. Rising costs are partly accounted for by inflation. *Source*: Central Statistical Office and *Annual Abstract of Statistics*.

they left school until they were eighteen. Facilities were to be made available for adult educational classes, infant schools, and for recreation and games. Provision of school meals, milk and religious instruction became obligatory. Indeed, there were few fields of education for which a local authority could be made responsible which were not covered in this extremely wide-ranging Act. It was not, of course, an achievement of the Attlee government; but it was during the period of Labour rule, when hope of more fair opportunities for all people in the new society was still so ardent, that it was put into operation.

Only a few comparatively minor additions to Butler's arrangements for the young and for education in its widest sense were made by Labour, but these deserve mention. The war-time Council for the Encouragement of Music and the Arts was maintained, as the Arts Council. Local councils were empowered to levy a penny rate for the support of the arts in their spheres of influence. In 1948 a Children's Act defined the responsibility of local authorities towards homeless children entrusted to them. And, also in 1948, the youth employment service was established.

---

[1] Hugh Dalton, *High Tide*, p. 64. Speech to Fabian Society 22.11.45
[2] Ibid., p. 93
[3] Women's Group on Public Welfare, *Our Towns* (Oxford University Press, 1943)

9

Labour, the Trade Unions and The Constitution

The support of the trade unions had always been an indispensable factor in the development of the Labour Party. Their size and influence had grown in unison. A high proportion of Labour M.P.s (generally at least half before 1945) had been sponsored by trade unions. In 1945 the unions had sponsored 125 candidates and 120 of these had been returned, 34 with the backing of the National Union of Mineworkers, 17 with that of the Transport and General Workers' Union, and 12 with that of the National Union of Railwaymen. Even if it were true, as Sir David Maxwell Fyfe claimed in October, 1949, that three million trade unionists were Conservatives, they certainly did not advertise their faith.

In these circumstances it was to be expected that one of the earlier pieces of Labour legislation would be the repeal of the 1927 Trades Disputes Act, which, apart from prohibiting the kind of sympathetic general strike which had occurred in 1926, had forbidden civil servants to affiliate to the T.U.C. and had obliged trade unionists wishing to contribute to their unions' political levies to signify their intention, in writing, to do so. The effect of rescinding the last stipulation and of reverting to the law of 1913, obliging members of a Union to contract out if they had no desire to contribute to a political fund, was to increase the trade unionist members of the Labour Party in one year from 2 635 000 to 4 386 000. In 1948, out of £164 000 received by the Labour Party in affiliation fees, trade unionists contributed £146 900. A similar proportion of a Labour Party development fund collected between 1947 and 1949 was provided by trade unions.

Labour's traditional hopes of achieving a greater degree of social equality were reflected in two important contributions to constitutional law. The first of these, a Representation of the

People Act introduced in 1948 by the Home Secretary, James Chuter Ede, abolished at the same time the twelve university seats and the business premises votes, and thus ensured that graduates and business men with their homes in one constituency and their means of livelihood in another should henceforth, like other citizens, have only one vote. The same Act, with the aim of leaving no constituency with more than 80000 electors, rearranged the boundaries of all but 80. Five hundred and twenty-eight constituencies emerged with altered boundaries. Apart from the university constituencies, 26 were swept away altogether, including the City of London, most of the electors of which had voted by right of their business premises. The total number of seats was reduced from 640 to 625. Churchill attacked, as 'a disreputable job',[1] the retention of a number of seats in industrial cities which had, in the original form of the bill, been doomed to disappearance; but the whole operation may well, in the end, have benefited his own party. Dalton, who had counselled delay until the country had finally settled down after the war, believed strongly that it was Ede's bill that deprived Labour of a working majority at the election of 1950.

The second measure affecting the constitution was one designed to reduce the power of the House of Lords to delay bills already passed by the Commons from two years to one. The Lords resisted, but after two years the bill was passed in December, 1949, under the terms of the 1911 Parliament Act. Its opponents asserted that the real purpose of the change was to ensure that the peers should be rendered incapable of delaying the bill for the nationalisation of the iron and steel industries until the electorate had had a chance of rejecting both the bill and the Labour ministry. The government denied the validity of such a view; and its spokesmen supported their case by quoting from speeches made by Churchill during the crisis of relations between Lords and Commons before the passage of the Parliament Act of 1911. However, only a few Labour extremists suggested the total abolition of the Upper House. Impartial observers suspected, in fact, that the standard of debates in the Lords was often higher than that in the Commons. Newly created peers did, after all, include elderly but able politicians, retired colonial governors, experts on economic issues, all with both knowledge and experience and under no obligation to consider the impact of their speeches on the electors in the constituencies. It was particularly on these men that the conduct of affairs fell.

The corporal punishment of criminals was abolished in 1948. An Act of 1949 made provision for legal aid to be given to those who were too poor to pay for it themselves. Of less certain benefit to the many young men concerned was the retention of peacetime conscription for twelve months in the forces. The period of service was raised to eighteen months in 1948 and to two years in 1950. It was not brought to an end until the end of 1960, and the last group of conscripts did not regain their freedom until 1962.

---

[1] Hugh Dalton, *High Tide*, p. 299

10
Labour foreign policy

With Ernest Bevin as a Foreign Secretary whose virtues were appreciated as much by the Conservatives in Parliament as by the moderates in his own party, no serious dispute was likely to arise about the main principles which were to influence Britain's policy abroad. Only an ineffective group on the extreme left criticised. Inevitably, the government was preoccupied in its initial stages with the settlement of the German problem; and, as time passed, with an increasingly disturbing relationship with Russia. Equally inevitably, Britain was in no position to reconstruct the world by itself. Its policy was to be evolved, in the immediate future, in close co-operation with the United States, and to be determined largely by the attitudes adopted by Russia. The situation was not one which would allow its rulers to strike out on a line of their own, even if they had wished to do so. This did not mean that it had been left by the war in the position of a helpless puppet. It possessed, after all, the reputation of a country that had, from the outbreak of war to its end, never surrendered to the Nazis, and its Foreign Secretary was both resolute and respected. It did mean, though, that much more effective collaboration with other countries than had been achieved during the lifetime of the League of Nations was a prerequisite of any policy. Conditions of peace had to be restored, and no country could lay these down by acting in isolation.

PEACE WITH GERMANY

The terms imposed in 1945 on Germany were based on American recommendations, which were readily accepted by the other Allies. Germany was to be completely disarmed. Any associations which threatened to perpetuate its militarism were to be abolished. Everything associated with Nazism was to be elimi-

nated. Active Nazis were to be removed from office, war criminals were to be tried and the racial laws abrogated. Government
was to be under the direction of an Allied Control Council and
such of Germany as had not been placed under the administration of the Poles was to be divided into zones controlled by the
Russians, Americans, British and French. To the British fell the
north-western region, reorganised in 1946 into four *Länder*:
Hamburg, Schleswig-Holstein, Niedersachsen and Nordrhein-
Westfalen. At the same time, political parties were to be encouraged, and local self-government, free speech, free Press and
Trade unions were to be restored. An American suggestion that
German society should become purely pastoral was abandoned
in favour of the restoration of a decentralised and decartelised
industry of a pacific nature; but in the early days after the war
the adoption of differing economic policies in Eastern and
Western zones was not envisaged, and their later emergence
was to symbolise the increasingly strained relations which
developed between Russia and the Western Allies. From the
beginning the collection of reparations in the form of industrial
equipment was allowed. It was stipulated, though, that sufficient resources should be left to enable the German people to
exist without foreign aid and that the Germans should be able
to pay for the goods that the Control Council permitted them
to import.

The problems that emerged from these scarcely well-defined
initial provisions were to become sources of substantial embarrassment to the ex-Allies during the next three years. In the
early months of 1946 it was agreed that German industries of
potential military importance, including those producing certain
machine tools and radio equipment, should be banned and that
other industries should be allowed to produce only a limited
percentage, varying between eleven and eighty, of their pre-war
output. The German merchant navy and Germany's overseas
assets were to be confiscated as reparations. Living standards
were to be kept at the level experienced during 1932, when the
Slump had been at its peak. Attitudes quickly changed, however. By September, 1946, James Byrnes, American Secretary
of State, was admitting that 'Germany is part of Europe, and
recovery in Europe, and particularly in the states adjoining
Germany, will be slow indeed if Germany, with her great
resources of iron and coal, is turned into a poorhouse.' It was

becoming evident that if too many German factories were dismantled, if too high a proportion of the country's limited coal stocks (only about a quarter of the pre-war total, mostly mined in the British zone) were taken and if it were deprived of its principal sources of invisible income, hopes of a balance of trade surplus by 1949 must be abandoned. Britain, at least, could not face this situation with equanimity. With German refugees from Eastern Europe crowding into the zone for which the British were responsible (more than 17 per cent of its population were refugees in June 1947) the British government found itself paying more than £80 million a year to preserve its former antagonists from starvation, and since the necessary supplies could be obtained only with the limited British reserves of foreign exchange, the obligation threatened catastrophe. In the hope of bringing to an end this currency drain, Britain merged its zone with the American zone in July, 1946. In the expectation of obtaining Marshall Aid for their zone of South-east Germany by amalgamation, the French, who had by this time abandoned an idea of fragmenting Germany into a number of small states, joined the British and Americans in 1948. Since the Russians consistently refused to follow suit, the division between Western and Eastern Germany had moved yet another stage towards crystallisation. The development of this rift was an unhappily characteristic feature of post-war diplomacy and was of sufficient significance to deserve closer consideration later.

PEACE WITH ITALY

The position of Italy was far less straightforward. From 1940 until September, 1943, it had been involved in the war on the German side; but thereafter it had readily changed allegiance. For nearly two years Italians had given as much support as they could to the Allies. More than 100000 had been killed during those years fighting, either as members of the regular army or as volunteer partisans, alongside the British and Americans. Six hundred thousand members of the Italian forces had been interned in Germany after their country's surrender, and very many of their civilian compatriots had been compelled to work in Germany along with more than four million Slav, French Dutch, and other people seized by the Nazis. The dominating figure in Italian politics when the war ended, Alcide De Gasperi, successively Foreign Minister and Prime Minister, had been imprisoned for four years by the Fascists and had afterwards spent years of virtual exile from public life in the Vatican library. Yet these factors did not spare Italy from peace terms which seemed, at least at the time, to be humiliating.

Britain was concerned particularly with the division of Venezia Giulia and the possession of Trieste and with the disposal of the Italian colonies. The first of these presented an especially intractable problem with Italian and Slav populations so intermingled as to make any entirely satisfying frontier quite impossible to define. The Yugoslavs claimed the whole territory. In May, 1945, Tito's forces occupied Trieste and withdrew only on Western persuasion to a line which left Trieste and Pola in the hands of the British and Americans. A Boundary Commission, composed of American, British, French and Russian representatives, met in 1946, but failed to reach agreement, and in the end a solution was adopted which left Trieste under Anglo-American control and handed over the surrounding territory, including Pola and Fiume, to Yugoslavia. The zones produced by this arrangement were intended to be temporary, but in fact the frontier that had been created could not clearly be improved, and after several years of dispute it was accepted. Britain handed Trieste back to Italy in 1954.

Equally little agreement had originally been possible among the war-time Allies about the treatment of the African colonies. Italy wanted to retain them. Britain refused to allow this. A compromise between the two countries was arrived at in 1949, only to be rejected by the United Nations Assembly. Finally the U.N. produced its own solution: Libya was to become independent on 1 January, 1952, and was to be guided and aided by the British; Somaliland was to become a United Nations Trust Territory, administered by the Italians until it gained independence, after ten years; Eritrea was granted to Ethiopia.

Although Britain, with the United States and France, renounced any claim to reparations from Italy, Russia did not. All were responsible for imposing terms concerning the armed forces which the Italians found particularly onerous. It was agreed by the Allies that the Italian navy, which had voluntarily joined them in 1943, should now be confiscated, that Italy should be permitted no fortifications on the Adriatic coast, Sicily or Sardinia and that the Italian armed forces should be

greatly reduced in numbers. Terms of this kind evoked De
Gasperi's comment that the peace treaty, signed in Paris in
February, 1947, was hard beyond all expectation. As it happened, however, the humiliation was of brief duration. Italy
benefited, like the other West European countries, from American Marshall Aid. In 1949, despite the initial reluctance of De
Gasperi and Count Sforza (then Italian Foreign Minister) to
commit their country to either of the great power blocs that were
developing, Italy joined NATO. Russian opposition kept it out
of the United Nations until 1955, but by this time it was already
becoming involved in the European Economic Community and
was about to enter a period of phenomenally rapid economic
growth. Its losses were made in retrospect to seem scarcely
worth the anxiety that they had at first caused.

RELATIONS WITH RUSSIA: THE COLD WAR

The difficulties of establishing a harmonious relationship with
Italy were insignificant compared with the difficulties of maintaining such a relationship with the supposed ally, Russia. At
first, despite recollections of the Molotov-Ribbentrop Pact that
had preceded the war in 1939, of the attacks made by Russia
on Poland and Finland in 1939 and of the imperialistic Soviet
retention of the Baltic States, Eastern Poland, Ruthenia and
parts of Romania after 1945, a large amount of sympathy and
good will for Russia existed in Britain. Regrets were felt that the
British government did not do more to co-operate with the
U.S.S.R., and a number of Labour M.P.s took a lead in seeking
for closer links. There was a tendency to regard the United
States with less favour. An amendment to a Commons debate
on foreign affairs in November, 1946, deplored the government's
'subservience' to America, and the harsh conditions of the
American loan encouraged such an attitude. Yet the symptoms
of the cold war between the Communist world and the allegedly
capitalist West had been perceptible even before the conclusion
of the fighting, and long before the end of the 1940s it was
perfectly clear that while Western Europe and America were
still united on all essentials, the Soviet Union remained a constant source of anxiety.

As early as 1945 a London conference of Soviet, American
and British foreign ministers failed to achieve anything once its

procedure had been denounced by Molotov, the Soviet representative. The Russians had claimed that the arrangements made at Potsdam for regular meetings of the foreign ministers had not allowed for the representation of France, and on this legal technicality they had been prepared to break up the conference. At a second meeting, held in Paris, they insisted on French participation. In January, 1946, bitter clashes broke out in the Security Council of the United Nations between Russia and one or more of the Western powers over the continuing presence of Russian troops in Northern Iran, British troops in Indonesia and Greece and French and British troops in Syria and Lebanon. The Soviet attitude to the last of these was symptomatic. Syria and Lebanon had appealed to the United Nations to arrange for the withdrawal from their territory of the foreign forces, and they had been supported by the Russians. The British and French accepted every major demand, and the Syrians and Lebanese accepted the concessions. The Russian delegate, Vishinsky, then vetoed the resolution on the ground that it was not worded precisely as he wished. This was the first of the occasions on which the Russians used the veto, which could block proceedings in the Security Council. During the next four years they were to veto thirty other propositions.

Dissension between the Communists and the West over the nature of the International Refugee Organisation and over Trieste were among the other symptoms of the Cold War's initial stages. To meet Soviet objections the other powers created a weaker Refugee Organisation than had been originally intended; and then the Russians refused to join. Soviet acceptance of an apparent solution to the embarrassing problem of possession of Trieste was followed by months of endeavour by the Russians to manipulate the compromise in such a way that Communist Yugoslavia would in fact have control. To the West it appeared as if the purpose of Russian diplomacy was to prevent settlements rather than to bring them about, never to agree to anything the first time it was discussed and to assume automatically that the aim of the West was to create an anti-Soviet bloc. An American view was expressed in 1946 to Molotov, the Russian Foreign Minister, by James F. Byrnes, President Truman's Secretary of State: 'The difference between us,' he claimed, 'is that we start with the facts and try, however falteringly and even selfishly, to reach true and fair conclusions, while you start with the conclusions you want and try to select and twist the facts to your own ends.'[1]

Ernest Bevin was no more impressed than Byrnes by Molotov's diplomacy, believing, in Dalton's words, that 'if you treated him badly he made the most of the grievance, and if you treated him well he only put his price up and abused you next day.'[2] It was almost impossible for the West to appreciate the Russian attitude. To them Stalin appeared still to be fighting the battles of earlier decades when he justified this attitude by quoting Lenin to the effect that 'The world has been severed into two camps, the imperialist and anti-imperialist . . . it is inconceivable that the Soviet Republic should continue to exist interminably side by side with the imperialist states. Ultimately one or another must conquer.'[3] Time was to suggest that conquest, in the Russian view, did not necessarily involve recourse to arms, especially so long as the Americans possessed atomic bombs while the Russians did not; but at least until 1953, when Stalin died, it was impossible for the West to feel confident of perpetual peace in Europe. The disillusionment which had developed even before the end of the war was merely confirmed by the failure of diplomacy in the years that followed.

From 1947 the U.S.A. was increasingly drawn into European affairs and began to share with Britain the full force of Soviet hostility. During this year Communist domination of Eastern Europe was emphasised by the trials of a number of leaders whose orthodoxy was supposedly doubtful. Communist contestants for power in Greece were being equipped through neighbouring Communist countries. In October the Cominform (Communist Information Bureau) was created to co-ordinate Communist activities in Eastern Europe and also in Italy and France. In the two Western countries, where Communism was strong, dock and transport strikes were aimed at disrupting the distribution of grain sent under the terms of the American Marshall Plan, which Molotov had denounced in Paris and which the countries of Communist Eastern Europe had been constrained to reject. In February, 1948, a Communist *coup d'état* in Prague and the unexplained death of the Czech Foreign Minister, Jan Masaryk, whose sympathies lay with the West, reaffirmed the determination of Communism to gain control wherever possible. Meanwhile, foreign ministers' conferences continued to be held without result; the fifth was adjourned *sine die* in November, 1947, and no other was convened until May, 1949. The peace treaty with Austria was held up until 1955.

Above all other causes and symptoms of dissension lay Germany. From the early days after the war the Russians, regardless of the expectation that Germany should be permitted to recover sufficiently to pay for its own imports, had removed from their zone not merely industrial equipment, but also a substantial proportion of current industrial production. For this they were strongly criticised by the British and Americans, who still hoped that the whole of Germany could be treated as an economic unit in accordance with an agreement reached at Potsdam. Molotov's demand that the fusion of the British and American zones should be cancelled convinced George Marshall (American Secretary of State from 1947 to 1949) that the Russians were hoping for an economic collapse of Europe which would pave the way for a Communist triumph. Bevin was no less convinced of the dangers presented by Communism. The events of 1947, 1948 and 1949 in Germany seemed to justify their fears. When Molotov walked out of the Paris discussions on the co-ordination of Marshall Aid, the Eastern zone was deprived of the assistance which was henceforth given to West Germany. By April, 1948, when the Russians imposed restrictions on travel between East and West Germany, four-power joint control of the country had effectively come to an end. When the Western Allies, in June, 1948, introduced a new Deutsche Mark to replace a currency which had come to be regarded as valueless and was being superseded by barter and black-market transactions, the Russians refused to accept the Western notes in their zone, hurriedly introduced a new currency of their own and imposed on all freight entering Berlin the same restrictions that had already prevented the free movement of people. For the West only the air corridors from Hamburg, Bückeburg and Frankfurt remained open. Accordingly, an air lift of all the supplies required by the citizens of West Berlin was instituted and kept going until May, 1949, when the Russians, perhaps because an Allied counter-blockade of goods passing from West to East was becoming effective, at last ended their restrictions on road and rail traffic. Before they did so, separate elections in East and West Berlin had produced two separate city governments, neither of which recognised the other. No pretence that Germany could hope for restored unity could be sustained any longer, nor could any hope that, at least in the immediate future, the attitudes of the Communist world and of the Western democracies could be reconciled.

WESTERN RESISTANCE TO COMMUNIST THREATS

The West was bound to resist. It could not depend on the international organisations which had already been created. Quite clearly, the United Nations Organisation could not, by itself, provide the world with any greater assurance of peace than the League of Nations had been able to provide. Its Security Council, designed to investigate disputes which might threaten peace, could be rendered powerless if one of its five permanent members (Britain, the United States, Russia, France and Taiwan—usually described as Nationalist China) used the veto.

In November, 1947, the U.S.A. managed to create an Interim Committee of the General Assembly which could evade the Soviet veto in Security Council sessions. Yet, as an answer to Communist threats, this was not sufficient, and accordingly the West started to draw together in other ways. In March, 1947, Britain and France had pledged joint resistance to any possible revival of German aggression and had provided for constant consultation on economic and other matters of concern to both countries; and in March, 1948, this agreement was expanded by the Treaty of Brussels, which united Britain, France, Belgium, Holland and Luxemburg, nominally in defence against German aggression, but equally against possible threats from Russia. In April, 1948, the Organisation for European Economic co-operation was established to assist the recovery which the Americans were encouraging with aid under the Marshall Plan. In July, 1948, British airfields were made available to American bombers and their atomic weapons. In April, 1949, the North Atlantic Treaty Organisation came into being, and Britain, the United States, Canada and nine Western European countries began to co-ordinate their forces for the preservation of peace. West Germany, brought into closer friendly contact with its former opponents by the Berlin blockade and the Allied airlift, was gradually restored to the concert of Europe after Dr Adenauer's Christian Democrats had won the first post-war elections in 1949. In September, 1950, the Western foreign ministers agreed to end the state of war with Germany, and the Federal Republic's readmission to an increasingly reunited Western Europe thereafter proceeded steadily. Since the outbreak of the Korean war occurred when 175 Russian divisions in East Germany and other East European neighbours were faced by only 4 properly equipped divisions in West Germany, a NATO meeting decided that West Germany should be permitted to rearm. Neither the Germans nor their new allies were enthusiastic. The Germans had suffered quite as much as others from their own past militarism and had no wish to see their country with its reviving economy, becoming once again the theatre of war, this time between the Communists and the West. But the Americans insisted that they should make a contribution to Europe's defence if the financial aid to Europe from the United States were to continue. In 1950 the French Prime Minister, René Pleven, evolved a plan for a European army which would include a German force. This issue, though, was still under discussion when the British Labour government was replaced by a Conservative one; and it did not in the end come into being in the form originally proposed by Pleven.

Britain's own defence policy was necessarily closely bound up with its foreign policy. During the years of hope immediately after the war the numbers in the forces had been reduced from about five million in 1945 to less than one million in March 1948; and the defence estimates, still £1667m for 1946–7, were less than £700m for 1948–9. The Cold War against Communism and the announcement in September, 1949, that Russia had successfully tested an atomic bomb two months previously brought to an end this progressive reduction in defence costs. In 1949 the White Paper on defence, in a reference to the United Nations, regretted that the establishment of collective security had not been achieved, and heralded the production of 'unconventional' (i.e. atomic) weapons. While the number in the forces continued to decline (they were less than 700000 by March, 1951) the estimates began to rise again.

In June, 1950, the Communist North Koreans invaded the South, and the Security Council of the United Nations (boycotted temporarily by the Russians and consequently allowed to operate effectively) approved the despatch of military aid to the South Korean government. The war lasted for a year, and spasmodic conflict continued until July, 1953. The United

Nations forces were commanded by the American General MacArthur, and it was on the United States that the main burden fell of resistance to the North Koreans and, after November 1950, to their Chinese allies, but Britain was among the fourteen other countries to send troops to Korea, and the effect on its defence programme and its economy was critical. A naval force and an army division were sent to the East to participate in a series of advances and retreats during which, it was estimated, the death roll approached 2¼ million. At home, in September, 1950, a three-year defence plan was announced, involving expenditure of £3600m on forces which were again to increase in number, to 800000; and in January, 1951, the pro-gramme was revised to allow an outlay of £4700m. These developments, which were made necessary by the fear that war in Korea might grow into conflict with China and Russia, were depressing. It was possible though, that Attlee's visit to America in December, 1950, may have influenced President Truman's decision not to authorise the use of the atomic bomb in Korea. At least the worst imaginable consequences of war were avoided.

For Britain, Korea was not the only theatre of strife. Twenty thousand of its troops had been involved since 1948 in a guerilla war in Malaya against Communist terrorists. This struggle is described in Chapter 32.

INTERNATIONAL COOPERATION

The cold war had ensured that Britain should not retire into splendid isolation or neutrality. So had membership of the United Nations Organisation and its Security Council, of its newly created subsidiary bodies dealing with such issues as Food and Agriculture, World Health, Refugees, Education and Science, and of such survivals from the inter-war period as the International Labour Organisation, the International Court of Justice and the Trusteeship (Mandates) Council. In certain quarters hopes were expressed that the British would play an even greater part in the affairs of the Continent. The potential strength of Britain's position in Europe after the war was recog-nised, for example, by the Belgian Foreign Minister and Secretary-General of NATO, Paul Henri Spaak, who declared that while the continental countries had suffered severely, both morally and physically, under enemy occupation, Britain had been spared and could consequently have provided Europe with a moral leadership which would have been readily accepted. Such ideas were echoed, to some extent, among the British themselves. Churchill raised them when he suggested at Zürich in 1946 that a kind of 'United States of Europe'[4] should be created. Bevin took the initiative in 1947 in welcoming the Marshall Aid proposals and in organising the Paris conference which drew up the arrangements required by the Americans. He helped to negotiate the Treaty of Brussels. British delegates played a part in the creation by the Brussels Treaty powers of the Council of Europe at Strasbourg in January, 1949. It was Churchill who urged that Germany should be represented on the council, as it was from June, 1950. When it had been decided that delegates to the Assembly should be chosen by the governments of the member countries and should reflect the proportionate strengths of the main parties in each national parliament, the British representatives, in 1949 and 1950, included politicians who were, or were later to be, well known in Europe: Dalton, Maurice Edelman, James Callaghan, Denis Healey and Anthony Crosland, Churchill, Harold Macmillan and Robert Boothby. Each party had its enthusiasts for the unity of Europe.

However, beyond participating in these international transactions, or allowing its supporters to do so, the Labour government was not prepared to go. It was not interested in the elaborate projects for European integration which, immediately after the war, the Continent might have accepted. Bevin did not envisage a supranational authority which might deprive states of their traditional sovereignty. Nor did Attlee, who, a decade later, was to denounce the negotiations for British admission to the Common Market. Cripps told Maurice Petsche, the French Finance Minister, that he did not think the time was ripe for anything beyond conventional commercial treaties. In 1950, when Jean Monnet (who had been responsible since 1947 for planning the modernisation and equipment of France) sought to include Britain in the European Coal and Steel Community, he found only reluctance in government circles in London to the idea of joining any organisation which might limit national control over important industries. Bevin was implacably opposed to membership of the Community. So, at this stage, were some of the leading Conservatives. Even Harold Macmillan, one of the more earnest of the Conservative advocates of European solidarity, felt obliged to inform the Council of Europe at Strasbourg that 'our people are not going to hand to any supranational authority the right to close down our pits or steel works. We will allow no supranational authority to put large masses of our people out of work.'[5] The Conservatives did suggest, as an alternative, inter-governmental committees to concert development plans, but the Continent remained unimpressed.

At the same time, when the question arose of surrendering any real authority to the Council of Europe, the British were as reluctant at the end of the 1940s as were the French. They had no wish to accept any organisation which might override their links with the Commonwealth, the work of such bodies as the United Nations, NATO or the O.E.E.C., or the essential features of their welfare services and the nationalised industries. They rejected the idea that the Council should aim for the creation of a federation of the European countries, and opted instead only for 'functionalism', the bringing together of experts on particular issues in *ad hoc* gatherings such as the European Payments Union. They may have found, as Churchill did, that it was easy enough to be visionaries when out of office, yet when confronted with the realities of government they hesitated considerably longer than many of their European contemporaries.

Herbert Morrison, who succeeded Bevin as Foreign Minister in March, 1951, made no alteration to his policy. Only after 1960, when the success of the European Economic Community was clear, was a British government to accept the idea of a limited surrender of national sovereignty in economic and political as well as in military spheres.

---

[1] James B. Reston, 'Negotiating with the Russians', *Harper's Magazine*, August 1947
[2] Dalton, *High Tide*, p. 155
[3] Stalin, *The Problems of Leninism*
[4] Churchill at Zürich, 19.9.46
[5] Macmillan at the Strasbourg Assembly, 16.8.50

11

Britain and India

The British may have hesitated when the surrender of sovereignty to a supranational European organisation was at stake. Confronted with the more familiar problems of India, however, their government acted with a decisiveness which made a profound impact on the entire colonial empire. Within two decades sovereignty had been abandoned over all but the smallest of the dependencies.

Although the ultimate transfer of power to the Indians had been foreseen for decades, the rapidity with which it would in the end be carried out had certainly not been realised in 1939. The embarrassments arising from the antagonism felt by Hindus and Muslims for each other, and the supposed incapacity of Congress and the other Indian parties to guarantee either internal stability or resistance to aggression from outside seemed to rule out any really dramatic developments. Lord Zetland, the Secretary of State for India, writing to the Viceroy, Lord Linlithgow, had expressed the view that the rate of advance was 'much more likely to be that of a stage coach rather than an express train';[1] and although he had doubted the wisdom of his prediction once the war had broken out, Linlithgow had continued to feel astonishment at the idea that the British would 'seriously contemplate evacuation in any measurable period of time'.[2]

WAR-TIME PROPOSALS FOR INDEPENDENCE

Yet Indian leaders were not inert, after all; they had no wish to wait indefinitely; and their demands for self-government had been stimulated in 1939 when the Viceroy had declared India a belligerent without consulting the central legislature. The White Raj had been quickly forced to recognise that its years were numbered. It had accordingly offered dominion status to

75

the Indians once the war was over, and detailed propositions had been formulated by Sir Stafford Cripps in 1942 when Japanese seizure of the British possessions in the Far East had made Indian help in the face of threatened invasion imperative. These propositions had not found acceptance. They had been spurned both by the predominantly Hindu Congress party and by the Muslim League. Congress had objected particularly to the suggestion put forward by Cripps that provinces might opt out of joining the projected dominion, while the League rejected the proposals on the entirely opposite ground that the idea of a separate Muslim state was not contemplated. Gandhi in particular had contributed to the failure of Cripps' mission with his demands that the British should leave at once, even if this meant bequeathing India to chaos and the Japanese. Clearly, the British could not comply with Gandhi's requirements, and when widespread disorders had followed the inauguration of a 'Quit India' campaign, the Mahatma was gaoled, as were some 36000 others by the middle of 1943. It was fortunate for the British that a majority of Congress supporters, including Jawaharlal Nehru, believed that the Japanese should be resisted, that the Muslim League took no part in the campaign of civil disobedience, and that most of the Indian army remained stalwartly loyal.

By the end of the war it had become evident not merely that independence for India could not be delayed but that the unity which the British had bestowed on the country was unlikely to be perpetuated. Since 1940 Mohammed Ali Jinnah had been expounding a two-nation theory and under his leadership the creation of a separate Pakistan had become the determined policy of the Muslim League. The British, who had always feared the possible bitterness and bloodshed which division of India along religious lines might produce, greatly regretted this. The Hindus were equally unwilling to contemplate partition. Gandhi and Nehru believed that the communal rift was essentially a domestic problem which Indians would resolve once they had obtained self-government. Gandhi predicted that when freedom from bondage had been gained 'an interim solution will be found to be easy.'[3] Nehru, an agnostic, whose ideal was a secular state, never envisaged a country divided along religious boundaries. The general Congress view was that conflict was being stimulated by the British with the conscious intention of dividing and ruling. Such judgments could scarcely have been more faulty.

THE CABINET MISSION 1946

Early in 1946 elections were held for both central and provincial assemblies. In the central assembly every reserved Muslim seat was won by the League and all the 'general' seats by Congress. These two parties also gained very substantial majorities of the seats in the provincial assemblies: Congress was left with absolute majorities in eight of the eleven provinces, including Assam (which Jinnah had claimed for Pakistan) and the North West Frontier Province (where Abdul Ghaffer Khan ensured the loyalty to Congress of an overwhelmingly Muslim population). In the Punjab a coalition including Sikh and Congress members emerged, leaving the League in opposition. The League held office without absolute majorities in Bengal and Sind. Such were the conditions prevailing in India when, in March, 1946, a Cabinet mission arrived consisting of Lord Pethick-Lawrence, the Secretary of State for India, Sir Stafford Cripps, now President of the Board of Trade and A. V. Alexander, the First Lord of the Admiralty.

Since the main Indian parties failed to produce a scheme of their own for the future government of the country, the mission was itself obliged to put one forward. They suggested the immediate establishment of an interim government in which all positions should be held by Indians and, as a long-term solution, the creation of a federal government which would leave the central authority with control over foreign affairs, defence and communications, and would give other issues to the provincial governments. A novel feature of the federation was to be the organisation of the provinces into three groups, one predominantly Hindu and the others predominantly Muslim. This system, the mission hoped, would make their scheme acceptable to the League, whose demands for an entirely separate state were rejected on the grounds that it would have been incompatible with Indian defence needs, that it was not desired by the great majority of Indians apart from League supporters, and that the administration and communications which had been developed to serve India as a whole would suffer from partition. The mission could not fail to observe that the League was laying claim to Assam, where there was no Muslim majority, and to Bengal and the Punjab, where there were very large non-Muslim minorities.

Discussion of these suggestions took place in Simla, but the cool climate and the remoteness from the passions of Delhi had no effect. Jinnah was contemptuous of 'a mutilated, moth-eaten and truncated Pakistan' and no agreement could be reached. Accordingly the mission published alternative proposals designed to bring members of the various communities together in an indirectly elected assembly, representing both princely states and British India, to draw up the final constitution. At first the response to these proposals was not unfavourable. The Congress leaders, however, changed their minds about entering the provincial government. When the Viceroy (Lord Wavell) slightly altered the allocation of government posts to be offered to each group (giving 6 to Congress and only 5 to the League, instead of 5 to each) Jinnah also changed his mind, resentfully withdrew his acceptance of the mission's proposals and planned to procure a separate Pakistan by force. The sixteenth of August 1946 became 'Direct Action Day'. The campaign began with communal riots in Calcutta which resulted in 4000 dead and 10000 injured.

DISUNITY AND DISORDER

The increased distrust which now developed between the Viceroy and the Muslims made co-operation between the Viceroy and Congress easier. Congress leaders changed their minds again and accepted the seats offered to them in a revised Interim Government, which consisted at first of 5 members representing the Hindus, 3 non-League Muslims and single representatives of the Scheduled classes, the Sikhs, the Christians and the Parsees. The League at first regarded this government as outrageous, despite an assurance that it was at liberty to nominate 5 more members of its own. Its members were advised by Jinnah to fly black flags from the housetops 'in silent contempt for the Hindu government'.[4] Then, in October, it accepted its 5 seats—though the *volte-face* was performed with the declared intention of campaigning for Pakistan from within, and henceforth Muslim ministers carried on their own policy with little reference to the policies of the non-Muslims.

Under this disunited government the disorder which had begun in Calcutta spread to the whole of Bengal and Bihar, where massacres continued throughout the autumn. Muslims were the principal victims. People whose families had lived contentedly among Hindus for generations were systematically murdered; and although it was never possible to discover who was behind the murders, they clearly represented a well-organised plan of extirpation. Nehru tried energetically to have the killing stopped, but the death roll rose nonetheless to at least 5000 and possibly twice this figure. Over 1000, perhaps 2000 Muslims were killed at a Hindu religious fair in the United Provinces. In the mountainous borderlands between the Frontier Province and the Punjab Hindus were the victims. Both communities continued to suffer in Calcutta. Strikes and sabotage in industry and mining occurred throughout Bengal. At the pressing invitation of Attlee, the Viceroy and five ministers from the Interim Government visited London, but the discussions that took place there had no result.

In December, 1946, a constituent assembly met at Simla. Congress was elated. Nehru still hoped to be able to introduce a constitution which would satisfy all the people of India. However, he gained the support of neither League nor princes, and the situation seemed yet again to have reverted to deadlock. In these circumstances the Labour government in Britain, determined to bring to an end interminable, irreconcilable argument and to oblige the Indian leaders to face the realities of rule, announced flatly in February, 1947, that the White Raj would be surrendered by June, 1948.

The effect of the British announcement on the politicians was bracing. Unhappily, it did not bring communal peace to India. In fact, in the Pubjab a very ominous struggle developed which presaged even greater trouble when British withdrawal eventually took place. While the Muslims of the province conducted a civil disobedience campaign and filled the prisons to overflowing, the coalition government of Sikhs and Hindus resigned, leaving a vacuum which obliged the Governor, Sir Evan Jenkins, to resort to personal rule. This explosive situation came to a head with savage rioting in Lahore at the beginning of March, 1947. Within two days much of Amritsar and Multan was in flames. Arson and rioting spread to other towns of the Punjab, and from these to the villages. In central and East Punjab the

Sikhs and Hindus were principally responsible, though in the north, where Muslims were in a large majority, they were the victims. About 20000 troops helped to restore an ephemeral order, but the experts who predicted a recurrence of the violence were unhappily prescient.

The antagonisms which divided Indian society were reflected in doctrinaire and unyielding leaders. The difficulties created for the British by Jinnah were obvious. Gandhi created problems of a different kind. His obstructiveness was recalled much later (1964) by Earl Attlee: 'Stafford Cripps' mission to India would have succeeded if Gandhi had not been so difficult. Not only was he stubborn: he was unpredictable. . . . Winston . . . thought Gandhi absolutely hopeless.'[5] Nehru, who had been educated at Harrow, Cambridge and the Inner Temple, seemed to Attlee 'altogether easier to deal with, practical, rational and flexible, and with singular personal charm'; yet, even so, he contributed much to the failure of the Cabinet mission's proposals in 1945, and Attlee was obliged to admit that 'Winston always regarded him as quite impossible.'

Confronted with the problems raised by the incompatible demands of the Indians, the Viceroy and his chief Service advisers (as Attlee wrote in his autobiography) 'were despondent and could only suggest a progressive retirement from India, province by province, which was in my mind a counsel of despair. I had a great admiration for Lord Wavell . . . but I did not think he was likely to find a solution. I did not think that he and the Indians could really understand each other. New men were needed for a new policy.'[6] Wavell had been considered by the Germans, at the start of the war, as the ablest soldier in the British army. He was scholarly yet practical as well, and fair, but he was taciturn and reticent and was interested neither in display nor in the trivialities of social life at a time when the opposite qualities may have been advantageous. He was replaced in March, 1947, after only three and a half years in office, his withdrawal being hurried and not very tactfully explained in England. The new Viceroy was Earl Mountbatten, who, like Wavell, had achieved great distinction during the war but was in other respects a notable contrast. Aged forty-six in 1947 (Wavell was sixty-three), with a royal background, sociable, he had a lively interest in politics. In Attlee's estimation he was the ideal new man for a new policy.

MOUNTBATTEN AND INDEPENDENCE

Mountbatten's arrival could not, unfortunately, make any difference to the communal strife that had now seized India. Nine of the eleven provincial governments were now ruling by decree, with powers to ban meetings and to inflict drastic punishments. These powers did not serve as deterrents, and unrest spread at the end of March to the Frontier Province where a zest for looting and destruction was added to the usual communal antagonisms. The Interim Government in Delhi was in no condition to lead the country back to peace since it was as disunited as ever, with rival wings at permanent loggerheads and failing to consult each other on issues of importance. British hopes that day-to-day contacts would teach ministers to co-operate proved to be quite unjustified.

The British now determined to lay down their burden even earlier than they had planned in February. The Indians were informed that they would have to accept self-government in August, 1947, ten months earlier than originally proposed. Furthermore, it was becoming quite clear that they would have to accept partition. During April the Congress leaders began to concede the necessity for Pakistan, if only because they realised that without partition they would never be able to establish the strong central government that they desired. During May Mountbatten, with the advice particularly of V. P. Menon, set to work to devise a future for India based on the assumption that two countries with separate governments would emerge. At the beginning of June the partition plan was formally made public, and, with forebodings amongst those who knew that it would lead with absolute certainty to mass slaughter, at least in the Punjab, it was unanimously accepted. The independence bill was passed by the British Parliament, in the face of Churchill's vigorous opposition, in July.

For a short time violence abated. The Muslim League called off a civil disobedience campaign in the Frontier Province and Assam. But incidents did not cease altogether, particularly on the south-east border of the Punjab; and the members of the Interim Government showed no more inclination than before to co-operate with each other. Furthermore, ominous symptoms of potential trouble among the Sikhs began to be observed. Mountbatten admitted that only after the plan for partition had

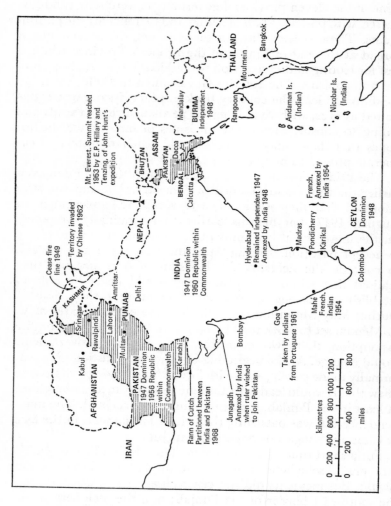

India, Pakistan, Burma and Ceylon after 1945

been devised had he discovered that the Sikh population would be cut in two; and neither Jinnah nor Nehru appear to have had much greater knowledge of this important section of the Punjab community. The future was to show that the problem was a serious one.

India and Pakistan gained their independence on 15 August, 1947. They were granted the right to leave the Commonwealth if they wished, though statesmen from other dominions hoped that they would not do so. The South African Prime Minister, Field-Marshal Smuts, spoke of the advantages of Commonwealth association as outweighing all inducements to chart a course alone, while Peter Fraser, the Prime Minister of New Zealand, exerted considerable influence when he asserted that the people of the British dominions did not regard dominion status as 'an imperfect kind of independence. On the contrary, it is independence with something added, and not independence with something taken away.'[7] Both India and Pakistan remained members of the Commonwealth and became the first dominions in which governments were not in the hands of the descendants of white settlers.

Independence could not, of course, come about without consideration of the princes. The Maharajahs of Bikaner and Patiala agreed readily that their representatives should co-operate in drawing up the new constitution. Others were influenced by Nehru's blunt declaration that states which did not join the new India would be treated as hostile. Few were in a position to bargain and those which were large enough to do so were given no encouragement. Mountbatten urged them to join on terms which would leave them with 'all the practical independence' they could possibly use while surrendering to the government control over foreign affairs, defence and communications. He indicated to them that they could no more run away from the neighbouring dominion government than they could run away from the subjects for whose welfare they were responsible. The Viceroy's powers of persuasion, aided perhaps by his prestige and his membership of the British royal family, had the desired effect, and, when the British withdrew, only Hyderabad, the unimportant state of Junagadh, and Kashmir had adhered to neither dominion. India was shortly to seize the first two. Kashmir was to become a more lasting problem, even after its annexation by India. As a Commonwealth failure it was unavoidably a matter of concern to Britain, but the British government had no power to impose a solution.

THE CONSEQUENCES

There was never doubt that the North West Frontier Province, Baluchistan, Sind, and the Sylhet district of Assam would opt for incorporation in Pakistan. Boundaries in Bengal and the Punjab, however, could not be straightforwardly defined so two commissions were set up to undertake the task. Each of these consisted of two Hindu and two Muslim judges, with a single British chairman, Sir Cyril Radcliffe. As it happened, the Hindu and Muslim judges failed completely to agree and decisions had in practice to be reached by the chairman, who collated information and announced his verdicts in Delhi. In Bengal a complication was introduced by the existence of a Bengal national culture which made many educated people of both creeds reluctant to adopt the partition which religious differences seemed to make inescapable. The possibility of remaining outside both dominions was discussed, but in the end the issue was forced by the determination of a majority of Muslims in East Bengal to join Pakistan.

The partition of the Punjab was even more difficult. While the Muslim population lived mainly in the west and the Hindus mainly in the east, the Sikhs were scattered throughout the province, so that wherever the boundary might be drawn, nearly two million Sikhs would find themselves under Muslim rule, which their leaders refused to accept. The fierce communal riots in which they had been involved earlier in the year had made necessary the creation of a Boundary Force under British officers, but the civil war which developed in August rapidly grew beyond control. District officers were helpless and the Boundary Force was incapable of preventing large parts of the Punjab cities from being burnt down. In rural areas, apparently organised and disciplined bands of Sikhs made systematic attacks on Muslim villages. The atrocities became quite out of hand after independence day. To the accompaniment of bloodshed and conflagration the East Punjab was cleared of its Muslim survivors. Unplanned and desperate mass migration followed, yet the refugees could never be sure that they would reach safety. They were attacked as they journeyed. Trains were derailed and their occupants were dragged out and massacred. It was estimated that by the beginning of November eight million people had crossed the frontier in one direction or the other, with hundreds of animals. Enormous camps were set up to accommodate these *émigrés* until permanent settlements could be found for them. Food supplies were dropped from the air by the Royal Indian Air Force. Doctors were rushed to the boundary with drugs and vaccines. For those who survived each government had to find work—not so hard for the peasantry (though seeds and tools were needed and maintenance until crops had grown) but more difficult for the urban classes, since the previous occupations of Muslims did not necessarily correspond to those of Hindus and Sikhs.

Difficulties of dividing the personnel of the civil government and the armed forces were small in comparison with the problems set by civil war and refugees, though even here bitterness was unavoidable. Particularly acrimonious were the discussions on the distribution of military equipment. Sir Claude Auchinleck's task as Supreme Commander became impossible, and negotiations broke down amidst harsh recriminations. Meanwhile, the requests for transfer from one dominion to the other of nearly 160000 employees of the Railway Department alone indicated the magnitude of the problem presented by civil officialdom. Most of the buildings and equipment required by a central government were at Delhi. It was much harder for the Pakistanis in Karachi. For the British who had ruled so much of India for nearly two centuries there could be little satisfaction. They were obliged now to stand aside and see their work of unification and pacification overturned. Those who had predicted that withdrawal would at once release the forces of disorder created by communal passions were plainly shown to have been quite right. And yet, unless they had wished the assaults to have been made on themselves, they could not possibly have persisted in imposing a white domination.

[1] Nicholas Mansergh, *Survey of British Commonwealth Affairs 1939–52*, p. 200, Oxford University Press for Royal Institute of International Affairs (London 1958), *Lord Zetland to Lord Linlithgow*, 1939
[2] Ibid., p. 200   [3] Ibid., p. 204   [4] Ibid., p. 221
[5] Attlee, *The Observer*, 31.5.64   [6] Attlee, *As it Happened*, p. 183
[7] *New Zealand Herald*, 5.6.47

12

Ceylon and Burma

Progress towards self-government in India was inevitably accompanied by similar movements in Burma and Ceylon. Burma's independence developed from the chaos left by the war and came into being in difficult conditions. Ceylon, on the other hand, moved steadily forward with neither crisis nor bitterness to mar its advance, providing an example which only a few of Britain's smaller dependencies were able to emulate in the future.

Ceylon's political progress had resulted from unemotional agreements between its own leaders and British governments. There had been no need for the creation by the former of a mass following, liable, as in India, to get out of control. The island had consequently been spared the violence and the gaol sentences from which the Indians had suffered. Before the war its organs of government had consisted of a State Council (for the most part elected, on a territorial, not communal, basis) and a number of executive committees presiding over different government departments and composed of members of the State Council. Towards the end of the war the Soulbury Commission recommended further changes, and accordingly, the executive committees were replaced in 1946 by Cabinet government under a Prime Minister. Ceylon became a dominion in February, 1948.

These changes were not dramatic. Lord Soulbury remained in Ceylon as the first Governor-General and not until 1954 was a Ceylonese appointed to the office. Don Stephen Senanayake, Prime Minister since 1947, remained until 1952. The same anglicised, upper middle-class *élite* ruled as ministers both before and after independence. Until 1957 the British retained a number of the naval bases which they had held during the years when they controlled the politics of the island. Only after 1958, when Solomon Bandaranaike launched his Sri Lanka Freedom party with emotional appeals to the masses and aroused their religious and linguistic prejudices against the anglicised *élite* did violence disturb a hitherto tranquil country—violence leading eighteen months later to Bandaranaike's own murder by a Buddhist monk.

Until the end of the First World War Burmese political consciousness had remained undeveloped. There was little native leadership. The British, with some Indians and Chinese, controlled most of the large businesses. Industrial labour was largely Indian or Chinese. Burmese held most of the junior posts, but the senior posts were occupied almost exclusively by British civil servants. Only after 1923 had the appointment of Burmese to the higher positions been encouraged. The Burmese legislature, introduced in 1897, had been entirely nominated. In 1923 a parliament had been created with a wide franchise and a large Burmese majority; but permanent officials continued to control the Treasury and only half the ministerial positions were left to Burmese. Not until 1937 had Burma obtained genuine self-government. The officials ceased to sit in parliament, Burmese ministers received all the portfolios, a Senate was established which contained only a few Europeans, the lower house became overwhelmingly Burmese and was entirely elected. Burmese government was separated from that of India. However, the Governor had retained control of foreign affairs and defence, and had remained responsible for the administration of the frontier highlands which the Burmese had never dominated.

Concessions stimulated aspirations for an even greater degree of independence, and during 1941 thirty young patriots received secret military training from the Japanese in the expectation of taking active measures against the British. They had their opportunity in 1942 when they led about 4000 Burmese who helped the Japanese to conquer Burma. However, their endeavours to set up local administrations in each district as it was occupied by the Japanese were accompanied by such excesses and revealed such incapacity that the Japanese disbanded their force and reformed it, under Aung San, as the Burma National Army. The Japanese then accepted Ba Maw as the head of the state, and after a proclamation of Burmese independence in August, 1943, their puppet declared war on Britain. Disillusionment followed rapidly among the patriots. The Burmese soon realised that the Japanese promise of independence was not

going to be honoured. The treatment to which they were subjected within the Japanese Co-Prosperity Sphere was contemptuous and humiliating. Accordingly, in 1944, Aung San made
secret overtures to the British.

The negotiations at first brought some embarrassment to the
British. General Slim, who was leading the campaign against the
Japanese in Burma, and Lord Mountbatten, the commander
of the forces in South-East Asia, both considered that if they did
not support Aung San's Anti-Fascist People's Freedom League
they would be obliged to fight it. Mountbatten compared the
Burmese with the Italians, who had come to be regarded as co-
belligerents against the Germans. However, the civil authorities
warned the forces that support for the A.F.P.F.L. would bring
serious difficulties in its train and advised the arrest of Aung
San as a war criminal. The Governor, Sir Reginald Dorman-
Smith, was initially particularly unwilling to include Aung San
in any administration. The uncertainty resulting from quite
contrary recommendations was reflected in London. In time,
though, both Dorman-Smith and the new Labour government
realised that Aung San now had too much influence to be disregarded. It was decided that the A.F.P.F.L. should be supported, and a new Governor, Major-General Hubert Rance,
was appointed to implement the decision.

The embarrassment created by Aung San was not the only
one left for the British authorities by the retreating Japanese.
The physical destruction in Burma was very evident: the docks
at Rangoon were in urgent need of repair after bombing and
the roads were disintegrating beneath the military traffic.
Without their reconstruction economic life could not revive,
trade would remain at a standstill and uncontrolled inflation
resulting from the almost complete disappearance of consumer
goods would continue. Insecurity had brought an increase of
crime. Great areas had gone out of cultivation. Towns had been
burnt and deserted. Nor, at first, was there an active civil administration to restore order where it had collapsed during the war.
The British administrators had been enrolled in the forces or
had struggled for survival in the abominable Japanese prisoner-
of-war camps. The Japanese themselves had revealed only very
limited capacity for governing a conquered territory. Many of
the Burmese had taken refuge in obscurity and persuasion had
to be exercised to bring some of them out of it. In short, few of

the new states of the post-war decades moved towards their independence in more discouraging circumstances.

In September, 1946, Aung San became virtually Prime Minister when his followers received a majority of the seats on the Executive Council. In January, 1947, he went to London where his plan for Burmese independence was sympathetically considered. In April the A.F.P.F.L. was overwhelmingly successful in a general election, winning 173 out of 210 seats.

Aung San's experience of high office was, however, short-lived. He was assassinated, with six other ministers, in August, 1947. The villain responsible was U Saw, who had been Prime Minister from 1940 to 1942 and was now unwilling to take second place. His gesture brought him only execution, after a trial before Burmese judges, and it was, instead, U Nu who succeeded as Prime Minister. In October, an Anglo-Burmese treaty was signed in London, and as a result of this Burma became an independent republic on 4 January, 1948, at 4.20 a.m., which the astrologers regarded as an auspicious time. U Nu admitted that the Labour government had shown wisdom and vision and had been at pains to win Burmese good will. The British had placed no obstacle in the way of Burmese withdrawal from the Commonwealth. As an act of friendship they had liquidated the debt owed to Britain by Burma. During the early years of independence, when the country was faced with all the problems of inexperience, political rivalries and revolt among the Karens, they provided loans to Burma amounting to about £75m, of which little more than £1m was ever repaid.

The initially close association between Britain and independent Burma gradually weakened as recollections of British rule faded. Trade, at first important, progressively declined in the 1950s as Burma's links with other Eastern countries developed. The close educational connection and the use of the English language diminished. Burmese methods of government, which had been much affected by British practices, became in time increasingly different. The British military mission, which helped the Burmese forces in the earlier years of independence, was withdrawn in 1954. Perhaps, though, personal relationships became more cordial once the British had ceased to be responsible for the government.

13

The Labour government and the Middle East

British soldiers had served for decades in the Middle East. They had been stationed in Egypt since it had become an area of particular concern to Britain in the 1880s, and in Palestine, Transjordan and Iraq since these countries became mandated territories for which Britain was responsible after the First World War. When the Second World War ended many were still serving throughout the region. Their power appeared to be as great as ever. In reality, the impression was quite misleading. Arab nationalism on one hand and, on the other, the obligation felt in the Western world to allow Jewish survivors of Nazism to strengthen their national refuge in Palestine combined with Britain's financial weakness to make the traditional position increasingly untenable during the two years which followed the collapse of Germany.

The original Labour view, explained in a policy statement accepted by the party in 1944, had been that all Jews who wished to settle in Palestine should be allowed to do so. 'Let the Arabs be encouraged to move out as the Jews move in,' the statement had advised. 'Let them be compensated for their land and let their settlement elsewhere be carefully organised and generously financed. . . . We should re-examine also the possibility of extending the present Palestinian boundaries, by agreement with Egypt, Syria or Transjordan.'[1] In the light of subsequent developments such a policy was highly unrealistic. It could not really be expected that the terms would find acceptance among the Arabs. They were, however, adopted also in the United States by Presidents Roosevelt and Truman. In October, 1944, Roosevelt had declared his hopes of 'the opening of Palestine to unrestricted Jewish immigration and colonisation.'[2] In August, 1945, Truman asked the British government, as an emergency gesture of humanitarianism, to issue 100000 certificates for Jews seeking admission to Palestine. Confronted with the probable consequences of unrestricted settlement, the government became anxious. Its Foreign Office, Colonial Office and service advisers considered that implementation of the Labour policy declaration could result only in catastrophe. Consequently, some limitation on Jewish immigration was accepted as necessary. The compromise, inescapable though it may have been, brought satisfaction to neither Jews nor Arabs, and during the next two years the discontent found expression in a series of terrorist outrages against British troops and administrators in Palestine which proved beyond the powers of military and police forces to suppress. The terrorism culminated in an explosion which caused a hundred deaths in the King David Hotel, the British administrative headquarters in Jerusalem, in July, 1946.

Meanwhile, Arab nationalism was also developing as a factor which the West could no longer ignore. The Arabs expected the British to act in accordance with Bevin's conviction that his countrymen should abandon for ever the idea that one people could dominate another; and they became impatient when the withdrawal was delayed. The Egyptians grew particularly restive when the British, reluctant to alter substantially the terms of the treaty drawn up in 1936, hesitated to transfer their troops from the Nile Valley to the Suez Canal zone. Only Jordan accepted the re-negotiation of a pre-war treaty, and even here King Abdullah was strongly criticised for consenting that British troops should remain in his country for another twenty-five years. Furthermore, Britain was in debt at the end of the war to Middle Eastern states: it owed nearly £70m to Iraq and nearly £400m to Egypt.

Despite all these evident problems, the British were still thinking, immediately after the war, in terms of their traditional role as military defenders of lines of communication and of oil supplies. When, by 1947, they had been compelled to admit that a permanent base in Egypt could no longer be envisaged, they began progressively to transfer their military stores to Palestine. Yet Palestine was no more secure a base than Egypt in the prevailing conditions of intense hostility between Jews and Arabs. It had, indeed, already become a millstone which Britain could no longer support. Between January, 1945, and November,

1947, at a time when the British balance of payments difficulties were acute, when foreign currency reserves were draining rapidly away and domestic recovery after the war was making heavy demands, endeavours to maintain order in Palestine cost the British one hundred million pounds. In an attempt to reduce the burden the British government sought American help. Notwithstanding the differences of attitude which had developed between the British and American governments on unrestricted Jewish immigration into Palestine, President Truman accepted the responsibility. The British thereupon determined, in September, 1947, to give up their mandate to keep the peace in Palestine, to bring to an end the transference of military equipment from Egypt to Palestine and to leave the final solution in the hands of the United Nations. While undeclared war developed between Arabs and Jews, the United Nations, by a narrow majority, voted for the partition of Palestine. The Arabs opposed this, but since they were disunited and unprepared to take over the power abandoned by the British, their opposition was ineffectual. Israel emerged, after all, as the country of the Jews, Jordan gained part of central Palestine and Jerusalem was divided between Israel and Jordan. Great bitterness continued to fester throughout the region but at least Britain was no longer burdened with the sole responsibility for keeping the contestants apart.

Britain's position in the Middle East was clearly crumbling. In 1951 advantage of this was taken by the Persian government of Dr Mussadiq. Persian xenophobia combined with Mussadiq's search for a scapegoat to distract attention from internal failures, and the outcome was the nationalisation (or seizure) of the oil refinery and other installations at Abadan which had been developed since the Anglo-Persian Oil Company, in 1909, had leased the land from the local sheikh. The Labour government in Britain could take no effective action to regain control at Abadan, and when Anthony Eden succeeded Herbert Morrison as Foreign Secretary in October, 1951, the Anglo-Iranian Oil Company had ceased to operate and the export of oil from Abadan had for the time being come to an end.

---

[1] Dalton, *High Tide*, p. 145
[2] Ibid., p. 148

14

Labour's last two years and the return of the Conservatives

In February, 1950, Labour still had a lead of 166 seats in the Commons over the Conservatives and a clear majority of 136 over Conservatives, Liberals, Communists and Independents. Since 1945 it had not lost a single by-election. Its strength, however, was ebbing much more rapidly than these facts suggested. As the very honest memoirs of Hugh Dalton revealed, the 'glad, confident morning' had clouded over at the time of the fuel crisis in February, 1947, the self-confidence of the Cabinet had weakened and personal antagonisms had thereafter increasingly divided the ministry. Dalton himself found Emanuel Shinwell (Minister of Fuel and Power from 1945 to 1947) unco-operative, self-centred and long-winded. Some of their Cabinet associates regarded Bevan as 'a spendthrift, an Empire-builder and a difficult colleague'.[1] Cripps believed that Morrison was 'quite out of his depth' and 'incapable of handling planning',[2] while Morrison criticised Cripps for seeming never 'to hear the other side.'[3] Bevin and Morrison deeply distrusted each other, and both at different times strongly criticised Attlee. In the summer of 1947 an ephemeral movement to dislodge Attlee from the premiership developed. These were, certainly, issues of which the public remained ignorant at the time, and it was not until 1951, when Bevan resigned, that any dramatic breakdown occurred. Plainly, though, Labour was less vigorous in 1950 than in 1945, and with so large an amount of important legislation already to its credit, it had less to offer the electorate.

Dalton suspected that the unpopularity of economic controls and the remains of the war-time rationing system combined with the continuing housing shortage to deprive Labour of support. He also suggested that nationalisation had ceased to be an attractive policy. Public ownership of sugar, cement, under-used farm land, 'all suitable minerals',[4] water supply, meat distribution, perhaps of chemicals, all 'had more strong opponents than strong supporters. All probably, therefore, lost us votes.'[5] None of these matters had received sufficient consideration before the election and Labour candidates had not been supplied with enough information to be able to expound with conviction the problems connected with them. Perhaps the truth in 1950 was that no Labour policies would have exercised much influence over large numbers of voters, particularly of the middle classes, who had boldly experimented with the so-called Left in 1945 but had now decided, possibly for no very clear reasons, to revert to a more characteristic Conservatism.

THE GENERAL ELECTION 1950

As it happened, the number of votes cast for Labour candidates at the general election of 1950 (13 266 592) represented an increase of more than $1\frac{1}{4}$ million since 1945. They still held 315 seats. The Conservative vote, however, had increased by more than $2\frac{1}{2}$ million to 12 502 567, and had given them 298 seats. Since the Liberal Party, with 9·1 per cent of the poll, had contrived to save 9 seats, the Irish Nationalists had won 2 and an Independent Liberal had been returned, the Labour overall majority was precariously small. To avoid parliamentary defeats on crucial issues every available supporter had to be brought to the House. The functioning of the Standing Committees, in which, normally, bills at their committee stage were debated, became particularly difficult. As these committees always reflected the total strength of each party in the Commons, the government had now only the narrowest of majorities on each one and major bills had to be considered in Committee of the Whole House, greatly increasing the time taken to introduce the legislative programme. On minor issues the government was in fact defeated on seven occasions. Controversial legislation of importance, the failure of which might have obliged the ministry to resign, was necessarily abandoned. No attempt was made to nationalise sugar, cement or anything else to which reference had been made in the election manifesto; nor, during the twenty months which elapsed between the elections of 1950 and 1951, was any other significant bill passed.

The period was significant, however, for the loss of three leading personalities in the Cabinet. Sir Stafford Cripps resigned on grounds of ill health in October, 1950, and Hugh Gaitskell took his place as Chancellor of the Exchequer. Ernest Bevin resigned for similar reasons in February, 1951, being succeeded at the Foreign Ministry by Herbert Morrison. In April 1951, Aneurin Bevan left the government after the announcement by Gaitskell of budget changes which included a requirement that the recipients of spectacles and false teeth should pay 50 per cent of the cost. Bevan argued that money allocated, because of the anxiety caused by the Korean war, to the stockpiling of military stores and raw materials could not be spent since the materials were unprocurable, and that it could more sensibly have been spent on the preservation of the free benefits of the Health Service. Events proved Bevan to have been right on the question of raw materials; but his manner angered many of his colleagues. Dalton described him as 'truculent, arrogant, rhetorical . . . determined either to bend the Cabinet or break it.'[6] The Cabinet backed Gaitskell, and the only other sympathetic resignations from the government were those of Harold Wilson, the President of the Board of Trade, and John Freeman, Parliamentary Secretary to the Minister of Supply. But the Labour Party suffered seriously during the next few years from the divisions which had developed. Bevan was popular among the constituency representatives at party-conferences. His supporters, Tom Driberg, Ian Mikardo and Barbara Castle, were elected to join him on the National Executive of the party. In 1952 and 1953 he challenged Herbert Morrison for the deputy leadership of the party. Factions developed which did not end with Bevan's resignation from the Labour Shadow Cabinet in 1954, and it was only after Gaitskell had decisively defeated both Bevan and Morrison in the poll among the Labour members of the Commons for the leadership on Attlee's retirement that these feuds moderated. In 1956 Bevan became Shadow Foreign Secretary, retaining the position until his death in 1960.

These developments were the problems of the future for a party out of office. In 1951 far more serious national and international issues preoccupied Labour during its last months of power. The economic effects of the Korean war, the enormous balance of payments deficit which was threatened, the alarming increase of wages and prices in 1951 and the seizure by the Persians of the Abadan oil installations all contributed to the weakening of the government. The great exhibition on London's South Bank, known as the Festival of Britain, indeed revealed the technological skill and architectural imagination of a resilient people and it aroused widespread interest; but it was not the Labour Party whose reputation was enhanced.

END OF THE LABOUR MINISTRY

In their election manifesto of 1951 the party appeared virtually to have abandoned its once dominating idea of public ownership. No more was predicted but that 'we shall take over any concerns which fail the nation and start new public enterprises wherever this will serve the national interest.' This vague gesture did not avail to save the day. Nor did Labour advocacy of the prohibition of retail price maintenance, the withholding by manufacturers of goods to traders who sold them for less than a stipulated price. Once again, it was true, the total vote for Labour candidates went up, to 13 948 605; and the proportion of their votes also rose, from 46·1 per cent in 1950 to 48·8 per cent. But once again the Conservative poll increased to an even greater degree. It was now, 13 717 538, or 48·0 per cent of the total. Since the British electoral system was never designed to allow Parliament to represent exactly the wishes of the electorate, and since Labour gained most of the unnecessarily very large constituency majorities, particularly in South Wales and County Durham, these results left the Conservatives with 321 seats and Labour with only 295.

The change may have been brought about by a greater transference of Liberal votes to Conservative than to Labour candidates. In 1950 the Liberals, hoping always for a revival in their favour, had had 475 candidates. Only 9 had been returned. Three hundred and nineteen deposits (£150 each) had been lost. The party was insured against the loss of only 200 and was in no state to contest the 1951 election on a similar scale. It ran only 109 candidates and gained only 2·5 per cent of the total poll, whereas twenty months previously it had gained 9·1 per cent. Whether or not Conservatives benefited substantially from these alterations of fortune, they were left with a majority over the other parties of 17, and this proved sufficient to enable them to govern for three and a half years with no further general election.

In 1955 the majority of 17 was converted into one of 60. Fewer people, only 13 286 569, bothered to vote for the Conservatives in this election than in the previous one (the total poll was only 76·8 per cent of the electorate entitled to vote, instead of 82·6 per cent), but Labour supporters were even more apathetic, declining by 1 543 635. The Conservatives won 344 seats, Labour 277. Hugh Gaitskell, Aneurin Bevan and Earl Attlee agreed that Conservative organisation was better and attributed the government's victory also to the country's prosperity (of which the foundations had been laid down between 1945 and 1951 by the Labour ministries). Gaitskell sadly admitted that the disunity of the party of which he was now leader had proved a handicap. On the question of further nationalisation and on Britain's retention of an independent nuclear weapon serious dissension had broken out among Labour supporters and personal rivalries still simmered, whereas Conservatism presented a spectacle of confident unity.

Liberal fortunes in 1955 showed no change. The party had only one more candidate than in 1951, gained almost the same number of votes, and as in 1951 won only 6 seats.

Churchill returned to the premiership in 1951. According to Harold Macmillan he was 'supremely happy'[7] to be back in office, facing once more the challenge of government with his old colleagues. He was to hold more Cabinet meeting than his predecessor, encouraging argument and discussion and never regarding the occasions as merely a 'formal method of registering decisions already taken'.[8] Macmillan admitted that he was not a good chairman, as Attlee had been, if by good chairmanship one implied consideration of the agenda 'as rapidly as may be with some kind of decision on the record'.[9] Some ministers may have found his procedure 'dilatory and tiresome'. Yet 'there was hardly a word . . . from him, whether of playful humour or of historical reflection or pregnant thought for the future, that was not memorable'.[10] His great days, however, were now behind him, and although he retained his interest in imperial and foreign affairs and in the improvement of living conditions, little of outstanding significance was to be associated with his name during the years after 1951, and a certain impatience was in time to be felt among some of those around him as he found various reasons for deferring his retirement from office. He remained Prime Minister until 1955, living thereafter in sheltered retirement until his death at the age of ninety on 24 January, 1965.

RETURN OF THE CONSERVATIVES

His principal lieutenant, as expected, was Anthony Eden, who now returned to the Foreign Office and became at the same time Deputy Prime Minister. Born in 1897, educated at Eton and Christ Church, Oxford, M.P. for Warwick and Leamington since 1923, Eden had been associated with foreign affairs almost continually, as long as his party was in office, since he had become Parliamentary Private Secretary to Austen Chamberlain, the Foreign Minister, in 1926. His record, like the records of such other leading Conservatives of the 1950s as Macmillan and Churchill himself, had not always been one of docile conformity: in 1938 he had resigned from Neville Chamberlain's Cabinet in protest against the policy of appeasement of the dictators, and had won widespread acclaim for having done so. Events had justified his action. In 1939 he had returned to the Cabinet as Dominion Secretary, and in 1940 had been made War Minister in Churchill's government; but later in 1940 he had gone back to the Foreign Office and had remained there until 1945. His succession to the premiership on Churchill's retirement in 1955 was regarded as inevitable. The only cause of surprise during the next few years was to be the brevity of his premiership and the general denunciation that accompanied the failure of his Egyptian policy and combined with illness to end his active part in public life.

Among the notable creators of the new Conservatism in the Cabinet were Lord Woolton, R. A. Butler and Harold Macmillan, who became respectively Lord President of the Council, Chancellor of the Exchequer, and Minister of Housing and Local Government. Lord Salisbury (educated, like so many Conservative leaders of this period at Eton and Christ Church, Oxford) became Secretary for Commonwealth Relations, Sir David Maxwell Fyfe went to the Home Office, Oliver Lyttelton to the Colonial Office, Walter Monckton to the Ministry of Labour and Peter Thorneycroft to the Board of Trade. A number of less important ministries or offices were held by

M.P.s who were to rise to greater prominence in the years to come. Selwyn Lloyd, a barrister and war-time brigadier, became Minister of State at the Foreign Office and was later (1955) to succeed to the Foreign Secretaryship and (1960) to the Chancellorship of the Exchequer. Iain Macleod was Minister of Health 1952–5 before going on in turn to the Ministries of Labour and the Colonies and to the Leadership of the House of Commons and the Chairmanship of the Conservative party organisation. At the Scottish Office in 1951 was Alexander Douglas Home, the fourteenth Earl of Home (Eton and Christ Church), who had sat in the Commons between 1931 and 1945, before inheriting his title, as member for South Lanark.

---

1 Dalton, *High Tide*, p. 365
2 Ibid., p. 241
3 Ibid., p. 236
4 Ibid., p. 242
5 Ibid., p. 339
6 Ibid., p. 365
7 Harold Macmillan, *The Tides of Fortune*, p. 485
8 Ibid., p. 486
9 Ibid., p. 486
10 Ibid., p. 488

PART TWO

15

The continuity of government policies

Disraeli once ventured to suggest that governments found most of their legislation in the pigeon holes of their predecessors. Few politicians of the 1950s would have been so cynical, or so honest, as to admit that this was still true, Attacks on the policies of rivals for power remained the essential feature of political controversy; and controversy became, in some ways, more intense. Far fewer members were returned to Parliament unopposed than had been unopposed before 1939. Whereas in 1900 243 had been returned without a contest, and whereas at no pre-war election since 1900 (apart from the exceptional one of 1929) had fewer than 32 members been returned unopposed, the idea of forgoing the election battle almost perished after the war: in 1945 there were only 3 unopposed returns, in 1950, 2, in 1951, 4, and in 1955, 1959, 1964, 1966 and 1970, none at all. Labour and Conservative parties contested a constantly increasing number of seats, and Liberal candidates stood in as many constituencies as they could afford. Increasingly, also, these parties supplied the candidates at local government elections and added to their strength at the expense of Independent councillors or those sponsored by such organisations as Ratepayers' Associations. Party political broadcasts became regular features of radio and television programmes.

THE SIMILARITY OF PARTY PROGRAMMES

To what extent, though, did party labels represent fundamentally divergent policies? The nationalisation of iron and steel and of road transport, and the Labour undertaking at the 1950 election to hand over various other industries and services, including sugar, to public corporations undoubtedly provoked fierce resentment. Conservatives pledged themselves to de-nationalise iron and steel and road transport when they returned to power, and the gulf between the parties on this issue appeared to be unbridgeable. In fact, though, the solutions adopted after 1951 did not represent a reversion to the original, pre-war conditions. The steel industry, with the exception of the firm of Richard Thomas and Baldwin, was indeed restored to private ownership; yet the Conservatives did not seek to reintroduce a cut throat rivalry between the different companies. The Iron and Steel Board which they set up in 1953 was empowered to determine maximum prices, to supervise investment programmes and to promote research. This was a compromise solution, combining characteristics of both public and private ownership. So, in the end, was the solution found to the problem presented by road transport. The Road Transport Disposals Board established by the Conservative government was able to sell back to private owners only a little more than half of the 35000 vehicles in its possession; and in 1956 a new Act increased the number of vehicles which the British Transport Commission was authorised to retain. Meanwhile, the Labour party leaders also showed a readiness to compromise.

Herbert Morrison's view that the nationalisation of iron and steel had been undesirable has already been referred to (see p. 48). So has his party's election manifesto of 1951, which omitted the nationalisation projects announced at the previous election and contained only the provision that concerns which failed the nation should be taken over. By the 1960s, although Labour still proposed to nationalise water, iron and steel, and such road transport undertakings as were not already publicly owned, the idea of further nationalisation had been abandoned by all but the extremists. When a leading socialist writer like John Strachey, ex-minister of Food and of War, could admit (in 1956) that capitalism was changing into something 'which it would be an abuse of language to call capitalism at all',[1] the old battle cries of the Marxist class war were bound to appear obsolete and unnecessary.

Apart from nationalisation, the issues which provoked the strongest emotions among the main contenders for power during the 1950s were the proportion of the country's wealth absorbed by taxation, the Conservative reduction of food subsidies in 1952, the adoption of a policy of so called 'Conservative freedom' and the abandonment of many of the war-time controls of food supplies and imports which Labour had, necessarily, maintained, the establishment of comprehensive schools, the Suez war of 1956 and the Rent Act of 1957. During the Conservatives' last five years in office conflicts also developed over the government's endeavours in 1961 to check inflation by limiting further wage increases for six months, over the negotiations for Britain's entry into the European Economic Community, and over the bill restricting the immigration from Commonwealth countries of all who wished to come to Britain. By the time of the 1964 election controversy centred round the continuing possession by Britain of its own atomic weapons and over the methods which should be used to prevent land prices from soaring uncontrollably upwards, especially in South-East England.

Yet retrospective consideration of the party battle fought on these issues might well provoke doubt as to whether all the

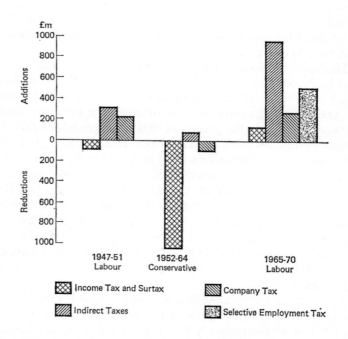

Total additions or reductions in taxation under Labour and Conservative Governments. *Source: The Economist*

differences were as deep as they appeared at the time. R. A. Butler wrote in 1949 that 'It is on the weight of taxation that the clash between Conservative and Socialist policies is the sharpest,'[2] and there was certainly a general tendency between 1947 and 1964 for Labour to increase taxation and Conservatives to reduce it. However, it would be wrong to exaggerate this tendency. The proportion of the Gross National Product taken in taxation fell during the 1950s only to a limited extent: from 34·5 per cent in 1950 to 30·6 per cent in 1959. The character of the taxes imposed did not greatly alter during the first eight years of Conservative rule: taxation of incomes amounted to 15·5 per cent in 1950 and 12·6 per cent in 1959, while taxes on expenditure declined only from 13·6 to 12·9 per cent. The reductions, moreover, were more the result of growing national wealth and improved terms of trade than of any real change in the objects of expenditure. The graphs of rising outlay after 1950 showed no appreciable fluctuations. Both parties followed a policy which had the effect of leaving the lower-paid classes relatively better off. Both had to take into account the wishes of such pressure groups as Trade Unionists and old-age pensioners, industrialists, farmers and professional associations. Not until after 1964 did developments in the sphere of taxation really appear to justify Butler's distinction between Conservatives and Socialists.

On the question of food subsidies the Conservatives had a strong case. While the subsidies made certain foods cheaper for the less prosperous, they had the same effect for wealthier purchasers, who did not require them, and it was considered better to save money here and to increase pensions and benefits for those in need. Sir Stafford Cripps had been well aware of the extravagance of the subsidies. In 1948, partly to encourage wage restraint, they had been allowed to rise to £485m, and when in 1949 they seemed likely to increase to £570m if the policy were not changed, the Chancellor had proposed, in the budget, a ceiling of £465m.

Freedom from controls was by no means an exclusively Conservative policy. The progressive elimination under the Conservatives of the war-time controls of imports and industry was in reality only the continuance of a policy already begun by the Labour government. Nor was the issue of the comprehensive schools fought on clearly defined party lines. A large number of

Conservatives, led during the 1960s by one of the chief Conservative spokesmen on education, Sir Edward Boyle, were quite ready to accept at least some of the experiments advocated by Labour, and only a minority was prepared to resist to the last. Doubts about the virtues of the 11-plus examination as an instrument for providing the evidence on which pupils were separated for grammar and secondary modern schools were widespread within all the parties. On the Suez issue in 1956 a number of Conservative M.P.s, including two ministers, Anthony Nutting and Sir Edward Boyle, sided with the Labour opposition. The Conservative wage freeze of 1961 was essentially the same kind of policy that had been tried by Sir Stafford Cripps in 1948. When the Conservative government was engaged in negotiations with the European Economic Community it was supported by about eighty Labour M.P.s and all the Liberals; and entry into the Community was later to become the official policy of Harold Wilson's ministry. After 1964 Labour felt compelled to retain, even to tighten up, the legislation limiting immigration. Some Conservatives admitted after their election defeat in 1964 that land prices would have to be prevented from rising by stronger measures than they had originally envisaged. The official lines of the parties on atomic defence turned out to be more akin than the election struggles of 1964 had suggested.

If it were hard to discern many basic differences of political philosophy in these controversial issues of the 1950s and early 60s, it was quite impossible to find them in most of the other important issues with which governments had to deal during this period. The essential features of the Welfare State had never been matters of genuine political controversy. Questions of foreign policy were normally regarded as bi-partisan, receiving the backing of the whole nation, not of a limited section of it. The grant of independence to the colonies in Asia, Africa and the West Indies was a policy pursued by Labour and Conservatives alike. The need for industrial and agricultural expansion was universally accepted as an axiom. Indeed, disunity within the parties after 1945 was sometimes more significant than disputes between them. Aneurin Bevan resigned from the Ministry of Labour in 1951 and Peter Thorneycroft from the Chancellorship of the Exchequer in 1958 on questions of principle which appeared, at least at the time, to be important. The Labour party, in opposition, was deeply divided, Hugh Gaitskell (leader from December, 1955, until his early death in 1963) endeavouring to follow a programme of moderate and practical character in the face of a strong challenge from more radical opponents. Even the Liberal party, which was too small to be able to afford fragmentation, tended during the first five years after the war to divide, some inclining towards Labour while others seemed sufficiently Conservative in their attitudes for their leader, Clement Davies, to have been offered a government post in 1951 by Churchill. Internal dissensions such as these had, of course, a long tradition behind them in the history of British party politics.

With wide variations of opinion inside the parties it was inevitable that both Labour and Conservatism should contain their more extreme elements, vocal and striving to exaggerate and perpetuate inter-party differences. However, the Labour minority who sought closer relations with Russia between 1945 and 1947, and those others whose hatred of private capitalism impelled them to demand a far greater amount of nationalisation were idealists to the left of most of their leaders. A decade later the Conservative Suez Group, who were anxious to preserve British influence in old spheres of imperial activity, were prepared to employ methods which most of their party would have regarded as outdated. Most of those who actually held ministerial office, or hoped to do so, were moderate, realistic, influenced by the same Civil Service advisers, compelled by the day-to-day obligations of governing to concede that extremist courses were undesirable. That this was so has doubtless been the saving grace of British politics. Without extremists of the Nazi type Britain was spared the fate of Germany under Hitler's dictatorship between 1933 and 1945. Without a large Communist party in Parliament (there were only two Communist members between 1945 and 1950, and none at all thereafter) British democracy enjoyed much easier conditions than did French or Italian democracy after 1945. There was in Britain too much common ground for lives to have been lost in political conflict.

CONSERVATIVE REFORMERS

Conservative readiness to face the need for change and reform after 1951 requires explanation. It was in fact not entirely novel. Disraeli's Tory Democracy had been as radical a movement in

the 1870s as any in the nineteenth century. Salisbury's lack of
confidence in the seriousness of demands for social reform had
left his party with a reputation for hesitancy where domestic
policies were concerned; yet more had been done to meet the
distress of the 1930s than was generally remembered during the
general election of 1945. Speaking at the Conservative conference in 1947 on the Industrial Charter, Anthony Eden emphasised the reforming tradition which, earlier in the century, had
been commended by the Labour leader, Keir Hardie. 'We are
not a party of unbridled, brutal capitalism . . .', he claimed.
'Although we believe in personal responsibility and personal
initiative in business, we are not the political children of the
laissez-faire school. We opposed them decade after decade.'[3]
Had any Conservative believed the contrary, the 1945 election
must have convinced him that any policy statement which did
not contain proposals for the removal of social injustices would
not win the support of a majority. War had levelled. All had
suffered in one way or another. A return to the social *status quo
ante bellum* was impossible.

The realisation of this produced a Conservative party which
could introduce some remarkably radical measures. In surrendering control over an empire, in aspiring to achieve
economic integration with Europe and in admitting life peers
and women to the House of Lords, it was undoubtedly far removed from the Salisburian conservatism of half a century
earlier, when the Prime Minister could recommend that his
party's bills should be 'tentative and cautious, not sweeping and
dramatic.'

Among the individuals who provided the Conservatism of the
1950s with a radical sense of direction none offered more than
Richard Austen Butler. After four years as a Fellow of Corpus
Christi College, Cambridge, he had become M.P. for Saffron
Walden in 1929. As President of the Board of Education he had
been responsible for the Education Act of 1944. In 1946 he
became chairman of the Conservative Research Department,
which had been established in 1929 to consider possible long-
term policies. His liberalising influence was exerted particularly
on the Conservative Industrial Charter (1947), which recognised workers' needs for greater security of employment and
suggested a strong government lead in economic planning. It
was also exerted in the sphere of penal reform: the study of

criminology, and the abandonment, for many offences, of birching, flogging and the death penalty. Butler had inherited the ideals expressed in 1914 by his uncle, Geoffrey Butler, in a book on *The Tory Tradition*. He believed that his party could no longer 'sit in entrenched positions or rely on holding old-fashioned fortresses' and that it would have to accept 're-distributive taxation to reduce the extremes of poverty and wealth, and repudiation of *laissez-faire* economics. . . .' These were ideals which attracted reformers. The Conservative Research Department attracted Iain Macleod, Reginald Maudling and others who later became ministers. The Tory Reform Group gave political opportunities to Quintin Hogg (Lord Hailsham) and Peter Thorneycroft.

Another individual whose impact on Conservatism was significant was Harold Macmillan. Descendant of Arran crofters and grandson of the founder of a flourishing publishing business, Macmillan had been educated at Eton and Balliol, had served during the war in the Grenadier Guards, and had afterwards become aide-de-camp to the Governor-General of Canada, the Duke of Devonshire, whose daughter he married. The upper-class background did not, however, blind him to the needs of the less fortunate. As M.P. for Stockton-on-Tees from 1924 to 1929 and from 1931 to 1945 he had opportunities to see the effects of poverty, and was provoked to advocate measures which, for the Conservative party at the time, were very radical. Regarding planning as inescapable, he supported the creation of public corporations to control the railways, the coal mines and electricity. He joined a number of Labour and Liberal writers in publishing *The Next Five Years—an Essay in Political Agreement*, and, for his criticism of government policy of unemployment in 1938, received the applause of Labour M.P.s who realised that his experience of a distressed area had left him with ideas which were not dissimilar to those of socialists. At the same time he emerged as an opponent of Chamberlain's foreign policy: he was the only Conservative to vote against the abandonment of sanctions against Italy in 1936, defying a three-line whip to do so and remaining in the Commons as an Independent Conservative for about a year thereafter. Despite these gestures Churchill made him Parliamentary Secretary to the Ministry of Supply in 1940. Later he became Under-Secretary at the Colonial Office and Resident Minister at Allied H.Q. in North

Africa and Italy. In 1945, heavily defeated at Stockton-on-Tees, he returned to the Commons as M.P. for Bromley.

A different factor behind the regeneration of Conservatism after the war was the stimulus given to the party organisation by Frederick Marquis, Earl Woolton. Bringing to the party talents which had made him a notably efficient war-time Minister of Food, Woolton appealed successfully for £1m, which enabled the Conservatives to train 278 new agents and to pay salaries high enough to attract men of ability. Advertising campaigns and serious efforts to find capable parliamentary candidates may also have helped to give the party its majority in 1951.

---

[1] John Strachey, *Contemporary Capitalism*, Victor Gollancz Ltd (London 1956)

[2] *Political Quarterly*, Vol. XX, No. 4, 1949, p. 320

[3] Conservative Party Conference, 1947

[4] R. A. Bulter, *Art of the Possible*, pp. 133–4, Hamish Hamilton Ltd (London 1971)

16

The economy under a
Conservative government

The economic inheritance of the Conservatives was not encouraging. The loss of reserves reached its peak in October, 1951, the month in which the new government took office. Fears of a second devaluation of sterling were causing further speculation against the pound. Since American stockpiling had slowed up, the overseas sterling area's sales of raw materials were falling. Britain was moving towards a balance of payments deficit which was to amount to £700m and a new round of wage increases had been inaugurated by a demand for more pay by the railwaymen. Restraint appeared to have ended.

Clearly, if the new government were to prove its worth it would need, before anything else, to take firm action to remedy the balance of payments crisis and the loss of Britain's gold and dollar reserves. The primary responsibility rested on Gaitskell's successor as Chancellor of the Exchequer, R. A. Butler. The measures that he introduced combined in due course with good fortune to overcome the difficulties that had troubled the Labour government during its last year, though the Conservative financial policy differed so little from that of its predecessors in essentials that *The Economist* coined the term 'Butskellism' to suggest the continuity. The civil servants at the Treasury did not, of course, change. Sir Robert Hall, who had been appointed Director of the Economic Section of the Cabinet Office in 1947, retained that title until 1953 and remained Economic Adviser to the Government until 1961. Both halves of 'Butskell' based their policies on the mixture of planning and freedom associated with Lord Keynes, and if one half seemed to enjoy a more successful tenure of office than the other, it was more the result of changing circumstances than of superior financial skill.

Early in November, 1951, measures were announced which

would reduce imports, particularly of unrationed foodstuffs, by £350m in a year, would curtail the stockpiling of materials for purposes of defence, and would cut the travel allowance for British tourists abroad from £100 a year to £50. Since the balance of payments continued to be adverse and the reserves continued to fall, more stringent measures were applied early in 1952. Imports were again cut and the travel allowance went down to £25 a year. Churchill admitted the impossibility of fulfilling the Labour undertaking to spend £1250m during the first year of the three-year armament programme. A moratorium was imposed on all new building projects, apart from house building. The Bank Rate (the interest charged on Bank of England loans) was raised from 2 per cent to 2½ per cent, and then to 4 per cent. Food subsidies, which had artificially kept down the prices of many essential purchases, were reduced from £410m to £250m. Hire-purchase sales were restricted.

These measures had two essential purposes: to check the drain of sterling overseas, and, by limiting the amount of money in circulation, to reduce sales at home and allow goods to be exported instead. Fortunately for the government, circumstances began to turn in its favour and to permit its aims to be achieved. In 1951, when the United States ended its stockpiling of raw materials, it may have checked trade in those materials but it also allowed inflated prices to fall to a more normal level. At the same time, the suppliers of these materials, having earned large sums during the previous year, were in a better position to buy the exports which the British were so anxious to sell. The desired results were soon apparent. The drain of the gold and dollar reserves ceased during the second quarter of 1952, and by the last quarter these reserves had begun once more to rise. Balance of payments surpluses on current account were once again recorded, and the final balance for 1952 amounted to £126m (Defence Aid, £121m, is omitted) in Britain's favour. Once again the government could apply itself to the task of restoring fully peace-time conditions by eliminating the remaining war-time controls over industry, trade and consumption, and by permitting greater freedom of enterprise.

'FREEDOM' AND EXPANSION

'Conservative freedom' from government control over imports, the allocation of raw materials and food rationing was sometimes in the late 1950s proclaimed to have been the essential factor behind Britain's growing prosperity and rising standard of living. Actually, the expression was misleading. The controls had, after all, not been evolved by the Labour government but had been bequeathed to them by the war-time coalition, and many of them had been repealed, as soon as expedient, by Labour. Some had necessarily been restored when the conflict in Korea broke out, but there had been no intention of making these permanent; and once the military crisis had passed, the Conservatives were able to continue a process which was already well advanced.

The renewed assault on controls began in December, 1952, with the abandonment of the war-time utility furniture scheme, which had limited output for the home market to the simple and cheap. During 1953 restrictions were ended on the use of steel, and softwoods; private trading was allowed in grain and a number of metals and metal manufactures; and 'bulk buying' of raw materials overseas by the government was stopped. Board of Trade price controls over petrol, nearly all raw materials and consumer goods other than foodstuffs were removed. Sweets, sugar and eggs were derationed, and white bread again became procurable. Endeavours were made to restore road transport and the iron and steel companies to private ownership. Such developments as these were continued in 1954, and by the end of this year the rationing of butter, fats and cheese, meat and bacon had disappeared, the Ministry of Materials had been brought to an end and the international commodity markets reopened, and the limitations on the proportions of houses built by private firms and by local authorities had been lifted. Most of the traditional liberties appeared to have been restored.

Indications remained, however, that Conservatism had not reverted entirely to industrial *laissez-faire*. Railways, coal mines, electricity and gas industries remained in public hands. The British Transport Commission continued to hold nearly half the vehicles entrusted to it by Labour. After 1953 the Iron and Steel Board ensured that the steel industry should develop as a whole and not as a collection of rival fragments. The aircraft industry could advance only with government assistance and this entailed increasing government regulation. Although Conservatives were reluctant during the 1950s to return permanently to ministerial controls they did nonetheless retain, until 1959, a Capital Issues

Committee, empowered to examine the borrowing and share issues by companies in order to ensure that their projects were in the general interest and were likely to make the best use of available resources. Between 1956 and 1957 the Committee could still reject about 15 per cent of the applications made to it.

During the early 1960s the Conservative outlook changed. Planning was restored to fashion and a National Economic Development Commission was set up. With it came the realisation that some kind of government control, albeit not identical with that of the post-war period, was indispensable. The apostles of 'Conservative freedom' of the 1950s became the advocates of new forms of centralised planning in the 1960s. These changes are considered at greater length in Chapter 22.

The repeal of so many of the war-time controls in 1953 and 1954 would scarcely have been feasible had British trade and industrial productivity not shown further welcome symptoms of recovery. Benefiting from an expansion of world trade in manufactured goods and from the fall in raw material prices which occurred once the boom of the initial stages of the Korean war had subsided, the productivity of British factories increased by about 5 per cent in 1953 and by about 4 per cent in 1954. These developments helped to stabilise the cost of living: whereas costs had risen by nearly 10 per cent during 1951, the increase in 1953 was less than 2 per cent. It was true that the balance of payments position deteriorated slightly during 1953 and 1954 and that an adverse balance of more than £200m was recorded at the end of each year on visible trade; but invisible earnings, such as the shipping and insurance facilities that Britain could offer, the income from overseas investments and the money brought into the country by tourists, more than counterbalanced this deficit. And, with more goods exported to America and fewer imported from that source, Britain at last found itself approximately in balance on dollar account. Meanwhile, unemployment fell from 450000 at the beginning of 1953 to 280000 at the end of 1954. Early in 1955 there were twice as many vacant jobs as there were unemployed to fill them.

R. A. Butler provided a further stimulus for industry in the 1954 budget by reducing the tax assessments of firms which bought new machinery and encouraging thereby both investment and output. In 1955 he cut taxation by about £150m.

STOP . . .

However, even at a time when the economy appeared to be flourishing indications that the situation was not so healthy after all had begun to show themselves. Had it been possible to foresee future developments it would have been realised that the alternation of crisis, recovery and renewed crisis, despondency, congratulation and despondency, was to set a pattern from which no government between 1945 and 1970 was able to escape. Labour, while in opposition, condemned the Conservatives for responding by adopting measures alternately of Stop and Go, but once in office they too found themselves caught up in processes of a similar nature and were even less able than the Conservatives to discover a rapid and lasting solution.

Symptoms of crisis began to appear towards the end of 1954. Cheering though the over-all picture of that year may have been, the achievements of the second half were in reality less satisfactory than those of the first half. Imports rose sharply, the increase in the reserves during the last six months was less than half the increase during the first six, and prices started to rise again. Early in 1955 the reserves fell yet further, confidence abroad in the pound weakened, and a substantial round of wage increases was not paralleled by the rise in productivity which would have been necessary to maintain price stability. A dock strike in the early summer paralysed foreign trade for a month. It became increasingly clear that this was to be another year in which Britain was to suffer an adverse balance of trade.

The consequence of Butler's tax reductions was that people found themselves with greater spending power at a time when a decade of peace in the West had allowed the shops once again to be well stocked with desirable purchases and when import prices had again started to rise. The demand for goods resulted in an increase during 1955 of $11\frac{1}{2}$ per cent in the volume of imports; and these imports had gone up 15 per cent in value. A quarter of the increase was accounted for by imports of coal and steel, a large proportion of the latter being bought, especially from the United States, by the vehicle industry.

The government's response to these unwelcome trends was to introduce in July a number of measures designed to absorb spending power, to reduce home sales and to permit more British goods to be sold overseas. Hire-purchase deposits on cars, electrical goods and television sets were raised. Coal and steel prices were also raised. The nationalised industries were required to cut their investment programmes and banks were asked to cut their advances to clients. In October an autumn budget, while introducing no alterations to the income tax concessions made in April, sought to reduce spending by imposing extensive increases in purchase tax on sales. Harold Macmillan's succession to the Chancellorship in December involved no changes of policy, and early in 1956 hire-purchase charges were again raised on goods of all kinds, the Bank Rate was raised to 5½ per cent, public investment was cut and the concessions made by Butler in 1954 to industrialists investing in new plant were suspended. The budget of 1956, aiming to provide the government with a surplus of at least £150m, brought further cuts in government spending; and, in the hope of encouraging private saving, it introduced premium bonds and enabled purchasers whose numbers were by chance selected to acquire up to £25000.

Premium bonds evoked the criticism of those who disapproved of gambling. Criticisms were also made of the withdrawal of the investment allowances for industrialists. Macmillan himself later thought that the measure had been an error, since tough measures were unfortunately liable to solve one problem only at the cost of creating another. Those of 1956 may have averted calamity. They may also, by denial of financial incentives to industrialists, have contributed to the failure of industrial production to expand during 1956.

. . . GO—AND STOP AGAIN

Apart from this disservice, it might have been claimed that the measures taken by Butler and Macmillan were effective. While imports remained at the same level during 1956 as in 1955, 6 per cent more goods were exported than had been exported in 1955, and the balance of payments position by the end of 1956 was £209m in Britain's favour. The early months of 1957 were months without financial crisis, in spite of Anthony Eden's prediction before the Suez war of November, 1956, that any prolonged interference with traffic through the Suez Canal would seriously dislocate industry in Britain. Oil supplies were not as damagingly interrupted as had been feared. Industry and transport did not, after all, grind to a halt. The output of the car industry (dependent on expectations of oil supplies) may have been 30 per cent below its 1956 output in the first three months of 1957; but it was 30 per cent higher in the second quarter, and had reached a new peak by the end of the year. Otherwise the war had a remarkably limited permanent effect on the economy. Peter Thorneycroft, Chancellor of the Exchequer after January, 1957, when Macmillan succeeded Eden as Prime Minister, was able again to reduce the Bank Rate and, in the 1957 budget, to reduce taxation. Industry was able to emerge from its year of stagnation, and, during the summer months to increase its output by 4 per cent.

However, recovery was very short-lived. In August, 1957, rumours that sterling was to be devalued made overseas traders hesitant about the payment of their sterling debts, and within two months £186m, a quarter of the gold reserves, drained out of London. The problem was exaggerated by financiers who were buying dollar securities in North America with funds which they had transferred to Kuwait. The Bank of England intervened to make such transactions impossible for British citizens, but by this time at least £70m was estimated to have seeped out of the country. Furthermore, the normal support for Britain from other countries of the sterling area was not forthcoming, since raw material prices were falling during the second half of 1957, and export earnings were falling correspondingly.

Another factor allegedly contributing to the uneasiness abroad about the strength of sterling was the inflationary trend attributable to yet another round of wage increases in the early months of 1957. This interpretation was to be emphasised in the government's Economic Survey for 1958. The Radcliffe Committee in 1959 was to take a quite different view, believing that the weakening of sterling was 'quite unconnected with the domestic programmes of the U.K.' The statistics of average weekly earnings might have strengthened the Committee's case: whereas between 1947 and 1955 earnings had risen by an annual average of more than 7 per cent, they had risen by no more than 5·8 per cent between October, 1956, and October, 1957. Nonetheless, Thorneycroft adopted the view expressed by the Economic Survey and acted on the assumptions that inflation was the essential enemy and that it would have to be resisted by limiting any increase in government spending. Accordingly, in September, 1957, the Bank Rate went up from 5 per cent to

7 per cent, its highest level since 1921 and one which was designed to deter expenditure and thereby to restrict the amount of money in circulation. At the same time the banks were instructed to limit their advances to a level no higher than the average of the previous year, and investment in the publicly owned industries was cut. The Chancellor, backed by two subordinate ministers, Enoch Powell and Nigel Birch, and by the Bank of England, insisted also that government expenditure should not be raised in the next budget. Hopes that development programmes for the railways, roads, electricity and mines would stimulate development in private industry as well appeared to be doomed.

That inflation was a menace was doubtless true. Whether it was responsible for the sterling crisis or could be cured by the September measures was open to question. In the end the rest of the Cabinet, fearing, like Butler, to overturn 'policies in social welfare to which some of us have devoted our lives'[1] by pegging expenditure, declined to support the Treasury ministers. Thorneycroft, Powell and Birch consequently resigned in January, 1958. Derick Heathcoat Amory became Chancellor of the Exchequer.

. . . AND GO ONCE MORE

Heathcoat Amory had the good fortune to succeed to his office at a time when the economy was once more moving towards recovery. Before the end of 1957 exports had again begun to rise and the year had, despite all its problems, brought Britain a balance of payments surplus of £216m. During 1958 conditions continued to improve. A fall in world commodity prices reduced the cost of British imports by about a tenth, each 1 per cent fall in prices entailing a saving of about £35m of foreign exchange. In the end, of course, the overseas sellers would find themselves with less money, and the sale of British manufactured exports would therefore decline; but this development was felt in only a limited degree in 1958. A particularly lucrative market was found for British goods, especially cars, in the United States. At the same time foreign purchasers, no longer hoping that the devaluation of the pound would enable them to buy the same quantity of goods for less money, paid their bills with greater alacrity. The flight from sterling, which had caused so much trouble in 1957, was replaced by a run on the dollar instead.

Investment in industry reached its highest level since the war.

Progressively, Thorneycroft's emergency measures were withdrawn during 1958. The budget in April proposed some increase in expenditure after all; and in the later months of the year the banks were again permitted to lend as much as they wished and the Bank Rate was reduced in stages to 4 per cent. An increase in the number of unemployed prompted the government to allow further aid for industries in areas where particularly large numbers were out of work. However, the country as a whole could welcome the largest balance of payments surplus (£345m) since the war. In the circumstances, Heathcoat Amory aimed at encouraging a steady but not excessive expansion in production. The 1959 budget took 9d off income tax, reduced purchase tax, and restored investment allowances for industrialists. It was not the Chancellor's intention to make this a 'spending spree budget', yet with larger sums remaining in people's purses and with less purchase tax to pay, sales were in fact greatly stimulated. The budget was followed by a boom. Within a year industrial production rose by nearly 11 per cent, and since unemployment remained comparatively high, with more than 400000 still out of work at the end of 1959, the increase in output had clearly been achieved by fuller use of existing industrial capacity rather by the use of a much larger labour force. The effect, as the 1960 Economic Survey indicated, was that the expansion had been achieved with only negligible increases in prices. This helped overseas sales as well as home purchasers, and 1959 was the fourth year in succession in which a balance of payments surplus was achieved.

In December, 1958, sterling held by foreigners had been made freely convertible into dollars. This move, undertaken in agreement with most other European countries, implied that Britain was now prepared to give dollars in exchange for sterling if they were required. The currencies of the other countries became subject to similar arrangements.

Before the end of 1959 the Conservative party had gained an even larger overall majority in the Commons. The economic developments during its final administration, between 1959 and 1964, are considered in Chapter 22.

---

[1] *The British Economy in 1950s*, p. 58, Ed. by Worswick and Ady, Oxford University Press (1962)

17

Successes and failures
of the 1950s

'Go round the country, go to the industrial towns, go to the
farms, and you will see a state of prosperity such as we have
never had in my lifetime—nor, indeed, ever in the history of this
country.'[1] Harold Macmillan's claim, made in a speech at
Bedford in July, 1957, was not an unreasonable one. Nor was his
assertion that 'they have never had it so good' without justification, even though cynics were later to deride it. For a majority
of people in Britain conditions were improving, and they continued to do so. The support given to the Conservatives in the
general election of 1959 suggested that developments were
recognised and found widely acceptable.

RISING LIVING STANDARDS

In 1938 the average weekly earnings of male manual workers
over 21 had been £3 10s 11d (£3·54½). By 1951 they had risen
to £8 8s 6d (£8·42½). In 1959 they were £13 6s 6d (£13·32½).
It was true that rising wages were paralleled by rising prices and
that not all the increases represented gain. However, in real
terms (judging, that is, by the amount that money would buy)
the British were considerably better off. Between 1951 and 1958
their average wages rose in value by 20 per cent and as the
decade ended they were still rising. Particularly rapid increases
occurred in the incomes of the young and unskilled manual
workers. At the same time a 20 per cent increase in consumption
was registered, an improvement in less than a decade as great
as that which had taken more than a quarter of a century to
accomplish before 1939. In 1955 the average British household
expenditure was £19 a week. By 1959 it had risen to £25 10s
(£25·50). The status symbols of the mid-twentieth century were

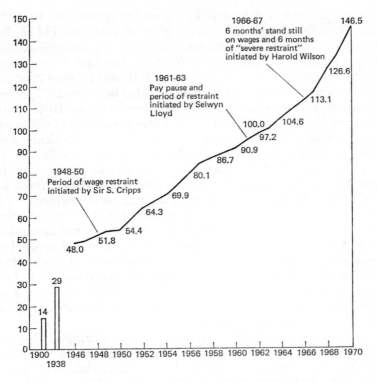

Average weekly wage rates of men employed in manufacturing.
Index numbers 1963:100

Average weekly wage earnings in
decimal currency of man employed in
manufacturing.

	£
1900	1·40
1933	3·545
1944	6·135
1950	7·71
1955	11·39
1960	14·99
1965	19·80
1969	25·10

Average earnings of male salaried workers were generally
about 20% higher than the wages of men employed in manufacturing. *Source*: Based on figures compiled by the London
and Cambridge Economic Service.

being acquired in very rapidly mounting quantities. In 1950 the monthly average of newly registered cars was 11 117. By 1960 it was 67 218. The total number of private cars rose during this period from 2 258 000 to 5 526 000. The monthly average sales of television sets in 1950 was 42 400, and in 1959 229 500. The number of television licences doubled between 1955, when 40 per cent of households already possessed sets, and 1959. More than 9m licences were issued in the latter year. Sales of refrigerators, washing machines and vacuum cleaners, furniture and electrical equipment were rising almost equally rapidly.

Since not all of these articles were bought outright, hire-purchase debts were rising correspondingly: from £208m in 1951 to £849m in 1959. The government took advantage of this when it realised that simple administrative decisions altering either the amount of initial deposit to be paid or the maximum repayment period were the most effective means of regulating expenditure; and between the first regulation in 1952 and 1960 the terms of hire purchase were altered eleven times. However, despite such changes, large numbers of people continued to enjoy the use of comparatively expensive articles without having first to engage in years of saving.

An increasing number of people were owning their own houses, even though they may not have completed the payments for all their contents. An increasing number, also, were taking holidays away from home. Whereas before the war only 1½m workers were receiving holidays with pay under collective agreements, the total had risen to 14m receiving a single week's holiday with pay by 1945. In 1951 one third of all workers were estimated to have been granted a fortnight's paid leave; and during the later 1950s this became an almost universal benefit. The number taking holidays outside Britain rose from about 2m in 1955 to nearly 6m a decade later.

Complaints were still to be heard about the stratification of society into distinguishable social classes, and the cynical professed to see a 'meritocracy' of the academically successful taking the place of industrial magnates and landed gentry. But there were also signs that some class distinctions were diminishing. By 1954, for example, the London County Council's principal school medical officer could report that the marked differences that had existed in the measurements of children from different parts of London had largely disappeared.

Furthermore, as educational opportunities increased and the influence of social background became less important, social mobility became more evident. By the early 1950s only one man in three fell into the same social category that his father had belonged to. More than half the men in the top professional categories were the sons of men whose positions had been less exalted. Whereas in 1914 the average unskilled worker was receiving only 59 per cent of the wage rate paid to the average skilled man, the percentage had risen to 77 in 1940 and 84 in 1963.

INFLATION

Yet notwithstanding this increased popular affluence, the advances in social welfare which accompanied it and the apparent resilience of the economy, some substantial failures remained to mar the record and to earn the condemnation of critics. Inflation had proved impossible to check for more than very short periods. Wage claims which were largely responsible for the inflation had proved impossible to resist. Government economic policies designed to cure balance of payments problems had failed at the same time to ensure stability of prices or to permit as much investment in industry as was desirable. Considerable though industrial expansion may have been, it was ominously falling behind the expansion of leading competitors by the late 1950s. Enormous sums of money continued to be spent on defence. Only limited satisfaction could be gained from the knowledge that some of these weaknesses were shared with other countries and from the fact that at least none was catastrophic in its effects.

The most persistent and evident weakness was the constantly increasing cost of living. It worried in turn both Labour and Conservative governments, and neither proved able to restrain it for more than a short time. It was described in the *Cohen Report* on prices (1958) as 'the one big failure in the post-war years of economic success'. It was, indeed, a development that Europe had known for centuries and one from which other countries suffered as much as Britain; but these factors brought little consolation to those who had to witness the inexorable decline of the purchasing power of their pounds. Goods which in 1938 had been priced at £100 were, on an average, costing £184 in 1950. A decade later costs were about three times as high as they had been before the war, and nobody could confidently expect that they would be stablised. They did, in fact, continue to rise.

In the years immediately following the war three principal factors operated to create rising costs. The traditional inflationary situation prevailed, in the first place, of too few goods coupled with a plentiful supply of money. The six years during which industry had been directed towards war production had left consumers with a strong desire to buy once more. Money saved from wages which had increased by 80 per cent during the war was available. The goods were not available in sufficient quantities. As it happened, the continuance of rationing, at controlled prices, and the exercise of restraint by those with commodities to sell prevented serious breakdown, and when industry and world trade began to regain a normal peace-time character after 1948, this cause of inflation was reduced in importance. Its disappearance, unfortunately, did not end the increasing cost of living. The prices of raw materials and manufactured goods imported from abroad had risen during the war and continued to rise, though with pronounced fluctuations, after the war had ended. Over this second cause of inflation no government could easily exercise control.

Over the third cause, rising wages and salaries, serious attempts at control would probably have caused so much discontent and would have required such far-reaching powers that no government dared, ruthlessly and consistently, to practise them. It was, moreover, recognised in 1945 that certain industries, mining in particular, were badly remunerated and that no objection could be raised to substantial increases in the wages paid to the workers in these industries. Inevitably, though, the entire economy was in time affected. Higher incomes for miners, for example, involved higher costs of coal. These were passed on to the railways, which in turn were obliged to increase freight charges. The goods carried by rail became, unavoidably, more expensive for consumers. At this point one industry after another would submit claims for additional wages to meet the additional cost of living. The position of organised labour in conditions of full employment was strong. Outside less prosperous regions, Northern Ireland in particular, no pool of unemployed labour existed, in normal circumstances, to fill vacancies. Men could not be dismissed by employers with any certainty that their places would be filled by others; and it was hard for employers to resist demands for higher wages when the trade unions were always in a position to threaten strike action if claims were rejected. All industries were affected. The fear of falling behind stimulated each in turn, and once wage increases had been conceded in a nationalised or other major concern, demands from other branches of industry (and, though generally less belligerently, from the professions) were inevitable.

Wage increases would not, by themselves, have added to living costs if industrial productivity had kept pace with them—if a 5 per cent increase of pay had been paralleled by a similar expansion of each man's output. Unfortunately this did not happen. The first *Cohen Report* showed that whereas between 1945 and 1958 the expansion of production had risen on an average by about 3 per cent a year, wages, salaries and profit income had increased by about $7\frac{1}{2}$ per cent a year (wages and salaries rising faster than profit income and dividends). Furthermore, income increases could not always be justified by rising living costs. While the latter had gone up by 84 per cent between 1938 and 1950, basic wage rates had risen by 97 per cent. When overtime bonuses were taken into account, earnings were found by 1950 to have increased by 140 per cent. Throughout the 1950s (and the 1960s as well) these wage demands were the essential cause of inflation. They continued to be made and met long after the post-war shortages had ceased to influence prices, and at periods (1951 to 1954, for instance) when the costs of imported raw materials were not rising and were therefore having no appreciable effect on the increase of British domestic prices.

More and more, in the late 1960s, economists began to regard a substantial annual increase in the supply of money as a factor causing inflation and not merely as a response to it. Whereas its precise effect was a matter of debate, and while there may have been valid reasons for it, it clearly could not continue to be disregarded if rising prices were ever to be checked.

It was true that other countries were also suffering from inflation. The problem was world-wide, and as long as it continued to be so there were only limited dangers that a country like Britain would find itself completely excluded, on grounds of price, from foreign markets. British industrialists could still sell overseas, provided that such factors as punctual delivery and

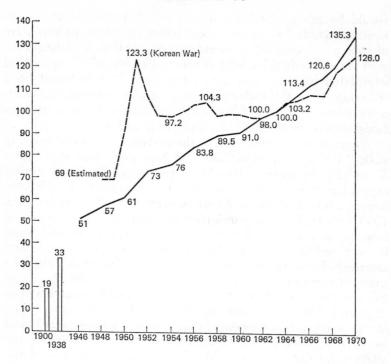

Prices: ————. Index numbers of increasing prices (all items):
— — —. Index numbers of wholesale prices of materials and
fuel used in manufacturing. 1963: 100. Methods of calculation
were changed in 1949 and earlier index numbers are not
exactly comparable. The graph of rising prices compared with
that of rising wages (see p. 119) shows that prices generally
rose less steeply and suggests a progressive increase of real incomes as well as of money incomes. *Source*: Based on figures
compiled by the London and Cambridge Economic Service.

efficient after-sales service could be guaranteed. However,
according to an International Monetary Fund report, France
was the only important industrial country whose export prices
rose more in the 1950s than Britain's prices, and the United
States the only other whose prices paralleled Britain's. British
merchants inevitably suffered a disadvantage at a time when
strong overseas demand for their goods would have provided a

very desirable stimulus for industry. Inflation mattered, moreover, in quite different respects. The trend could be a very unwelcome one for people with fixed incomes and for those with no powerful trade or professional union to press their case. In addition, it was not at all uniform, and prices of certain requirements threatened at times to rise out of all control. By the early 1960s, for example, land and houses, particularly in South-east England, had soared in price far more than other commodities. Whereas the London County Council was paying on an average £8800 an acre in 1951, by 1963 it was paying £61 800. House prices in the South-east rose by 63 per cent in the five years after 1958.

Curiously, in the light of what happened, the Labour government had felt more apprehensive in 1945 about the possibilities of an unsettling fall in prices, deflation, rather than its opposite. When it was realised that prices were, instead, rising steadily, an earnest attempt was made by the government, Sir Stafford Cripps in particular, to check the development. Labour was no more willing than Conservatives were to be later to intervene directly in wage negotiations between workers and management, but it did endeavour to place moral pressure on employers and arbitrators in wage disputes not to cause a general increase of wages. This policy had some success. Wages which had risen annually since 1940 by between 6 per cent and 8 per cent rose by only 4 per cent in 1948, less than 2 per cent in 1949, and not at all during the first half of 1950. Unfortunately, other factors conspired during 1950 to raise the cost of living: gradually, the effects of the devaluation of sterling (which made British exports cheaper for foreign purchasers but increased the price of imports) combined with the higher import prices developing as a result of stock-piling during the Korean war. In these circumstances it was difficult to maintain a wage freeze in Britain. By the end of 1950 the Labour policy had begun to disintegrate. The Conservatives, in 1951, inherited a new inflationary trend.

Conservative policy, initially, was one of appeasement. Churchill was particularly anxious to avoid industrial strikes, and he had appointed a notable conciliator, Sir Walter Monckton, to the Ministry of Labour. Conciliation tended to mean concession. Employers and workers may have been brought successfully together, but the resultant bargains were often highly inflationary. In December, 1953, for example, government pressure obliged the Transport Commission to avert a threatened railway strike by allowing a higher wage increase than an independent tribunal had already recommended. Lord Woolton frankly asserted that surrender of this kind 'greatly disturbed some of us in the Cabinet';[2] but a majority of his colleagues were prepared to rely on appeals such as R. A. Butler's request to both sides of industry, in 1952, that the national wage bill should not be allowed to outstrip National production. Most ministers accepted Butler's view that 'we do better through relying on voluntary moderation.'[3]

Unfortunately, even by 1954, all the evidence was that 'voluntary moderation' was ineffective. The pattern had already been set in 1952 when engineers, ship-builders and railwaymen employed strike threats or overtime bans to gain their wage increases. Between 1953 and 1954 wages and salaries rose by $7\frac{1}{2}$ per cent though output per man had gone up by only $2\frac{1}{2}$ per cent. In the boom conditions of the first half of 1955 nearly $10\frac{1}{2}$ million workers received increases, and by August most of these had already formulated claims for yet another rise. Characteristic of conditions of the 1950s were the initiatives often taken by workers in the nationalised industries. In 1957, for instance, the Transport Commission offered a 5 per cent increase to the railwaymen, similar increases were granted to electricity supply workers and coal miners, and it then became impossible for engineering and ship-building employers to resist demands from their own workers for comparable rises. Inevitably, higher incomes involved, in due course, higher prices; and higher prices provided the trade unions with their excuse for perpetuating the inflationary spiral.

If successive Chancellors showed themselves unwilling to insist on the maintenance of stable incomes, the Trade Union Congress repeatedly made clear during the 1950s that any more determined policy would have inspired strong resistance. In 1952, on the grounds that if incomes outran productivity the government was to blame, it refused to take any action which might be incompatible with voluntary collective bargaining on wage questions between employees and managements. It was not deterred by prophecies of the development of an ominous wage-price spiral. By 1956 its attitude had not altered. The government was once again made responsible for inflation, and the withdrawal of controls and food subsidies together with the inadequacy of family allowances and increases in purchase tax were blamed. While the employers' associations and the nationalised industries undertook to work for price stability, the T.U.C., in September, 1956, was loudly applauded when it passed a resolution opposing wage restraint. The inevitable result was that, despite good intentions in many quarters, prices rose by about 6 per cent in 1957.

By the end of the 1950s doubts at last began to be voiced about the possibility of ever obtaining stable prices as long as very full employment remained the first priority. Such heresies had for some time occurred to an inaudible minority, but recollections of the calamitous unemployment of the 1920s and 1930s were so unnerving that they were not openly discussed until the Cohen Committee, in 1958, hinted that the demand for scarce manpower was so strong that employers were always willing to offer higher sums to attract it and retain it. This was the position exploited by the Trade Unions. Commenting on an unemployment rate of 1·8 per cent in January, 1958, the Committee stated frankly that 'no one should be surprised or shocked if it proves necessary that it should go somewhat further.' The new doctrine seemed to be reflected in the attitude of Heathcoat Amory, the Chancellor, when he claimed that price stability and the strengthening of the pound would be the government's dominating aims and that nothing whatever would take precedence over them. Unemployment, in May, 1958, had risen to 2·1 per cent (448000), and the Chancellor recognised, in his budget speech, that the figure might continue to rise. It did do so, to 2·8 per cent (621000) in January 1959; and it coincided with both a lower average increase of pay in 1958 than in 1957 and a relaxation of trade union demands towards the end of 1958.

The problem was not one which could be easily or permanently solved, however, and the history of the 1950s was to be repeated, with only minor variations, throughout the next decade.

COMPARATIVE INDUSTRIAL DECLINE

A second cause of anxiety during the Conservative 1950s was Britain's failure to increase its industrial productivity at the same rate as many of its trading partners on the continent of Europe and elsewhere. The problem was not merely a failure of productivity to keep pace with incomes, with resultant inflation. It was an international issue. Whereas in Britain productivity per man rose between 1950 and 1960 by 25 per cent, in Germany it rose by 59 per cent and in France by 77 per cent. Towards the end of the decade France was increasing its proportion of the world's manufactured exports three times as fast as Britain, Germany and Italy six times as fast. In 1957 Britain was superseded as a ship-building country by Japan, despite an

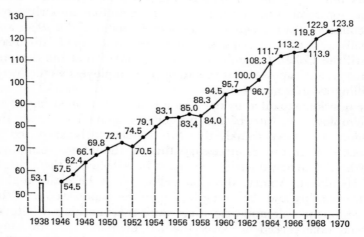

Index of industrial output. 1963: 100. *Source*: Based on figures compiled by the London and Cambridge Economic Service.

earlier high reputation, which it had maintained during the war. British ship yards were producing less in 1957 than in 1913. The Germans and Swedes, as well as the Japanese, were building vessels twice as fast as the British were building them. Meanwhile, in all spheres, the graphs of Russian output were soaring upwards with a rapidity which eclipsed completely the upward movement of British production. It was, of course, true that Britain was by no means stagnating and that its not easily measurable technological skill continued to command respect. However, the comparisons were disconcerting to those who believed that it should never have been necessary to make them and asked themselves why, in 1957, Britain should ever have become a net importer of motor cycles or why it was Germany and Japan which were leading in the construction of giant oil tankers.

Critics of Britain's achievements were quite ready to suggest explanations for the apparent loss of Britain's nineteenth-century reputation as the workshop of the world. Some blame, inevitably, was placed on conservative trade unions which were more concerned with the preservation of the jobs occupied by their members and the avoidance of unemployment than with increased efficiency, automation, or other novel methods which might enable one man to do what had previously been done by two. George Woodcock, the General Secretary of the T.U.C., himself condemned some union practices: demarcation disputes, which arose when members of one union claimed sole right to do a particular piece of work and refused to collaborate with outsiders; closed shops, in which unionists employees of a firm refused to allow non-unionists to work with them; and unofficial strikes such as those which cost industry most of the 8 412 000 days lost in 1957 alone. The T.U.C. could exercise very little control over the members of about 190 separate unions, which were increasingly dominated by some 200 000 unpaid shop stewards. The part played by unions in forcing up prices has already been considered. Clearly, without these difficulties industry could have advanced more smoothly.

However, the work force was certainly not the only cause of failure in the sphere of productivity increases. Critics were quite as severe in their condemnation of the inadequacy of investment in industry and of government policies which did not always encourage investment. They could not rightly claim that nothing was done, but they could assail British gestures as insufficient or inconsistent. Cripps, in 1949, permitted tax remission on 40 per cent of any profits ploughed back on new plant; but during the economic emergency of 1951 the concession was withdrawn by Gaitskell. Butler restored investment allowances when prospects were encouraging; and Macmillan withdrew them in 1956 when crisis again threatened. The process was to occur yet again before the end of 1960, until six changes of policy had taken place within a decade. The theory behind all this was comprehensible. Periods of 'Stop' were designed to reduce the amount of money in circulation, to check inflation and to increase overseas sales. Periods of 'Go' were supposed to permit industry to forge ahead. In fact, it was arguable that the lack of continuity did more harm than good, unsettling industry and perhaps inhibiting technological modernisation. At all events, whatever the value of the fluctuating policies may have been, British investment certainly did not parallel that of other countries. In the early 1950s about 5 per cent of the net national product was invested in industry, and the figure rose in the middle of the decade to rather more than 7 per cent. However, Italy was investing 12 per cent, Germany 15 per cent, and Norway more than 20 per cent; and, at a time when expansion depended on costly technological innovations, these differences were important. It was not good enough that between 1951 and 1954, when Germany and Japan were re-equipping their ship yards on an extensive scale, only a little more than 3 per cent of the average annual income of the British yards was being spent on fixed assets, not sufficient even to replace worn-out plant.

Undoubtedly, certain continental countries had enjoyed initial advantages in the post-war years. Germany, France and Italy all possessed rapidly expanding labour forces, the first as a result of the immigration of millions of East European Germans and the others as a result of the settlement in industrial regions of large numbers of under-employed agricultural workers. The stimulus given by a need to reconstruct on a large scale operated particularly in Germany. Russia had infinite natural resources still to exploit. None of these factors existed in Britain. Moreover, Britain's endeavours to remain a first-class military power, despite its comparative disadvantages, were diverting to defence needs money and materials which could more profitably have been devoted to peaceful development. In 1953, even though the Conservative government had reduced its original programme, the official *Economic Survey* could not evade the admission that 'important sectors of the engineering industries are heavily engaged in defence work when they might otherwise be concentrating their main energies on the export trade.' Total expenditure on defence in the year 1953–4 amounted to £1 364 500 000. It rose in 1954–5 to £1 435 900 000, and remained at approximately the same level throughout the later 1950s. Only later could suspicions be confirmed that this was largely money wasted.

Later, though, another suspicion gained ground that at least some of these excuses were no longer valid, or that they could equally have been made by other countries, the records of which had surpassed the British record. If the British were underlings, less successful than they might have been, the fault was not in their stars but in themselves. The early 1960s were to see serious attempts to discover remedies and to apply stimuli.

---

[1] Anthony Sampson, *Macmillan*, p. 159, Penguin Books Ltd (1968)
[2] Samuel Brittan, *Steering the Economy*, p. 194, Penguin Books Ltd (London 1964)
[3] Budget Speech, 1954

18

The Conservatives and the Welfare State

The Conservatives had no intention of altering the essential features of the Welfare State. All the parties had played a role in its creation and had come to regard the social responsibilities of the state as inescapable. Such developments were characteristic of all the wealthier nations of Europe, and although different countries tended to stress different aspects of the benefits bestowed by governments (France was particularly generous with its family allowances, West Germany with its pensions, Britain with its health service) the essentials were generally accepted.

The figures of British government expenditure on the social services indicated very clearly that the substitution of Conservatism for Labour involved no important change of policy. During the last year of Labour power, 1950–1, total expenditure on social services amounted to £1964m. During Conservatism's last year, 1963–4, the figure had risen to almost £5280m. Education, which had cost the central government £355m in 1950–1, cost £1317m in 1963–4. Expenditure on the National Health Service went up from £484m under Labour to £1077m in the last year of Conservative control. Family allowances rose from £66m to £151m, national insurance from £417m to £1525m, housing expenditure from £365m to £647m, national assistance from £70m to £240m. Each year these services had cost more than they had cost the previous year. Outlay on school meals and milk and on child welfare rose similarly. It was true that the increased costs reflected to a large extent the constant inflationary trend of the period and the accompanying decline in value of the pound. To some extent they reflected an expanding population of schoolchildren and students and of old people. They also suggested, though, that with growing wealth, expectations grew: better school buildings, modern housing, a greater amount of medical attention were required, and all these were costly.

In one sphere, the Health Service, costs were indeed rising so rapidly when the Conservatives came into office that they imposed a charge of a shilling on each medicine prescribed by a doctor under the Service. They thereby aroused Opposition wrath, though the Opposition had in fact, when in power, already recognised that such a charge might be necessary to defray expenses which were much higher than had been anticipated. In other respects party attitudes did not diverge.

HOUSING

As the population increased and its standards of living rose, housing became a matter of special concern. The Conservatives aimed to exceed the Labour achievement by building 300 000 new houses a year. Responsibility for carrying out the policy was given to Harold Macmillan and to Ernest Marples, a junior minister with experience of building, Sir Percy Mills, a Birmingham business man, and Dame Evelyn Sharp, the Secretary at the Ministry of Housing. Macmillan acknowledged a debt to

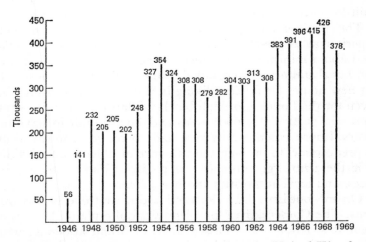

Number of permanent houses completed in the United Kingdom.

his predecessor, Hugh Dalton, from whom he had inherited plans for easily constructed, comparatively inexpensive dwellings. Dalton, he admitted, 'is the pioneer of simplification, he has shown the way, and I am merely following humbly in his track'.[1] He followed very effectively. In 1953 some 327 000 houses were built, and thereafter, while the Conservatives remained in office, the total number of new houses fell below the target of 300 000 in only two years, 1958 and 1959.

A characteristic development under the Conservatives was the increased encouragement given to private builders. In Labour's last year a local authority had been able to licence only one house built privately for every four built by the council itself. In fact, in 1951 only 25 000 were put up by private builders, compared with 166 000 for which local authorities were responsible. From 1952, however, local authorities were empowered to licence as many privately built houses as they were constructing themselves; and from 1953 further relaxation of the law in favour of the private builder was introduced. With the revocation of war-time regulations licences ceased to be necessary for such builders after November, 1954. By 1956 private builders were responsible for 41 per cent of new houses, while local authorities and the New Towns Development Corporations were responsible for 56 per cent, and government departments and voluntary associations for the remainder. In 1959 private builders constructed 153 000 houses, while only 125 000 were built for local authorities.

The government gave practical encouragement to such experiments as pre-cast concrete and steel-framed houses. Like the Labour ministry it continued the policy of subsidising housing. Local authorities were aided by the Exchequer in constructing new houses for families living in slums. Subsidies were also given for the building of high blocks of flats on expensive sites, houses in particularly poor areas and houses built to serve industry. Improvement grants were made by the government, as by its predecessor, to prolong the existence of older properties. By 1956 the central government was paying £78m for these purposes, and local authorities another £29m.

On only one issue did serious and lasting controversy develop: rents. The Conservatives' problem was quite plain. A series of Rent Restrictions Acts, passed since 1915 and applying, with few exceptions to unfurnished houses below a certain rateable value, had limited the rent which a landlord could legally take from his tenants, and had given those tenants, in normal circumstances, security of tenure. Theoretically such arrangements were fair and in the interests of classes who were insufficiently wealthy to buy their own homes. The Acts, however, did not keep pace with the inflation and declining value of the £ in the years following the outbreak of war; and although a Conservative measure of 1954 had allowed landlords intending to improve their property to raise their rents, the landlords could still claim in 1957 that while average family money incomes after taxation were about 80 per cent higher than in 1938, rents had increased by only 13 per cent. Many tenants were paying unrealistically low prices for their homes, while many owners were finding their incomes absorbed almost entirely by the cost of repairs. To remedy this the Rent Act of 1957 removed the limits on the rents of about 810 000 houses, the rateable values of which were more than £30 (or £40 in London and Scotland); and it allowed some increases of rent for 4 300 000 others, based on their gross value as assessed in November, 1956.

The Labour Opposition echoed the protests of many of the tenants and threatened to repeal the Act when they had the opportunity; and certain scandalous examples of profiteering by unscrupulous landlords which came to light in the next few years in dilapidated parts of London lent substance to their case. In fact, though, the effects of the Act were less remarkable than had been anticipated. The number of decontrolled houses was found to be not 810 000 but only 317 000. The automatic decontrol of 320 000 others during the next two years occurred only when the landlords recovered vacant possession of them. Furthermore, although conditions were not uniform throughout Britain and some tenants suffered, average rent increases were not crippling: unfurnished accommodation that had cost 19s 10½d (99p) in 1951 still cost only 25s (£1·25) in 1959, and the ratio of outlay on housing to the total outlay of the average family rose merely from 7 per cent to 8·1 per cent. In order to limit injustices, a Landlord and Tenant Act of 1958 required the owner of a decontrolled house who wished to regain possession to take the matter to a competent court. It could not be shown that the 1957 Act had much effect on the movement of tenants or any effect at all on the question of the 'under-occupation' of a house.

TOWN AND COUNTRY PLANNING

During the 1950s the effects of Labour town and country planning became evident. Eight new large towns were grafted on to
smaller ones to absorb London's overspill population: Stevenage, Harlow, Crawley, Welwyn, Hatfield, Hemel Hempstead,
Basildon and Brackneu (see Fig. 20). Cumbernauld and East
Kilbride were built to take Glasgow's surplus. Glenrothes was
developed in Fife, Peterlee and Newton Aycliffe in Durham,
Corby in Northamptonshire, and Cwmbran in Monmouthshire. It was intended ultimately to house 550 000 people in the
English and Welsh towns, and 125 000 in those in Scotland. The
towns were not designed as suburbs for commuters to the cities
but as new, self-contained communities with all the requirements for life and work, education and entertainment, and
as centres to which industry would gravitate. They were also
intended to preserve older cities from unbearable population
pressures which could only produce interminable suburbs where
green belts were needed. Some, it was hoped, would help to
develop less prosperous parts of Britain. In due time the number
was augmented. Skelmersdale, Livingston, Dawley and Runcorn
became new towns during the 1950s and early 1960s. A Town
Development Act, passed in 1952, provided for the expansion of
twenty-nine other places, though as most of these were in regions
which were already highly developed, such as the periphery of
London, they did not result in any large-scale redistribution of
population.

During the 1950s the effects of Labour policy were also seen
in the 'Development Areas' where stagnation and unemployment had been so especially demoralising before the war.
Between 1945 and 1947 the control exercised by the government
over the grant of licences had influenced the siting of one-third
of all new industrial buildings in these areas. By the 1950s new
light industries in the Tyneside region were employing more
people than the traditional ship building and ship repairing,
while in South Wales new steel and tinplate works and large
numbers of new factories for such products as nylon and watches
were preventing the sort of emigration that had depopulated
the area in the 1930s. Only one person left South Wales in the
1950s for every seven who had left in the 1930s. The success of
government policies for the location of new industry was, indeed,

sufficiently evident to encourage some relaxation in the middle 1950s of the vigour with which these policies were administered; but when such indications as regional unemployment figures suggested that the prosperity of the South East and Midlands was increasing at the expense of prosperity elsewhere, the attack on the problem of industrial location was resumed. In 1958 the government was empowered, by the Distribution of Industry Act, to give financial help to any firm which consented to settle in a region regarded as liable to suffer unemployment.

Concern for the centres of industry was paralleled by concern for the open spaces. The National Parks Act of 1949 had resulted by the 1950s in the preservation of twelves areas of particularly fine scenery: the Lake District and the Peak District, the Cheviots, the North Yorkshire Moors and Dales, Snowdonia, the Brecon Beacons and the Pembroke coast, Exmoor and Dartmoor. By 1957 fifty-six stretches of country had been designated Nature Reserves; by 1966 seventy-four. The Cairngorms was one of the largest in Europe. The National Trust became one of the major landowners in Britain. The construction, in regions of great natural beauty, of such monuments to technological progress as electricity pylons generally aroused the strongest protests. So did the establishment of the Trawsfynydd power station in the heart of Snowdonia, prospecting for phosphates on the moors near Whitby and the carving of a new motorway over the Chilterns. Protests may not have been effective in diverting progress, but they at least forced planners to bear the appearance of the environment in mind when advancing their interests.

Endeavours of a quite different type to preserve the environment found expression in the Clean Air Act of 1956. Realisation of the costly consequences of pollution of the air was certainly not a discovery of the 1950s. The Coal Smoke Abatement Society had been founded as long before as 1899. In December, 1952, however, three days of smoke laden fog ('smog') were estimated to have caused 4000 deaths among people already prone to bronchial illnesses. Moveover, in 1953 the Beaver Committee found that smoke associated with inefficient combustion of fuel, corrosion resulting largely from sulphur-dioxide in the air, damage caused to plant growth by air pollution, illness and reduction of daylight connected with a contaminated atmosphere were altogether costing the country at least £250m a year. These facts made legislation urgent. The 1956 Act, recognising that domestic coal fires were the main cause of pollution, provided for the creation by local authorities of smokeless zones, where bituminous coal should not be burned in open grates. The local authorities were obliged to pay seven-tenths of the cost of installing new grates. At the same time new industrial furnaces were to be fitted, so far as was practicable, with smoke and dust arresters. The measures were, incidentally, expected to save some 19m tons of coal a year.

---

[1] Anthony Sampson, *Macmillan*, p. 99

19

Foreign policy 1951—56

The Conservative government introduced no changes of policy, and indeed, since foreign relations were as usual dictated largely by developments elsewhere, they were scarcely in a position to do so as long as the international situation remained unaltered. The dominant factor, for the Conservatives as for their predecessors, was still the Cold War. In Korea, although a halt had been called to full-scale war in July, 1951, spasmodic conflict continued for two years more. In Eastern Europe, where the leaders of the non-Communist parties had been liquidated within three years of the final collapse of Germany, a new wave of terror, directed against supposedly deviationist or Titoist Communists, began in 1949; and as Rajk in Hungary, Kostov in Bulgaria, Patrashcanu in Rumania and Clementis and Slansky in Czechoslovakia met the same fate as so many Russian Communist leaders between 1936 and 1938, the Western view that Stalinism remained a dangerous menace was inevitably strengthened. At United Nations meetings the Eastern European Communist countries voted invariably with the Soviet Union, while the Western democracies consolidated their own association. Disarmament talks, when they were held, were prolonged and barren, even after 1954 when the possession by both the United States and Russia of nuclear weapons added urgency to the negotiations.

Stalin's death on 5 March, 1953, gave rise to hopes that international tension might be relaxed; but the suppression by the Red Army of the anti-Communist rising in the Soviet sector of East Berlin and the simultaneous failure of similar movements in other parts of East Germany in June, 1953, suggested that over-sanguine expectations of a revival of individual freedom among Russia's satellites and a consequent *détente* between East and West would have been premature. Two years later Harold Macmillan, who had followed Eden as Foreign Secretary, remained pessimistic despite the successful conclusion of a peace treaty with Austria. A conference of foreign ministers produced yet another clash. Molotov remained inflexible, and Macmillan felt moved to write that 'instead of taking another step forward, at the best we are locked in stalemate, at the worst we have taken a step backward. . . . We are back in the strange night-mare where men use the same words to mean different things.'[1] Another year passed and pessimism was reinforced. The inter-vention by Soviet forces to crush the Hungarian bid for indepen-dence in October, 1956, showed that even after Malenkov had been replaced by Khrushchev as the power behind Russian politics, most of Communist Europe could still not hope for freedom and the rest of the world could not hope confidently for good East-West relations.

DEFENCE PACTS

The West continued to seek means of closer military co-operation. In order to allow West Germany to participate in the defence of the democracies without once again developing the power to assail European peace by itself, the French introduced the idea of a European Defence Community, designed by its originator, René Pleven, to be a more closely integrated group than NATO, with an international army. For nearly four years the Pleven Plan was debated; but in the end, after ratification by Germany and Italy, Belgium, the Netherlands and Luxem-burg, the French National Assembly rejected it and the project collapsed in August, 1954. So far the British government had shown no inclination to help. Now, however, anxious that Germany should assume a full role in Europe, it intervened. Anthony Eden toured Western European capitals and gained the glory of contributing to the creation in October, 1954, of Western European Union. The six countries of the abortive European Defence Community participated, along with Britain, which promised to maintain its existing forces in Europe (be-tween 50000 and 60000 men) or whatever the Supreme Com-mander might consider requisite.

The restoration of West Germany to the concert of European powers was undoubtedly one of the finer achievements of the powers and the German rulers alike. The developments of the late 1940s were quite rapidly completed in the early 1950s. In March, 1951, the Federal Republic regained control of its foreign relations, and its representatives were consequently able to take part in the discussions on European defence on an equal footing with the representatives of other countries. In May, 1952, the Treaty of Bonn restored full German sovereignty and the Allied High Commission was brought to an end. The fact that this treaty was supposed to depend on the completion of the E.D.C. arrangements, which the French jettisoned, made no practical difference. Within a decade of Nazi totalitarianism, West Germany had once again become a prosperous and respected country. Its political life and popular liberties, its Press and scholarship, its evident desire to bring its war criminals to justice, and, indeed, the reluctance of its young men to join the armed forces, all encouraged confidence in the West that militarist aberrations had at last been replaced by a genuine acceptance of democratic ideals. Relations with Britain remained harmonious, in marked contrast at times during the 1950s and 1960s with the strains felt in the *entente* with France. At a conference in Berlin in January, 1954, of the foreign ministers of the four powers which had occupied Germany after the war, it was Eden who presented a plan for the reunification of Germany to follow free elections in both West and East. If the division remained, it was because the Russians refused to accept either of Eden's propositions. West Germany was invited to join NATO in 1955.

NATO and Western European Union were supplemented by two other defensive organisations in which Britain was involved, extending barriers against possible advances by hostile powers into South-East Asia and the Middle East. The first of these, the South East Asia Treaty Organisation, was provoked by the capture of Dien Bien Phu by the Communist Vietminh in 1954 and the collapse of the French position in Indo-China. It was brought into being by a treaty signed at Manila in September, 1954, by Australia, France, New Zealand, Pakistan, the Philippines, Thailand and the U.S.A. as well as by Britain. Britain was particularly concerned with the security of Thailand and, ultimately, of Malaya. At the time the threats were, no doubt, still largely theoretical. Not every country of South East Asia was conscious of the need for defence. India, Burma and Indonesia doubted the value of the organisation. Yet the West could not allow the situation to go by default, and the organisation may have been a stabilising factor in a region where the long drawn-out war between Communists and non-Communists in Vietnam illustrated the potential dangers that existed. Symptoms that this war was liable to spread to other neighbouring countries (Laos and Cambodia in particular) did indeed appear, if not for fifteen years after the creation of SEATO.

The other arrangement designed to contain the advance of Communism was the Baghdad Pact. This developed from a defence pact concluded by Turkey and Pakistan in February, 1954. Between January and October, 1955, it was joined by Iraq, Britain and Iran.

DEFENCE EXPENDITURE AND NUCLEAR TESTS

Britain's defence expenses remained high. In 1954–5 they amounted to £1 495 900 000, and there was no significant change before the end of the decade when they began to increase. Between 1952 and 1957 about 10 per cent of the money collected in taxation was spent on defence. It occupied about 7 per cent of the working population and absorbed about one-eighth of the output of the metal industries. After 1954, when a British force was stationed in Germany under the terms of Western European Union, the costs had to be met in Deutsche Marks, which had somehow to be earned. Once full sovereignty had been restored to Germany, these costs, amounting to about £50m annually, could no longer be exacted from a German government which made clear that it did not recognise an obligation to contribute. Even when the British balance of payments was encouraging, the burden remained substantial.

Total military expenditure abroad amounted, in the mid 1950s, to an average of about £160m. In 1956 the Suez war, considered in the following chapter, forced expenses up to £178m.

The most significant single development in the sphere of defence was probably the creation of the thermo-nuclear, or hydrogen, bomb, which was announced in the White Paper on Defence of 1955, after tests on the Montebello Islands off northwest Australia (1952) and at the Woomera rocket range in central Australia (1953). The government's view was that this deterrent had 'significantly reduced the risk of war on a major scale'.[2] Churchill considered that the stakes were now too high for any power to embark on war. 'It may well be,' he said in the Commons, 'that, by a process of sublime irony, we shall have reached a stage in this story where safety will be the sturdy child of terror and survival the twin brother of annihilation.'[3] He may have been right. However, in a sphere where certainty was not possible fervent passions were to be aroused among opponents, many of whom were little stirred by other political issues. The magnitude of the disaster which a single explosion could cause inspired these opponents to demonstrate constantly against British possession of so enormously dangerous a weapon. Moreover, far more people than those who marched each Easter from the atomic research station at Aldermaston to Trafalgar Square in symbolic protest were worried by the 'fall-out' of various constituents after tests in the air: iodine 131, which, by contaminating milk, could affect the thyroid gland; strontium 89 and strontium 90, which in large enough quantities would affect human bones; caesium 137, which could affect the whole body. The crew of a Japanese fishing boat suffered accidentally after an American hydrogen bomb test in March, 1954. Yet during the next eight years, fears of contamination by fall-out were balanced by governments' fears of falling behind in a race for security, and accordingly, despite an atmosphere of increasing anxiety, the tests went on.

While these ominous developments were taking place, one comparatively small-scale problem, inherited from the Labour government, was successfully settled: the conflict over the Abadan oil refinery, which Dr Mussadiq's government had taken over in 1951. The Persian ability to run the concern alone had not been clear, and in August, 1954, it was agreed that the oil installations should be worked by a consortium in which the British Petroleum Company (the old Anglo-Iranian Oil Company) should have 40 per cent of the interests, and various American, Dutch and French companies the other 60 per cent. The Iranian government was to receive 50 per cent of the earnings.

Unfortunately, Britain's relations elsewhere in the Middle East were moving, stage by stage, towards complete breakdown. Hostility to the British among the Egyptians was intensifying, and several years before the agreement with Iran was brought about, problems were developing which were far less easy to resolve.

---

[1] Sampson, p. 107. Macmillan's closing speech at the Geneva Conference, 9.11.55

[2] *White Paper on Defence Estimates 1955*

[3] Sir W. S. Churchill, House of Commons Debate on *Defence White Paper* 17.2.55, *Keesing's Contemporary Archives 1955*, pp. 14093–4

20

Britain and Egypt and the Suez war

In October, 1951, the Egyptians denounced the treaty made with Britain in 1936. Sabotage and guerilla actions against the British who still remained in the Canal zone followed. Colonel Nasser, the leader of a *coup d'état* which obliged King Farouk to abdicate in July, 1952, predicted such terror that the British would find it 'far too expensive . . . to maintain their citizens in occupation of our country.'[1] By 1954, when Nasser became Prime Minister of Egypt, the British, deprived of local civilian labour, were on the defensive behind barbed wires. In October, 1954, they agreed to withdraw from their base. They could justifiably claim that it was no longer essential, that they had insufficient troops to police the world and that Turkey's membership of NATO had altered the military situation in the Middle East. Yet it was still humiliating to leave under pressure; and the next two years showed that hopes of improved Anglo-Egyptian relations resulting from their withdrawal had no foundation.

In September, 1955, Nasser announced that Egypt had purchased from Czechoslovakia arms which he admitted later were of Russian origin. By November, 1956, the British had reason to believe that these acquisitions included at least 50 jet bombers, 100 jet fighters and about 300 tanks, as well as armoured troop carriers, guns, rocket launchers, radar and wireless equipment, worth altogether at least £150m. At once the Anglo-American hopes of maintaining a balance of arms between Arabs and Jews collapsed; yet, to prevent Nasser from becoming entirely a protégé of the Communists, they were obliged to go on helping Egypt. Nasser particularly wanted aid for the construction of a high dam which would create a lake 300 miles long on the Nile, regulate the flow of the waters and

145

allow the irrigated area of Egypt to be increased. The World Bank was unwilling to lend the entire sum necessary, but it agreed to lend $200m if the United States lent $56m and Britain $14m. The arrangement did not lead to harmony. Egyptian radio attacks on every remaining vestige of British influence in the Middle East accompanied the riots in Jordan which met General Templer's attempts to induce the country to join the Baghdad Pact; they accompanied the dismissal by King Hussein of Jordan of General John Glubb after twenty-six years' service with the Jordan army and seventeen years spent as commander of it; and they took advantage of the anti-British riots which greeted Selwyn Lloyd, the British Foreign Secretary, during a visit to Bahrein. Eden was infuriated. Moreover, doubts were beginning to arise about Egypt's ability to repay the loans which had been agreed upon, since its cotton crop had been pledged for several years in order to pay for the Soviet arms. In America the Secretary of State, John Foster Dulles, was as dissatisfied as was Eden. The consequence was that on 19 July, 1956, the United States withdrew its offers of a loan for the dam. Britain did so too the following day, and the World Bank offer, which was conditional on American and British loans being paid, automatically lapsed. Thereupon Nasser, determined to obtain money from some other source for the dam, announced, on 26 July, the nationalisation of the Suez Canal Company. He at once put Egyptians into the controlling positions, and informed the shareholders that they would be bought out at prices prevailing that day on the Paris Stock Exchange and that subsequent revenues would be used to pay for the dam.

The background to Nasser's action requires some explanation. For decades Egypt had obtained no direct income from the Canal. In 1937 it accepted a rather paltry £300000 per annum. In 1949 the Egyptian government was allowed to appoint five directors to the Canal Board and to take 7 per cent of the profits. It was restrained from demanding more partly by the presence of British troops in the Canal zone and partly by the knowledge that in any case the Canal was due to become Egyptian in 1968. The feeling was widespread that the days of the Company were numbered. Not that this consoled Britain and France when nationalisation finally occurred. Two days afterwards, on 28 July, the British Treasury ordered that all Egypt's sterling balances and assets should be frozen; and within a week the

French and American authorities had done the same. On 30 July, Eden ordered a ban on the export of any further war materials to Egypt. Early in August 20 000 British army reservists were called up and reinforcements were despatched to the Eastern Mediterranean. The Prime Minister concluded, as he made clear in communications to President Eisenhower, that economic pressures were unlikely, by themselves, to be effective, and that the only way to break Nasser was to use force without delaying to negotiate. Force was in fact not used at this stage. Eisenhower advised caution; and the British service chiefs, who had been instructed to prepare plans, considered that the distance of their bases made immediate military retaliation impossible. Accordingly, Eden convened a conference of the maritime powers in order to assert the international character of the Canal. This was unsuccessful. Some of the powers were unprepared to go to extremes. The Americans made clear that they would not countenance force. Contradictory advice came from France, Russia, the British embassies in the Arab states and from India. Meanwhile, Nasser denounced the deliberations of the Canal users and Egyptians continued to run the Canal, to the surprise and embarrassment of the West, without any of the predicted catastrophes.

PREPARATIONS FOR WAR

In these circumstances the British made military plans on the assumption that if the situation developed into war they would meet strong Egyptian resistance stiffened by Russian pilots and technicians. The French, intensely annoyed by their belief that Nasser was encouraging the Algerian rebels who were so seriously taxing France's strength, entered (without at first informing the British government) into closer association with Israel, which had for several years been involved in intermittent border conflict with Egypt. French representatives were, in fact, planning a means of capturing the Canal, in collaboration with the Israelis, at the same time as a mission led by the Australian Prime Minister, Robert Menzies, was in Cairo endeavouring to persuade Nasser to negotiate. The details of the events which followed remained for most of the next decade a subject for conjecture. At the time, Labour Opposition charges of collusion between the British government and the Israelis were denied both by Anthony Eden and by Selwyn Lloyd. It was only in

Nasser in the dismissal on 1 March, 1956, of Glubb Pasha by the King of Jordan. Eden, ignoring the likelihood that this was a personal gesture by the King, convinced himself that Nasser lay behind it; and from this time onwards, ill and impelled by considerations of pride and prestige, he could envisage no alternative but the removal and destruction of Nasser, even though it might mean 'anarchy and chaos in Egypt'.[4] It is of course, never altogether safe to analyse another man's motives. Yet it is hard to escape the conclusion that British participation in the war was brought about almost entirely by the Prime Minister. Nutting endeavoured to prevent the adoption of the French plan, but Eden was determined to go ahead and was able to obtain Selwyn Lloyd's unhappy acquiescence. The British government was consciously involved in a war of aggression on the side of the aggressor.

WAR

The preliminaries may at the time have been obscure. The facts from 29 October were perfectly plain. On that day the Israelis attacked Egypt to eliminate the army posts in the Sinai Peninsula from which Egyptian raids on Israeli territory had been made. On 30 October an Anglo-French ultimatum demanded that both Israelis and Egyptians should withdraw to lines ten miles from the Canal and requested that Egypt should accept temporary Anglo-French occupation of Port Said, Ismailia and Suez. If answers were not received within twelve hours Britain and France would intervene with force. Israel was prepared to accept the ultimatum, but Egypt, as was anticipated in the Anglo-French plan, refused to do so. Accordingly, to the dismay and bewilderment of British diplomatic representatives in the Arab countries (Sir Humphrey Trevelyan in Cairo in particular), Britain and France intervened.

The avowed justifications for this war were to preserve the Canal from damage, to end a conflict which might have developed into a more widespread war, to safeguard the interests of British citizens in Egypt, to guarantee supplies of Middle East oil for the West and to prevent Cairo from becoming the scene of rivalry between Russia and the West culminating in the sort of bloodbath which had just overwhelmed Budapest. It was, however, quite impossible to regard Britain and France as

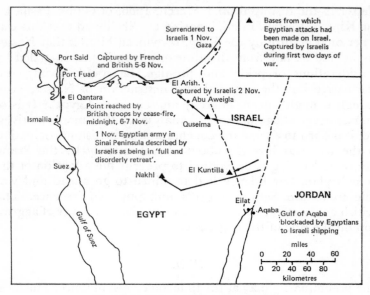

The Suez War, November 1956.

impartial referees in the fight. The demand for the withdrawal of troops from the Canal had the effect of allowing the Israelis to remain well inside Egyptian territory and to occupy almost all of the Sinai Peninsula, though at the time of the ultimatum they still had not got within ten miles of the Canal, and, as the published records of the Israeli Chief-of-Staff, General Dayan, later made clear, had no intention of carrying the war so far into Egyptian territory. Thereafter the British concentrated their bombardment on Egyptian targets, particularly airfields (from which Russian and Czech advisers and pilots at once removed the Ilushin bombers which Nasser had acquired). Inevitably the British appeared to the world not as policemen parting the combatants but as unashamed allies of the Israelis. When the Security Council, on an American motion, called on all members of the United Nations to refrain from using or threatening to use force in Egypt and demanded that the Israelis should withdraw to their original lines, Britain and France for the first time used their veto (30 October). Their bombardment continued for five days while landing craft and armour were brought 936 miles from Malta. Port Said was taken in the face of stiff resistance. A third of the Canal zone was occupied. Then, making a virtue of submission to the United Nations, the operation was called off at midnight on 6 November after unconditional acceptance by both Israel and Egypt of a ceasefire.

The French wished to go on. Part of their Cabinet was prepared to continue even without Britain. However, for Britain, American pressure was irresistible. President Eisenhower and the Americans had deliberately been kept uninformed and events had taken them by surprise. To Eden's chagrin they played a leading part in the United Nations' censures of Britain. Furthermore, the war caused a sterling crisis worse than any since 1945. At the beginning of October the reserves stood at about $2 800 000 000 and the situation seemed stable; but British intervention in Egypt precipitated withdrawals amounting on balance to $400 000 000. Sterling could be saved only by borrowing from the International Monetary Fund for general purposes and from the Export-Import Bank for essential goods which were being bought in the United States—and these loans would have been unobtainable had the fighting continued.

THE CONSEQUENCES

The consequences of the adventure were profound. The world was against Britain and France. Even within the Commonwealth only Australia and New Zealand gave support to the war, while others, like Canada, were as forthright in their condemnation as was the United States. The Arab states, inevitably, were alienated. Even the pro-British Prime Minister of Iraq, Nuri-es-Said, was constrained to suggest the ejection of Britain from the Baghdad Pact. The Jordan government dismissed the few remaining British officers still serving with its forces and abrogated the Anglo-Jordanian treaty. Nor could this general condemnation be silenced by a successful conclusion of the operation. None of the principal aims of Britain and France was in fact achieved. The safety of the Canal was not preserved, since the Egyptians sank nearly fifty vessels in it and until these were salvaged (April, 1957) it was unusable, and shipping was obliged, after all, to voyage round the Cape. Oil supplies were not safeguarded: the Syrians blew up pumping stations between Iraq and the coast; Saudi Arabians refused to pump to British-held terminals and into British ships. British citizens, many of whom had originated in Malta and had spent most of their lives in Egypt, were not safeguarded; many of them came, destitute, to Britain. It was not clear that any Middle Eastern city had been saved from a Communist take-over; most of the East European technicians discreetly withdrew from the scene of action and were not implicated in the war at all. Nasser remained more firmly in control than ever, and was indeed to retain power far longer than any member of the British or French governments in 1956, dying in office in 1970. The Israelis, who had expected to crush Egypt within forty-eight hours if left to themselves, were deprived of their victory.

At home, this episode did more to divide the nation than any other since the war. So great was the authority of the Prime Minister and so strong was a sense of party loyalty that only seven Conservative members of the Commons opposed the government, and only two ministers, Sir Edward Boyle, the Economic Secretary to the Treasury, and Anthony Nutting, resigned. Only two Labour M.P.s supported the government. After a session so turbulent that the Speaker was obliged to suspend the sitting for half an hour, the government survived a vote of censure by 324 votes to 255. But the divisions in Parliament along party lines, as if the debate had been on some comparatively trivial issue, could not conceal the strong feelings that had been aroused in the country, in Parliament and among the permanent officials of the Foreign Office. Few would have justified Nasser's recent actions; but many doubted whether either the methods adopted against his country or the timing of the intervention were moral or sensible. With Nutting they believed that Britain, the theoretical champion of the rule of law, had resorted, in a 'mad imperialist gamble',[5] to the law of the jungle. The Liberal Party, for several years close to extinction and often indistinguishable from Conservative party, found in opposition to the government a basis for its resurgence during the next few years. On the other extreme, a substantial section of the Conservative party voiced strongly the opinion that the British should have gone on with the fight and should have reached the southern end of the Canal; they assailed the government not for an action of doubtful wisdom but for premature surrender to the demands of a United Nations which had itself been so ineffective in dealing with an explosive situation.

Sir Anthony Eden, deeply disturbed though he had been by British isolation in the United Nations and by the censure which his policy had drawn from the United States and the Commonwealth, did not resign for several weeks. Despite illness which obliged him to take three weeks' holiday in Jamaica at the end of November, he remained Prime Minister until January, 1957, when Harold Macmillan succeeded to his office.

---

[1] E. Monroe, *Britain's Moment in the Middle East*, p. 173, Chatto and Windus Ltd (London 1963)

[2] Anthony Nutting, *No End of a Lesson*, pp. 164, Constable & Co. Ltd (London 1967)

[3] Ibid., p. 14

[4] Ibid., p. 35

[5] Ibid., p. 139

21

Foreign relations after the Suez war

Harold Macmillan had at first strongly supported the Suez adventure. As Chancellor of the Exchequer at the time, though, he had not been able to disregard the sterling crisis which the war had brought upon Britain. Denunciation of the government's actions had been all too audible even within the Conservative party. Having become Prime Minister, Macmillan propounded as his first objective the restoration and maintenance of unity within the party. Calmly, without the unpredictable interventions and tenseness by which Eden had irritated his colleagues, he sought to revive confidence in the government and self-confidence in the country. In a broadcast he called for an end to suggestions that Britain had become a second-class power. 'This is a great country and do not let us be ashamed to say so. . . . There is no need to quiver before temporary difficulties.'[1] His ministers were impressed. Lord Kilmuir could not over-emphasise the Prime Minister's personal contribution to 'the renaissance', while Dr Charles Hill, Postmaster-General and later Chancellor of the Duchy of Lancaster, admired the judgment and 'superiority of mind'[2] which he brought to the chairmanship of Cabinet meetings.

A number of ministerial changes were made, including the appointment to the Chancellorship of the Exchequer of Peter Thorneycroft and to the Parliamentary Secretaryship at the Ministry of Education of Sir Edward Boyle, who had resigned from the government in protest against the Suez war. Selwyn Lloyd remained Foreign Secretary. Macmillan's interest in foreign affairs was such, however, that he tended to dominate, rather as Eden had dominated when he had become Prime Minister and Macmillan had himself been at the Foreign Office. Britain's relations with other countries in the late 1950s were

1964 that French, Israeli, American and Canadian authors began to discover and publish the truth. Not until 1966 did Christian Pineau, the French Foreign Minister during the Suez crisis, reveal, in a B.B.C. interview, what had occurred in France. Only in 1967 was the British part in the preliminary negotiations divulged by Anthony Nutting, who, as Minister of State for Foreign Affairs in Eden's government, was deeply, though very reluctantly, involved in them.

When the truth was at last exposed it became clear that by early October the Israeli Prime Minister, David Ben Gurion, had agreed to provide a pretext for the French (and perhaps also for the British) seizure of the Canal by attacking Egypt across the Sinai Peninsula and by clearing the Egyptians out of Gaza and the Tiran Strait leading to Israel's Red Sea port of Eilat. The French had promised to deliver 100 Super-Sherman tanks, among other vehicles, in return. Ben Gurion had made one important condition, though: Israel had to be safeguarded against retaliatory bombing by Nasser's Russian-equipped air force. Only Britain had bomber bases sufficiently close to permit this. Britain, consequently, had to be drawn into the plot.

On 14 October two French emissaries met Eden in great secrecy at Chequers to unfold the plan of the campaign which, in most essentials, was to be carried out a little more than a fortnight later: Israel should attack across Sinai; France and Britain should then order both sides to withdraw from the Canal; and France and Britain should then intervene to preserve the Canal from harm. This was indeed what happened. The only major feature of the plan which was not in the end to be carried out was the capture of Suez as well as of Port Said. According to Pineau, Ben Gurion had flown to Paris on 23 October and had the next day signed an Anglo-French-Israeli treaty which had assured him of the required British bomber support; and Selwyn Lloyd had been present at this meeting.

The British acceptance of the plan seems to have been the responsibility essentially of the Prime Minister. Why ever did he embark on a course which at the time entailed deceiving, for various reasons, Arab states, the Americans, the British people, even members of the government, and which was, a decade later, to be described by Anthony Nutting as 'a sad and sordid chapter of history',[2] 'morally indefensible and politically suicidal'?[3] Nutting found the origin of Eden's intense dislike of

consequently largely affected by the Premier's own journeys, initiatives and negotiations. A visit with Selwyn Lloyd to President Eisenhower in Bermuda in March, 1957, did something to repair the damage done to Britain's reputation by the Suez war, even though Eisenhower feared that the Englishmen were still too obsessed with the idea of unseating Nasser to be able to consider objectively and realistically possible methods of operating the Canal in the future. In the end they were obliged to accept Nasser's terms, despite Lord Salisbury's protests against the surrender. The Canal was in fact worked with unexpected effectiveness by the Egyptians.

A more successful British gesture than the Suez war, though one involving a difficult decision for Macmillan, was the despatch of 2000 parachutists to Jordan, in July, 1958, at the request of the government of Jordan, in order to protect King Hussein after massacres in Iraq had produced yet another unsettled Middle-Eastern situation. On this occasion the Americans were also involved. They responded to a similar appeal by the Lebanese government.

Intervention in Jordan was a small issue. A very much larger one, with which Macmillan was preoccupied as long as he remained Prime Minister, was the need to improve relations between Russia and the West. These relations remained very uneasy, even after Khrushchev's great speech in 1956 which damned relentlessly the evils and errors perpetrated by Stalin and appeared to portend a break with everything associated with the Stalin dictatorship. The White Paper on Defence (1958) estimated that Russia still faced westwards with some 200 divisions, about 20000 aircraft and a fleet which included 500 submarines. The success of the first Russian *Sputnik*, the rocket which heralded the age of space exploration, in October, 1957, inspired the fear that there could now be no limits to the development of inter-continental missiles and made some real move towards disarmament seem quite essential. Khrushchev's announcement in November, 1958, that he was about to sign a peace treaty with East Germany and to end the rights of the Western Allies in the Western sector of Berlin underlined yet again the need for a détente.

In the hope of reducing the tension which these developments had created, Macmillan, Selwyn Lloyd and a substantial retinue visited Moscow in February, 1959. Eisenhower,

Adenauer and de Gaulle had few expectations that the gesture would produce any favourable results, and the early meetings appeared to justify their doubts. The final stages were more cordial, and at least agreement was reached on the possibility of investigating arms limitation and the chances of checking nuclear tests. From Moscow Macmillan went on to Paris, Bonn and Washington to report on his achievement, if it could be so considered. The Foreign Ministers of Britain, Russia, France and the United States (Selwyn Lloyd, Gromyko, Couve de Murville and Christian Herter) met in Geneva, though with little effect. Conferences also took place on the suspension of nuclear tests, with equally little effect.

Nothing positive had been achieved by these activities. However, it could perhaps be said that the situation was not growing worse. The suspicion was gaining ground in Britain, moreover, that although Russia might be suited by a condition of turmoil in the capitalist and allegedly imperialist world, its leaders were not prepared to risk the involvement of Soviet forces in an international war. Good reasons for this attitude were revealed by the 1959 census, which showed that Russia had nearly 21 million more women than men over the age of 32 (over 18 in 1945), although in the younger age groups the numbers were almost equal. Western demographers were left to conclude from this, and from the fact that the total population had risen unexpectedly slowly in two decades, that Russia may have lost 30 million people during the war, either killed or starved or unborn because of the deaths of potential fathers. Eight million may have been military casualties. No argument against active participation in another war could have been stronger.

---

[1] Sampson, p. 129
[2] Charles Hill, *Both Sides of the Hill*, p. 235, William Heinemann (London 1964)

22
Conservative economic policies 1959–1964

The Conservative election campaign in 1959, directed by Oliver Poole and Lord Hailsham, had been preceded by two years of professionally organised advertising at an estimated cost of £468000. Labour's recent history had been one of apparent dissension and division, and, although a fortnight before the poll Hugh Gaitskell was still hoping for victory, the general satisfaction produced by increasing prosperity, combined perhaps with Harold Macmillan's personal popularity, did in fact result not merely in a third successive Conservative triumph, but, in addition, an even greater majority than they had enjoyed previously. In defiance of earlier theories about the swing of an electoral pendulum between elections, the government increased its majority in the Commons from 60 to 100. The total number of Conservative seats was now 365, the total Conservative vote 13749830. Labour lost another 19 seats and was left with 258. Its candidates polled 12215538 votes, about 188000 fewer than in 1955. The Liberals, encouraged by victory in a recent by-election at Torrington, put up nearly twice as many candidates as in 1955, and the fact that they lost fewer deposits suggested that at last a revival in their favour was developing; but they still obtained only 6 seats, and 2 of these were won as a result of local agreements with Conservatives that their candidates should not oppose each other but should offer an undivided front against Labour. The invariable Liberal disadvantage at elections, after which their representation never reflected the proportion of votes cast for the party, provoked them, alone among the parties, to advocate the introduction of proportional representation. Joseph Grimond remained the party leader in the Commons.

The election was followed by a considerable number of alterations in the government: about half the ministerial positions changed hands. The personnel, however, changed very little. Ministers were merely moved from one office to another, and it was not until 1962 that any really radical developments occurred. Nor, for the time being, were any significant new policies introduced. Foreign relations, colonial policy, the welfare programme and domestic economic measures all continued to advance along lines similar to those followed previously.

THE NATIONAL FINANCES

Heathcoat Amory's pre-election budget had not been intended to inaugurate 'a spending spree'. Steady but not excessive expansion of production, designed to reduce an unemployment rate of 2·8 per cent without adding to the problem of inflation, was the Chancellor's purpose. Actually, the budget was followed by a boom which certainly reduced slowly the average monthly unemployment figure for Britain and Northern Ireland, from 512 000 in 1959 to 392 000 in 1960, but at the same time encouraged an almost 11 per cent expansion of industrial output, profits of nearly 12 per cent and rapidly rising imports with their attendant problem of another balance of payments deficit in 1960. Ultimately the deficit on visible imports turned out to be £408m, and even with a favourable balance of British invisible exports, the deficit was still £275m. Before the extent of this reversal of financial fortunes was fully clear, however, Heathcoat Amory had resigned his position. Selwyn Lloyd was the new Chancellor of the Exchequer. The Earl of Home succeeded him as Foreign Secretary.

The balance of payments deficit was, on this occasion, only transitory. Selwyn Lloyd's first year of office coincided with an improvement in the position: 1961 produced an adverse balance of no more than £5m. Unfortunately it also produced yet another sterling crisis of a different kind. This time an upward revaluation of the Deutsche Mark by 5 per cent inspired an idea that sterling would be devalued as a step in a general realignment of currencies. With the aim, customary at periods of such rumours, of withdrawing their sterling holdings before their value was reduced, overseas creditors started once again a run on British reserves. And once again a Chancellor found himself obliged to introduce crisis measures. In July, 1961, a 10 per cent customs and excise surcharge was imposed on various products, including drinks of all kinds, petrol, tobacco and sugar; purchase tax was increased by 10 per cent; government spending, at home and overseas, was reduced; and the Bank Rate was raised again, to 7 per cent.

At the time these measures appeared unavoidable. Later, though, they were to be condemned as having done more harm than good. They were introduced when the run on the reserves was already subsiding and when the balance of payments position was about to move in Britain's favour. They were, indeed, too late. Their only real result was to ensure that there should be nearly two years of industrial stagnation. Economic forecasting had, yet again, proved to be a hazardous undertaking.

In certain other respects Selwyn Lloyd's career as Chancellor was enterprising and significant. The establishment of the National Economic Development Council and a National Incomes Commission opened up prospects both of industrial planning and of resistance to Britain's never-ending inflation such as not even the post-war Labour government had attempted. Appeals for long-term planning had already been made in 1960 by a small group of business men, influenced particularly by the chairman of the Federation of British Industry's Economic Policy Committee, Hugh Weeks. To these leaders of industry the contrast between the slow expansion of British industry and that of some continental countries, especially West Germany and France, was as disturbing as the rapid changes of government financial policy, the 'Stop-Go', which rectified some problems only at the cost of undermining confidence in investment. Selwyn Lloyd appreciated the need for more effective planning, and although at first opposed by most of the Cabinet, he found support for his plans increasing as the sterling crisis of 1961 drew renewed attention to Britain's weaknesses. Accordingly, the N.E.D.C. came into being in 1962. Since Conservatism was instinctively inclined to dislike the idea of excessive government interference in private industry, and since neither the experience of nationalised industries nor of Treasury influence on the management of the economy in the 1950s had been altogether encouraging, the new council was designed to be an independent body which could exert pressure on the government as well as on industry. It was composed of six employers, six representatives of the trade unions, two representatives of the nationalised industries, two independent members and three ministers. Its Director was Sir Robert Shone, previously Director of the Iron and Steel Board. Its initial aim was to plan future growth, over-optimistically estimated at 4 per cent a year, at least until 1966, and at 50 per cent during the next decade.

A PAY PAUSE

Selwyn Lloyd's incomes policy began with an attempt to gain acceptance for a pay pause. The constant upward movement of prices, brought about primarily by the obligation of employers to pay ever higher wages, seemed to make this inescapable. The government's *Economic Survey* had pointed out that earnings during the second half of 1960 had been 6½ per cent higher than during the previous year, while the Bank of England had issued a plain warning that further wage demands made early in 1961 would lead to an over-valued currency which could be remedied only by devaluation. Support came from the Ministry of Labour for a policy which would end the everlasting surrender to the unions when wage demands were formulated. And particularly significant condemnation of the ineffective measures previously adopted to check wage inflation was published in 1961 in a review by the Organisation for European Economic Co-operation of rising prices in Britain. 'On the strength of its record to date,' asserted this survey, 'the U.K. must be judged to have failed to respond satisfactorily to the new problems posed by full employment . . . given the antiquated nature of the institutional arrangements in a number of industries, the weakness of the central bodies on both sides, the lack of any clearly defined norm for arbitrators, . . . there can be no assurance that wage increases will in future be kept in line with the growth potential of the economy.'

Whether the pay pause was particularly effective was not clear. Inflation slackened for a short period, though this may have been the result of unemployment, the monthly average figures for which were higher in 1962 than in 1961. Some of the public may at last have realised the need to take action, though no sooner had the pause ended, on 1 April, 1962, than wage demands revived. Indeed, a number of settlements had been made even before the end. In November, 1961, workers in the nationalised electricity industry gained a wage increase, and altogether, critics of the government complained, more than seventy trades and professions had broken the pause, only those helpless or honourable enough to make no effective demands being obliged to observe it. The Chancellor himself had permitted the pause to coincide with the raising of the surtax level from £2000 to £5000, and although there may have been sound arguments for this gesture, the moment for it was ineptly chosen and Selwyn Lloyd could not convincingly explain it to a critical public.

The pay pause was designed as a temporary measure to be followed by a period during which it was hoped that wage increases would not exceed $2\frac{1}{2}$ per cent a year (raised in 1963 to $3\frac{1}{2}$ per cent) and outrun expected increases in productivity. The National Incomes Commission, on the other hand, was intended as a permanent organisation, examining incomes from all sources and endeavouring to exert an influence over what was now clearly the main cause of almost continuous inflation. The trade unions, unfortunately, refused to play any part in the N.I.C. At the Trade Union Congress in September, 1963, both Frank Cousins and Ted Hill, leading members of the General Council of the T.U.C., and members of the N.E.D.C., condemned any form of wage restraint which might interfere with traditional methods of collective bargaining. Non-unionists were left wondering how, if an incomes policy were not permitted to operate effectively, long-term economic planning could be expected to function satisfactorily either. The two seemed to be, at least to some extent, interdependent.

A factor which introduced complications into any discussion of wage increases was the payment, particularly in the engineering, electrical and ship-building industries, of supplementary wages above the recognised hourly rates and overtime. In 1961 the British Employers' Federation estimated that in addition to an agreed national wages bill of approximately £6500m and overtime amounting to about £600m, excess payments cost employers about £1500m more. Furthermore, during the last years of the Conservative government this 'wage drift' was always in an upward direction. Ministry of Labour statistics suggested that it never rose by less than ·2 per cent in any year and that in 1964 it increased by as much as 2·4 per cent. It was a factor which could never easily be influenced by any Commission or by any directive from the Chancellor of the Exchequer.

CONSERVATIVE RADICALISM

Selwyn Lloyd's chancellorship was significant for several other departures from tradition, apart from the establishment of the N.E.D.C. and the N.I.C. Some impetus was given to the planning of government expenditure along lines suggested by the Plowden Committee appointed by Heathcoat Amory: a branch of the Treasury was to be established to consider the long-term effects of public financial policy on such issues as monopolies, the employment of skilled workers, industrial costs and prices and productivity. Decisions involving the expenditure of public money were to be subjected to forecasting techniques; and the competing demands of different ministries were to be considered in the light of probable requirements over several years. In addition, on the recommendation of Sir Frank Lee, the Permanent Secretary to the Treasury, powers were given to Chancellors to vary taxes when necessary between budgets. Such developments implied not merely that the attitude of the Conservatives of the 1960s towards planning differed substantially from their attitude during the previous decade, when many believed that the government had already taken over too much. It suggested, indeed, that Conservatism, in its approach to planning, had become considerably more radical than Labour had been in the 1940s. The facts of government control of the economy were now too clear to be ignored.

Total public expenditure, including interest on the National Debt, had never, in any full year of Conservative power, been below 40 per cent of the Gross National Product (the sum total of all domestic incomes received by individuals and corporations, together with net incomes received from abroad). In 1962 it was 44 per cent. The so-called Public Sector (the central government, the local authorities and such public bodies as the nationalised industries) was responsible for more than 40 per cent of all fixed investment in such assets as buildings, plant and machinery and vehicles. It was responsible for 50 per cent of all building work. Central and local governments employed three million people and paid 15 per cent of all wages and salaries. In these circumstances the government was evidently in a position to exert, for good or evil, a powerful influence on the country's economy. The discovery was, of course, not altogether new, but the degree to which the government acted upon it really did denote change. The impulse to introduce the change seems to have had its origin in Harold Macmillan, though it was with Selwyn Lloyd that many of the most obvious developments were associated. Unfortunately for the Chancellor, when, in July, 1962, as a gesture symbolic of the new spirit, Macmillan replaced about a third of the ministry by younger men, technocrats and radicals, Selwyn Lloyd was one of the victims. He was suddenly and unexpectedly obliged to give way to a more youthful colleague, Reginald Maudling.

23

Social welfare, government planning and the constitution 1959—64

EDUCATION

The growing affluence which may have contributed to the Conservatives' third successive election victory in 1959 also stimulated the production of a series of projects for the expansion of educational opportunities of all kinds, the improvement of communications, the extension of the town planning schemes of the forties and fifties, and the development of new methods and technical skills in a wide variety of industries. The period was distinguished by a succession of Reports advocating modernisation and, inevitably, increases in public expenditure. In economic life long-term planning, symbolised by the establishment of the N.E.D.C., was the dominant characteristic, and something of this spirit pervaded equally the recommendations for the future of British society and geographical appearance.

On various aspects of education five Reports were published between December, 1959, and October, 1963. The first was the report of a committee under the chairmanship of Sir Geoffrey Crowther to consider the education of people aged between 15 and 18 in relation to changing social and industrial needs. It recommended the raising of the school-leaving age to 16 and the introduction, by the 1970s, of compulsory part-time education for young men and women of 16 and 17 who had left school. Two months later, in February, 1960, the Countess of Albemarle's committee on the youth service advocated a ten-year programme involving the extension and modernisation of youth centres and an increase in the number of full-time trained youth leaders. The impact of the Albemarle recommendations had already been felt before the life of the Conservative government

164

ended: by 1962 429 projects, costing £3¾m, were under way, and 99 others had been prepared. Nearly a 1000 leaders were employed by the middle of 1963.

In January, 1961, a government White Paper on technical education advised the introduction of new, longer courses and the expansion of the day release scheme. By 1962 about a quarter of a million young people were being released by their firms for educational purposes.

The last two reports on education appeared within a few days of each other in October, 1963, and both aroused a great deal of attention. The first, produced by a committee under John Newsom, was concerned with pupils aged between 13 and 16, of average and less than average ability: those in, or recently in, the secondary modern schools. The report claimed that the potential ability of these pupils was possibly much greater than had been generally assumed and that they should be given every opportunity to develop their talents. Such claims were in line with a belief, which was being expressed ever more frequently, that ability, of whatever kind, was too valuable to be wasted. Like the *Crowther Report*, the *Newsom Report* called for the raising of the school-leaving age to 16 for all pupils entering secondary schools from September, 1965, and expressed the hope that the last year at school would be used to initiate these pupils into the work and leisure opportunities of an adult world. The authors of the *Report* were impressed by the achievements of the schools, observing with satisfaction that the number of young people remaining at school after the age of 15 had risen from 26·1 per cent in 1951 to 39·8 per cent in 1961. They were particularly struck by the steady growth in the standards of literacy, but recognised, as others had done before them, that for many pupils examinations were inappropriate. They advocated instead the encouragement of extra-curricular activities.

The *Newsom Report* was followed by one on the universities. Already, since the war, important developments had taken place in this sphere. Between 1948 and 1957 the status of full university had been granted to a number of colleges which had previously been affiliated to the University of London and had awarded London degrees: Nottingham, Southampton, Hull, Exeter and Leicester. In 1949 the University College of North Staffordshire had been founded at Keele, with A. D. Lindsay, hitherto Master of Balliol, as its first principal. The early and

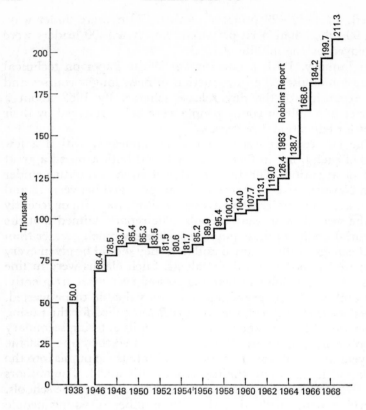

Full-time university students

Older Universities

Oxford, Cambridge	Reading 1926
Durham 1832	Wales (Aberystwyth,
London 1836	Bangor, Cardiff, Swansea,
R.C.A. 1837	Lampeter) 1893
Manchester 1851	St Andrews 1411
Newcastle 1852	Glasgow 1451
Birmingham 1900	Aberdeen 1494
Liverpool 1902	Edinburgh 1583
Leeds 1904	Belfast (Queen's) 1908
Sheffield 1905	Dublin (Trinity) 1591
Bristol 1909	National University of
	Ireland 1908

Post-war Universities

Keele, University
College 1949,
University 1962
Sussex (Brighton) 1961
East Anglia (Norwich)
1963
York 1963
Lancaster 1964
Essex (Colchester)
1964
Warwick 1965
Kent (Canterbury) 1965
Loughborough University
of Technology 1966
Aston in Birmingham
1966

The City University
1966
Brunel (Uxbridge) 1966
Bath University of
Technology 1966
Bradford 1966
Surrey (Guildford) 1966
Salford 1967
Strathclyde (Glasgow)
1964
Herriot-Watt (Edin-
burgh) 1966
Dundee 1967
Stirling 1967
Ulster (Coleraine) 1965
Open University 1969

University Colleges granted
University status
Nottingham 1948
Southampton 1952
Hull 1954
Exeter 1955
Leicester 1957

mid '60s had seen the creation of universities at Brighton, York, Norwich, Colchester, Lancaster, Warwick and Canterbury; another had been proposed for Stirling. The committee under Lord Robbins (Professor of Economics at the London School of Economics) estimated that, compared with 216000 students in 1963, there should be about 390000 by 1973 and 560000 by 1980, representing about 60 per cent of the young men and women leaving school. Six new universities should be established at once. University status should be bestowed on some ten regional colleges and colleges of further education. Existing institutions should be expanded, and about a quarter of the students in teachers' training colleges should take four-year courses for a degree in Education. Post-graduate studies should be pursued by about 30 per cent of the university students, as opposed to the 20 per cent undertaking them in 1963. The

Robbins Committee believed that a large number of able young persons were still not receiving the higher education of which they were capable and that the substantial increase in the numbers at college would not result in a decline of academic standards. In the atmosphere of hope which this *Report* inspired, and which few dared openly question at the time, the government immediately accepted the main recommendations, even though they would have involved an increase in expenditure on higher education from £206m in 1963 to £742m by 1980. No ministry could have permitted Britain's educational facilities to fall behind those of the United States or Russia, or could have suffered the reproach that vital ability was being squandered through neglect.

The most evident repercussions of the *Robbins Report* were the creation, or the re-establishment with a higher status, of a number of new technological universities. The Universities of Aston in Birmingham, Bath, Bradford, the City (Finsbury), Loughborough, Surrey, Strathclyde (Glasgow), Herriot-Watt (Edinburgh), Brunel (Acton, later transferred to Uxbridge) and Wolfson College, Oxford, all came into being or were given their new dignity between 1963 and 1966.

The expansion of the senior forms in the schools was equally rapid. Even before the production of the *Robbins Report* the numbers staying at school until the age of 18 had been rising faster than the total population of that age. The number entering universities had also been increasing. After the issue of the *Report* in 1963 these trends became more marked still. For every 100 at school at 18 in 1962, nearly 152 were at school in 1966, though the total population of the age of 18 had risen by only 30·2 per cent. More than half as many again left school with two or more A-level passes in 1966 as had left with such qualifications in 1962. For every 100 admitted to universities in 1962, 154 were admitted in 1966.

Central and local government expenditure on education of all sorts amounted in 1963 to £1266m. About half the money collected in rates was being spent on education.

TOWN PLANNING AND REGIONAL POLICY

A second issue which attracted more and more attention, from members of all parties and of none, was town planning. As the population continued to expand, to migrate from one part of the country to another, and to expect more comfortable and convenient homes for a smaller number of persons (an average of 3·2 in 1951 compared with 4·5 in 1911), a series of reports and projects was published, and expenditure on new or expanded towns remained high: £1135m in the year 1963–4. The drift of large numbers of people to the South East of England continued to be a matter of particular concern. Eight of the fifteen original New Towns had been in the South East and had been designed to absorb the excess population of London; and in the 1960s town planning was still largely concerned with the development of this region.

The prospects were disturbing. Whereas in 1963 there were in the Home Counties, outside built-up London, about eight acres of open country for each built-up acre, it was predicted that by 2000 there might be only four, and that there might be even fewer unless the high density of buildings constructed in the suburbs during the early 1960s were maintained in future decades. The prophets foretold that if each household were to have a separate dwelling, some 900 000 houses would be required in the Home Counties in the decade 1961–71 instead of the 670 000 for which plans had been made shortly before their prognostications were published. They expected that during this decade road traffic in the area would double, as would the number of commuters by rail. In 1964 the *Buchanan Report* confirmed their expectation of the rise in the number of motor vehicles.

One consequence of these trends was that the land and house prices which had been rising all over the country continued to rise with more than average rapidity in the South East. As building land became increasingly scarce builders found it necessary to buy, along with the land, antiquated houses, which had to be demolished before modern homes could be erected. The falling value of the pound was also partly responsible for the inflated prices. But the problem remained for years a nettle which few wished to grasp, however eagerly they might urge others to act. Ultimately, in 1964, the Labour Party developed the idea of a Land Commission which should provide a solution by imposing a levy on the increased value of urban land sold for building purposes. This was, in theory, supposed to preserve some price stability.

Another solution to the problems arising from the over-population of the South East was suggested in a report, published in 1964, which advised the development of Bletchley, Newbury and the region between Southampton and Portsmouth as new cities, and advocated substantial urban expansion at Ashford (Kent), Stansted, Ipswich, Peterborough, Northampton and Swindon. Further recommendations were contained in plans brought out at about the same time for the development of North-east England and Central Scotland so as to increase the prosperity of these areas and thereby to discourage the drift towards the over-crowded South East. In North-east England public investment was to increase from £55m in 1962–3 to £80m in 1963–4 and to about £90m the following year. Newton Aycliffe and Peterlee were to expand still further, and another new town was to grow up at Washington. Tyneside, Teesside and County Durham between the Great North Road and the coast were to become 'growth zones'. Expenditure on roads was to be increased from £54m in 1964 to £85m by 1969. The housing programme was to be accelerated to produce 25 000 houses a year instead of 18 000. Regional government offices were to be endowed with greater authority or newly established. Seven per cent of total public investment was to be bestowed on an area in which 5½ per cent of the country's population lived. The plans for Central Scotland followed similar lines. Public investment there was to increase from £100m to £140m (11 per cent of the total for 7½ per cent of the population). New trunk roads were to be built. A new town at Livingston was to be created, in addition to those at East Kilbride, Cumbernauld and Glenrothes. Extensive districts were designated Growth and Rehabilitation areas. One hundred million gallons of water a day were to be obtained from Loch Lomond, and 30 000 houses a year were to be built in place of 23 000.

Continuing earlier Conservative and Labour policies of encouraging industry to settle in the less affluent parts of Britain, the government introduced in 1960 a Local Employment Act, by which any area, not merely a particular Development Area, became eligible for assistance if threatened with a high level of unemployment (4·5 per cent of the labour force, or whatever may later have been decided). Factories in these regions could be leased at moderate rents or sold on deferred terms. Capital grants of 25 per cent of costs were to be made available for industrialists building their own factories, and government assistance was offered to local authorities clearing derelict sites or improving their services. Among the results of this Act were the establishment of steel-rolling mills in Scotland and South Wales, and the extension of the activities of the motor industry to Merseyside and Scotland. Between 1960 and 1963 the Board of Trade spent £81m in encouraging such developments and helped to create 90 000 new jobs.

Unfortunately, instead of declining, unemployment rose, from a monthly average of 377 000 in 1961 to 500 000 in 1962 and to 612 000 in 1963. It remained a reason for particular anxiety in Northern Ireland and was above the average in Scotland, Wales, and, at times, in Northern England. Accordingly, Reginald Maudling's 1963 budget offered further facilities to those willing to establish or expand their firms in these areas. Capital grants for both building and equipment were increased. A sum of £10m was provided to double the number of government training centres, especially in Scotland and Northern England. Loans were offered to underdeveloped countries with which to buy equipment from Britain's areas of higher unemployment. At the same time, a directorate for regional development was created at the Board of Trade and wider powers were bestowed on the regional offices of the various ministries. It was increasingly realised that effective improvements could take place only on an extensive scale. Since factories producing different commodities tended to be interdependent, piecemeal development of isolated and widely separated concerns was of only limited value. Moreover, without good roads, power supplies and new homes, industry could scarcely be established successfully.

During the final stages of the Conservative administration, when Edward Heath had been accorded the title of Secretary of State for Industry, Trade and Regional Development, and Lord Hailsham had been given special responsibility for the North East, these measures appeared to be having encouraging results. Between 1963 and 1964 there was a considerable increase of applications for Board of Trade assistance, and 435 plans were accepted and aided. Loans for the construction of the Wiggins Teape paper mill near Fort William (Inverness-shire) had particularly noticeable effects. Over the country as a whole the unemployment figures declined once more, to a monthly average of 414000 in 1964 and to 360000 in 1965.

Long-term planning of industry was carried a stage further during 1964 with the creation of a number of committees known generally as 'Little Neddies'. While the N.E.D.C. concerned itself with over-all planning, these were designed to direct the futures of particular industries. Initially committees were established for confectionery, the distributive trades, chemicals, electronics, machine tools, paper, mechanical engineering and wool. During the two years that followed similar committees were set up for thirteen other industries.

SOCIAL AND CONSTITUTIONAL MEASURES

A greater degree of uniformity and organisation was imposed on the building industry by Geoffrey Rippon (Minister of Public Building and Works) and Sir Keith Joseph (Minister of Housing). Using powers bestowed on the government by the Labour government's Industrial Organisation and Development Act of 1947 they encouraged the adoption of such modern methods as the use of factory-made components designed for assembly on the building sites. In 1963 a Contracts of Employment Act asserted the principle, new to Britain, that there should be fixed minimum periods of notice for dismissed workers. One week was not enough if a worker had been with a firm for two years or more. Labour was not to be considered as no more than a commodity for normal sale. In 1964 the Industrial Training Act gave the government power to impose a compulsory levy on all firms in an industry to finance training, whether they wanted their men trained or not. Previously expenses had been borne by individual firms. Also in 1964 Edward Heath piloted through the Commons an Act to end Resale Price Maintenance, which was intended to prevent manufacturers from insisting on a minimum price below which their products could not be sold. Despite the fears of those who believed that the small shopkeepers would suffer in competition with the large chain stores which could afford more easily to cut their prices, this Act was welcomed by purchasers who realised its potential value in reducing the cost of living, and by a majority of each of the parties in Parliament. Insofar as there was opposition, it came mainly from Conservatives. The Labour Party, Hugh Dalton in particular, had advocated such a measure years before. Provision was made in

1964 for the establishment of a special tribunal to hear the cases of manufacturers who had special reasons for wishing that price maintenance should continue.

The Conservatives introduced a number of very radical constitutional measures affecting the House of Lords. Criticism of the essentially hereditary character of the upper House had been heard throughout the century. Accordingly, in 1958, life peerages were introduced for both men and women, apart from the Law Lords and Bishops who had traditionally enjoyed membership of the House of Lords. By 1965 there were eighty-four life peers, and it appeared likely that the hereditary principle would gradually disappear. The first four women to sit in the Lords were the Dowager Marchioness of Reading, Lady Elliot of Harwood, Baroness Ravensdale and Baroness Wootton of Abinger. Later, they were to be joined by Miss Florence Horsbrugh (Conservative Minister of Education 1951–4), Dr Edith Summerskill (a Labour M.P. since 1938) and Lady Violet Bonham Carter (the Liberal daughter of H. H. Asquith, Prime Minister from 1908 to 1916).

After a prolonged campaign by Anthony Wedgwood Benn to avoid becoming against his will the second Lord Stansgate, an Act passed in 1963 allowed peers and peeresses to disclaim their titles and to stand for membership of the Commons. Lord Stansgate once again became Mr Benn and an M.P. The second Lord Altrincham became again Mr John Grigg; and by 1965 six others had abandoned hereditary titles. The most notable of these were Sir Alec Douglas-Home, who ceased to be the fourteenth Earl of Home on becoming Prime Minister in 1963, and Mr Quintin Hogg, who renounced his title of Viscount Hailsham when he also became a candidate for the premiership.

Another provision of the reforms of 1963 was the permission granted to peeresses in their own right to take their seats in the House of Lords.

Apart from the changes in the House of Lords, the most significant constitutional development of the post-war years was the establishment of the Greater London Council, designed to replace the London County Council and a number of contiguous borough councils, municipal boroughs and urban district councils. For years the Metropolitan Police and the Water Board had covered a region considerably greater than that covered by the L.C.C., and the unsuitability of the L.C.C.

boundaries had become increasingly clear. Fears of the consequences of absorption, which were expressed by the authorities in some of the outer suburbs, resulted in the exclusion of certain of them, like Epsom, from the Greater London area ultimately created. But one fear that was not immediately justified was that the progressive and successful Labour dominated Council of the old L.C.C. would be overwhelmed by the Conservatism of the suburbs. It was not until 1967 that the Conservatives swept Labour out of office.

24

Foreign relations 1959—64

1959 was not, in most respects, a particularly significant year in the history of Britain's foreign relations. Fear of the consequences of nuclear bomb tests continued to grow. In an erratic manner, fear of a Russian threat to the West continued to weaken. Macmillan continued to seek, by personal travels and meetings, the restoration of European harmony. The one new feature of the foreign policy of Conservatism's last phase was the realisation that, prosperous though Britain might appear to be, its prosperity would probably be greatly enhanced if, belatedly, it could become a part of the European Economic Community. In this last sphere the Conservatives were to be disappointed. In the other spheres times were more propitious, advantage was taken of the opportunities, and something of value was achieved, even though slowly and not entirely surely.

ATTEMPTS TO BAN NUCLEAR TESTS

The Prime Minister's endeavours to obtain both a suspension of nuclear tests and an improvement of relations with Russia proceeded simultaneously, as indeed they were bound to, so closely connected were the issues. Already, in 1957, a committee had spent five months in London deliberating on disarmament, though at that stage the Americans had been too anxious about surprise attack and the Russians too determined to avoid international control and inspection of their activities for any really satisfying solution to have been expected. In 1958, when the Russians had temporarily suspended nuclear tests, a conference in Geneva had brought about a suspension of tests for a year by the British and Americans, despite the misgivings of the latter, who were worried about the possible continuance of underground tests which could not be detected. In 1959 Macmillan developed the idea of an annual quota of inspections which

175

should be accepted by Britain and the United States and by Russia as well; and by the end of the year this idea was adopted.

While he had been striving to bring an end to nuclear tests, Macmillan had also been seeking a 'summit meeting' of the heads of the states concerned in the manufacture of the bombs. Eisenhower, for two years, declined to take part in a conference which, he felt, could bring no effective results, and it was not until May, 1960, that Macmillan's hopes could be realised. The Prime Minister envisaged, in the first place, a series of trade agreements. These, he thought, might contribute to a relaxation of the tensions which had for so long affected Russian relations with the West and might enable the British to act as an indispensable link between the two major powers of the world. The aspirations were not unrealistic. Unfortunately, the opening of the summit in Paris coincided with the shooting down over Russia of an American plane, the pilot of which had evidently been engaged in spying. Khrushchev, furiously demanding an apology from Eisenhower and an undertaking that such flights should end, left the conference, and none of Macmillan's appeals availed to restore harmony. The Summit had become an even greater calamity than Eisenhower had anticipated.

Subsequent diplomatic activities in 1960 were less unfortunate. In August Macmillan visited Bonn and Rome to prevent the disintegration of NATO following a dispute between de Gaulle and the Americans over American bomber bases in France. In September, when Khrushchev used a United Nations meeting in New York as a forum for Soviet propaganda, Eisenhower and Macmillan also went, to ensure that the representatives of the rapidly increasing number of new nations should hear the views of the West as well. A meeting between Macmillan and Khrushchev was more cordial than that in Paris in May. Progress towards a détente certainly continued to be erratic. Imperialist bourgeois capitalism remained the object of periodic Soviet denunciation, and the Communist programme for the next twenty years, which was published in 1961, was quite as unyielding as any earlier polemic. However, the truth was that Russia was becoming even more concerned with a steadily more strained relationship with the rival source of Communist doctrine, the Chinese empire of Mao Tse-tung. Throughout the 1960s the terms in which the two Communisms denounced each other continued to be as forthright as those previously reserved for damnation of the capitalist West. As the danger of serious conflict developed in the Far East it receded in the West.

A danger which still showed no signs of receding in 1961 and 1962 was the contamination of the atmosphere and the poisoning of international relations as a result of nuclear tests; and it was on this issue that the British now concentrated their efforts. The need became all the more urgent when, between August and October, 1961, another round of Russian tests was carried out. By November, 1961, the United States had been responsible for 157 explosions, Britain for 21 (the later ones at Maralinga in the Great Victoria Desert of South Australia, and near Christmas Island in the central Pacific), and France for 4. All these were together equivalent to about 126 megatons, or 126m tons of T.N.T. Russia outstripped America, Britain and France combined if judged by the power of its bombs. By November, 1961, it had carried out more than 100 tests. In October of that year it exploded a bomb of 25–30 megatons; and a week later, despite American appeals, one of 57 megatons. The power of the Russian bombs, together, added up to about 170 megatons by the end of 1961, and tests continued, though on a smaller scale, the following year. Macmillan's attempts to dissuade President Kennedy (in office since January, 1961) from allowing the United States to engage in any sort of competition were unsuccessful, and in April, 1962, a new series of American tests took place on Christmas Island.

All the northern countries of the world were, in varying degrees, affected by the fall-out from the tests, which were universally denounced. In Britain, where a campaign for nuclear disarmament had been begun in 1958, supporters of a policy of unilateral abandonment of the bomb felt that their case had been strengthened. Would the risks of retaining nuclear weapons remain at all limited once France, China, and, perhaps, other countries possessed them in large quantities, as well as the United States, Britain and Russia? What might happen if a Hitler seized power in one of these countries? The questions were important, though the answers were never as certain as many believed. Divisions in the Labour party in the early sixties on the issue of unilateral nuclear disarmament reflected the perplexity better than the solid support given by Conservatives to the government attitude that the bomb should be retained.

The Liberal policy was to compromise: the West should retain the deterrent, but Britain should not retain its individual possession of it.

In October, 1962, a major crisis developed when missiles of Russian origin were found to have been set up in Cuba. American determination that Cuba should not become a Communist nuclear base brought about a Russian withdrawal, but it was clear that the situation was potentially too dangerous to permit a settlement of the nuclear question to be postponed indefinitely. In November, accordingly, the disarmament conference resumed its activities in Geneva. The views of the British and Americans were now closer, and although the Russians were still obstructive, they were evidently more prepared to compromise than previously. They were willing to accept a limited degree of inspection, and though this was less than the Americans wanted, the change of attitude was encouraging. At last it seemed clear to both sides that their long-term interests really required an end to the experimental rivalry. The end was reached in July, 1963, when American and British representatives, Averell Harriman and Lord Hailsham, went to Moscow and, instead of insisting on a comprehensive ban on nuclear tests which Khrushchev would have refused, signed an agreement with the Russians that at least tests above ground should be banned. Underground tests could, and indeed did, continue; but the most alarming and perilous consequences of the tests could, it was hoped, henceforth be avoided.

The achievement was largely Macmillan's. The fall-out had been stopped. Unfortunately, this did not involve the return of Britain to traditional means of defence. Enormous sums had already been spent on highly sophisticated equipment, and these expenses went on rising so rapidly that even after the end of conscription the defence bill continued to increase. In 1953, when the total intake into the forces had been 238000, defence estimates had amounted to £1364500000. Ten years later the intake was only 37000, and the total number in the forces was considerably less than half the number in 1953, yet the estimates had risen to £1791800000, and there was no indication that they could be held in check in the immediate future. Rising costs were not entirely accounted for by inflation. The 'independent nuclear deterrent' and various very elaborate missiles were both extremely expensive and, because they rapidly became obsolete, regrettably wasteful. A missile project known as Blue Steel was abandoned since it would have to be taken to within 100 miles of its target by bomber aircraft. It was followed by Blue Streak, a ballistic missile designed to be launched underground but cancelled on grounds of cost in 1960, when £100m had already been spent on it. Blue Streak was succeeded by Skybolt, a similar missile though with a much longer range, which Britain was to buy from the United States on the understanding that it would supply its own nuclear war-heads. When in 1962 the Americans themselves cancelled their Skybolt project, an arrangement was made between President Kennedy and Macmillan, at a conference in Nassau, that the United States would instead provide the so-called Polaris missile and the technical information about the nuclear-powered submarines from which this missile was to be fired. The British government thereupon resolved to build five such sub-marines, at a total cost of some £500m.

These developments in the sphere of defence coincided with a remarkable reversal of attitudes in government circles on the advisability of economic integration with Western Europe.

ATTEMPTS TO JOIN THE EUROPEAN ECONOMIC COMMUNITY

For six years after the rejection by the British of suggestions that they should join the European Coal and Steel Community (1950) British governments had pursued their traditional policy, avoiding anything more than a partial surrender of their sovereignty over control in Europe of their country's armed forces. In 1955 only observers from the Board of Trade and the Foreign Office had attended the meeting in Brussels at which a committee of continental experts had considered the problems involved in the merging of their national economies. The Common Market came into being with France, West Germany, Italy, Belgium, the Netherlands and Luxemburg as its members: not with Britain. The British government had at that time no wish to become a member of a group which, while lowering and ultimately eliminating tariffs among themselves, was working towards the adoption of the same tariffs on goods imported from other parts of the world. Harold Macmillan, then Chancellor of the Exchequer, explained his government's attitude: 'We could not expect the countries of the Commonwealth to give preferential treatment to our exports to them if we had to charge them full duty on their exports to us. . . . So this objection, even if there were no other, would be quite fatal to any proposal that the U.K. should seek to take part in a European Common Market.'[1] However, Britain could not altogether ignore the need for closer relations with the Continent. Macmillan therefore proposed, in November, 1956, a system to enable countries to reduce their tariffs among themselves while retaining their own differing external tariffs and leaving out of account foodstuffs, which seemed likely to produce particular difficulties; and Reginald Maudling, the Paymaster-General, was commissioned to interest Europe in the proposal. The British hoped that all the seventeen members countries of the Organisation for European Economic Co-operation (O.E.E.C.) could be associated in a free trade area.

Maudling had little success in Bonn and none at all in Paris. In November, 1958, by which time General de Gaulle had been in control in France for six months and French business men had learnt to expect more from the Common Market than from the wider but less competely integrated group proposed by the British, the French rejected the British plans. Endeavours to re-open negotiations during the next three months were unavailing, and Britain was obliged instead to turn for support to the smaller countries of Europe which had not already been drawn into the Community of the Six. It was with the representatives of Norway, Sweden and Denmark, Switzerland, Austria and Portugal that a fresh round of negotiations was begun by British delegates in March, 1959, and with them that a Convention was initialled in Stockholm on 20 November, establishing a European Free Trade Area (E.F.T.A.) with a commercial policy similar to that suggested by Macmillan two years before. The Convention was ratified by the Parliaments of the seven countries involved during March and April, 1960. It was opposed in neither House of the Parliament at Westminster.

It was not long, however, before a change of heart began to manifest itself in Britain. This change was encouraged by Sir Frank Lee, Joint Permanent Secretary at the Treasury, by Sir Gladwyn Jebb, British ambassador in Paris, and by several senior members of the European Department of the Foreign

Office. They believed that Britain should make a serious endeavour to join the European Economic Community. The idea was spread enthusiastically throughout government circles during 1960 and 1961. It was supported by a variety of journals: by *The Economist*, the *Financial Times*, the *Sunday Times*, the *Daily Telegraph* and the *Daily Mail* in particular. The Liberal Party backed it strongly. After its experience of frequent economic crises the business community was beginning to alter its views. Macmillan, perhaps before the end of 1960, ceased to doubt the value of joining. Selwyn Lloyd, the Foreign Minister, publicly regretted at Strasbourg that Britain had not been a member of the Coal and Steel Community from the start. Conservative back benchers with experience of Western European Union and Council of Europe meetings or with other European contacts, spoke on behalf of the trend. It was true that doubts existed, even at this stage, whether the French would welcome British membership of the Economic Community, but when Couve de Murville, the French Foreign Minister, asserted in March, 1961, that the Common Market would 'always remain open to any other European country desiring to join',[2] the British government determined to go ahead.

ADVANTAGES OF MEMBERSHIP OF THE COMMUNITY

Underlying all the very complex moves towards economic union were certain basic beliefs: that industry would sell more in a populous market (the Six contained nearly 170m potential purchasers) than in a small one; and that the elimination of tariffs and the consequent reduction of prices would have the effect of increasing sales still further. The Coal and Steel pilot scheme had been encouraging. Coal may have suffered universally from the competition of oil, but sales of steel, iron and scrap had all risen substantially. The general indices of industrial production in the Six had been even more significant They showed that between 1953 and 1961 production had increased in France by 75 per cent, in West Germany by 89 per cent and in Italy by 100 per cent. Increases in Belgium, the Netherlands and Luxemburg were not quite so high, yet in each case they were more remarkable than the 30 per cent increase in Britain. Not merely was the output of the continental countries rising

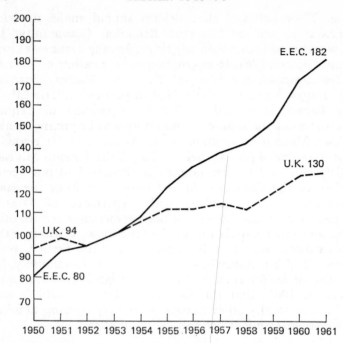

Britain and the Common Market countries. General indices of industrial production compared (1953:100)

1950	1961
U.K. 94	Italy 200
Belgium 93	Germany 189
France 89	France 175
Luxemburg 89	Netherlands 160
Netherlands 88	Luxemburg 142
Italy 78	Belgium 135
Germany 72	U.K. 130

faster than British: they had less unemployment. In Germany, in 1962, fewer than 100000 were without work, despite a large influx of foreign labour. France had only 110000 unemployed, despite the presence in the country of large numbers of Algerians and Italians. Italian employment figures had risen by 50 per cent in six years. On the other hand, Britain, in 1962, had 463000 workless, and the number at that time was growing. It was very evident that a wide market, combined with the stimulating effects of tariff reductions, was bringing benefits to continental industry that British industry was experiencing on a much more limited scale. It was equally evident (to many) that Britain's greatest hope of expansion lay in an increase of trade with the Six. Between 1958 and 1961 trade in this sphere had risen by 43 per cent compared with an increase of 39 per cent in exports to EFTA countries, of 18 per cent in exports to Canada and the rest of the non-sterling world, and a decline of 2 per cent in exports to the sterling area. The fact that during these four years the Six's imports had risen by 72 per cent suggested that their potential market was considerably greater than improved British trade with them indicated. It was, however, a market which would become progressively harder for Britain to enter as stage by stage it reduced its own internal tariffs while retaining against foreign countries the average tariff prevailing among its members (13·6 per cent in 1961).

All these developments coincided with certain changing features of British industry to make the future of that industry appear in 1961 enigmatic and even ominous. The group of British exports which clearly brought in more money than was paid for similar imports was at the same time the smallest group: commercial vehicles, some drugs, dyes and yarns, paper-making machinery and whisky. Imports which were rising faster than exports of similar goods were of textiles, ships, heavy electrical equipment, many metal manufactures, aircraft—from some at least of which so much had been hoped in the years after the war. In many other spheres imports had in recent years overtaken exports: goods in this category included clothing and shoes, motor cycles, cameras and toys. Such factors were constantly stressed during the months when British negotiations with the Six were at their peak. For example, the Federation of British Industries was obliged to report in October, 1962, that the level of production had remained unchanged during the previous four months, that nearly three-quarters of 700 leading firms reported shortages of orders or sales, and that two firms out of three were working below capacity. The Cotton Board revealed in the same month that Britain's share of West Europe's increasing market for cotton yarn had dropped from 25 per cent in 1951 to 2 per cent in 1962. Anxiety was expressed in December, 1962, about the failure of the engineering industries to increase their output appreciably over the previous year. In short,

Britain was, in comparison with the countries of the Common Market, falling behind and suffering serious and effective competition.

It was conceded in Britain that admission to the Community would create difficulties for certain industries with only limited powers of resisting competition. Cotton, leather goods and footwear were in this class; so were cameras and scientific instruments, toys, carpets and china. For other industries the prospects were mixed: some metal and rubber products, some machine tools and vehicles, some types of paper and electrical equipment might suffer; but other types would probably benefit. Drink and tobacco, aircraft engines and ships were not expected to be greatly affected. However, there was a substantial list of manufactures for which the prospects were hopeful, from chemicals and cement to computers, television and radio equipment, domestic electric appliances, commercial and sports vehicles, tractors and woollens. There were, moreover, compensating features of the Common Market system designed to help industries with special problems. The Commission and the Council of Ministers which regulated the development of the Market were not unaware of the need for provisions to minimise the dislocation experienced by various industries, for the retraining of workers who had to change their jobs and for financial help for less affluent regions. And since the elimination of tariffs within the Community was to be phased over several years, time was allowed for industries in trouble to adapt themselves to changed circumstances. Thereafter, the spur of competition and the very large market available were expected to provide a stimulus from which the efficient, at least, could only benefit. Such was the view held in Britain by a majority of the experts: an enquiry undertaken by the *Observer* suggested that four times as many leading economists favoured Britain's membership of the Community as were opposed to it.

Behind all the economic arguments was the hope, not stressed during the early years of the Market's existence but gradually emerging later, that economic unity would be followed in time by a far greater degree of political unity. With industry, agriculture and social services bound together by the Treaty of Rome and its subsequent development, the national differences which had constantly provoked wars between the powers of Western Europe in the past could no longer operate with the same disastrous results. The Common Market could in due course develop into a United States of Europe.

During the early summer of 1961 the British minister charged with the conduct of the negotiations, Edward Heath, and other ministers approached the EFTA and Commonwealth governments to ascertain their reactions to a British application for membership of the Community. Of the EFTA governments, those of Sweden and Switzerland, which valued their traditional neutrality, were the least sympathetic. The Austrians and Danes were anxious that Britain should go ahead. From the Commonwealth, prolonged discussions suggested at this stage that at least no serious opposition was likely to arise. Accordingly, on 9 August, the British government officially applied for the opening of negotiations. Ireland had already done so. Denmark followed suit on 10 August. The applications were particularly well received by Germany, Italy and the three smaller members of the Community.

THE NEGOTIATIONS

Britain's principal experts among the negotiators were Sir Frank Lee, Sir Pierson Dixon (ambassador in Paris) and Sir Eric Roll (an ex-professor of Economics at Hull and now a civil servant from the Ministry of Agriculture). Edward Heath, who presented the British proposals to the Six on 10 October, 1961, was to remain the leader of the British delegation until the negotiations ended in January, 1963.

Since these negotiations were ultimately to collapse, any detailed examination of the various phases through which they passed would be unnecessary; though since at some stage or other they were concerned with every aspect of trade policy and with Britain's relations with both European and Commonwealth countries, they had a significance which cannot be altogether disregarded. On one plane were comparatively trivial agreements on the abolition of duties on tea, cricket bats and polo sticks, tropical hardwoods, fish liver oil and kangaroo meat, agreements on special tariff arrangements for desiccated coconut, pepper and extract of mimosa, and the prolonged bargaining on Canadian tinned salmon, Australian tinned peaches, pears and apricots, and Cyprus sultanas. On another plane were very fundamental disputes about agriculture and Britain's relationship with the Commonwealth.

From the outset of the first session in Brussels, in November, 1961, the Six refused to accept any special, privileged trading links with the Commonwealth as a whole. This was an issue of profound concern to Britain. Although during the previous three years the value of its Commonwealth trade had not risen, and although the proportion of its exports going to Commonwealth countries was steadily declining, the preferential treatment received by these countries in the British market remained nonetheless important. Whereas Britain's non-preferential tariff (on 993 items) averaged 16·5 per cent, its preferential tariff for the Commonwealth averaged only 2·6 per cent. On such products as chemicals and plastics, base metals, earthenware, china and glass, the general British tariff was between 13·1 per cent and 16·4 per cent while no duty at all was charged on similar goods coming from countries which enjoyed Britain's preferential arrangements. The Six would not consider the retention of such a system. Britain, on joining the Community, would have had to accept the same tariff as the other Six, on Commonwealth and foreign goods alike.

At the same time this problem of Commonwealth trade was entangled with agricultural problems. On many vital agricultural imports Britain's general tariff was very much lower than that imposed by members of the Community, and even this low tariff had been eliminated by the preferential arrangements with the Commonwealth. On butter, for example, Britain imposed a tariff of 5 per cent on imports from foreign countries and none on imports from the Commonwealth; German, French and Italian duties were between 20 per cent and 25 per cent. The British tariff on imported beef was 3 per cent (Commonwealth beef was duty free); the French tariff was 35 per cent and German and Italian 18 per cent and 20 per cent respectively. Britain imposed no tariff on imported wheat; Germany imposed 20 per cent, France and Italy 30 per cent. On entering the Common Market Britain would have been obliged to bring its duties into line with those gradually introduced by the rest of its members. And unless special agreements could have been negotiated, the Commonwealth countries which produced foodstuffs likely to compete with the produce of Europe would have been compelled either to sell their goods more cheaply to Britain or to find alternative markets. Britain did in fact agree that its preferential treatment of manufactures from the older dominions should be progressively withdrawn (some of them had not hesitated to introduce tariffs on British manufactures when they wished to protect their own home industries); but this arrangement, combined with fears of the effect which the adoption of a common tariff would have on British imports of foodstuffs from the temperate dominions, caused most members of the Commonwealth to turn against Britain's entry into the Community.

As it happened, the British delegation had not given in over the question of imported foodstuffs when the negotiations ended. Heath had, on the contrary, warned the Six that unless they were prepared to restrain their own producers so as to allow Commonwealth farmers to go on selling in the enlarged Community markets there was no hope of Britain's coming in. The warning had created an impasse. The real rift lay between Britain and France. The French had agricultural surpluses to be disposed of. The British maintained that the French wished to monopolise the markets of the Community for the sake of their own producers. The other five Community members worked out amendments in the hope of reconciling the French and British viewpoints; the British also put forward amendments, long night sittings were held and a rift developed between France and the Five. However, the deadlock remained.

The tropical countries of the Commonwealth seemed likely to fare better than the older dominions. A comprehensive trade agreement was made with India, Pakistan and Ceylon, by which the Six pledged themselves to ensure that these countries should maintain their foreign capital earnings in order to enable them to finance their development plans. The newly independent British ex-colonies in Africa and the Caribbean were granted the same favourable terms that had been extended to the French ex-colonies. Heath obtained from the Six a concession that special trade agreements would be negotiated with African dependencies which did not want association with the Community. Actually, association would have brought substantial benefits to these countries. They would have obtained access to a vast market, their produce would not have been subject to heavy tariffs and they could have hoped for generous financial help. Unfortunately, suspecting perhaps that in some way their new independence might suffer from association, their representatives at the London Commonwealth conference held in the middle of the Brussels negotiations nearly all opposed British actions.

Problems of Commonwealth trade were paralleled by domestic agricultural problems. As has been mentioned, the countries of the Community protected their farmers (who were often smaller and poorer than British farmers) by imposing quite substantial tariffs on foreign imports. Britain's tariffs were negligible; but its farmers were instead given subsidies and grants, totalling in 1961 £351m. The effect of the subsidies was to keep prices low for purchasers while still giving the farmers adequate incomes. Wheat, for instance, fetched about £20 a ton on the market; but deficiency payments made this up to about £27 a ton for the farmers. This cost the government more than £73m in 1961; but it kept bread prices lower than they would have been without the subsidies. Prices of other foodstuffs in Britain were generally (though not always) cheaper than E.E.C. prices. The Six objected to the system, fearing that it must encourage over-production and lead to a flood of British produce on the continent. They wished Britain to adopt their own system and to abandon the deficiency payments as soon as it joined the Common Market. The potential embarrassment for Britain of such a change of policy could again be illustrated by the example of wheat: prices were expected to rise to the French price of about £34 a ton, and later to an even higher figure, since German prices were about £41 a ton and some sort of compromise was ultimately to be reached among the Six. Not merely would Britain have faced administrative difficulties of needless complexity; its food prices would have risen—though to what extent nobody could confidently say with certainty: various sums, from one shilling to ten shillings a week per person were quoted. There were, no doubt, compensating factors, such as increased national wealth as a member of the Community, which would have nullified the disadvantage of higher food prices. And it was generally thought that, on the whole, farmers (apart from those concentrating on sugar beet and horticulture) would be able to hold their own with Europe or to improve their positions. However, the tariffs and subsidies, like the matter of Commonwealth trade, produced a deadlock, and the compensating factors were never in the sixties to be put to the test.

The intractable nature of these agricultural issues was to be clearly seen in 1964 and 1965, when the E.E.C. itself almost disintegrated as a result of disputes over the prices of foodstuffs.

An isolated France was to find itself, during this crisis, in opposition to all its partners.

FAILURE

It was on French intransigence, also, that British hopes of joining the Community had already foundered. Sir Pierson Dixon, at least, had feared almost from the start that the negotiations might end with a French veto. During the autumn of 1962 a veto became increasingly likely. General de Gaulle was coming to believe that France's closest relations should be with Germany rather than with Britain; and he feared that Britain's admission to the E.E.C. would inevitably, in the end, augment the influence in Europe of its Anglo-Saxon ally, America. In his televised New Year message he regretted that Britain was not yet showing itself sufficiently European to qualify for membership of the E.E.C. On 9 January, 1963, the French cabinet learnt that he was growing more and more hostile to the Brussels negotiations. By 14 January he had lost all patience with compromise and conciliation, and his remarks at a Press conference for all practical purposes brought an end to a year and a half of endeavour to expand the Community. 'Britain,' he declared, 'is, in fact, insular and maritime, linked by her trade, her markets, and her supply routes to very varied and often very remote countries . . . the structure and present condition of England are widely different from those on the continent.'[3] It was not ready to renounce Commonwealth preferences, the privileges of its farmers and its pledges to EFTA. Moreover, if Britain joined the E.E.C. it would be followed by other applicants, and the E.E.C. would then unavoidably lose its cohesion. It would become a prey to 'a colossal Atlantic grouping, under American dependence and control.'[4] Its whole character would be destroyed.

Most of the negotiators at Brussels were shocked by this declaration. They were still endeavouring earnestly to arrive at compromises on a large number of issues, were reluctant to stop at once, and were indeed still deliberating on lead and zinc when the French Foreign Minister, Couve de Murville, suggested that negotiations should be adjourned. When Couve de Murville asserted that the differences between Britain and the Six were insurmountable and that the discussions were a waste of time, there was uproar in the conference room.

The French attitude was attacked by Belgian, Italian and German leaders. Dr Walter Hallstein, the head of the E.E.C. Commission, feared that the French might wreck the Common Market. France was isolated. Yet in the end it was manifestly impossible to pursue the negotiations without de Gaulle's support. On 29 January, in an atmosphere of anti-climax, and to the accompaniment of a series of speeches expressing the great regret of the representatives of each member country of the Six, apart from France, the meetings in Brussels were suspended indefinitely.

---

[1] Nora Beloff, *The General Says No*, p. 78. Macmillan, 26.11.56
[2] Ibid., pp. 106
[3] Ibid., pp. 163–4
[4] Ibid., pp. 163–4

25

Towards the end of Conservative government

The drastic ministerial purge of July, 1962, in which Selwyn Lloyd lost the Chancellorship, may have been designed to restore vigour to a Conservative party which had recently lost an apparently safe seat at Orpington to a Liberal, Eric Lubbock, and had suffered serious reductions in its majorities at other by-elections. While R. A. Butler, Home Secretary since 1957, became Deputy Prime Minister and First Secretary of State, and while Peter Thorneycroft was restored to the Cabinet as minister of Defence, the purge also allowed a number of younger M.P.s to be brought into the Cabinet. Reginald Maudling became Chancellor of the Exchequer, Sir Edward Boyle Minister of Education, Enoch Powell Minister of Health, and Sir Keith Joseph Minister of Housing. At the same time the suddenness of the changes evoked condemnation. Lord Kilmuir (Sir David Maxwell Fyfe) and Dr Charles Hill both later expressed regret at the undignified manner of their leaving the Lord Chancellorship and the Ministry of Housing and Local Government. Selwyn Lloyd, previously the object of mounting criticism, now gained the sympathy of his party in Parliament. In retrospect, indeed, it seemed that most of the really important developments of the last phase of Conservative government had already been inaugurated and that the Cabinet changes of 1962 merely ushered in a period during which the country's support was increasingly withdrawn from the Conservatives.

Initially the revised government enjoyed a certain degree of economic success, to compensate partially for the failure of its negotiations with the six countries of the Common Market. 1962 and 1963 were years of expansion. With the reduction of the Bank Rate to 5 per cent in March, 1962, the relaxation of hire-purchase conditions and of limitations on bank lending in June, and, in the winter, tax reliefs to encourage investment, industry was supposed to experience a stimulus. Tax reductions, combined with a substantial increase of government spending, even at a cost of a £687m budget deficit, were announced by the Chancellor in April, 1963. The aim was to secure an annual industrial growth rate of 4 per cent. Actually, between the last quarter of 1962 and the corresponding period of 1963, the Gross National Product rose by 7 per cent. A 7 per cent increase in exports in 1963, associated with the usual favourable balance for invisible exports, permitted the overall balance of payments, for the second year running, to be in Britain's favour. The country was on the verge of a very large increase in investment, public and private.

It was also on the verge of a period of miscalculation, mismanagement and misfortune.

MACMILLAN'S RETIREMENT

In the autumn of 1963, after nearly seven years as Prime Minister, Harold Macmillan fell ill and was obliged to retire. His retirement coincided with the annual Conservative party conference, and as a result the proceedings from which a new party leader was expected to emerge were all the more openly highlighted. There was no obvious heir, as Anthony Eden had been Churchill's heir for years before he succeeded in 1955. The choice was not even limited, as it had been limited to Macmillan and R. A. Butler when Eden resigned in January, 1957. This time Butler was the most experienced of the Cabinet ministers, and he was acting head of the party and the government while Macmillan was ill; but Viscount Hailsham, Iain Macleod, Edward Heath and Reginald Maudling were also contenders for the premiership. Even the Earl of Home was considered as having a chance of acceptance. Lord Hailsham (educated like Lord Salisbury and the Earl of Home, at Eton and Christ Church) had, as Quintin Hogg, been M.P. for Oxford City from 1938 until his succession to the peerage in 1950; he had in due course held various Cabinet appointments before becoming responsible for the Conservative party organisation. Iain Macleod (Fettes and Caius, Cambridge) had served as Minister of Labour, Secretary for the Colonies, Chancellor of the Duchy of Lancaster, and Leader of the Commons. Edward Heath

(Chatham House School, Ramsgate, and Balliol) had gained fame as Conservative Party Whip and had increased it during the Common Market negotiations. Reginald Maudling (Merchant Taylors and Merton, Oxford) had been M.P. for Barnet since 1950 and after holding a number of government offices had become Chancellor of the Exchequer in 1962. Alexander Douglas-Home had spent twenty years in the Commons before succeeding to the Earldom of Home in 1951, and since then had been in turn Minister of State at the Scottish Office, Secretary for Commonwealth Relations and Foreign Secretary.

The new Prime Minister was supposed to emerge as a result of consultations among the elder statesmen of the party, the Conservative M.P.s and the constituency parties. A consensus of opinion was supposed to make itself known. In fact it rapidly became all too clear that the process was not working easily, that there were too many candidates, and that none had overwhelming support. The country was left to assume that the leadership fell in the end on the candidate who evoked least hostility in the party. It was the Earl of Home who emerged. He renounced his peerage (as Lord Hailsham had done), was found a safe Conservative seat at Kinross and West Perth, and became Prime Minister.

In a B.B.C. interview in 1966 Lord Butler, now Master of Trinity College, Cambridge, reflected on the negotiations that had taken place: 'a very unsatisfactory business in my view— which I hope will never be repeated . . . to try to run a convention for the appointment of a leader coincident with a conference.' Looking back on his own defeat Lord Butler 'reached the conclusion . . . that it was almost inevitable that the Conservative party would choose a younger man.'[1] It had never occurred to him that Lord Home would become Prime Minister.

When, in August, 1965, the party once again had to choose a leader, the methods had been changed, and it was as the result of a ballot among Conservative M.P.s that Edward Heath succeeded Sir Alec Douglas-Home.

ECONOMIC SUCCESS—AND CATASTROPHE

1964 was superficially a prosperous year. The budget introduced by Reginald Maudling was having an effect. Considerable reductions in income tax and increases in old-age pensions

and national insurance benefits had left more money in circulation, had stimulated demand and had consequently reduced
unemployment. Investment in private industry rose by 16 per
cent, public investment by 15 per cent. Average hourly wage
rates went up by 5·7 per cent, and, taking overtime and 'wage
drift' into account, incomes rose, on an average, by 8·2 per cent,
exactly double the increases of 1962 and 1963. Since 1959 the
average weekly earnings of male manual workers over the age
of 21 had risen from £13 16s 6d (£13·82½) to £18 8s 10d (£18·44),
which, despite inflation, represented an increase in real terms, as
opposed to money terms, of 30 per cent. Whereas in 1959 £522m
had been spent on cars and motor cycles, expenditure in 1964
was £910m. Hire-purchase debts in 1959 amounted to £849m,
in 1964 to £1115m. The symptoms were those of continuing
affluence.

In fact the boost to demand had been excessive, the economy
had been 'over-heated', and the country was about to enter the
most prolonged crisis since the war. During the summer it
became increasingly evident that the year would end with a
massive balance of payments deficit. In June a deficit of £113m
was recorded, in July one of £87m. Although by this time lost
British pre-war investments overseas had been more than made
up and private overseas assets were far in excess of private overseas liabilities (£7950m compared with £2835m) the economic
research organisations were predicting yet another major crisis
later in the year. They were quite right. Military expenditure
abroad, loans to under-developed countries, long-term in-
debtedness to foreign governments, as well as the adverse trade
balance were all insupportably high. The N.E.D.C. plan was
not being realised. While imports during 1963 and 1964 increased by 16 per cent exports went up by only 10 per cent; and
the costs of the imported goods exceeded those of the exports.
In short, so much more were the British spending abroad than
they were earning that it was generally believed at the time of
the general election in October that their total deficit for the
year would amount to about £800m. Labour candidates at the
election were able to condemn the Conservative government in
almost the same terms as those used in 1951 by Conservatives
about the Labour government.

The deficit on overseas trade was not the only factor that
provoked critics to question the affluence of Britain. The Com-

mon Market negotiations had revealed that however rapidly British industrial strength might have appeared to be expanding, that of the Continent was expanding faster. Comparisons in 1964 continued to emphasise Britain's disadvantageous position. Between 1953 and March, 1964, West Germany's export prices had risen by only 7 per cent and its volume of manufactured exports by 233 per cent. French prices during the same period had gone up by 3 per cent, French exports by 136 per cent. Italy's prices had actually declined, by 18 per cent, and the volume of all its exports had rocketed by 303 per cent. British prices for manufactured goods, on the other hand, had risen by 19 per cent, and British manufactured exports by only 48 per cent. It was no consolation to know that the American export record was considerably worse. Nor could any prospect of price stability encourage an expectation of an early improvement. Inflation gathered impetus, despite the existence of the National Incomes Commission. During 1964 postmen, electricity workers and busmen all received increases above the government's $3\frac{1}{2}$ per cent 'guiding light'; postmen, indeed, obtained a $6\frac{1}{2}$ per cent increase. When the lead was given by the public sector no pretence could be maintained any longer than an incomes policy existed or that prices would not continue their upward trend in the wake of the higher wages.

At home the most disturbing single feature of the inflation was the soaring price of homes, particularly in the South East of England, where the houses built in the years following the Slump were changing hands in 1964 at prices nearly ten times as high as those for which they had been sold in the 1930s. The Conservatives centred their hopes on the development of industry and amenities in the less prosperous parts of Britain, assuming that this would eventually contribute to a reduction of the demand for houses and land in the South East, and would thus bring about a reduction of prices. The success of such a policy was not sufficiently certain to convince the electorate. Labour and Liberal parties at least made more specific recommendations for the control of the high land prices which were helping to force up house prices. The proposals may have been open to criticism, but they did suggest a greater awareness of the problems than Conservative remedies suggested. The Conservative image suffered.

The image suffered again from a small number of episodes,

not all of great importance in themselves, but exploited by the popular Press and by opponents of the government. The discovery that secrets had been betrayed to Communist agents had reflected adversely on security arrangements during the last year of Macmillan's premiership. The leadership crisis made a bad impression. A scandal developed when a junior minister was found to have associated with a prostitute and to have misinformed the House about it. Revelations of high profits being extorted from the hapless tenants of some squalid London slum properties provoked criticism of the government's housing policy and suggested that there were loopholes which should never have existed in the Welfare State. Such incidents were trivial in comparison with an adventure like the Suez war, from which the Conservative party suffered no serious electoral disadvantage. In the thirteenth year of the government's existence, however, they helped a pendulum to swing, however irrational the swing may have been. Chances of the survival of a Conservative government at the polls continued to diminish, and Labour hopes rose correspondingly.

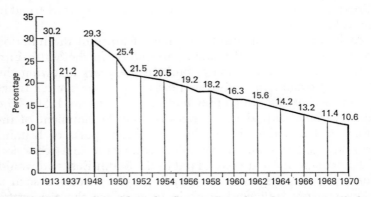

British share of world trade. *Sources*: Based on figures compiled by the London and Cambridge Economic Service.

In his autobiography, published two years after the election, Lord Kilmuir implied that the country had grown tired of the normal content of political controversy. 'We utterly failed,' he wrote, 'in these years [after 1959] to find a popular, non-materialistic policy for the party. . . . The return of idealism to politics caught both parties off balance, and the Conservatives suffered worst.'[2]

---

[1] *The Listener*, 28.7.66. BBC Interview
[2] Lord Kilmuir, *Political Adventure*, pp. 321–2, George Weidenfeld and Nicolson Ltd (London 1964)

PART THREE

26

The end of British imperialism in Africa

Nationalism of the kind that had brought independence to India, Pakistan, Ceylon and Burma in the late 1940s was much slower to develop in Africa. Substantial obstacles existed to its emergence in the colonies and protectorates artificially carved out by European powers in the 1880s. In the first place, African society was fragmented along tribal lines. In Nigeria, for example, the British had been obliged to recognise no fewer than 110 separate native administrations, and they were later, during the Nigerian civil war, to be forced to recognise the intense hostility that existed between certain of these tribes, even after independence. The Ashanti and Ga of the Gold Coast, the Kikuyu and Luo of Kenya, the Baganda of Uganda all shared their countries with many less numerous or less advanced peoples, and as independence approached or after it had been attained, the antagonism that they felt for each other, particularly in Kenya and Uganda, proved to be a serious obstacle to harmonious negotiation and stable government.

Tribal divisions entailed linguistic differences. It was true that in East Africa a widespread knowledge of Swahili provided a certain limited unity; but in the West there was no common vernacular. It was estimated that altogether about 400 major languages were spoken in British tropical Africa, and many of these were subdivided into dialects. Nigeria, at the time of its independence, had 248 languages. Animist religions, linked with the ancestors of each group, were also dividing factors, complicated in the nineteenth century by the teaching of Muslim, Protestant and Catholic doctrines. Outside West Africa insufficient consciousness of historical development existed to unite different peoples. Tribal traditions of ancestral heroes were not enough. Europeans had frequently added to the problem by defining their boundaries without regard to the tribes living in the annexed areas: the Masai, for instance, lived in both Kenya and Tanganyika, and Somalis moved from Somaliland to Ethiopia or Kenya whenever new grazing grounds for their animals were required. Sometimes the opposite mistake had been made, and peoples who had no wish to live together had been incorporated in one colony: the Ibo and the Hausa and Fulani of Nigeria, for example, or the Arabs and the Nilotic tribes of the Sudan.

These factors, however, could not permanently prevent the development of African nationalism. A strong desire for independence gripped an increasing number of Africans with experience of European university education or overseas war service. The desire was encouraged by British traditions of individual liberty. The example of the Indian independence movement was influential, and once it had infected the more advanced African territories (the Sudan and the Gold Coast in particular) it was inevitable that it should spread rapidly to other colonies. Bitterness engendered in African countries by the retention by Europeans of the most responsible positions, determination no longer to be regarded as inferior peoples, new opportunities offered for the expression of nationalist aims by the United Nations Organisation, and the vocal anticolonialism of both the United States and Russia, were all factors in the creation of what Harold Macmillan called 'the wind of change'. From the middle years of the war onwards demands for self-government gathered strength. Dr Nnamdi Azikiwe, an American-educated Nigerian Ibo, published in 1943 *The Atlantic Charter and British West Africa*, demanding immediate reforms and representative government. He founded in 1944 the National Council for Nigeria and the Cameroons. Then, for fear of domination by the inhabitants of Southern Nigeria, the Northerners, led by the Sardauna of Sokoto and Abubakar Tafawa Balewa, established the Northern People's Congress. In 1947 Dr J. B. Danquah founded the United Gold Coast Convention and in the same year the first congress of the Kenya African Union was held in Nairobi. In 1948 an African National Congress was brought into being in Northern Rhodesia. In 1951 Obafemi Awolowo, a Yoruba chief and London graduate, founded his Nigerian Action Group as a rival to Azikiwe's N.C.N.C. Henceforth developments were rapid, and parties proliferated in all the British colonial territories in Africa. French dependencies saw a similar trend.

A number of official reports encouraged these developments by stressing some of the disadvantages of white rule. A report issued by the East Africa Royal Commission in 1948 expressed the conviction that the conditions of life of the majority of urban Africans had been deteriorating over a considerable period, since wages were too low to allow them to pay for adequate accommodation or to support their families. A Gold Coast report of 1949 estimated that about half the money earned by exports of gold, manganese and bauxite was transferred out of the country. A United Nations investigation into the effects of federation on the Rhodesias and Nyasaland indicated that whereas in 1945 Africans had received about 25 per cent of the gross profits of the Rhodesian mining industry (£1 400 000 out of profits after royalty payments of £5 500 000), by 1956 they were receiving only about 8 per cent (£6 400 000 out of gross profits of more than £80 000 000). About £50m left Northern Rhodesia in 1956 as company and corporation profits for overseas shareholders, though the country was desperately in need of money to pay for education and other social services. The report of the East Africa Royal Commission 1953–5 showed that whereas the net cash product per head was about £100 in South Africa, in Ghana it was only £34, in Uganda £16 and in Kenya £14.

Why, it might have been asked, were educational facilities in East Africa (with a population of about 24m) so insufficiently developed that, however hard a limited number of expatriate civil servants and educationists may have worked, fewer than 2000 African boys and girls obtained school certificates in 1959, when each country was on the verge of independence. Why should Northern Rhodesia, with its mineral wealth, have only one school offering Africans a complete course in 1958 to Senior Cambridge Certificate level, and why should there be only thirteen Africans in the highest forms of the school system in Southern Rhodesia in that year? Up to June, 1959, only thirty-five Northern Rhodesian Africans and only twenty-eight Nyasalanders had completed university degree courses. Surveys revealed that, in terms of trained personnel, the colonies which were demanding independence were poorly prepared, especially those in East Africa. It was true that, following the recommendations of the Asquith Commission (1943), the British government had established university colleges in Sierra Leone, the

Gold Coast, and Nigeria, Uganda, the Sudan and Southern Rhodesia. Some of the money paid by British taxpayers under the terms of the Colonial Development and Welfare Act of 1945 was spent on the university or technical education of Africans. The number of schools was rapidly increasing. Yet British officials feared that not for at least ten or fifteen years could Africa find sufficient trained administrators of its own to ensure stable government.

27

West Africa

GOLD COAST

Among British African colonies the lead in constitutional matters was taken by the Gold Coast. The unsuitability of the climate for white administrators had made it desirable that Africans should be associated with the government as early as 1888; and for twenty years, by 1945, a third of the Legislative Council (corresponding to a parliamentary assembly) had consisted of elected Africans. In 1946 a new constitution established the first preponderantly elected Legislative Council in the British African dependencies, and further changes followed rapidly. Dr Danquah's United Gold Coast Convention, which aimed at complete self-government for his country, was a group of middle-class intellectuals with little understanding of the technique of building up mass support; but it had as its secretary an ex-schoolmaster who had studied in America and at the London School of Economics: Kwame Nkrumah. Nkrumah was far more extreme than the rest of the U.G.C.C. and showed a greater capacity for creating a popular following. In 1948 riots, which accompanied a rise in prices and the devastation of the cocoa farms by a disease known as 'swollen shoot', led to the imprisonment of both Danquah and Nkrumah; yet at the same time a committee was appointed under the African Judge Coussey to work out another constitution. The committee's recommendations led to the establishment in 1950 of a legislative Council of 84 of whom 38 were elected and others were representatives of the conservative and often illiterate chiefs. Eight out of eleven members of the Executive Council (corresponding to the ministry in more advanced countries) were elected by the Legislative Council.

Meanwhile, Nkrumah, free once more but sacked by the U.G.C.C., founded the Convention People's Party, to struggle

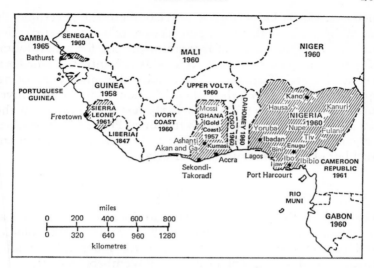

West African independence. The dates indicate the year in
which independence was gained. Principal tribes of Nigeria
and Ghana are indicated. British dependencies are shaded.

both against the British government and against the 'reactionary
intellectuals and chiefs'. The theoretically peaceful non-co-
operation or 'positive action' for which the new party was responsible so disturbed the government that it again arrested
Nkruman; but it continued nonetheless to allow the Coussey
constitution to function, and, in 1951, held elections which gave
the Convention People's Party 34 of the 38 elected seats.

Nkrumah was thereupon released from prison by the Governor,
Sir Charles Arden-Clarke, to become the leader of government
business and, a little later, Prime Minister. During the next few
years, under Nkrumah's direction, the Civil Service came to
consist increasingly of Africans and the power of the chiefs was
reduced by the creation of predominantly elected local councils.
Yet another constitution, introduced in 1954, established 104
single-member constituencies of the British type. The Convention People's Party gained 72 of the seats, and a number of
Independents joined them later. During the next few years
doubts developed about Nkrumah's allegedly dictatorial

methods. Cocoa farmers grew worried about the government's use of the profits of their crop; chiefs were reluctant to surrender their powers; advocates of federalism pressed for a devolution of governing power to such regions as Ashanti, the Northern Territories and Togoland. Yet despite the emergence of an opposition calling itself the Ashanti National Liberation Movement, the Convention People's Party lost little ground in the elections of 1956, and Nkrumah remained Prime Minister when his country, now known as Ghana, became an independent member of the Commonwealth in March, 1957.

NIGERIA

The basic pattern of Ghana's constitutional development was repeated, with slight variations, in all the other British colonies and protectorates which moved towards independence after 1945: a small minority of local, elected members on the Legislative Council was gradually replaced everywhere by an elected majority; and at the same time the number of these elected members chosen to serve on the Executive Council in place of British officials was increased by stages until the former colony was granted full self-government with Prime Minister and Cabinet of its own. Nigeria was a colony which, while passing through these phases of development, was also obliged, owing to its size and the differences between its peoples, to contend with the complications of federalism. Its constitutional advancement began in 1945, when Sir Arthur Richards was Governor, with a form of government which left a large amount of power with the chiefs but allowed direct elections in Lagos and Calabar. This did not satisfy Dr Azikiwe and other educated Nigerians, so in 1951 a revised constitution, introduced during the governorship of Sir John Macpherson, permitted three regional legislatures to elect members, indirectly, to a central legislature, and stipulated that four unofficial members from each region should join six officials on the Executive Council. It was still hoped ultimately to establish a unitary government which would not be obliged to delegate much of its work to regional assemblies. By the 1951 constitution no regional bill could become law without the consent of the central Executive Council. However, endeavours were made to meet the wishes of the nationalists, and during the next few years it became clear that only a federal constitution would give general satisfaction. Differences between North and South remained. The North was less anxious than the South for immediate independence; being more backward, it feared domination by Southern civil servants and officials. Accordingly, a conference held in London to consider revision of the constitution resulted in 1954 in the grant of separate executive councils with separate Prime Ministers to each of the three regions.

Perhaps, more than three regions should have been recognised, since not one of them was tribally homogeneous. The North contained substantial numbers of non-Muslim peoples, apart from the Hausa, Fulani and Kanuri. Such ethnic groups as the Tiv and the Nupe were more numerous than the entire populations of several newly independent states of Africa. Demands were later to grow for a fourth region, to be created between the Northern region and those dominated by the Ibo and the Yoruba; and eventually, in 1967, General Gowon was to establish a twelve-state system. But in the mid fifties anxiety among leading Nigerians to advance as quickly as possible towards independence resulted in the retention of the existing regional framework as a basis for a self-governing Nigeria, and subsequent conferences on the country's government confirmed the tripartite arrangement. To preserve some of the features of unity, the Federal House of Representatives was enlarged and provision was made for the election of the great majority. Further steps towards self-government were taken in 1957, when Sir Abubakar Tafawa Balewa, a Northerner, became Prime Minister; and complete independence within the Commonwealth was celebrated on 1 October, 1960. The last colonial Governor, Sir James Robertson, remained for a brief period as Governor-General before handing over his office to Dr Azikiwe.

SIERRA LEONE AND GAMBIA

Britain's two other West African colonies, Sierra Leone and Gambia, advanced towards independence unobtrusively and created fewer problems for Britain than Ghana and Nigeria had done. In Sierra Leone conflict might have arisen between the Creoles (a minority conscious of their historic ascendancy) and those who would outnumber them once a democratic electoral system had been imposed. That the transition to independence was actually peaceful was to the credit largely of Dr Milton Margai, who had turned from Sierra Leone's Medical Service to politics in 1950 and had been Chief Minister since 1954. Independence within the Commonwealth was attained in April, 1961.

The Gambia, with only 320000 inhabitants, smaller in area than Yorkshire, and depending on groundnuts to provide 90 per cent of its exports, had to wait for independence until February, 1965. Since it could not be self-supporting Britain promised to grant it £800000 a year for development purposes, and other sums were allocated to cover its budget deficit during the first two years of independence.

28

East Africa

In East Africa each colony presented its particular problems. Everywhere obstacles existed which made progress towards independence uncertain and future stability enigmatic. During the fifties it was in Kenya that the British colonial authorities found their greatest embarrassments. Here rather more than 60000 European settlers and 200000 Indians and Arabs combined with about 6m Africans, of various tribes, to create a multi-racial problem which greatly complicated advance towards self-government. The Africans, as in the other colonial territories in the East of the continent before the end of the war, were generally backward, illiterate, ill-nourished and leaderless. An increasing population was exhausting the fertility of the land available to the native tribes before methods had been learnt of restoring the fertility and of preventing erosion. At the same time the masses were confronted with an increased number of white settlers, many of them aspiring to a privileged status in a non-socialist paradise of cheap labour. Four thousand of these Europeans farmed some 16000 square miles of the Highlands of Kenya, about a quarter of the country's arable land, while the Africans had to be content with the rest. The settlers claimed that they had created prosperity in an area which had been empty when they arrived. The Africans asserted that they had left the Highlands unoccupied only temporarily. Resentment was to grow into great bitterness and to culminate in catastrophe.

Backward though they were, the Africans of Kenya could no more be kept in a condition of permanent tutelage than those of the West African colonies. War service had aroused new ideas and had exposed the European overlords in all their weaknesses and initial humiliations. The recovery of independence by

207

East and South African independence. The principal language
groups and dates of independence are indicated.

Ethiopia provided an example which might be followed by other African countries. African customs were breaking down under the impact of missionary teaching. The factories of Nairobi were encouraging a concentration of African workers. Above all, the return to Kenya in 1946 of Jomo Kenyatta, after seventeen years in London and Moscow, gave the Kikuyu, and ultimately the other tribes, a leader. The Kenya African Union, of which he immediately became President, sought such essentially moderate reforms as the creation of further educational and administrative opportunities for Africans and African representation on the Legislative Council.

It was never the intention of the British government to stand in the way of African advancement. An African had been nominated to the Council in 1944. Four had been nominated by 1948. At the same time these men continued to be heavily outnumbered by elected Europeans and even by the Asians whom both they and the white settlers generally disliked. Most Europeans remained jealous of their privileges and anxious that their own numerical superiority on the Council should be preserved.

Any complacency that might have existed was, however, destined to be seriously shaken after 1952 by the Mau Mau terrorist movement that grew up among some of the Kikuyu and two minor tribes. Symptoms of this had simmered beneath the surface already for five years without worrying the government of Kenya. Now it was impossible to ignore. Its aim, insofar as it had one, was the expulsion of the European settlers who had taken over the apparently unoccupied Highlands and had developed them with the assistance of African labourers. However, African chiefs and others who denounced the movement were as much the victims as were white farmers. Oaths of a barbarous character were imposed by the leaders of the rising on tribesmen who became terrified of disobeying them. Shelter for the movement was found in the forests. By the time the upheaval had been brought to an end 1875 civilians had lost their lives, 1786 of whom had been Africans. Five hundred and ten members of the security forces had been killed, more than 90 per cent of them Africans; and 7811 Mau Mau had died.

To eradicate the terrorists British troops were despatched to reinforce the local units, thousands of African labourers were transferred from European farms to already overcrowded reserves and more than £30m was spent on emergency measures between 1952 and 1955. The principal African political organisation, the Kenya African Union, was banned, and Jomo Kenyatta was sentenced to ten years' imprisonment for allegedly assisting in the management of the rising and for being a member of a proscribed cult. In the end, with increasing food problems and with forest hideouts overrun by patrols, the terrorism slackened; but although the worst phase was over by 1956, the movement had not been brought completely under control until 1959.

Despite Mau Mau, perhaps because of it, constitutional development continued. Provision was made in 1954, when Oliver Lyttelton was Colonial Secretary, for Asians and Africans to be appointed to ministries. In 1956, when Alan Lennox-Boyd was Colonial Secretary, it was announced that African members would be elected to the Legislative Council. African representation was doubled in 1958 in response to the demands of a future Minister of Justice, Tom Mboya, and his supporters. It was increased again in 1960. In 1960 and 1961 deliberations in London under the guidance of yet another Colonial Secretary, Iain Macleod, and of Michael Blundell, sometime Minister of Agriculture in Kenya, resulted in the introduction of a constitution which allowed Africans to dominate future elections to the Legislative Council. European control of Kenya's government was now effectively at an end. Meanwhile, it had been agreed that more educational facilities, homes, Highland villages and light industries should be made available for the Africans; and, under a scheme inaugurated in 1954, African farmers were being encouraged to exchange scattered holdings for compact fenced farms on which they could keep their animals and experiment with new crops and modern methods.

All these changes inevitably entailed difficult problems in so racially mixed a country. Among the white settlers, although Michael Blundell worked hard to establish racial co-operation, there was strong resentment at developments which were presumed to threaten the reduction of the best educated and most enterprising section of the people of Kenya to a helpless minority deprived, perhaps, of both influence and the farms which they had created. Problems of a different kind troubled the Africans. Divided into a National Union representing the strongest tribes (Kikuyu and Luo) and a Democratic Union of the minor tribes seeking respectively unitary government and federalism for

Kenya, they were faced for a time with the fragmentation of their country on the eve of independence. The leader favoured by most of the Africans, Kenyatta, was still under detention in the arid North of the state. Yet, notwithstanding these initial difficulties, Kenya survived its final moves towards self-government better than many other newly emancipated countries in an Africa where disillusionment, instability and military take-overs were too frequently to follow the withdrawal of European guidance. Kenyatta was released in 1961 and he became Prime Minister in 1963, shortly before Kenya's independence was achieved. The Europeans who remained in Kenya were not unimpressed by his speeches and actions. Age had endowed him with more wisdom than many younger African politicians possessed, and at the London Commonwealth conference in 1964 his role was that of an elder statesman. The divisions between the rival political and tribal groups disappeared. In short, Kenya, the future of which as a stable, self-governing country had seemed so enigmatic in the fifties, emerged as one of the less disturbed African states in the sixties.

TANGANYIKA

Tanganyika did not share Kenya's racial problems since not more than 20000 Europeans had settled there, and these were of mixed nationality. The Asian population created no great difficulties. Rivalry for land was unimportant. However, the dependency was Britain's poorest in East Africa. It had the lowest educational standards and the least developed economy. Sisal and the Williamson diamond mine were the only significant sources of wealth. An attempt was made in 1948 and 1949 to clear large areas of scrub and to grow ground nuts on hitherto unproductive land, but it foundered expensively during a dry first season and had to be written off by the Labour government as an economic and social failure.

A committee which travelled extensively in 1949 to prepare a programme of constitutional reform found, to its surprise, little desire for such reform. However, the usual processes, with slight variations, were put into operation. An African was appointed to the Executive Council in 1951. In 1955 ten Africans, along with ten Asians and ten Europeans, were nominated by the Governor as unofficial members of a Legislative Council which also contained thirty-one members pledged to support the government. Meanwhile a party known as TANU (Tanganyika African National Union) was being developed by Julius Nyerere, an ex-schoolmaster who had studied at Makerere and Edinburgh University. Nyerere's aims were the creation of a new political consciousness among the African masses of his country and the ultimate removal of control both by white administrators and by chiefs appointed by the colonial authorities. He hoped that racial co-operation could be maintained. The sort of tribal differences which emerged in Kenya and Uganda were not allowed to develop in Tanganyika, and in elections held in 1958 every successful candidate had the support of Nyerere's party. Europeans and Asians made no attempt to resist the inevitable trend towards a government dominated by Africans and during the next two years further constitutional changes allowed Africans greatly to increase their strength in both Legislative Council and government. A second general election, held in 1960, gave TANU fifty-eight unopposed successes and twelve of the thirteen seats in which contests took place.

In 1955 Nyerere had hoped for Tanganyikan independence in twenty or twenty-five years, and even this modest aspiration had been regarded with dismay in governing circles. However the situation very rapidly altered. Both the Governor, Sir Richard Turnbull, and the British Colonial Secretary after October, 1959, Iain Macleod, became convinced that Africans should be given responsibility much sooner; and the country actually received independence in December, 1961. A year later it followed the fashion set by India of becoming a republic within the Commonwealth, with Nyerere as President. Britain had agreed to make available in the form of grants or loans more than £22m during the next few years, to provide technical assistance and to support Tanganyika's own armed forces.

UGANDA

Unlike Tanganyika, Uganda was by African standards rich. Its people were socially more advanced than those in most other African colonial territories. Some important schools and the University College of Makerere had produced an intellectual élite; commercial life was not dominated entirely by Asians, as it tended to be in Kenya; and some Africans were prospering in a developing industry or in the cultivation, with British help, of coffee and cotton. To these more successful members of the community co-operation with the governing authorities seemed to offer more than would revolt, and consequently no strong nationalist movement developed in the fifties as it did in Kenya, Tanganyika and Britain's West African dependencies. A series of constitutional changes in the early fifties provided the Africans of Uganda with increasing opportunities, but they showed a surprising reluctance to take them.

However, the advance towards independence, once begun, was to prove as rapid as the advance in other parts of East Africa, and it was to produce problems quite as intractable as any experienced elsewhere. In the first place, the African masses were increasingly resentful of the power of a feudal aristocracy. In the second, tribal rivalries such as had created difficulties for the constitution-makers in Nigeria and Kenya showed themselves to be particularly unmanageable in Uganda. The dominant people, the Buganda, constituted only 17 per cent of the total population, and relations between them and some minor tribes were strained. Tension increased in 1953 when a new constitution provided that only a minority of the African members of the Legislative Council should be elected by the Buganda assembly. The assembly, fearing that the new body would overwhelm the traditional Buganda leaders, was unwilling to co-operate. This placed their ruler, the Kabaka Edward Mutesa II, in the embarrassing dilemma of either having to oppose his most distinguished subjects or having to disregard the British government and thereby to violate the 1900 agreement by which he and his people were bound to co-operate loyally with Britain in return for protection. He ultimately decided to take the latter course and to request that Buganda should be granted independence, notwithstanding the adverse impact which such a development would have on the other regions of the protectorate. Whereupon he was deported for two years to Britain by the Governor, Sir Andrew Cohen.

An agreement made in 1957 soon proved valueless. Parties emerged which demanded self-government with increasing insistence, yet were at the same time so unconstructively critical of British proposals that the existing government was all the less inclined to negotiate with them. It was, indeed, a matter for surprise that recommendations put forward in 1961 should have found general acceptance at a conference in London. Accepted they were, though, thanks to some unexpected party man-oeuvring in Uganda, and in the end the country quite peacefully adopted a strong central government which nonetheless permitted Buganda and some other regions to preserve a federal relationship with the centre at Kampala. The British could now withdraw without fear of leaving confusion behind them. Uganda became independent in October, 1962. Milton Obote, a representative of the Lango people, became Prime Minister with a coalition government composed of members of his own Uganda People's Congress and of the Kabaka's party, the radicals and the traditionalists. The Kabaka himself was installed as first President when Uganda followed the now customary routine of becoming a republic within the Commonwealth in October, 1963.

Difficulties were not quite at an end, however. The reconciliation between the new and the old rulers was merely superficial, after all. Tension between those who wished to establish a centralised state in which tribal antagonisms were eliminated and those who represented an older tradition was not laid to rest for ever in 1962; and when the Kabaka was once again to be constrained to leave his country, in 1966, it was as a refugee who had barely escaped with his life from a sacked palace. He was again to make his way to London. Dr Obote was to remain in control in Uganda.

ZANZIBAR AND SOMALILAND

Zanzibar had been a British protectorate, just as Uganda had been. The Arab sultan's foreign policy had been controlled by the British and a British Resident had given advice; but the sultan's authority over home affairs had not been surrendered. After elections in July, 1963, independence was gained in December, 1963. The regime survived less than five weeks. In January, 1964, revolution directed by a party representing the African majority in the islands of Zanzibar and Pemba brought about the flight of the sultan to London and the creation of a republic in which real power was rapidly seized by three men trained in Communist countries or with Communist associations. Three months after the revolution, Zanzibar and Tanganyika were amalgamated as Tanzania.

The fortunes of the Somali territories that had fallen under British and Italian rule were bound together. The Italians, in 1950, had resumed their trusteeship over the region which they had held before the war, but a limit of ten years had been imposed after which independence was to be granted. The British, in order to enable their own protectorate to be merged in a new Somalia, accelerated their grant of self-government by creating new ministerial posts for Somalis in 1959 and holding elections for an almost entirely elected Legislative Council early in 1960. British Somaliland was not really prepared for independence. Men with little or no training were rapidly promoted to senior positions in government service, and only the absence of tribal antagonisms and the existence of a small number of competent leaders, helped by some British administrators, prevented breakdown.

The protectorate became independent on 26 June, 1960. Its new national assembly at once passed an act of union with the Italian trusteeship territory and the Republic of Somalia came into being on 1 July. The new President was confronted with rivals for the premiership but solved the problem by appointing a third candidate and making the rivals foreign minister and defence minister. The British government agreed to provide £1½m for the first year of Somalia's independence and further aid in the future.

29
The Sudan

As a Condominium, in the government at which both Britain and Egypt had been involved since 1899, the Sudan presented quite different problems to those facing the British in other parts of Africa, though the stages of constitutional development through which it passed corresponded to the customary pattern in the British colonies. The stirrings of Sudanese nationalism had become evident with the foundation in 1938 of a General Congress of some of the better educated members of the community, who wished to express an interest in the establishment of schools and other social reforms. Most members of this association had been government officials who at first had had no intention of embarrassing their government; but by 1942 the Congress, under its secretary, Isma'il al-Azhari, had become more assertive, asking that the Sudanese right of self-determination should be conceded immediately the war ended.

The moves towards independence were to be complicated by the different characters of the northern and southern regions of the Sudan. The North was unified by Islamic culture and the Arabic language. The South was far less developed; it had been ruled by British officials, benevolently and capably, and missionaries had provided education based on English rather than Arabic. The two parts could not easily be harmonised. When in 1944 an Advisory Council, including twenty-eight Sudanese members, was established by the Governor-General, Sir Hubert Huddleston, it represented only the North, and misgivings were expressed at the exclusion of the South, though knowledgeable and experienced Southerners might have been hard to find. The creation of the Council, moreover, provoked the disapproval of the Egyptians, who were prepared to accept only a settlement by which Egypt and the Sudan were permanently united. The resulting disputes figured prominently in all the negotiations concerning the Sudan's future status which took place between 1946 and 1952. Ernest Bevin's declaration in 1946 that change would take place in the Sudan only after consultation with the Sudanese and that the existing regime would remain until the Sudanisation of the Civil Service and the development of self-governing institutions were more advanced did not satisfy everyone; and in 1947 Egypt brought the issue before the Security Council of the United Nations, though without result.

In 1948 Britain went ahead alone in establishing a Legislative Assembly and an Executive Council and in holding elections. The Governor-General was to retain extensive powers, including that of legislating by ordinance; and on certain issues, including the constitution and foreign relations, the Assembly was unable to legislate. However, at least half the Executive Council were to be Sudanese and the leading Sudanese member was to be, in effect, Prime Minister. Unfortunately, the parties favouring union with Egypt boycotted the elections, and Egypt refused to accept any settlement for the future of the Sudan which was also acceptable to Britain. In 1951 the Egyptian government unilaterally abrogated the Condominium agreement and proclaimed King Farouk 'king of Egypt and the Sudan'. The Sudanese government, supported by the British, denied the validity of these gestures, and in 1952, in face of Egyptian opposition, went on to provide for the institution of an all-Sudanese Council of Ministers with responsibility to a bicameral parliament.

During these years of abortive attempts to reach agreement with Egypt on constitutional matters, economic developments had gone ahead. British grants had helped education, agriculture and communications. The Gezira cotton growing scheme, from which the Sudan obtained a high proportion of its revenue, was largely under British control until 1950, after which it was rapidly transferred to Sudanese management. Improved farming in the Southern region was especially encouraged.

In July, 1952, the situation was dramatically altered when King Farouk was deposed by the Egyptian army. The new military government of Egypt was prepared to negotiate on the Sudanese question, and in 1953 an Anglo-Egyptian agreement was reached which settled the powers of the Governor-General, reaffirmed the desirability of the unity of the Sudan and arranged for another general election. The elections took place towards the end of the year. They were preceded by a vigorous propaganda campaign by Egyptian officials and wireless, and Azhari's pro-Egyptian party won a clear majority of the seats in both House of Representatives and Senate. Henceforth the substitution of Sudanese for British officials was rapidly accelerated. Fortunately, the British connection with the country did not terminate in a spirit of hostility. The officials who left received compensation. The South found that the British with whom they were familiar were preferable to the Muslim Arab Northerners who had replaced them; and when in 1955 a serious revolt occurred in the South against over-hasty changes introduced by these Northerners, British help was hoped for, though in vain. At the same time there was a rapid reaction against the Egyptian connection, and the government, once in office, revealed no urge for union with Egypt.

Towards the end of 1955 the final stages of the preliminaries to independence were completed. British and Egyptian forces were withdrawn, and the independence ceremonies took place on 1 January, 1956. Azhari, Prime Minister since 1953, remained in office. Democratic processes survived until, in 1958, disputes over the acceptance of American aid provoked General Ibrahim Abboud to take over the government in order to end what he condemned as a 'state of degeneration, chaos and instability'.[1]

---

[1] Broadcast 18.11.58. *Keesing* p. 16593

30

The Central African Federation

As demands for independence spread from one colony to another British governments were constantly obliged to face up to the supposed incompatibility of 'dominion status' and the poverty and small size of some of the countries which were clamouring for self-government. How, the British asked themselves, could one of its colonies or protectorates ever deserve political independence if it were destined never to be economically 'viable' but always to depend on the financial help of Britain or some other wealthy state? Perhaps the partial union of several colonies under federal systems of government, such as had operated in Canada, Australia and India, would be an answer. It was to be tried in Rhodesia and Nyasaland, in the Caribbean and in Malaysia. It was suggested for East Africa. It was doomed, in all these regions, to fail, entirely or partially, though the failure may have been ascribable more to intractable racial or personal antagonisms or to an ignorance among the newly independent of the importance of making it work than to a lack of wisdom on Britain's part. Britain had been forced to realise the incapacity of the small states of Europe to stand alone. They could neither resist the aggression of a Hitler nor, by themselves, give their inhabitants the advantages of rising living standards. Europe was moving, of necessity, towards the E.E.C., EFTA and NATO. It did not augur well for the future if the colonies could not move towards similar groupings. It had not served India and Pakistan well to have spurned the suggestion of a federation, which would at least have preserved some element of union and may have prevented the constant quarrels between the two countries (and, indeed, between the two regions of Pakistan) once separation had been accepted.

In North and South Rhodesia ideas of association had been considered long before the Second World War. In 1939 the Bledisloe Commission had approved in principle of union, though it had believed that differences between North and South on 'native policy' were too great to make such a development a practical issue. In 1950 a revival of interest, inspired particularly by Sir Andrew Cohen, followed a conference of officials in London; and by 1953, when rapid changes were beginning to take place throughout the colonial world, a federal solution appeared to the government in Britain to be the best answer to a number of problems. It would in particular allow a more flourishing economy to develop than would have been possible if Southern and Northern Rhodesia and Nyasaland continued to act in comparative isolation. Northern Rhodesia was largely dependent on wealth earned by its copper belt, and it needed new secondary industries. Nyasaland was an agricultural, thickly populated and poor protectorate with insufficient work for all its inhabitants. Southern Rhodesia's economy was more balanced but it needed a larger labour force for full development. The assets of these countries were, therefore, complementary, and would be benefited by closer association. A further consideration, less clearly expounded, was the need to preserve Southern Rhodesia from being drawn into the orbit of South Africa, subordinating Rhodesians of British stock to an Afrikaner majority and leading to the adoption of a similar policy of apartheid. Aligned with Northern Rhodesia and Nyasaland instead, it could become part of a separate, federal dominion, such as none of the territories could aspire to become, so it was believed, if they continued to stand alone. In Rhodesia itself the idea of federation was welcomed equally by Sir Godfrey Huggins, the Prime Minister of Southern Rhodesia, and by Roy Welensky, the most prominent Northerner, not only on economic grounds but because it appeared to guarantee the maintenance of white leadership.

The Federation was established in 1953. Matters of common concern were to be dealt with by a federal government of which the first Prime Minister was Sir Godfrey Huggins. Local concerns remained the responsibility of the three component parts of the Federation, each of which was to develop constitutionally in its own way while remaining a part of the whole. An African Affairs Board was to consider any legislation affecting Africans and to refer to the British government any Bill which it regarded as threatening African well-being.

From these arrangements the founders of the Federation

expected a prosperous future. They were to be disillusioned. Despite the existence of the African Affairs Board, opposition developed from the outset among Africans. No African representative could be persuaded to attend the final conference in London at which the character of the Federation was determined. They feared that the Federation, far from helping them to resist the apartheid characteristic of South African society, would only allow segregation to spread, and they may well have been justified. The operation of pass laws and a Land Apportionment Act in Southern Rhodesia suggested that most of the European settlers there were no more liberal than the white rulers of South Africa. So did the raising in 1951 of the property or income qualifications for voters to a level which excluded all but an insignificant fraction of the Africans. In Northern Rhodesia only eleven Africans had found a place on the electoral roll even as late as 1957. No elections to Nyasaland's Legislative Council were held before 1956. Federation seemed to Africans to represent a setback to their hopes of ultimate self-government. Although they outnumbered the white population of the Federation by twenty-seven to one, they were themselves outnumbered in the Federal Assembly by twenty-nine to six; and even the six were scarcely representative, being chosen by a preponderantly white electorate in Southern Rhodesia and only indirectly in the North. They felt no confidence that their demand for 'one man one vote' would ever willingly be granted by the white minority. They were unimpressed by arguments about the increased wealth which would follow the establishment of an integrated economic system and an expanded market for goods of all kinds. They suspected that only Europeans would benefit. When in 1957 constitutional amendments doubled the number of African seats in the Federal Assembly but simultaneously increased European representation from twenty-nine to forty-seven, they boycotted the election held to fill the seats.

Discontent developed at first most strongly in the most backward of the three partners, Nyasaland. It emerged on a local scale in 1955 when a new Nyasaland constitution was introduced, stipulating that a small number of Africans should sit in the Legislative Council but limiting the franchise to Europeans and Asians and leaving the Africans to be elected indirectly through provincial councils. The very small European community in

Nyasaland believed that these proposals went too far. An African leader, on the other hand, condemned them as 'arbitrary, oppressive and undemocratic'. Three years later the Africans found a leader in a London doctor, Hastings Banda, who had spent forty years away from the country of his birth but now returned to Nyasaland and was received as a national hero. Unfortunately, when the new Malawi Congress party called for non-co-operation and the secession of Nyasaland from the Federation, disorders occurred; the British Governor, Sir Robert Armitage, declared a state of emergency; and Dr Banda was among a large number who were arrested in March, 1959. He remained in gaol until April, 1960, though on his release was able to negotiate a new constitution with Iain Macleod, obtaining a dominating influence for Africans. There were too few European residents in Nyasaland to oppose the arrangement.

Meanwhile, the Southern Rhodesian Africans fared less successfully: their National Congress was outlawed, and when police opened fire on rioters in the outskirts of Salisbury, twelve Africans were killed.

The British government appointed two commissions to examine conditions in the Federation. The first, under Lord Justice Devlin, made no recommendations but drew further attention to the problems of the Federation. These were considered in detail by the second commission, under Lord Monckton, whose report was issued in October, 1960. The findings were saddening to those who had hoped for much from the association of the territories. 'The Federation cannot in our view be maintained in its present form. On the other hand, to break it up at this crucial moment in the history of Africa would be an admission that there is no hope of survival for any multiracial society on the African continent, and that differences of colour and race are irreconcilable. . . . We state our view that the three territories could best go forward if they remained linked in a federal association; but that it is too much disliked to survive in its present shape.' In an endeavour to make it more acceptable to the Africans the Commission made certain recommendations; some practices discriminating against Africans in local government, public services and industry should be ended, and a bill of rights should be written into the Federal and territorial constitutions. The franchise should be widened to include Africans 'with experience,' even though without education or property qualifications. More Africans should be admitted to the Federal Assembly. The three regional governments should gain responsibility for health, roads, prisons, non-African education and agriculture, while the Federal government's power should be limited to economic policy, external affairs and defence. Above all, Britain should permit the component territories to secede from the Federation if they wished.

The last provision made the ultimate break-up of the Federation inescapable. The final attempts made to save it by Sir Edgar Whitehead, the Prime Minister of Southern Rhodesia until December, 1962, and by Sir Roy Welensky, the Federation's Prime Minister since November, 1956, were unavailing. The British government was becoming increasingly unsympathetic to the white Rhodesian case, and when they allowed Nyasaland to secede from the Federation in December, 1962, and Northern Rhodesia to do so in March, 1963, the experiment of association had come to an end. It was formally abandoned a few months later at a conference at Victoria Falls presided over by R. A. Butler.

Nyasaland, renamed Malawi, became independent under the leadership of Hastings Banda in July, 1964. Northern Rhodesia, known henceforth as Zambia, gained its independence under Kenneth Kaunda, a former schoolmaster, in October, 1964. Only Southern Rhodesia, almost a dominion since 1923, remained without complete control over its affairs, and the consequences of this were before long to present to a new Labour government in Britain one of the most embarrassing of all the situations produced by a disintegrating Empire.

31

Cyprus and Malta

The possession of dependencies in Africa may have created problems for Britain in the 1950s of a kind which the empire-builders of the 1880s could never have envisaged. The possession of Cyprus created even greater problems. The British might well have regretted that when in 1915 they had offered Cyprus to Greece, on condition that Greece would aid Serbia against invading Bulgarians, the offer had been declined.

The difficulties in the late fifties arose essentially from the demands of the Greek Cypriots (79 per cent of the population of 549 000 in 1958) for the union of Cyprus with the country which had rejected it four decades previously. This ideal, known as 'Enosis', was bitterly opposed by the Turkish population of the island (17·5 per cent). Through disinclination to sacrifice a minority to the mercy of the majority as well as unwillingness to abandon their only remaining base in the Eastern Mediterranean, the British were unable to regard Enosis as a satisfactory solution.

Demands for Enosis had caused serious disturbances as early as 1931. After 1945 they were revived. In 1954 they were referred to the General Assembly of the United Nations, which refused to consider them; and this judgment was followed by four years of rioting and terrorism, negotiation and frustration. In the first place the anti-British demonstrations were the work largely of youths and schoolboys. Indeed, through all the years of upheaval, it was the young men who were most frequently responsible for acts of violence, inspired and directed by a movement known as the National Organisation of Cyrpiot Struggle (EOKA), the commander of which, Colonel Gheorghias Grivas, was a former officer of the Greek army. Behind this elusive figure lay the influence of the Cypriot church. Cypriots 'would

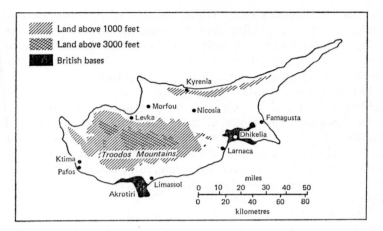

Cyprus

not abandon the struggle,' declared Archbishop Makarios in a sermon in September, 1955, 'even if the whole island were turned into one great prison.' Passive resistance would be sponsored by the church, 'so intense that it would disrupt the machinery of government.'[1] Attempts by a new Governor, Field-Marshal Sir John Harding, to negotiate with the Archbishop produced only stalemate; and by March, 1956, the evidence of his implication in terrorist acts was all too clear. Ammunition had been discovered in the archiepiscopal residence, and appeals to the Archbishop to denounce terrorism had met with no response.

In March, 1956, the Archbishop was exiled to the Seychelles, along with the Bishop of Kyrenia, an open advocate of violence who had helped to organise a youth movement from which EOKA had recruited supporters. The removal of these prelates did not end the implication of the church in politics. The evidence continued to accumulate. The seizure of Grivas's diary in the summer confirmed that Makarios had personally taken part in the planning of EOKA's initial operations and revealed that the Bishop of Kitium, the acting Ethnarch during Makarios's exile, had also been involved in the organisation of terrorist activities. By February, 1957, the British authorities had been provoked to detain no fewer than fifty-seven priests and to issue a statement condemning the Archbishop and deploring that the laity had 'become so indoctrinated by political propaganda, cleverly disguised in religious dress by their pastors, that hatred and even murder have become endowed in the eyes of many with the aura of sanctity.'

During the four years' emergency 506 people were murdered, British, Greek and Turkish, civilians, soldiers and policemen alike. Communal riots added more than 100 other Greek and Turkish Cypriots to the total killed. The terrorists, having shot their victims in the back or thrown their bombs at government buildings, usually contrived to escape, and, withdrawing to the mountains, tied down large British forces: 25000 were in Cyrpus by the end of the emergency in 1959.

The British government made repeated efforts to grant the island a constitution which would be acceptable to both Turks and Greeks. A conference in London in September, 1955, offered an assembly with an elected majority, safeguards for the Turkish minority, and control over foreign affairs, defence and internal security for the governor. This came to nothing. In 1956 Lord Radcliffe, who had presided over the Punjab and Bengal Boundary Commissions in 1947, was appointed to make further constitutional proposals. His suggestions also found no acceptance. In June, 1958, (by which time Sir Hugh Foot had replaced Sir John Harding as Governor of Cyrpus) Harold Macmillan put forward a seven-year 'partnership' plan, under which representatives of the Greek and Turkish governments should work with the British and with elected members of Greek and Turkish Cypriot Houses of Representatives in evolving a generally acceptable system of government. When objections were raised, particularly by the Greek government and by Makarios (who had left the Seychelles in April, 1957) Macmillan flew to Athens, Ankara and Cyrpus, and modifications were introduced into the plan. The Turks accepted the amended proposals but the Greeks were as obstructive as ever. Makarios placed on record 'our profound disappointment that the moderation we have shown in a spirit of good will and compromise . . . has met with no response whatever from the British government'.[2]

At least as late as August, 1958, Makarios was still insisting on complete self-determination, which was generally understood to mean union with Greece. He would not consider plans for self-government which would have involved written safeguards for the Turks and would have ruled out Enosis. Unfortunately, this extreme Greek attitude hardened the desire of the Turkish Cypriots to partition the island, separating the two communities. Since the populations were mixed in all the main towns and were nowhere clearly segregated in the countryside and villages, the British could not regard such a solution as practicable, and all their constitutional proposals avoided it.

The British were worried also about the international repercussions of the Cyprus dilemma. Both Greece and Turkey were members of NATO, but relations between them were inevitably tense. The Turkish government was normally restrained, though it indicated that it was not prepared to accept Greek annexation of the island. Athens was not at all restrained. Anti-British broadcasts over Athens radio, anti-British demonstrations in Greek cities and Greek encouragement of acts of violence in Cyprus, occurred throughout the emergency. When Makarios reached Athens from the Seychelles he was enthusiastically welcomed. When in October, 1958, Paul-Henri Spaak, Secretary-General of NATO, suggested a NATO conference to discuss Cyprus, the Greeks refused to participate, and then blamed Britain for 'incomprehensible and unacceptable intransigence' at a time when Greece had given 'proof of her conciliatory spirit and moderation'.[3] The conference collapsed.

Ultimately, in February, 1959, the Prime Ministers and Foreign Ministers of Greece and Turkey met in Zürich, and they followed their discussions with meetings in London attended by British and Cypriot representatives. From these deliberations Cyprus emerged as a republic which should neither unite, wholly or partly, with another state, nor be partitioned. A Council of Ministers was to be created with seven Greek Cypriot members and three Turks. Seventy per cent of the House of Representatives were to be Greek, 30 per cent Turkish. Agreements were also reached on the composition of the civil service, the forces, the judiciary and local government in the larger towns. A pact was signed by the three countries concerned, guaranteeing this constitution and the independence of Cyprus. It was also laid down that Britain should retain sovereignty over two areas of the island which were to be developed as military bases.

Apparently the emergency was at an end. An amnesty brought about the release of about a thousand detained terrorists.

Hundreds of others came down from the hills. In March, 1959, Makarios was received at Nicosia by some 200000 Greek Cypriots when he at last returned to Cyprus; and Grivas, in Athens, was rewarded for his activities by a state reception, triumphal drives through the city and the highest titles and decorations that could be granted by parliament, King and Academy. And yet . . . Cyprus had obtained an uncertain tranquillity. Within a few months Grivas was bitterly criticising the settlement, and attacks on Makarios were being made in the island both by the Bishop of Kyrenia and by Greek Cypriot mayors. When the Archbishop offered himself for the Presidency in December an opponent gained nearly half as many votes as he was given himself. Furthermore, independence planned for February, 1960, was delayed until August by prolonged negotiations over the British bases. The British envisaged the retention of areas amounting to about 120 square miles; the Cypriots were willing to surrender only 36 square miles and Makarios threatened a resumption of civil disobedience when deadlock appeared to prevail. Ninety-nine square miles was in the end agreed upon, mostly round Akrotiri, near Limassol, and Dhikelia, near Larnaca.

Britain agreed in 1959 to grant Cyprus more than £14m during the first five years of its independence. It was expected that the continued presence of British forces in the island would contribute between £15m and £20m to the economy and that some 15000 Cypriots would be employed at the bases.

Normally the British were not directly involved in the domestic history of their ex-colonies once independence had been granted. However, since they retained military bases in Cyprus their responsibilities there had not ended with the ceremonies of August, 1960, and in due time they were once more called upon to intervene to preserve the peace. In 1963 Makarios suggested constitutional changes. The Turkish government rejected his proposals, and during the upheavals which followed in Christmas week nearly 200 Cypriots were killed. In January, 1964, with the consent of the Greek, Turkish and Cypriot governments, British troops took upon themselves the task of maintaining order. An Anglo-American plan for a NATO force in Cyprus was rejected by Makarios, but in March the United Nations approved the formation of an international force under its own control, and contingents were sent from

Canada and several European countries. British troops, already on the spot, continued their peace-keeping work in the south of the island.

MALTA

The British authorities in Malta were spared the civil conflicts which made their dealings with the Cypriots so disturbing. They were spared none of the problems which could be created by unyielding politicians, divided among themselves, in an island with an exceptional share of social difficulties. Maltese constitutional development had never shown the steady progress from paternal absolutism to majority rule by elected representatives which most of Britain's other dependencies experienced. Advance towards self-government had been interrupted by controversies over marriages between Maltese and English, linguistic differences, taxation and relations between government and church. Between 1930 and 1939 the constitution had been twice suspended and once revoked altogether. Then followed the heroic years of war and the restoration in 1947 of complete self-government under a British governor. There also followed a period when, despite the emigration to such countries as Britain, Australia, the United States and Canada of almost one-third of the working male population, Malta became, with 320000 people in 1953, one of the most densely populated territories in the world, with one of the highest birth rates in the West.

An election in 1955 gave the Maltese Labour Front 23 seats out of the 40 in the Legislative Assembly. The Nationalist Party gained the other 17. In the same year a conference met in London to consider the future constitutional and economic relationship between the island and Britain. Labour, under Dominic Mintoff, favoured an integration with Britain which would have given Malta a status similar to that of Northern Ireland, with representation at Westminster. Nationalists, under Borg Olivier, preferred dominion status. In 1956 a referendum on integration produced 67000 favourable votes (about 75 per cent of those who voted); but it also produced 20000 opponents, a Nationalist party boycott and 62000 abstentions. The opposition expressed the fears felt by Roman Catholics of secular influences and British Protestantism, and the referendum marked the start of an ugly controversy between church and Labour party. The

British government found it hard to pursue the question of integration. It was further discouraged from doing so when, shortly afterwards, differences developed over a demand from Mintoff for a very steep increase of British financial aid to Malta, and when, at the end of December, 1956, both parties in the Maltese Legislative Assembly declared that the island would no longer be bound by its obligations towards Britain unless the British government provided firm guarantees concerning the future employment of Maltese workers in British government service. This unexpected threat, ignoring projects which would have ensured employment for Maltese, drew a strongly worded protest from Alan Lennox-Boyd, the Colonial Secretary: during the previous eleven months, British taxpayers had provided nearly £15m in aid to Malta, and offers had been made of another £25m, to be paid over a five-year period, together with very generous help towards Maltese expenditure on education and health. 'Not a penny by way of increased taxation has been raised by the Maltese government,'[4] wrote Lennox-Boyd. All recommendations that economies should be made had been disregarded.

Discussions on integration which were resumed in London in March, 1958, broke down in April. Mintoff returned to Malta and announced that the British government was responsible for the delays and for overriding Maltese opinion without consultation. He declined any longer 'to remain responsible for public peace and order'[5] and resigned the premiership. Dr Olivier refused to succeed him, so, amidst a strained atmosphere the Governor, Sir Robert Laycock, assumed direct control of the government and declared a state of emergency. The impasse continued even when Lennox-Boyd had announced that the Admiralty dockyard, the future of which was causing particular anxiety, would be taken over by a Welsh ship-repairing firm and converted to commercial use, so as to ensure the livelihoods of the Maltese employees. Mintoff asked the workers not to co-operate with the firm in question. Only the small Maltese Progressive Constitutional party, led by Miss Mabel Strickland, welcomed the dockyard plan.

In December, 1958, another round of constitutional negotiations broke down when Mintoff and Olivier refused to sit at the same London conference table as Miss Strickland. Malta then became once again a Crown Colony and was for three years directly ruled, for all practical purposes, by the British government. Their rule was benevolent. Already 80 per cent of the foreign exchange needed by the island to pay for its imports was supplied by Britain. Twenty-seven per cent of the Maltese labour force was employed by the British authorities. A considerable amount of money was spent in Malta by the British services. Now the Colonial Office offered to contribute in addition £29m over the next five years to help the development of new industries and to convert the dockyard to civil use. It also undertook to make good a £6½m budget deficit, to develop water resources, to carry out port modernisation and to encourage tourism.

The next British endeavour to settle the constitutional issue was made in October, 1960. Characteristically, the Maltese Labour and Nationalist parties boycotted the commission which was set up, and when it announced its recommendations in March, 1961, only Miss Strickland's party welcomed them. The British government none the less went ahead, and after an interlude during which a quarrel between the Maltese Labour party and the Catholic Church culminated in the placing of Mintoff under an interdict, a new constitution was promulgated in October. It came into operation early in 1962. Once more a Maltese government and parliament were to enjoy full legislative powers, only foreign affairs and defence remaining partly under British control. Once more Miss Strickland expressed satisfaction while Mintoff and Olivier issued denunciations. It chanced, fortunately, that Olivier's opposition was of limited duration and when in February, 1962, a general election gave his Nationalists half the fifty seats he formed a government.

The idea of Maltese integration with Britain had by now been practically forgotten. Both Mintoff and Olivier were demanding Maltese independence. In 1959 Lennox-Boyd had considered that independence was an 'apocalyptic vision'[6] which Malta was much too poor and small to sustain with success; but by July, 1963, when another Colonial Secretary, Duncan Sandys, presided over yet another London conference, and when Malta was receiving millions of pounds in aid not merely from Britain but also from the World Bank, the British had concluded that independence was indeed the only possible answer to prolonged deadlock. The July conference, like the others, ended in failure: the Labour delegation fell out with the other parties over the status of the church in Malta. However, Sandys, adopting the policy which had in 1947 compelled the Indians to face the future, announced nonetheless that Malta should become independent not later than May, 1964. To the last the negotiations lacked dignity. The leaders of three minor Maltese parties which had played little part in the developments of the fifties and sixties feared the consequences of independence. The larger parties refused to compromise on the position of the Maltese church and failed to agree on the terms of a referendum to determine the character of a constitution. When in April, 1964, a referendum was held, a majority of votes cast signified approval of the draft constitution; but since this majority represented only 40·4 per cent of those entitled to vote, Mintoff was able to assert that the result meant 'complete defeat'[7] for Olivier. Mintoff threatened to 'use all means to smash the constitution' if it were imposed. However, deadlock could not persist indefinitely. Olivier spent the summer negotiating in London, a defence agreement allowed British forces to remain in Malta for ten years, Britain agreed to provide up to £50m for the development of the Maltese economy and for higher education and emigration, and independence was celebrated (except by Mintoff's party) on 21 September, 1964.

---

[1] Sermon at Kalopsida, 25.9.55. *Keesing* p. 14514
[2] Makarios, replying to a letter from Sir Hugh Foot, 16.8.58. *Keesing* p. 16454
[3] Greek Government statement, 29.10.58. *Keesing* p. 16643
[4] A. Lennox-Boyd to D. Mintoff, 3.1.58. *Keesing* p. 15973
[5] Broadcast 21.4.58. *Keesing* p. 16362
[6] Lennox-Boyd in the House of Commons, 2.2.59. *Keesing* p. 16716
[7] Mintoff, 19–20.5.65. *Keesing* p. 20108

32

Nationalism in the Far East

The nationalism of India and its moves towards self-government produced only a delayed echo in the British dependencies further East. In Malaya, for example, the idea that Malays, Chinese and others should come together as a united, self-governing Malayan nation seems to have been undeveloped until it was put forward between the wars by Tan Cheng Lock, a member of the Straits Settlement Council; and it made little immediate impact. Forces of tradition remained strong in Malaya. British rule was accepted by Malay aristocrats and Chinese merchants alike. No educated middle class was in revolt against the traditions. No popular demand was made before 1939 for democratic government. Each ethnic group looked to the British for protection against the others. So paternalism survived, and in 1941 Britain was still firmly in control.

The tradition was shaken by calamity at the end of 1941. The Japanese invasion began on 8 December, and on 15 February, 1942, Singapore surrendered. Malaya became a Japanese colony, brutally and incompetently administered, its tin-mining equipment destroyed during the campaign, its rubber, though more or less unscathed, deprived of normal export outlets, particularly after 1943 when Allied submarine attacks ruined the Japanese merchant navy. The economy therefore stagnated. Unemployment and food shortages, inflation resulting from an excessive production of paper money, and the disintegration of first-class medical services characterised the occupation. About 60 000 Indian estate labourers were sent to work on the Bangkok-Moulmein railway, and more than 40 000 died.

Malaya was, however, spared the additional curse of the liberation war which had been planned for the autumn of 1945. British control was restored peacefully and was genuinely welcomed. Tin output slowly revived: down to 8000 tons in 1946 from 81 000 tons in 1940, it had climbed to 45 000 tons by 1948.

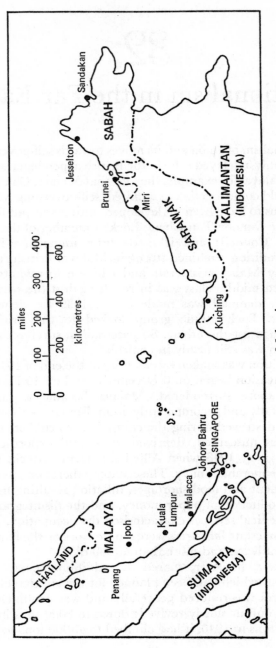

Rubber recovered more quickly, largely because the plantations had benefited from their enforced wartime rest: the 1948 output of 697000 tons was 150000 tons higher than the 1940 output. At the same time, it was understood that the old order could not continue unchanged indefinitely. As early as October, 1945, a new constitution merged the nine Malay states and Penang and Malacca (without Singapore) into a Malayan Union and provided for equal rights for all races; but since this union was imposed after inadequate discussion it produced a rapid reaction, led by Dato' Onn bin Ja'afar, a Johore aristocrat who had been educated in England. Accordingly, a different arrangement was made in February, 1948. A Federation of the nine states was now introduced, each with a Malay chief executive and a British adviser. A central government contrived to retain a large amount of control by taking wide financial powers.

Equal rights of citizenship for all races were once again insisted on. Unfortunately, though, the Federation evoked protests from sections of the Chinese and Indian communities; and advantage of the situation was taken by the Communists. A terrorist campaign was begun which was not to end until 1960. Its immediate aim was the dislocation of the economy by attacks on plantations and mines. Ultimately it was proposed that a popular revolt should lead to Communist control of the whole country. Support for the movement came essentially from the Chinese element in Malaya. Not more than four or five thousand terrorists were ever active at one time, yet 40000 regular soldiers, 70000 police and a quarter of a million 'Home Guards' were needed to keep them in check. The Emergency cost £20000 a day for several years. The isolated bungalows of planters required armed sentries, barbed wire fences and floodlighting. Individual planters on their daily rounds had to be protected by armoured vehicles. Yet despite these precautions, one planter in ten was murdered, buildings and vehicles were burnt and rubber trees were slashed. In October, 1951, the British High Commissioner, Sir Henry Gurney, was killed in an ambush.

In the end it was realised that a military solution to the war could be only a very distant prospect, so difficult was it for troops to make contact with the Communists in the jungle. A social solution was likely to be more effective. Consequently, large numbers of squatters who had settled on the fringes of the jungle and had been terrified into supplying the Communists with provisions were transferred in the early 1950s to new villages, fortified with barbed wire and provided where possible with piped water, electric light, schools and police stations. Here the squatters were safe from intimidation and were brought for the first time under government control. The terrorists, meanwhile, were gradually isolated. Their morale broke as food supplies dwindled and as they were subjected to bombardment and loud-speaker propaganda from the air. Many were captured and sent, with considerable success, to rehabilitation centres where they could learn a trade. By the end of the fifties acts of violence were confined to north Malaya. When Malaya gained its independence the Communists played no part in determining its character.

Despite the Emergency, the advance towards self-government continued. A nominated Legislative Council gradually gave way to an elected one. Shrewd leadership prevented racial rivalry from tearing Malaya part. As early as 1948, under the influence of Malcolm MacDonald, the British Commissioner General in South-East Asia, the different communities had formed a Liaison Committee to discuss possible remedies for racial friction. The chances of harmony grew stronger after 1951, when Tunku Abdul Rahman, brother of the Sultan of Kedah and a comparatively unknown barrister, succeeded Dato' Onn as President of the United Malay National Organisation. An 'Alliance' between this Organisation and the Malayan Chinese Association survived in spite of the forebodings of doubters. Indians also joined and by 1955, when elections to the Federal Council took place, the Alliance polled almost 80 per cent of the votes and won all but one of the fifty-two seats. The electorate was predominantly Malay, yet of the fifty-one successful candidates fifteen were Chinese, one Indian and one Ceylonese. An Alliance government took office and Tunku Abdul Rahman became chief minister. British officials continued to control defence, economic affairs, finance and the Civil Service, but they did not endeavour to oppose or overrule the elected ministers and in 1956 surrendered the ministries of defence and finance to Alliance colleagues. Most of the Malay ministers were aristocrats, the Chinese ministers were wealthy, and some had already gained experience as nominated members of the Federal Council. Therefore extremist policies were unlikely.

The Alliance had campaigned in 1955 for independence by 1959. In fact, although the British had originally been reluctant to grant *Merdeka* (Freedom) too rapidly while the Communist Emergency lasted, independence was celebrated on 31 August, 1957. The British left behind them some of the essential principles of liberal government: federalism guaranteed the survival of a certain amount of local independence; parliament brought together members of each racial group in a senate and an elected House of Representatives. Rules of citizenship were defined. More Chinese and Indians were to be enfranchised. Though Islam was to be the official state religion, freedom of worship was guaranteed. Malay was to be the national language; English was to be, for a decade, the second language.

SINGAPORE

The movement towards self-government in Singapore had no unusual features. The number of elected representatives on the Legislative Council was progressively increased between 1948 and 1955, and the political apathy of more than one and a half million overcrowded people diminished. Fortunately Singapore did not experience the racial clashes which might have been expected where Chinese outnumbered Malays by more than five to one and outnumbered all others by three to one. It could accept as its first chief minister after the introduction of the 1955 constitution a lawyer of Iraqi Jewish extraction, David Marshall.

Some difficulty arose for the British in determining the functions and responsibilities of their troops in times of upheaval. In the end the 1959 constitution declared that if a breakdown of internal security seriously affected British defence responsibilities the constitution could be suspended; and an Internal Security Council was set up, with three British representatives among its eight members.

The 1959 constitution also established an entirely elected assembly and a cabinet responsible to it. The British High Commissioner was left with diplomatic rather than administrative functions. The first elections after independence gave a very clear majority to the People's Action Party, and its leader, Lee Kuan Yew, a lawyer with an outstanding academic record at Cambridge, became Prime Minister.

MALAYSIA

Britain remained responsible for three regions of Borneo: Sarawak, Brunei and North Borneo. Sarawak had been a Protected State since 1888, though it was only ceded to Britain as a colony by the last Rajah of the Brooke family in 1946. North Borneo also became formally a colony in 1946; previously it had been a Protected State administered, since 1881, by the British North Borneo Company. Brunei, like Sarawak, became British protected in 1888. By 1960 the population of the three territories together was no more than 1282000.

British opinion, during the years when the old Empire was breaking up, was strongly in favour of federal solutions for the government of areas which by themselves could never have become prosperous or populous enough to have sustained the burdens of independence. Nowhere did federation succeed for long in the form originally planned. Yet the reasons for Malaysia seemed sound, and although Britain was no longer in a position to insist on it, its establishment was at first readily accepted. Fundamentally, federation in the East was inspired by Malaya's desire to introduce some measure of unity without the risk of being dominated by Singapore. Singapore, by itself, might have become so overwhelmingly important as a commercial centre as to endanger the newly acquired position of Malaya's capital, Kuala Lumpur. It had already become a centre of left-wing activity where Communists were allowed a degree of freedom which seemed in Malaya to be dangerous. It might have become a base for Chinese nationalism in opposition to Malaya. If the various territories combined all these potential hazards would have been reduced. In particular, if Sarawak and North Borneo (Sabah) were brought into the system, the Chinese would not numerically outweigh the other peoples of the region. Accordingly, the Federation of Malaysia was established in September, 1963, with Malaya, Singapore, Sarawak and Sabah as its component parts. Brunei did not join. Singapore soon left.

Britain's work in the East was not quite finished. Malaysia was faced, on the jungle frontier in Borneo, with a war provoked by Indonesia, which professed to disapprove of the new Federation, claimed (unjustifiably) that the Bornese territories had not wished for it and may well have sought expansion to distract the attention of the Indonesians from economic disintegration at home. The frontier on which the so-called Confrontation took place was long and very difficult to defend. Britain sent troops, helicopter landing-grounds were created in the jungle and at least the situation was preserved from getting out of hand until, in 1966, the fall from supreme power of the Indonesian President Sukarno brought about the end of the conflict.

33

The end of Imperialism in the West Indies

Too small, for the most part, to develop a flourishing economic and political life independently of each other and of Britain, the West Indies nonetheless provided an opportunity for a federal experiment. The idea was old, but only after the war, when independence was in fashion and federation was still a British panacea for areas of the Empire which were too large (like India) or too small (like the West Indies and the Bornese territories) or economically complementary (like Central Africa), was any positive attempt made to bring it into being. A conference at Montego Bay, Jamaica, in 1947, set up a Standing Closer Association Committee; and in time this inspired the creation of organisations to control the economic development, labour and air communications in the islands.

In 1956 it was decided that a federation should be set up, and this was ultimately done in January, 1958. The Federation was endowed with a Governor General (Lord Hailes) and a Council of State, a Senate composed of one member from Montserrat and two from each other island, and a House of Representatives with seventeen members from Jamaica, ten from Trinidad, five from Barbados, two each from Antigua, St Kitts, Dominica, Grenada, St Lucia and St Vincent, and one from Montserrat. It was arranged that defence, foreign policy, migration and overseas borrowing should be dealt with by the federal government, that certain issues should be dealt with by both federal and island governments, and that everything else should be managed locally. After long argument it was settled that the federal capital should be developed with British aid in Trinidad. Sir Grantley Adams, Prime Minister of Barbados, became federal Prime Minister, none of the other leading contenders (Dr Eric Williams of Trinidad, Sir Alexander Bustamente and

240

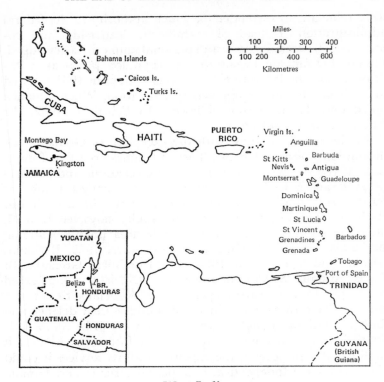

West Indies

Norman Manley of Jamaica) wishing to leave their islands.

With similar histories and a common culture and language, with similar social problems arising from over-population, and with needs for close economic links, the federation should have been effective. It was not. Insular prejudices proved too strong. The larger and richer islands feared that they would find themselves supporting the smaller ones and that their progress would thereby be delayed. Trinidad, comparatively wealthy, was as unwilling as the mainland territories, Honduras and Guiana, had been to accept large numbers of immigrants from the poorer islands. Jamaica, with more than half the population of the islands, considered itself entitled to a proportionate number of seats in the federal legislature. All the local island governments were reluctant to surrender too much authority to the federal administration. Instead of enthusiastic leadership and co-operation, friction, intrigue and personal animosities developed. Finally Bustamente began to campaign for Jamaican with-drawal from the federation, and a referendum in 1961 resulted in a victory for forces opposed to federation. When Jamaica opted out, Trinidad soon followed. In February, 1962, the federation was dissolved.

To the smaller islands, with the exception of Grenada, the dissolution was a misfortune. They still considered that federa-tion offered the best means of achieving economic and political progress, and indeed reached an agreement amongst themselves on the creation of a new, limited federation, with a capital in Barbados. This never developed successfully, however. Instead, after the establishment of a free-trade area linking Antigua, Barbados and British Guiana in December, 1965, Barbados became independent, in 1966, and Dominica, Grenada, St Lucia, Antigua, St Vincent and St Kitts-Nevis-Anguilla agreed to accept a form of near-independence as Associated States with Britain. Britain was to conduct and subsidise their defence and foreign relations, though otherwise they were to be responsible for their own development; and if in the future any island felt itself capable of bearing the expense of all its services it could claim complete independence. Expanding sugar and banana production, the establishment of secondary industries, and the development of tourism were envisaged as prerequisites for such independence.

In 1969 a conflict between the 6000 people of Anguilla and their government in St Kitts obliged the British to send troops and officials to the island. Clearly, even Associated Status was not a final solution to West Indian difficulties.

Meanwhile, British Guiana was also advancing uneasily to-wards independence. Inheriting from its colonial past an un-usually complex racial composition, it possessed a population of East Indians (163000 in 1946), Negroes (143000), Amer-indians (16000), Portuguese, Chinese, British and people of mixed descent, who had been insufficiently integrated for any straightforward development to be likely. In the late 1940s the balance was upset by the elimination of malaria from the territory. This had dramatic effects on the birth rate, especially among the Indians, who had hitherto suffered, in rural areas, more from the disease than had the Negroes and Europeans. Within twenty years the Indian population had almost gained a clear majority over all the other groups together. A different complication was the domination of economic life by the plantation sugar-growing firm of Booker. Only in recent years had peasant rice farming in the coastal belt and bauxite mining in the interior brought diversity into the economic system.

Despite these unprepossessing circumstances, a commission on constitutional reform recommended in 1951 the immediate introduction of universal suffrage. This produced a majority for the People's Progressive Party, led by an Indian, Cheddi Jagan. Within a short time the party's Marxist character had aroused fear among both racial minorities and sugar-growing interests. To preserve the rights of the minorities and to safeguard the economy, the British Governor, Sir Alfred Savage, accordingly suspended the constitution in 1953. Democracy, it was argued, demanded the freedom of smaller groups as much as government by a majority. In due course, embarrassingly, Jagan and his followers won other elections. As independence approached, however, the British government introduced proportional representation; and this had the effect of putting Forbes Burnham a London-educated negro lawyer, into the premiership. Independence was finally granted in 1966 and Burnham remained Prime Minister. The government's policy was to restore a racial harmony and commercial confidence and to avoid alienating Britain or the United States by the adoption of doctrinaire economic policies.

PART FOUR

34

Population

The population of Britain in 1931 was 44 795 000. By 1951 it had grown to 50 383 000, and by 1961 to 52 825 000. Substantial though these increases may have appeared, they were actually not nearly so dramatic as the increases of the Victorian decades. The decline of the rate of increase during the 1920s and 1930s had been so marked that some demographers had predicted that by the end of the century the population would have been halved. Events, however, proved their forebodings to have been unjustified. The trend was arrested in the years following the Second World War. A birth rate in 1947 of 20·7 per thousand helped to produce what was popularly known as 'the bulge'; and although this rate, the highest since 1921, was not maintained, the number of births per thousand continued during the late 1940s and early 1950s to be higher than the number in the years preceding the war. A slow increase after 1955 suggested that the bulge might, after all, have been no ephemeral phenomenon. In 1961 the birth rate was 18 per thousand.

Improved medical attention, as well as a rising birth rate, helped to confound the more pessimistic prophets of the thirties. In the mid-twentieth century mortality from the main childhood infections was less than one hundredth of the mortality in the mid-nineteenth century. Scarlet fever, typhoid and diphtheria were, by the 1960, only very rarely causing death. Diphtheria had, indeed, almost disappeared by the sixties. Such smallpox cases as occurred usually resulted from contacts overseas. Whooping cough became far less common. Poliomyelitis was a very disturbing threat in the early fifties, but it was mastered so effectively that in 1963 only fifty-five cases were recorded.

There was a marked decline during the post-war years in deaths from tuberculosis, syphilis and rheumatic fever. The fatal diseases which were increasing were those generally associated with the elderly: heart ailments, pneumonia and bronchitis, and cancer, particularly cancer of the lung. A series of medical surveys, in other countries apart from Britain, plainly showed the connection between the last of these and heavy cigarette smoking.

Between 1900 and 1961 the infant mortality rate was reduced by 80 per cent, while maternal deaths were nearly halved in the eight years between 1934 and 1942, reduced to slightly over one-sixth of the 1934 rate by 1956 and to about one-eleventh by 1961. Furthermore, a greater number of potential mothers married. By the 1950s a higher proportion of women under 40 were married than ever before. They were marrying younger: whereas in 1911 only 24 per cent of women between the ages of 20 and 24 were wives, by 1960 55 per cent had been married. The number who married before they were 20 steadily increased, and the number who were still spinsters at 35 declined. At the same time, improved conditions of working and living, better medical facilities and nutrition contributed to a constantly rising expectation of life. In 1871 the expectation of life at birth had been only 42 for men and 45 for women. In the early 1920s the figures had risen to 56 and 60; in the early fifties to 66 and 72; in the sixties to 67·5 and 74.

EMIGRATION AND IMMIGRATION

Population figures were inevitably affected by the large amount of emigration and immigration which took place at various times. Between 1800 and the middle of the twentieth century about 25m people born in Britain are estimated to have emigrated. The movement of British citizens was certainly a rather erratic one: in the 1930s large numbers who had settled in overseas countries of the Empire after the First World War returned, disillusioned, to England; countries which had been as badly affected as Britain by the Depression refused to accept immigrants; and consequently, during this decade, more people entered Britain than left it. The trend was once again reversed, however, after the second war. Between 1946 and 1951 another wave of emigration to the Commonwealth developed. A peak of 85000 in the net outflow was reached in 1951, but this time there was to be no repetition of the experience of the 1930s. Even though the advance of the colonies to independence closed some earlier outlets, like the White Highlands of Kenya.

emigration did not come to an end. In 1963, for instance, 59 500 people left Britain to live in Australia, while 37 100 left for countries of Western Europe. During each of the next four years more people emigrated than came to settle in Britain. From the middle of 1967 to the middle of 1968 293 000 immigrants entered the country; but 312 000 left it.

The fluctuating pattern which was a feature of the settlement overseas of people born in Britain was equally characteristic of the immigration into Britain of foreign and Commonwealth citizens. During the 1930s refugees seeking asylum from oppression on the Continent had outnumbered emigrants, and Britain's net gain during the twenty years following 1931 was about half a million, despite the revival of a movement towards settlement abroad in the late forties. The 1951 census showed that about 1·7m people in the United Kingdom had been born outside it. About one-fifth of these had come from independent Commonwealth countries or from the colonies, about one-third from the Republic of Ireland and nearly half from foreign countries, particularly Poland, Germany, Russia and the United States. Since 1931 the number born in Commonwealth countries had increased by about a third, those born in Ireland by about two-thirds, while the numbers of foreigners had approximately doubled.

COLOURED IMMIGRANTS FROM THE COMMONWEALTH

In the late 1950s, apart from the Hungarian refugees who settled in Britain after their abortive endeavours to secure a greater degree of freedom and independence in the face of Russian force, the largest group of immigrants came from the West Indies, India and Pakistan. The 1961 census indicated the presence in Britain of 172 000 West Indians, 81 000 Indians, 25 000 Pakistanis and 80 000 other Commonwealth citizens (mainly West Africans and Chinese). They made their homes particularly in the conurbations where the demand for labour was especially high: in London, Birmingham, Wolverhampton and the other towns of the Black Country, Bradford, Leeds, Halifax and Liverpool. Many found useful employment in spheres where the white population was reluctant to seek work, such as the railways and buses, or in the hospitals. Whatever popular opinion may have thought, there was clear evidence that, since a high proportion were of working age, they put more into the economy than they took out in the form of social services. Despite the troublesome problems created for the education authorities by the presence in the schools of Indians and Pakistanis who could not speak English, and despite the pressures placed on those responsible for housing a rapidly increasing population in areas which were already overcrowded, the immigrants were on the whole more of an asset than a burden.

One enquirer, Professor Maurice Peston, concluded that immigration had probably been conducive to growth and anti-inflationary. A study of juvenile crime by John Lambert showed that Asian children were 'markedly less delinquent in terms of approved school attendance than a comparable English age group',[1] and that while West Indian boys were less good, they were still better than their English contemporaries. Complaints that the presence of coloured neighbours was affecting property values were not shown to have been justified by such surveys as were undertaken, in Southall (Middlesex), Oxford and West Yorkshire. Furthermore, though the Indians and Pakistanis may have imported a culture of their own, the West Indians, at least, had generally been taught in English-speaking schools and had imbibed from their background many of the conventional English ideas on 'respectability', cleanliness and the value of education for their children.

Notwithstanding the findings of the surveys of immigrant communities, however, anxiety in Britain mounted. As the population explosion of the twentieth century affected islands with limited space or countries with limited opportunities, the annually increasing number of immigrants seeking their fortunes in Britain threatened to get out of control. The racial prejudices which responsible statesmen had deplored and condemned in America or South Africa began to obtrude themselves in the English cities as soon as coloured immigrants ceased to be an insignificant minority and began to compete with the white residents for accommodation. The government, which had been reluctant in the fifties to erect barriers against the admission of holders of British passports and had felt a moral obligation as an ex-colonial power to let them in, was in the end forced to take a stronger line. The Commonwealth Immigrants Act of 1962 allowed it to limit permission for entry into Britain to those with assured prospects of employment or adequate means of self-support, and to deport those who proved unsuitable. The measure aroused the strong opposition of the advocates of a free right of entry for all Commonwealth citizens, and it was assailed by people who suspected that in practice it would operate against the coloured populations of the Caribbean, India and Pakistan, but not against the white Irish. Yet it was, in fact, rapidly accepted as necessary. The number of coloured residents had been rising so fast, and, in spite of the Act, continued to rise, that by the end of 1964 430000 West Indians, 165000 Indians, 100000 Pakistanis and 125000 other coloured people were living in Britain. In 1965 the Labour government, which in opposition three years earlier had attacked the Conservative measure, tightened up the law further by introducing a Bill to prevent the illegal immigration of persons claiming, with no clear evidence, to be dependants of others already in Britain, or students, or visitors. No voice of condemnation was heard in Parliament.

A census taken in 1966 showed the total coloured population of Britain to be 924000. Of these 454000 had their origins in the West Indies (273700 in Jamaica), 223600 were Indians (80 per cent of them Sikhs, coming predominantly from two districts of the Eastern Punjab), 119700 were Pakistanis and 50800 West Africans. These groups accounted for 92 per cent of Britain's coloured people. Between 1966 and 1968 the numbers were believed to have increased to 1113000. Figures of white and coloured births during March and April, 1969, indicated that at least one-fifth were coloured in Wolverhampton, Bradford and a number of London boroughs (Brent, Haringey, Lambeth, Hackney, Hammersmith, Islington and Ealing). By this time the issue was no longer one which the politicians could minimise. At the 1964 general election, when the tide was flowing strongly in Labour's favour, a Conservative candidate at Smethwick who adopted a bluntly realistic policy on the social strains created by the race problem actually won a seat from Labour, defeating Patrick Gordon Walker, whom Labour had cast as Foreign Secretary if they were returned to office. Enoch Powell, sometime Conservative Minister of Health, insistently emphasised the risks arising from an excessive concentration of coloured citizens in a limited number of areas and advocated assisted repatriation. He was accused of exacerbating existing difficulties, was furiously denounced and was deprived of his position in the Shadow Cabinet; but he was in fact only bringing into the open the views of large numbers of less articulate white people.

The extent of the moral and practical difficulties raised by Enoch Powell was indicated yet again during the debates in 1968 on another Act introduced by the Labour government. This had the effect of making almost impossible the entry into Britain of a great many Kenya Asians, holders of British passports, who had been deprived of their means of livelihood by an African government. The measure was passionately opposed by some members of both main parties (including Iain Macleod and Sir Dingle Foot) and by all the Liberal M.P.s. But it was supported, albeit with regret, by a great majority of Conservatives as well as by a majority of Labour members on the grounds that about 230 000 Asians in Kenya, Tanzania and Uganda were eligible to come to Britain if they wished and that so large a number could not possibly be absorbed. The Act caused considerable bitterness. At the same time, though, the government did make some attempt to safeguard the position of the coloured people who had already settled in Britain. Race Relations Acts passed in 1965 and 1968 imposed legal penalties on overt symptoms of racial discrimination directed towards such people when housing, employment, education, recreational facilities or various forms of service were at stake. A Race Relations Board, under the chairmanship of a former Liberal M.P., Mark Bonham Carter, was created to supervise the administration of the Acts.

No Act of Parliament could ensure that discrimination would disappear overnight. All the surveys of immigrant living and working conditions showed that a dark skin entailed disadvantages which nothing could easily eradicate. While in normal circumstances the unemployment rate among immigrants was under 3 per cent, it tended to rise more rapidly than the average when the employment situation became less favourable. Immigrants were over-represented in occupations which white people regarded as undesirable, and only a limited proportion of them could aspire to the more responsible positions. Their housing conditions were less satisfactory than the conditions in which white Britons lived. In London in the late sixties 70 per cent (twice the average) of all immigrant households were sharing dwellings. Almost inevitably, they were more over-crowded, with about one person per room compared with a national average of 0·6 per room. Whereas white families tended to leave city centres when they could, coloured families remained. Very few coloured immigrants obtained council houses: 6 per cent, by 1966, compared with 28 per cent of Irish immigrants and about one-third of the resident English. A proportion of coloured people far higher than the national average occupied furnished rented accommodation (in London 44 per cent), yet such homes were, by the late sixties, becoming increasingly difficult to find. By 1970 the position particularly of the West Indians in Britain was deteriorating. Expecting more from Britain than Asian immigrants expected, their sense of rejection was all the greater. For their children, transferred frequently from a village to a decaying part of an English city and left to their own devices during the day by their mothers, two-thirds of whom were at work, the educational and social future must have appeared enigmatic.

THE MOVEMENT OF PEOPLE INSIDE BRITAIN

Most of these immigrants came from parts of the world where population was beginning to outrun resources. Unfortunately, living space was also contracting in Britain. By 1961 the density of the population of England and Wales had grown to 790 per square mile, a figure exceeded in Europe only in the Netherlands, which had 893 per square mile. More than half the people of England and Wales were concentrated in 156 urban areas with populations of more than 50000. More than a third lived in the six conurbations of Tyneside, West Yorkshire, Southeast Lancashire, Merseyside, the West Midland towns with Birmingham as their centre, and Greater London. As urban populations increased, the more remote and less affluent parts of Britain lost inhabitants, and had indeed done so since the First World War. Between 1921 and 1938 the population of North and Central Wales had declined by 4·8 per cent that of South Wales by 8·1 per cent. Between 1951 and 1961 six of the twelve Welsh countries still showed a decrease. The populations of Cornwall and Westmorland declined, both before and after the Second World War. In Scotland numbers declined in twenty-seven counties in the 1920s and in eighteen out of thirty-three in the fifties. Between 1951 and 1961 the crofting counties of Argyll, Caithness, Ross and Cromarty, Sutherland, Orkney and Zetland lost 2·8 per cent of their inhabitants, while 6·3 per cent left the Border counties. About half moved to other parts of Britain, particularly to England, and half went overseas. Total emigration from Scotland between 1931 and 1951 was estimated at just under a quarter of a million. Between 1951 and 1961 it was rather more than 254000. This redistribution did not, it was true, represent an absolute decline in numbers for the whole of Scotland, but it did mean that while the population of England and Wales expanded in the 1950s by 5·3 per cent, that of Scotland expanded by only 1·6 per cent.

In England the most remarkable increases occurred in the Midlands and South East. Between the wars the population of the Midlands went up by 11·6 per cent, the counties of Nottingham, Leicester and Warwick gaining very substantially, Worcester, Stafford, Cheshire and Derby rather less so. After 1945 the thriving industries of the Midlands, such as iron and steel, brick-making and chemicals, continued to attract workers, while the coal-mining and textile-manufacturing areas of the North had far greater difficulties in retaining either their prosperity or their people. Meanwhile, the changes in the South East were even more remarkable. Between the wars the number of residents here expanded by 18·1 per cent. Greater London and the rest of the South East each gained about half a million people in the years following the Depression of the early thirties. The Drift after the war became so pronounced as to create major social problems. It happened that the population of inner London itself declined between 1951 and 1961 by 2·3 per cent; but the number living in the outer suburbs increased during this period by 39·7 per cent, and the number living in an area spreading into Kent, Sussex, Berkshire, Bedford and Essex rose by 20 per cent. In the rest of the South East the population expanded by 9·6 per cent. Even in London's precious Green Belt, which had a population of less than a million in 1938, more than half a million additional people were living by the early sixties. Altogether, an area containing just over 28 per cent of the land of England and Wales contained 38 per cent (18m) of their people. For many of these, desire or need to live away from town centres entailed the problem of commuting between home and work. In central London, in 1955, a resident population of 225000 was augmented during business hours by 1027000

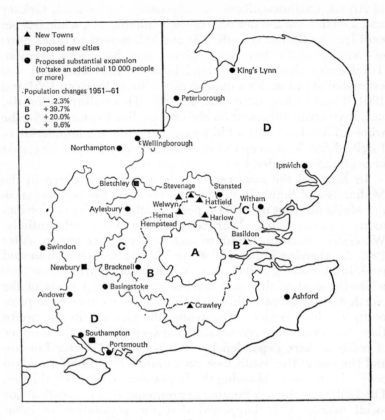

South-east England, town planning and population changes.

Towns for which population growth of 5000–10000 was planned	Plans for growth of 1000–5000
Letchworth	Canvey Island
Banbury	Frimley and Camberley
Bury St Edmunds	Houghton Regis
Haverhill	Luton
Mildenhall	Huntingdon
Sudbury	St Neots
Thetford	Grantham

Source: Based on information provided in the *South East Study 1961–81* (Ministry of Housing and Local Government, H.M.S.O. 1964)

workers. Endeavours to decentralise made only a very limited impression on London's dominating position as an administrative, financial, commercial and artistic capital.

The drift of people to the South East was accompanied by a migration of industry and other forms of employment. In 1962, for the 38 per cent of the population of England and Wales who lived in it, the South East could offer 40 per cent of the jobs. During the previous three years Category I industry (industry in which jobs increased by 20 per cent or more) had expanded by 54 per cent in this region, whereas in the North it had expanded by only 22·7 per cent and in the Midlands, prosperous though it was, by 15·9 per cent. When occupations of all kinds were considered the same dominance of the South East was evident. Between 1955 and 1962 more than three-quarters of a million new posts were created here, while no other region had more than a third of this number. The Midlands, with about a quarter of a million, ranked next.

For the town planners and for a government which was anxious to restore wealth to older industrial regions and to the more remote parts of Britain, these trends were disturbing. The attempts that were made to divert new development away from the South East and the Midlands and to limit unmanageable congestion in more affluent districts are considered in Chapter 38.

---

[1] E. J. B. Rose and others, *Colour and Citizenship,* Institute of Race Relations and Nuffield Foundation, Oxford University Press (1969)

35

The Labour revival

The general assumption in 1964 that the period of Conservative power was coming to an end was proved by the results of the election in October, 1964, to have been justified. Whereas in 1959 Conservative candidates had been supported by 49·4 per cent of the electors and had amassed 13 750 935 votes, they now attracted only 43·4 per cent of the electors and their total poll declined to 12 002 407. They gained 5 seats, but lost 63; and were left with only 304. The Labour party profited correspondingly. Although its popular support in the country showed no signs of having rallied since 1959 (its total poll actually fell, from 12 216 166 to 12 205 576) its representation in the Commons was increased by 56, rising as a consequence to 317. The Liberal party, led still by Jo Grimond, the member for Orkney and Shetland, was the only one of the three to have enlarged its vote since 1959. With 3 093 316 supporters (more than at any election since 1929) and 11·2 per cent of the votes cast, its hopes of a revival might have seemed reasonable; yet it could still obtain only 9 seats.

THE MINISTRY

Harold Wilson became Prime Minister. Born in Huddersfield in 1916 and educated at Wirral Grammar School, Bebington, and Jesus College, Oxford, he had become a Fellow of University College, Oxford, in 1938, Director of Economics and Statistics at the Ministry of Fuel and Power during the later years of the war, and, as an M.P., Parliamentary Secretary to the Ministry of Works in 1945, Secretary for Overseas Trade in 1947, and, in October, 1947, President of the Board of Trade. On Hugh Gaitskell's death he had been elected leader of the Labour party by his parliamentary colleagues in a ballot which had at least avoided a repetition in 1964 of the unseemly rivalry for the Conservative leadership that had contributed to the weakening of the previous government. During the six years of his premiership his influence was to be felt, so it seemed, behind every aspect of government. The Wilson Administration was no metaphorical expression. Commentators even suggested, particularly during the election campaign of 1970, that Britain was moving towards a presidential form of government under which the Prime Minister was no longer content to remain merely *primus inter pares*.

At the same time the early twentieth century image of the Labour party as a group of sincere and earnest but scarcely intellectual, articulate or politically experienced Trade Unionists with a small number of Fabian leaders had, for a generation, ceased to be tenable. It was possible for Wilson to find able occupants for an unusually large number of ministerial offices. George Brown became Minister for Economic Affairs, James Callaghan Chancellor of the Exchequer, Herbert Bowden Lord President and Leader of the Commons. Denis Healey was appointed to the Ministry of Defence, Sir Frank Soskice to the Home Office, Arthur Bottomley to the Commonwealth Relations Office, and Douglas Jay to the Board of Trade. Michael Stewart became Minister of Education and Science, Richard Crossman Minister of Housing and Local Government, Ray Gunter Minister of Labour. Barbara Castle was given the newly created Ministry of Overseas Development; and Frank Cousins was drawn from Trade Unionism (the secretaryship of the T.G.W.U.) to take over another new post, combining the Atomic Energy Authority, the National Research Development Corporation and the Department of Scientific and Industrial Research under a Ministry of Technology. Outside the Cabinet, the minister who was destined to rise furthest during the next six years was Roy Jenkins, appointed in 1964 to the Ministry of Aviation.

Initially, an unexpected problem was presented by the Foreign Secretaryship. Patrick Gordon Walker, who was expected to take over the office, was defeated at Smethwick by a Conservative who had earned widespread denunciation for expressing the popular view on coloured immigrants. A supposedly safe seat was then created at Leyton by the grant of a life peerage to Reginald Sorensen. Gordon Walker, however, suffered another defeat and was obliged to resign. Michael Stewart became Foreign Secretary instead.

LABOUR INTENTIONS—AND PROBLEMS

The Labour party embarked on the problems of government to the accompaniment of general condemnation of the thirteen allegedly 'wasted years' of Conservative rule and proclamations of the intention that the later sixties should be a period of technological progress, of managerial revolution and of rapidly increasing productivity. The age of Conservative Stop-Go was to end: no longer should industrial expansion be subject to frequent alternating encouragement and limitation in futile endeavours to stimulate overseas sales and, at the same time, to check domestic spending and inflation. Britain was instead to experience a period of sustained economic growth and of high and stable employment combined with such restraint over wage demands that incomes would not outrun productivity. Its new rulers' hopes for its future, both at home and abroad, were symbolised by the new ministries: Land and Natural Resources, Technology, Disarmament and Overseas Development. The new emphasis on economic expertise was symbolised by the recruitment for the Department of Economic Affairs of outsiders from the higher ranks of industry and banking and by the appointment of dons from Oxford and Cambridge, Thomas Balogh and Nicholas Kaldor, as special advisers of the government.

Six years later critics who suspected that in practice one government was much like another, whatever the party label, were to find ample scope for their cynicism. They might have conceded, however, that the Labour inheritance in 1964 was not an easy one. The balance of payments position, while preserved by the postponement of debt service payments to the United States and Canada from being quite so serious as the pessimists had feared during the late summer of 1964, was still very ominous. The unfavourable visible trade balance for the year amounted to £519m, compared with £80m in 1963 and £102m in 1962. An advantageous invisible balance in 1964 could not prevent an adverse current balance of £382m. The costs of imports were far outstripping the earnings of exports. Exports in fact fell, while imports, at higher prices than in 1963 soared. The quantity of manufactured consumer imports, which had increased by 8 per cent in 1962, rose by 23 per cent in 1963 and again by 23 per cent in 1964. Imports of manufactured capital goods such as machinery rose by 31 per cent in 1964 compared with an increase of only 2 per cent the year before. These disquieting developments coincided with a progressive decline of Britain's share in world trade in manufactured goods: in 1954 this share had amounted to more than 20 per cent; by 1964 it had dropped to less than 14 per cent. The Common Market countries and Japan were taking the place that Britain was losing. Britain was laying itself open to condemnation in a survey by the Organisation for European Co-operation and Development as the only major developed country apart from the United States which had not increased its gold and foreign currency reserves since 1958.

It spite of its discouraging financial position, British overseas expenditure remained high. Whereas in 1952 such expenditure amounted to £74m, by 1964 the total was almost £500m, of which £350m was draining away on military commitments in the Far and Middle East and in Germany. And although incoming interest on the long-term private capital investments which continued to flow overseas was ultimately to be anticipated, it could provide no immediate solution to a disastrous balance of payments deficit in 1964. Current balance of trade figures, combined with these other overseas payments, had produced a total deficit of £744m by the end of the year.

THE GOVERNMENT'S RESPONSE

The government lost little time in introducing measures intended to remedy the position. A White Paper published ten days after its formation announced that a temporary 15 per cent surcharge would be imposed on all imports except foodstuffs, basic raw materials, unmanufactured tobacco and works of art, that exports would be encouraged by rebates of indirect taxation on such goods, and that plans for increased productivity in essential industries would be examined immediately. James Callaghan's supplementary budget in November imposed an additional sixpence on income tax and an extra sixpence a gallon on petrol. Bank Rate was raised from 5 per cent to 7 per cent. A massive loan of $3000m (£1071m) was accepted from foreign countries which were represented in the Bank of International Settlements. A further sum, of $1000m (£357m), was borrowed in December from the International Monetary Fund, in order to restore the stability of British trade. An $80m loan was received at the same time from Switzerland.

The recovery programme was extended during the early months of 1965. In January Douglas Jay announced the establishment of a Commonwealth Council designed to stimulate exports. In February the construction of TSR2 military aircraft was cancelled on grounds both of expense and of the excessive absorption of scarce reserves of highly skilled technicians. In April Callaghan's second budget aimed at reducing public expenditure and increasing taxes still further, in the hope that, with less money left in citizens' pockets, fewer goods would be purchased at home and more be made available for export. A capital gains tax was introduced, directed particularly at speculators who had grown wealthy through untaxed sales at favourable moments of shares which were rising in value. Business men whose 'expense accounts' had hitherto been exempt from taxation were no longer to enjoy this widely criticised fiscal loophole. A new Corporation Tax was to be imposed on company profits. At the same time the Chancellor aspired to reduce the net outflow of long-term capital, privately invested abroad, by at least £100m a year. One important possible measure he ruled out, however: devaluation. 'As a result of this budget and of a changing attitude on the part of management and others,' he said, 'we have now reached a stage where not even the most doubting Thomas believes that the pound is likely to be devalued. I can say that not only is there no case for it, but . . . I do not believe that anybody can force us to devalue.'[1]

This last forecast was not to prove to have been justified. The budget, despite its new features, could not cure the economy, and in May, 1965, Britain was once again obliged to call upon the International Monetary Fund for a loan. This time a sum of $1400m (£500m) was borrowed. Another $40m were lent by the Swiss National Bank. In June arrangements were made for German payments to Britain to offset some of the costs of the British Army of the Rhine. And to convince European creditors that determined efforts were being made in Britain to restrict extravagant spending at home, limits were imposed on expenditure on housing, school and hospital building and the armed forces. Meanwhile, direct overseas investment outside the sterling area was to be restricted, the time allowed for the payment of goods acquired on hire-purchase was to be reduced, and special certificates were to be obtained by those wishing to build factories or offices in the prosperous South East, the Midlands and Eastern England. Additional credit facilities were to be made available for exporters. In September the leading banks of Western Europe, America and Japan agreed with the Bank of England to provide further very large sums to defend sterling against speculators.

By the end of 1965 it could at least have been claimed that the foreign trade figures suggested an improvement after the calamities of 1964. Receipts on invisible transactions remained much the same as they had been during each of the recent years: £188m. The visible trade balance on imported and exported goods amounted to — £237m and the current balance to a deficit of £49m, compared with the £382m deficit of the previous year. Gold and foreign currency reserves rose and the net outflow of long-term capital investments fell. The situation, though, was still very disturbing. It remained true that no economic measure introduced by a government could be guaranteed to cure every problem simultaneously. Loss as well as profit was involved in the remedies put into operation by the Chancellor. Restriction of government expenditure, high taxation and a raised Bank Rate might have reduced the amount of money available for domestic purchasers and might have been intended to check inflation and divert industrial products, at stable prices, into export markets. Without being very evidently effective, however, the measures also tended to discourage investment in industry, to make expansion difficult, and, for the sake of an immediate advantage, to create future stagnation. At the same time, Britain had incurred enormous debts, particularly to the I.M.F. It was becoming increasingly obvious that it no longer had the resources to sustain the power and influence in Asia in which it had gloried in the past. Its government, by endeavouring through the 15 per cent surcharge (reduced in 1965 to 10 per cent) to restrict imports, had defied a trend towards reduced tariffs and greater freedom of trade, and had especially alienated its partners in the European Free Trade Association, who had not been consulted. An excessively high bill for imports might have been prevented; but strong criticisms of Britain by Scandinavians, Austrians, Swiss and Irish, by

GATT[2], by the Organisation for Economic Co-operation and Development (O.E.C.D.) and by the Council of Europe could not be.

While the Chancellor and the Treasury had been contending with the forbidding problems of international trade and finance, George Brown and the Department of Economic Affairs had been working bravely and hopefully on a National Plan for the development of every aspect of the economy during the next five years. Output was to expand by 25 per cent. Annual growth rate was to rise, well before 1970, to 4 per cent a year. Individual output was to rise by 3·2 per cent, and wages and salaries were to increase no more than expanding productivity permitted, in order that British prices overseas should remain more favourable than those of competitors. Industrial modernisation and reorganisation were to be planned by the Development Councils which had already been created. Investment in industry, technological and business education, personal and public expenditure, and the reduction of government expenditure abroad, especially on armed forces, were all to play a part in changing a trade deficit to a surplus. Every aspect of industry and agriculture, fuel and power, transport and education was covered. The Plan was so unexceptionable and optimistic that it was accepted by Parliament without a division. Unfortunately the five years that followed revealed, as might have been anticipated, that the most sanguine projects were liable to founder when faced with the divergent expectations of intractable human beings. The National Plan was to remain, to a large extent, an academic exercise.

During moments which, in retrospect, appeared to have been more realistic, the government continued to introduce welfare legislation. At the height of the economic crisis, in November, 1964, increases in income tax and petrol duties were accompanied by increases in national insurance benefits: 12s 6d (62½p) more for single people, 21s (£1·05) per week more for couples. In February, 1965, the prescription charges on medicines were ended, a concession which produced a steeper rise in costs in a year (21·9 per cent) than in any similar period since the Health Service was introduced. Nearly 250m medicaments prescribed during the next twelve months cost £128m, compared with the £105m spent on 208m prescriptions during the previous year.

Less controversial than the issue of prescription charges was the Redundancy Payments Act (August, 1965), which provided that people losing their jobs as a result of redundancy should receive compensation as of right and laid down a scale varying according to age and years of service.

---

1 Callaghan, winding up Budget debate in House of Commons, 13.4.65. *Keesing* p. 20757

2 GATT: the General Agreement on Tariffs and Trade, introduced in 1947, and accepted by more than sixty countries with the aims of reducing tariffs and of promoting international trade and economic development. The Organisation for Economic Co-operation and Development was the name adopted by the Organisation for European Economic Co-operation in 1960, when it was joined by the United States and Canada.

36

Labour government 1966–7

Little had occurred by March, 1966, to convince the country that the government had really mastered its domestic and overseas problems. Britain was no more obviously the beneficiary, or the victim, of startling changes of political philosophy than it had been in 1951. The promised era of technological progress had made no dramatic impact. Labour was not very clearly saving Britain. At the same time, though, there was no evidence that the decline of support for the Conservatives had been arrested. The Opposition had even lost a by-election at Roxburg, Selkirk and Peebles to the Liberal candidate. Accordingly, in expectation of an increase in the number of Labour members of Parliament, the Prime Minister staked his party's future on the results of another general election, in March 31, 1966. He won convincingly. Labour backing rose from 44·2 per cent of those who had voted in 1964 to 47·9 per cent, and this substantial minority of the voters gave the party a substantial majority of the Commons seats: 363 out of 630, a net gain of 48. The Conservatives, with only 41·9 per cent of the poll in place of the 43·4 per cent they had gained in 1964, lost 51 seats. They saved 253. The Liberals, though prevented by comparative poverty from putting up as many candidates as in 1964, gathered a little more support in North Scotland and South West England and managed to return 12 members to the House to compensate for 104 lost deposits. A single Republican Labour condidate was victorious in Belfast, but otherwise the minor parties suffered badly: the Communists lost all 57 of their deposits; and no Welsh and Scottish Nationalists or Independents came within sight of success. The Speaker was returned, as convention prescribed.

Only six weeks later, local government election results in the boroughs of England and Wales suggested that a fickle electorate had already begun to change its mind. Labour suffered a net loss of 171 seats while Conservative candidates enjoyed a net gain of 263. Conservatives took control of Birmingham, Cardiff, Plymouth and fifteen other boroughs which they had not previously held. Two months after the local elections, at a Parliamentary by-election at Carmarthen following the death of Lady Megan Lloyd George, the Welsh Nationalist, Gwynfor Evans, raised his party's vote from 7416 to 16179 and decisively defeated his Labour rival. These were ominous symptoms for Labour of a decline in support which was to bring it, during the next three years, to a level of unpopularity inconceivable during the rejoicing of March, 1966.

FINANCIAL ISSUES

Inheriting the readiness of the Conservative government to introduce radical financial measures, and co-operating closely with Sir William Armstrong, the Joint Permanent Secretary to the Treasury, James Callaghan had already, in 1965, imposed corporation and capital gains taxes. In his 1966 budget he brought in a Selective Employment Tax. The main purpose of this tax was to ensure that burdens which had hitherto fallen on industry should be shared by the far more rapidly expanding services of all kinds. It was estimated that the value of manufactured goods subject to purchase tax and excise duties was about £6000m, of which taxation accounted for about 40 per cent, whereas the sum paid for services amounted to about £7000m, of which only about 1 per cent was accounted for by taxation. To redress the balance and to encourage the transference of manpower from services and distributive and constructional activities (in which numbers had increased by more than a million since 1960) to industry (in which the labour force had risen by only 142000) employers would be charged, for each man employed, a weekly 25s (£1·25), which would be refunded with an additional 7s 6d (37½p) to manufacturers, would be refunded without an addition to certain categories of employers such as those engaged in transport, and would not be refunded at all to the providers of services or to those involved in building. The measure was strongly opposed, denounced as potentially inflationary and was threatened with ultimate repeal by the Conservatives. However, Labour was to find it sufficiently useful later to enlarge the sums paid for employees in services. Not merely did the government wish industry to expand, it also anticipated an enormous expansion of the social services. The estimates published in 1966 predicted that between 1964 and 1970 housing subsidies would increase by 68 per cent, education costs by 32 per cent, health and welfare costs by more than 23 per cent, the costs of various benefits and assistance by 38 per cent, and expenditure on roads by 40 per cent. In these circumstances SET promised to be a most productive form of revenue.

It was during Callaghan's years at the Exchequer that a series of important White Papers on public expenditure and on the objectives of the nationalised and other industries was published, and that the introduction of a decimal currency was successfully started. Unfortunately, success continued to be denied the Chancellor in the sphere of international financial transactions. During its first eighteen months in office Labour had followed a policy, pursued by the Conservatives during the Chancellorship of Reginald Maudling, of working for the steady expansion of industry in the expectation that, with increased productivity, balance of payments difficulties would be cured automatically. The loans contracted by the government were intended to tide the country over a limited period, until this increased productivity had been achieved. The policy, in fact, foundered. A balance of payments surplus was still not in sight in the summer of 1966. Despite endeavours to limit people's spending power at home by imposing high taxation and a high Bank Rate, and thus to free manufactures for export, domestic demand for goods remained persistently higher than anticipated. One reason was that the government itself, while taking with one hand, was giving back with the other: public expenditure had grown by 5·5 per cent in 1963, 5 per cent in 1964 and 7 per cent in 1965. A second reason was the failure of productivity to rise as had been hoped, with the consequent failure of supply to satisfy demand. A third was the apparent impossibility of restraining excessive wage increases and the inflation that followed almost automatically from them. In 1965, when increased productivity earned an additional £600m, wages and salaries increased by £1300m. White Papers, ministers (George Brown especially) and the more responsible Trade Union leaders might agree that wages should not outrun an estimated annual productivity increase of 3 to $3\frac{1}{2}$ per cent; yet during the first three months alone of 1966 hourly earnings in manufacturing industry went up by 7 per cent. Products inevitably increased in price, and although they might still find sales at home, their success in foreign markets would depend on a comparable degree of inflation in those foreign countries. The trade statistics for the first half of 1966 revealed, in reality, only that Britain's exports, month after month, were earning less than the sum which was being paid for imports. Once again gold and foreign currency reserves were falling. A strike of seamen which lasted for nearly seven weeks in May and June and eventually immoblised more than 900 ships in British ports made an unsatisfactory situation worse still.

Commentators were beginning to suggest that sterling was over-valued, and that no amount of effort would avail unless the government overcame its reluctance to countenance devaluation. For the moment, however, such a measure was ruled out. The more customary expedients of loans, economies and restrictions on wage increases were resorted to instead. In June new arrangements were made to support the pound at a meeting of the leading West European, United States, Canadian and Japanese bankers, and although transactions of this sort remained as usual confidential, the Press estimated that $1000m had been borrowed. A further $52m was borrowed from the Export–Import Bank to cover the purchase of military aircraft. And on 20 July, 1966, the Prime Minister, who had only eight days previously assailed 'the defeatist cries, the moaning minnies, the wet editorials'[1] of critics of the government, announced a series of emergency measures designed to reduce public and private expenditure at home and, it was hoped, to improve the balance of payments. Purchase tax, surtax, postal charges and hire-purchase payments were all increased. Surcharges were imposed on spirits and petrol. Further controls were imposed on building, particularly of office blocks in Southeast England and the Midlands. Government expenditure was to be reduced, especially on investment in the nationalised industries, on defence and on aid for foreign countries. At the same time, the foreign travel allowance for individuals was to be limited to £50 a year, and there was to be a six months' standstill on increases of wages, salaries and dividends, followed by another six months of 'severe restraint'. Legislation on prices and incomes, which had been initiated early in July, was to be put into operation, obliging industry to give forewarning of intended wage, dividend and price increases, and bestowing power on the Prices and Incomes Board (the successor of the Conservative National Incomes Commission) to examine and to reject proposals for increases. Meanwhile, the government agreed to use its influence to persuade industry and Trade Unions to eliminate over-manning and such restrictive practices as those which had delayed the operation of the freight liner train services.

Harold Wilson optimistically explained all these measures as being intended, ultimately, 'to provide industry with the opportunity to achieve a major increase in productivity by streamlining production and labour utilisation. They [were to] be seen against a background of policies designed to speed the application of scientific methods and techniques . . . , to increase efficiency in private industry and in the public sector.'[2] George Brown, still Minister for Economic Affairs and Deputy Leader of the Labour party, was far less happy. Although he had himself sought limitations on wage and price rises and an end to inflation, the emergency restrictions on investment threatened to check industrial expansion and consequently to ruin his National Plan. He offered to resign. Since so flamboyant a gesture would have damaged even further the Labour party's image at a critical time, though, he became Foreign Secretary instead, while Michael Stewart, Foreign Secretary hitherto, took over his position at the Department of Economic Affairs.

A member of the government whose resignation mattered less was Frank Cousins, the Minister of Technology. After a career as a Trade Union leader he was unable to accept any surrender by the Unions of control over their wage bargaining powers. He approved neither of the control to be exercised by the Prices and Incomes Board nor of official pressure to freeze wage increases. He would not accept the view that an inflationary situation had been created by a cycle of higher wages. He was replaced at the Ministry of Technology by Anthony Wedgwood Benn. The other members of the government, whose ideals were not affronted by the measures which had been forced upon them, could only wait hopefully for these measures to take effect.

APPARENT RECOVERY

In some ways the harsh policies were quite successful. 'Broadly speaking,' said Callaghan in April, 1967, 'the measures are doing what the government expected of them, namely restoring our fortunes abroad while giving us an uncomfortable time at home. . . . The freeze and squeeze have been worth it. . . . The slackening of domestic demand has helped the export drive.'[3] Over the last two years exports had risen by over 14 per cent. Exports to the United States had risen by 50 per cent. Later, balance of payments statistics showed that the deficit on visible trade had declined from £237m in 1965 to £73m in 1966, and that, when invisibles were also taken into account, an adverse current balance of £49m in 1965 had turned into a favourable one of £84m in 1966. The end of the year brought the establishment of the proposed free-trade area among the members of EFTA, three years earlier than originally planned.

Meanwhile, at home, a number of other symptoms of economic recovery inspired an ephemeral hope that all would be well. Weekly wage increases (3·3 per cent) could be shown to have been less steep than in any year since 1959. Investment in industry was maintained better than had been anticipated. Bank Rate went progressively down. Gold and foreign currency reserves rose. Some of the money borrowed from the International Monetary Fund and Switzerland could be repaid. When, early in 1967, the defence estimates predicted expenditure of £2 205 120 000 during the coming year (an increase of £33m) and the civil estimates proposed expenditure of £7 746 503 250 (an increase of £1144m) it might have been supposed that the need for economies had passed. Such a view might have been confirmed in July, when increased family allowances for about 6 500 000 children were introduced at a cost of £83m, less than a third of which was to be saved by increasing school meal and milk charges. Prices and incomes were permitted, also in July, to enter a phase of 'moderation' following the periods of 'freeze' and 'severe restraint'.

AND FURTHER OMINOUS SYMPTOMS

And yet the now customary pattern of crisis, recovery, and renewed crisis had not, after all, come to an end. Despite all the encouraging signs, Britain's international financial position was moving quickly towards the most prolonged of the periods of misfortune that the Wilson government was to face. As usual, adverse balance of payments and declining reserves were the symptoms. Reserves fell each month from May to September, and only another Swiss loan prevented further deterioration of the position in October. An ominous £46m trade deficit in September developed into a calamitous one of £107m in October. Several factors contributed to this reversal of fortunes. War in June between Israel and its Arab neighbours had resulted not only in the defeat of Egypt, Jordan and Syria but also in the withdrawal of Arab funds from London, and, much more important to Britain, the closure of the Suez Canal and an addition of between £15m and £17m a month to the British fuel and freight bill. At the same time, dock strikes at home appeared to harm exports more than imports, perhaps being responsible for nearly half the deficit recorded during October. The withdrawal in November, 1966, of the import surcharge, originally imposed in 1964, may also have encouraged the purchase abroad of more goods in 1967 than during the previous two years. So may the Final Act of the so-called Kennedy Round of tariff reductions, signed at Geneva in June, 1967. This approximately halved tariffs on a wide range of imports, from cars to photographic equipment and shoes; and it reduced them in varying degrees on steel, textiles and chemicals. Such a move towards freedom of trade was designed, of course, to bring only benefits. However, at a time when wage increases in Britain were rising twice as fast as productivity and adding to the cost of British wares, it was more likely to exaggerate British weaknesses in a competitive world.

Once again, drastic action was clearly necessary. It was no longer sufficient to twice raise the Bank Rate. Accordingly, after a week of rumours of yet more massive loans to Britain from overseas banks and the open announcement that the Bank for International Settlements had lent about £90m to permit the repayment of Britain's debt to the International Monetary Fund, the government was at last, on 18 November, obliged to do what it had consistently tried to avoid: to devalue the pound. The old rate had been $2·80 to the pound. Devaluation of 14·3 per cent changed the rate to $2·40 to the pound. Britain's lead was followed by some of the smaller members of the Commonwealth in the Caribbean and West Africa, by Cyprus and Malta, Malawi, Ceylon and New Zealand. Iceland, Ireland, Israel and Spain also followed; and Denmark, Hong Kong and Fiji devalued to a lesser extent.

Devaluation was accompanied by further international credits to Britain of $3000m, by a third increase in the British Bank Rate (which now rose to 8 per cent), and by the announcement of another round of government economies. It was also accompanied by the resignation of James Callaghan, who had been forced by circumstances to disregard a pledge to preserve the parity of the pound. The new Chancellor of the Exchequer was Roy Jenkins. Callaghan took over the Home Secretaryship, which Jenkins had relinquished.

---

[1] Harold Wilson, speech welcoming Sir Robert Menzies at Guildhall 12.7.66
[2] Wilson, House of Commons debate, 20.7.66. *Keesing* p. 21533
[3] Callaghan, Budget speech, 11.4.67. *Keesing* p. 22028

37

The struggle for
economic stability

By itself devaluation could not bring about recovery. The struggle for economic stability had to go on. Britain was deeply in debt to foreign lenders and the deficit on visible trade, amounting in 1967 to £557m, could not possibly be compensated for by an improved invisible balance. Britain's exports were likely to cost purchasers about one-seventh less than they had been paying previously, as long as the British advantage was not eroded by inflation at home unparalleled by comparable inflation elsewhere. However, the costs of imports from countries which had not also devalued, including the costs of the raw materials of industry, were bound to rise by an approximately similar amount, and demands were in the end likely to arise at home for increased incomes to meet rising prices. In fact, month after month throughout 1968 and the first half of 1969, nothing happened to suggest to the British public that devaluation and all the other restrictive measures that had accompanied it were having any effect at all. The government's popularity, judged by election results, ebbed away to such an extent that comparatively few Labour seats seemed unassailable. Only after August, 1969, did the actions of 1967 at last appear to have been justified.

HARSH MEASURES

Further cuts in the government's future programmes were announced in January, 1968. The withdrawal of the forces from the Far East (apart from Hong Kong) and the Persian Gulf was to be accelerated and completed by the end of 1971 instead of by the mid-seventies. An order for fifty F1-11 military aircraft was cancelled. The raising of the school-leaving age was to be deferred from 1971 to 1973. Free milk in secondary schools was to be brought to an end. Financial aid from the Ministry of Education to the Direct Grant schools was to be reduced. A charge of 2s 6d (12½p) was to be made on medicines prescribed under the National Health Service, more than had been imposed under the Conservatives and abolished in Labour's earlier, ardent days. Expenditure on housing, roads and technological research was to be cut. To many Labour M.P.s, especially the Left-wingers, these measures, particularly the reduction of funds for the social services, were very regrettable, and, just as Miss Margaret Herbison had resigned from the Ministry of Social Security when the price of school meals had been raised in July, 1967, so now Lord Longford resigned from the office of Lord Privy Seal as a protest against the postponement of the plan to raise the school-leaving age. However, the government, which had in comparison with the Conservatives been extravagant, felt obliged to stand firm. Roy Jenkins predicted a hard budget later in the year—though, according to his critics, by ill-chosen timing of this forecast he allowed the public two months of undesirable hard spending before new tax burdens were imposed.

Jenkins's Budget speech, in March, 1968, emphasised the need

The trade deficit and ultimate surplus under Labour. *Source:*
The Economist

for a 2 per cent reduction in consumption, both to make more goods available for export and to reduce imports. To achieve this, additional taxation amounting in a full year to £923m was imposed. Among other measures the Selective Employment Tax was to be raised by 50 per cent, so that the Treasury would now receive and retain 37s 6d (£1·87½) a week for each employee in service trades. The Chancellor sought to reconcile the country to SET by indicating that the total cost of employing labour in services in Britain would still be less than in any country of the E.E.C. 'Our over-all figure will be about 14 per cent,' he said, 'as against about 16 per cent in Luxemburg and Germany, 19 per cent in Holland, 27 per cent in Belgium, 37 per cent in France, and 45 per cent in Italy. The on-costs of employing manufacturing labour here will, of course, be only a fraction of those in any of these countries.'[1] Conservatives remained anxious to repeal SET when the chance was offered, though they could not deny the need for draconian measures to rectify the persistent weaknesses of the economy.

The Budget was followed in May by renewed restrictions on bank lending. In June another loan, of £583m, was received from the I.M.F. In July, in the face of opposition from twenty-three Labour M.P.s as well as from Conservatives and Liberals, a Prices and Incomes Act extended the powers of the government to delay increases of prices from seven months to twelve, imposed a ceiling of 3½ per cent on wage increases, and provided that excessive dividends should not be paid. In September another large sum, £833m, was borrowed from the Bank of International Settlements. In November, since in spite of the Chancellor's budgetary discouragement the British public appeared still to be spending no less than it had spent in the second half of 1967, another round of hire-purchase regulations was promulgated. And, also in November, in the hope of reducing imports without imposing tariffs, importers of most goods other than basic foods, fuel, raw materials and certain goods from developing countries were required to deposit with the Customs 50 per cent of the value of the goods before the Customs would release them. The deposits would be refunded after 180 days, but the government expected that the restrictions on bank lending would make it difficult for importers to procure the required sums and that they would consequently be deterred from buying overseas. The scheme, which was intended to operate for a year, affected just over a third of Britain's total imports.

Notwithstanding all the regulations, restrictions and taxes, the situation at the end of 1968 remained extremely disappointing. Debts to foreign and international banks had reached their peak of £3363m. Reserves were no higher than £1009m. The balance of payments deficit was almost as high as the 1967 deficit. The volume of imported manufactures, even at the higher prices brought about by devaluation, still rose by 16 per cent, far higher than expected. It was widely feared that the advantages of devaluation were being whittled away by the inflation which was persistently increasing the costs of British exports. Yet, in a democratic country, there was a limit to the amount of compulsion that a government could exert over the citizens who had elected it. Not much was left for Labour now except to wait in anticipation that its measures would belatedly produce the required results in 1969.

1968 had at least provided evidence that Britain was not alone in all its dilemmas. In March the United States' balance of payments problems, the decline of its gold stock and rumours about future developments contributed to a rapid and unprecedented increase in the demand for gold and a corresponding failure of confidence in paper currencies. On this occasion it was the dollar that was particularly affected, though the solution to the crisis, the adoption of a two-tier gold price system, was one of world-wide significance. Eight months later expectations of an upward revaluation of the German mark and fears of a French devaluation of the franc resulted in a massive flow of capital into Germany and ominous losses by France; and although at the time both the German and French governments adopted measures other than an alteration of the parity of their currencies to restore financial stability to Western Europe, in the end expectations were fulfilled and both revaluation and devaluation had to take place.

Inflation was also an international problem, by no means peculiar to Britain.

BELATED RECOVERY

In the summer of 1969 British fortunes appeared at last to change for the better. In August a trade surplus of £40m was achieved, and surpluses were thereafter recorded each month until April 1970. Over 1969 as a whole the surplus on current account was £444m, invisible earnings having brought in a quite exceptional total of £587m. Exports had risen by 12 per cent in value. British trade with the E.E.C. and the EFTA countries, with the developing countries of the sterling area and with Japan flourished particularly. Imports, owing to higher prices, were up by 5 per cent in value but only 2 per cent in volume. In his budget speech in April, 1970, Roy Jenkins described the statistics as showing 'the largest positive figures ever recorded either for current account alone or for current and long-term capital account combined.'[2] Figures published in March, 1970, actually revealed a visible trade surplus for the previous nine months of £87m, a state of affairs all the more encouraging since visible surpluses had been earned in only two years since 1822. It became possible at last to pay off a very substantial proportion of the debt to the international banking organisations. In January, 1970, limitations on the foreign currency allowances for travel in non-sterling countries could be ended. Import deposits could be reduced in May.

The extent to which this reversal of fortunes had been brought about by government economies and other restrictive policies and the delayed part played in it by devaluation in November, 1967, could not, of course, be exactly defined. The welcome accorded to it both at home and overseas, though, was very clear. Confidence in sterling had revived. The fact that recovery had occurred despite such disregard of the continuing need for moderation over wage claims that wages and salaries had not been prevented from rising in 1969 by 8 per cent brought about an impressive revival of confidence in the Labour government as well. Not until just before the 1970 general election did the May trade figures suggest that, after all, the situation may not have changed permanently for the better.

---

[1] Roy Jenkins, Budget speech 19.3.68. *Keesing.* p. 22756
[2] Jenkins, Budget speech, 14.4.70. *Keesing* p. 23970

38

The economy, planned and unplanned, under Labour

PLANNING FOR EXPANSION

The planned economy, traditionally a theoretical aspect of Labour policy, and put into operation even more fervently by a Conservative government, continued without interruption after the 1964 election. George Brown, at the head of the Department of Economic Affairs, was entitled First Secretary of State and endowed with a dignity greater than that of any other member of the Cabinet apart from the Prime Minister. Under him, the National Economic Development Council, initiated by the Conservative ministry, continued to plan. The nine so-called Little Neddies which had come into existence by the summer of 1964 to plan the futures of individual industries, multiplied until there were twenty-one, covering about two-thirds of the firms that remained in the private sector. Eleven economic planning regions were created, each with a council which included representatives of local government, industry and commerce, the trade unions and universities. A similar number of planning boards, composed of civil servants, came into being, to coexist with the established local offices of the various government departments. The First Secretary's elaborate and ambitious National Plan for all aspects of the economy was published in September, 1965.

An essential feature of the planning of the sixties was the emphasis that it laid on the development of each region of Britain, particularly of Scotland, Wales, Northern England and Northern Ireland, which had not experienced prosperity comparable to that which had since the war increased the wealth of the South East and the Midlands. There was, at least until the beginning of the next decade, no party disagreement about

275

policies to be followed in the less affluent development areas. While limitations were maintained on the building of new office blocks and factories in London and its commuter belt and in the Birmingham area, every encouragement was given to those who wished to establish their firms in more remote regions. Half the new factories approved in 1965 were to be built in Scotland, Wales and Northern England; only 30 per cent in the South East, the Midlands and Eastern England. Even more generous financial help (45 per cent of the costs) was granted for building and equipping factories in Northern Ireland. The Board of Trade continued a policy of creating industrial estates, moving in 1965 into Lanarkshire and Teesside. It continued, also, to help private industry to open new factories: £42m was allotted to this type of aid in 1965, among the recipients being Imperial Chemical Industries at Ardeer (Ayrshire) and Ford at Swansea. When in 1967 the Selective Employment Tax was introduced it was arranged that an extra premium should be paid back to employers in development areas as an additional incentive to the establishment or expansion of industry in these parts of the country.

A Northern Ireland Economic Council and a Highlands and Islands Development Board were added in 1965 to the similar bodies for Wales and North-East England. The Highlands Board was designed to promote the economic and social development of the seven crofting counties of North Scotland by buying land, building, introducing industry, arranging grants or loans for farmers and industrialists, providing training facilities and encouraging tourism. It was followed by a series of other new Boards, Councils, Corporations and Commissions. In the end, few aspects of economic life were not covered. Those of which most was heard, the Industrial Reorganisation Corporation and the Prices and Incomes Board, must be considered in this chapter. Reference is made in Chapter 48 to the involvement of government, Conservative and Labour alike, in particular industries which were confronted either by exceptionally large research costs or by abnormal difficulties liable to result in serious social distress.

The Industrial Reorganisation Corporation was provided with resources amounting to £150m which it could use to enable industry to enhance its efficiency. In bestowing its loans it required proof that they would be used to benefit the national economy, that money was not available from other sources, and that a profit could reasonably be expected from the project which had been assisted. It gave particular encouragement to the merger of companies where fragmentation appeared to have been harmful to the industry concerned: for example, to the merger in 1968 of Leyland and the British Motor Holdings, of the General Electric Company and Associated Electrical Industries, and of G.E.C. and English Electric. By 1970 it had become especially concerned with the production of machine tools, a sphere in which West German output had gone rapidly ahead of British. A loan to Leyland depended on the Company's purchase of British-made machine tools. Twenty million pounds was loaned to Rolls-Royce, £6m to the ailing ship-building firm, Cammel Laird, £10m to the Lancashire textile industry to encourage re-equipment in an increasingly competitive world and the amalgamation of small firms. The Corporation was also interested in international reorganisation, bringing together British and European companies.

Mergers of shipyards were stimulated by the Ship Building Industry Act of 1967, which empowered a board for the industry to make large loans to assist reorganisation. Among the principal beneficiaries were the Scottish companies which combined as Upper Clyde Shipbuilders. Reorganisation was here clearly desirable. Rising costs, among other problems, were contributing to the difficulties facing the industry, and by the end of the sixties Britain had been left far behind as a shipbuilding nation by Japan, and had also been passed by Sweden.

None of these developments was, at the time, politically controversial, though by 1970 Conservatives had reached the conclusion that it was no longer desirable to spend large sums on special concessions to manufacturers establishing industries in the development areas, and others had decided that the endeavours to limit new office building in London were futile and that redevelopment of twilight areas might, after all, be allowed to take place. In one other industrial sphere party antagonism was as pronounced as ever: renationalisation of iron and steel. A White Paper proposing this in April, 1965, was accepted in the Commons as a basis for legislation only by a margin of 310 votes to 306. Only after the general election of 1966, which gave Labour a very safe majority, did the government act. The Bill was introduced in July, 1966, and passed in

March, 1967, after the longest committee stage in Parliament's history. A new justification for the measure was the existence of twenty-two foreign companies outside the Communist world which had a greater capacity than Britain's largest, the already nationalised Richard Thomas and Baldwin. Labour claimed that only a state-owned industry could compete with the even larger overseas consortia planned for the late sixties and seventies. On the other hand, the Liberal spokesman, Richard Wainwright, condemned the bill as 'a wholly unnecessary and ill-timed political luxury',[1] and in the Lords Lord Erroll of Hale referred to a loss by Thomas and Baldwin's of £30m in the previous four years. In the end, however, only thirteen other large companies, previously nationalised and later returned by a Conservative government to private ownership, were involved. Nearly 200 companies, producing about 60 per cent of Britain's steel, remained in private hands. Richard Marsh, the Minister of Power, looked forward to a 'process of genuine competition' between private and public sectors.

A Bill to nationalise the docks aroused far less wrath. It was, in any case, brought to a halt by the general election of 1970.

PROBLEMS CONFRONTING THE EXPANSION PROGRAMME

The 1965 National Plan, which was intended as a realistic survey of future achievements, expressed the hope that gross domestic output would increase by 3·8 per cent a year and that exports would rise by 5·2 per cent a year. Actually, domestic growth amounted to about 2·2 per cent, while exports increased by about 3 per cent. Between 1963 and 1970 the percentage output per man hour in manufacturing rose less in Britain (where it rose 27 per cent) than in any other industrial country apart from the United States. The Italian increase was 50 per cent, the Japanese 102 per cent. The increase in industrial production in Britain (23 per cent) was lower than that in any other industrial country. Japanese increase amounted to 122 per cent. Wage cost per unit of output in manufacturing rose by 20 per cent in Britain, by 10 per cent or less in Italy, France, Germany and Japan. In 1963 the British share of the world's exports was 15·4 per cent; by the end of the decade it was less than 11 per cent. Such results were all the more disappointing in view of the efforts lavished on economic development by politicians and experts alike and of the emphasis placed on growth in every advanced country of the world. To have spoken of Britain's failure would doubtless have been to exaggerate; but those who were concerned with the performance of the nation were bound to consider why it had not done better. Each individual company might have suggested its particular reasons. Two factors which concerned many of them merit some consideration: the inadequacy, despite measures of encouragement, of the investment programme, and the wave of industrial strikes that held up output, especially during the later years of the Labour ministry.

The short-comings of an apparently inescapable 'Stop–Go', whether practised by a Conservative government or by Labour, and the tendency for drastic measures to rectify one weakness only by creating another have already been indicated. To cut down domestic consumption and check inflation, and thereby to make available at stable prices an increased quantity of goods for export, and to solve successive blance of payments crises, governments were constrained to restrict the amount of money in circulation by requiring the banks to limit their lending, by raising Bank Rate, by reducing government spending and by imposing heavier taxation. These measures might have solved immediate problems. But they also involved a reduction of the investment without which industry could not easily expand its output. A government survey, *The Task Ahead* (1969), admitted that while investment in the non-manufacturing spheres of the private sector had risen, investment during the middle sixties in the manufacturing industries on which British exporters depended had 'lagged badly'. Between 1962 and 1967 all increases in industrial investment had occurred in the public sector, government concerns and the nationalised industries. Most of Britain's main competitors were devoting a higher proportion of their total resources to investment than were the British.

STRIKES

To overemphasise the impact of strikes during the earlier years of Labour administration would not be realistic. Professor H. A. Turner doubted whether they deprived the country of more than one-thousandth of the annual national product. It was easy to show that the number of million working days lost between 1907 and 1926 or during the 1890s was very much higher than the number of days lost at any time since the Second World War, or indeed since the General Strike of 1926. The International Labour Office, reporting on the decade 1959 to 1968, could show that, with an annual average of 262 working days lost for each thousand employees, Britain's record was better than those of Japan (282 days lost), France (312), Canada (784) and the United States (1114).[2] The average British workman on strike between 1962 and 1968 withdrew his labour for only two or three days at a time, whereas between 1892 and 1931 the number of days lost by strikers during each five-year period had not fallen below fourteen and had risen as high as forty-four. However, at a time when Britain was striving to rectify pronounced economic weaknesses and was witnessing a progressive decline of its share of world trade, these arguments brought limited consolation. The I.L.O. report, while showing that other countries suffered even worse labour problems, also revealed that between 1959 and 1968 West Germany had lost through strikes only 20 working days for each thousand employees and Sweden only 15, while some smaller countries, such as Belgium, the Netherlands and Switzerland, had better records than Britain. Moreover, only five other countries had a greater number of strikes than Britain. With an annual average between 1952 and 1968 of about 2300 the position was considerably worse than at any period during the previous half century. Moreover, strikes of small groups of men tended to disrupt other branches of industry, with resultant losses of output far higher than those revealed by the strike statistics.

A government analysis of the strikes which occurred between 1964 and 1967 showed that more than 96 per cent were unofficial, were not inspired by the trade union leadership, were generally started in defiance of union arrangements for settling disputes and were responsible for about three-quarters of the working days lost. The average annual number of unofficial strikes during these years was 2125, the average number of workers involved 663 300, whereas there was an average of only 82 strikes begun with union approval, involving only 84 700 employees. While in earlier decades the industry most prone to stoppages had been coal-mining, the worst records of the sixties,

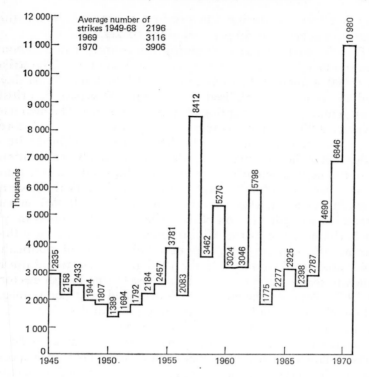

Working days lost through industrial disputes 1945–70
Years between 1900 and 1945 when more than 10m working
days were lost through industrial disputes (thousands)

1908	10 790	1921	85 870
1911	10 160	1922	19 850
1912	40 890	1923	10 670
1919	34 970	1926	162 230
1920	26 570		

judged by the number of days lost for each 1000 employees,
were those of the dockers, the vehicle builders and the ship
builders, with 1766 days, 831 and 412 days lost respectively,
compared with an annual average for all industries of 84. The
commonest motive was the achievement of a higher wage,
though even in 1970, when demands for wage increases exceeded

any put forward during the previous twenty-five years, this factor provoked only 59 per cent of the strikes.

Clearly, some strikes confronting the country while Labour was in office had far wider repercussion than others. The strike of 27000 seamen in the early summer of 1966 lasted for 47 days and eventually immobilised more than 900 vessels in British ports, entailing the disruption of trade of all kinds. The men had received a 25 per cent pay increase only just over a year before. They were now demanding a further increase combined with a reduction of the working week, which would involve calculations of overtime, particularly difficult when ships were at sea. Concessions were eventually granted, though only after the government had declared a state of emergency, and Harold Wilson had broadcast a condemnation of the strike as 'totally unnecessary'. In Parliament the Prime Minister had expressed the view that behind the dispute lay 'a tightly knit group of politically motivated men' who had, in the 1966 general election, 'utterly failed to secure acceptance of their views by the British elector-ate'.[3] Challenged to be specific, Wilson named eight Communists, whose ultimate aim he considered to be the ruthless destruction of the government's prices and incomes policy.

Strikes by dockers inevitably had repercussions as wide as those following a seamen's strike: ships were held up, exports lost, trade diverted to continental ports. The first really effective assault on Labour's policy of incomes restraint was made at the end of 1967 by an unofficial dock strike at Liverpool, which also illustrated the inability of the Transport and General Workers' Union leadership to control a large proportion of its members. At other times disputes over the use of containers caused disruption: fear of redundancy tended to prove stronger than desire for the efficiency which the introduction of containers of standard size would denote. Sympathetic strikes also characterised unrest in the docks. Merseyside militancy infected dockers elsewhere.

The stoppages affecting the motor industry were significant not merely because their progressive increase in number during the sixties made vehicle builders the most turbulent single section of the industrial community by the end of the decade, but also because they inescapably affected a potentially very lucrative overseas market and showed plainly the chain effects liable to follow from a strike by a small group of workers: for example, strikes at a Bromborough brake factory, or by a number of fork-lift truck operators at Linwood, Glasgow, by workers on a Cardiff gear box and transmission plant, or by the employees at Pilkington's glass works at St Helens eventually created difficulties which caused hundreds of others to be laid off in other factories. All the major vehicle concerns in the end suffered from the breakdown of relations or from the unquenchable desire for higher wages.

Forthright condemnation of the men who had brought about conditions of this sort came in 1969 from Ray Gunter, Minister of Labour until his resignation from the government in June, 1968, and, earlier, for eight years President of the Transport Salaried Staffs Association. 'We have had the spectacle,' he said, 'of the Prime Minister and his Ministers being bullied and threatened by a tiny but powerful handful of trade union leaders' whose authority rested on only a very small fraction of their Union membership—as low as 6 per cent in one case. At the same time 'small groups of men can exert tremendous power, what appears sometimes as blackmail. Two hundred men can by strike action put 8000 men out of work within a week.'[4] Gunter believed that strikes such as were occurring in the sixties represented a complete breakdown of communication between the various classes involved in industry.

In the hope of cutting down the number of strikes and re-establishing the essential communication, the government introduced, in January, 1969, a White Paper entitled *In Place of Strife*. Along with a number of concessions designed to strengthen the unions and to encourage their acceptance of the other intended legislation, this proposed to check 'wildcat' strikes in breach of agreed procedure for settling disputes by imposing a compulsory twenty-eight days' 'conciliation pause' during which enquiry should be made and solution, if possible, be reached. The White Paper also suggested that a ballot indicating approval or disapproval should precede any potentially damaging official strike and that, in certain circumstances, inter-union disputes should be ended by an imposed solution. Barbara Castle, now Minister for Employment and Productivity, fought with great determination for acceptance of these measures. They were, as *The Times* hinted, 'the least that any government could put forward in the present climate of opinion.' The Conservatives, and the Confederation of British Industry, would have been more content with more drastic legislation. And yet no Bill was permitted to reach the statute book. The outcry from the Labour back benches was so intense and the prospect of the disintegration of the party so unnerving that in the end Barbara Castle and the Prime Minister, who had backed her, were obliged to surrender. Nothing, after all, had been gained other than a solemn and binding undertaking by the T.U.C. that it would henceforth make determined endeavours to prevent unofficial strikes.

Developments of the next eighteen months suggested that the solemn undertaking was practically worthless. When the President of the Amalgamated Union of Engineering and Foundry Workers, Hugh Scanlon, announced that his policy committee could not delegate, either to the government or to the T.U.C., responsibility for determining workers' wages and conditions he was in effect ensuring that one of the most important and most militant unions, at least, would accept no remedy that it did not devise itself. More than ever, the impression gained ground that the unions had become pressure groups against which Parliament was no longer effective.

In 1969, 3116 strikes occurred and 6·8m working days were lost. In the first six months of 1970 2296 strikes deprived the country of just over 5m working days and showed substantial increases in all but five of the twenty-six sectors of industry distinguished by the Department of Economic Affairs. The statistics for the various branches of engineering were particularly disturbing. Underlying the discontent were demands, made over and over again, for higher wages.

INCOMES

The incomes policy instituted by the government had indeed been no more lastingly successful than earlier attempts to prevent wages from outrunning productivity. It could be shown that despite constant moralising, during the period 1953 to 1967 productivity per head had increased annually by only 2 to $2\frac{1}{2}$ per cent, while the average annual wage increase amounted to about 6 per cent, higher than both prices and company profits. A Prices and Incomes Board, under the chairmanship of an ex-M.P., Aubrey Jones, was established in 1965 to replace the National Incomes Commission, with which the

Unions had always refused to co-operate; and the fact that by the end of 1969 about 30 per cent of the labour force was covered by productivity agreements may have indicated that this body had achieved a certain success. However, the 8 per cent wage increases granted to the average manual worker between October, 1968 and October, 1969, and the considerably larger increases of the next six months plainly denoted ultimate failure. Freeze and severe restraint and a requirement that an 'early warning' (thirty days' notice) should be given of intended price and wage increases could be made to operate for a limited period, but by 1970 neither main party any longer felt real confidence in their effectiveness.

By January, 1970, demands for higher incomes had become explosive, and all classes had been affected. Teachers went on strike for an additional £135 a year. Air-line pilots demanded an extra £85 a week for flying Jumbo jets. Car workers at Fords demanded 38 per cent more, to give them parity with Rootes workers at Ryton, near Coventry. Seamen aimed at a 50 per cent rise. The more extravagant demands were not conceded, but increases of 10 per cent or more had been awarded by April, 1970, to construction workers, nurses, postmen, teachers, police, local government employees and electricity supply workers, and so many other awards had been made or were under consideration that the Treasury was predicting an average rise of 13 per cent during the course of the year. What was particularly surprising about demands on this scale was that they had been made, and conceded, at a time when, for several years, unemployment had been comparatively high: above, or not far short of 600000. It was clear that fear of losing an occupation was no longer an effective disincentive to the presentation of a renewed wage demand. Clearly, also, the end of inflation was nowhere in sight.

---

[1] Debates, House of Commons, 25.7.66. and House of Lords, 13.2.67. *Keesing* p. 22170–1

[2] *Statistics of Strikes*, I.L.O. Report, *Keesing* p. 23716. For Professor Turner's views see *The Times* 15.5.69

[3] Wilson, House of Commons, 20.6.66. *Keesing* p. 21548

[4] Ray Gunter, speech at Manchester, *The Times*, 2.10.69

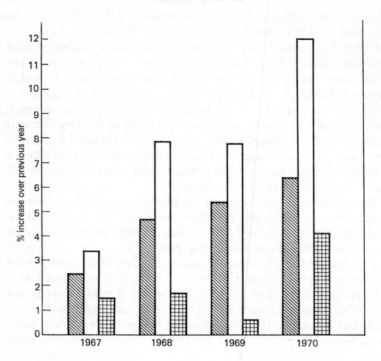

Rising prices and incomes 1967–70. *Source*: *The Times*, based on information from the Central Statistical Office and Department of Employment.

▨ Retail Prices

▢ Average earnings (of all employees in Great Britain)

▦ Personal disposable income at 1963 prices (an approximate indicator of the real increase in personal purchasing power)

39

Social developments
under Labour

By 1964 the essential features of the Welfare State had been so thoroughly established that little of fundamental significance could be added. The Labour party under Harold Wilson's leadership sought, however, to earn the reputation of a dynamic and vigorous body in an age of rapid technological development. It was therefore not to be expected that the government would adopt a Palmerstonian view that nothing needed to be done. The later sixties were indeed characterised by the passage of a series of measures of very varied nature if not of outstanding importance. Some of the measures were controversial, though divisions of opinion did not always evolve along party lines. Only two developments were essentially socialist or egalitarian in character; and only one of these, the renationalisation of iron and steel, which is considered elsewhere, would have been quite unimaginable under a Conservative ministry. The second was a progressively more determined endeavour to establish comprehensive schools throughout Britain.

EDUCATION AND SOCIAL EQUALITY

The comprehensive system had been pioneered in Britain in the late forties by a small number of councils: London above all, the West Riding, Coventry and Bristol. During the years of Conservative government a number of other councils, notably Leicestershire, introduced variations on the theme, devised particularly to eliminate selection at the age of eleven, which increasingly caused anxiety, not merely in Labour circles. By 1965, when a Department of Education circular 'requested' local authorities to prepare plans, 262 comprehensive schools were already in existence, catering for 8 per cent of the school

287

population. It was left to the councils to determine the type of schools that they would establish. In some regions the simple expedient of sending all pupils to the same school for the duration of their educational careers was adopted. Some other councils established separate schools to take pupils aged between eleven and thirteen or fourteen and the older pupils. Sixth-form colleges, combined with normal comprehensives for those under sixteen, also came into being. An infinite variety of difficulties arose. It was not always easy for schools to enrol either the social or the intellectual cross-sections which the most zealous theorists regarded as desirable. Only in a limited number of areas, such as Anglesey, did it prove possible to establish an entirely comprehensive system, and generally comprehensive schools and established grammar schools had to co-exist, often, as in London, to the disadvantage of the former, which had difficulty in attracting the academically more able. Since the creation of many entirely new schools big enough to educate about 2000 pupils would have been prohibitively expensive, older buildings, sometimes widely separated from each other, had to be used by the same school. Once the comprehensives had been brought into being, the decision whether to stream into forms of different ability or to abandon selection altogether had still to be made.

Always, doubts remained about the wisdom of sacrificing successful grammar schools with centuries of tradition, and perhaps of outstanding achievements, behind them. As a result, only a very small number of local authorities had gone over entirely to a comprehensive system by 1970. The independent schools, 179 Direct Grant schools, and more than a thousand local authority or voluntary aided grammar schools survived, albeit anxiously and uncertainly. Out of the 163 local authorities responsible for education 22 had either refused to submit plans for any type of comprehensive school or had drawn up projects which the Labour Ministry had rejected as unsatisfactory. However, the need for comprehensives had become, by 1970, an article of Labour faith, and in that year Edward Short, the Secretary of State for Education, introduced a Bill to compel councils to prepare acceptable plans. Bolton, Bournemouth, Bury, Kingston and Richmond on Thames, Rutland, Westmorland, Worcester, Buckinghamshire, Norfolk, Salford, Torbay and Warley were now to produce obligatorily what requests had failed to elicit. Birmingham, Gloucester, Harrow,

Hillingdon, Nottingham, Plymouth, Southend, Sutton and Wolverhampton were to make a renewed attempt. The passage of the Bill was checked, though, by the general election, after which a final decision was again left, at least for the time being, in the hands of the local authorities. By this time about 1200 comprehensive schools, with 26 per cent of the country's school pupils, were already in existence.

The notable reports produced on various types of education under the Conservatives had still not exhausted the themes on which committees and commissions could make recommendations. Important surveys of primary and Public School education were published in 1967 and 1968. The first of these, compiled by a committee under the chairmanship of Lady Plowden, was concerned with the 21 000 schools which served the four million primary school children. It advocated particularly special aid towards the provision of better buildings, more generous equipment and a greater number of teachers for the schools in poor areas. It was characteristic of the time that the report should deplore the losses both to the children of poorer neighbourhoods and to the community arising from an avoidable, and consequently intolerable, inequality of educational opportunity. A similar concern with youthful victims of social disadvantages was expressed by the *Newsom Report* on the Public Schools, which recommended that at least half the places at such schools should be allocated to the children of broken or migratory homes, orphans, or those with special aptitudes not catered for near their homes. 'The independent schools are a divisive influence in society,'[1] agreed a majority of the commission. Ninety per cent of their pupils came from the professional classes. 'There is no sign that these divisions will disappear if the schools are left alone. They themselves deplore it. It is time we helped them to change a situation which was not of their making.' After the publication of this advice the commission was reconstituted under Professor D. V. Donnison and issued a second report, recommending that the Direct Grant schools[2] should fall into line with the moves towards comprehensive education.

The essential theoretical aim of the educational reformers was the encouragement of talent in whatever social environment it might be discovered. Critics were emerging during the late sixties, however, who feared that in their concern for granting equal opportunities to all and for sparing any child the stigma of failure the theorists were in reality, even though unintentionally, weighting the scales against their really able pupils. Intense competition in spheres of sport was not merely permissible: it was to be encouraged. In an academic sphere competition was, as far as possible, to be eliminated. Academic egalitarianism, though, was beginning to provoke a backlash.

CURRENCY, ABORTION, CENSORSHIP, JUSTICE, THE ELECTORATE

A change of a different sort, which the public accepted calmly, was the progressive introduction of a decimal currency, plans for which were announced in December, 1966. By 1970 10 penny, 5 penny and 50 penny pieces were in use, though still popularly referred to in terms of shillings. Halfpennies and half crowns had become as obsolete as farthings. Metric measurements were also bringing Britain into line with the Continent. Measures which aroused more passionate debate were the Acts rescinding legal punishments for homosexual relations between consenting adults (July, 1967) and (October, 1967) allowing abortions to be obtained legally on a greater number of grounds than previously, thereby preventing the birth of thousands (54000 in 1969) of unwanted or illegitimate children. Another Act ended the censorship of plays, though nobody could believe that this was as effective a method of encouraging drama as the enlightened state patronage, directed by Jennie Lee (Mrs Aneurin Bevan), the Labour Minister for the Arts, for such organisations as the Royal Shakespeare Company and the National Theatre and for English opera.

Endeavours were made, by Roy Jenkins's Criminal Justice Act (1967), to speed up procedure in the criminal courts, to permit agreement by ten out of twelve jurors in criminal cases to suffice, and, while encouraging the law to 'be consistently liberal and rational in its approach',[3] to enable it more effectively to deal, in the Home Secretary's words, with 'the most menacing crime situation with which this country has recently been confronted.' At the same time the comparatively novel iniquity of dangerous driving, with its expanding total of victims killed and wounded, was assailed by regulations and propaganda directed against drinking and driving, and by the introduction of the breathalyser to test the quantity of alcohol drunk by a driver. In December, 1969, on a free vote, Commons and Lords agreed that the death penalty should be permanently abolished.

Various projects for the alteration of the machinery of government continued to attract the legislators. In November, 1968, a White Paper on the reform of the House of Lords suggested that heredity should no longer be an automatic qualification for membership and that the House's powers to delay a Bill should be restricted to six months. In 1969 a major reconstruction of the areas of local government was proposed. More immediately effective was the Representation of the People Act 1969, which reduced the voting age from 21 to 18. This concession was expected to add 2·8m new voters to the register. Psephologists claimed that since working-class families tended to be larger than those of the professional classes, and since young voters were inclined to follow the voting habits of their parents, the Labour party would enjoy a potential advantage; but that this might be nullified by the fact that about 10 per cent more young Conservative supporters registered than Labour supporters. When the issue was put to the test, first at a by-election at Bridgwater and then at the general election of June, 1970, it was found impossible to draw any significant conclusions about the political allegiance of the newly enfranchised. The decline of the proportion of the electorate who voted did not suggest that the 1969 Act had injected any substantial new enthusiasm into the processes of party rivalry.

URBAN DEVELOPMENT

The Labour government maintained the policies of its predecessors in connection with urban development and the dispersal of Britain's population. Plans were suggested in 1966 for the creation of populous new cities on Humberside (between Goole and the sea), Severnside (a region stretching from Gloucester and Bristol to Newport) and Tayside (from Dundee to Perth). In 1967 a decision was taken to develop a new town of at least 250000 people in North Buckinghamshire, round Milton Keynes. Peterborough, Ipswich, Northampton, Warrington, Leyland and Chorley (south Lancashire) and Dawley (incorporating Wellington and Oakengates in Shropshire) were listed by the planners as towns to be greatly expanded, as counter-attractions to existing conurbations. The enlargement of the New Towns of the fifties in England and Scotland was also considered. In Northern Ireland, which had hitheito not figured prominently in the movement for urban expansion, Craigavon, linking Lurgan and Portadown, was designated a new town to take the overspill population of Belfast, while a region of forty square miles including Antrim and Ballymena and stretching from Lough Neagh to the Glens of Antrim was also to be developed, though without sacrificing its finer scenery and farmland. Coleraine, Portrush and Portstewart were to become the focal points of a growth centre.

The house-building programme, whether it was conducted privately or by local authorities, resulted in 1968 in the completion of a record total of 413700 homes. Although shortages still existed in the conurbations, the more acute insufficiency of houses of earlier years was elsewhere at last disappearing. Unfortunately, an official admission that more than two million houses in Britain were, by modern standards, unfit for habitation indicated that much remained to be changed. The slums of Glasgow continued to earn particular condemnation, despite the city's twenty-year clearance scheme which had begun in 1960. The organisation known as Shelter, one of the most successful voluntary undertakings of its time, gave wide publicity to the squalid conditions surviving in some poorer city regions. A quite different problem was the soaring cost of house-building. It was calculated, by the Co-operative Permanent Building Society, that between 1964 and 1969 prices rose by 34 per cent. Materials cost about 15 per cent more, the average weekly earnings of building workers rose by nearly 30 per cent and land prices increased by nearly 70 per cent. During their election campaign in 1964 Labour candidates had expressed particular anxiety about land prices; but there was widespread suspicion that their government's Betterment Levy, which took 40 per cent of the difference between the original value of the land and its market value once planning permission had been obtained, was contributing to the inflation. Whatever the truth may have been, house prices undoubtedly illustrated the worst features of the apparently unconquerable rise in the cost of living.

As the population grew and an increasing area was absorbed

by expanding towns, emphasis by scientists and newspapers on the damage being caused by pollution of the environment became more insistent. Reports of one and a half million tons of grit and ash poured each year into the air over Britain, two million tons of smoke and five million tons of sulphur gases would have been disturbing even if the costs of the resulting corrosion had not been assessed at about £350m (or even £600m) a year. Moreover, these reports were accompanied by accounts of lifeless rivers, polluted by factory waste or an excessive quantity of nitrates washed by rain off agricultural land, of beaches polluted by unsatisfactory methods of sewage disposal, and of sea birds and marine life dying as a result of the discharge of ship's oil into the sea. Revelations of damage to the environment were, it was true, no novelty; but with the approach of 1970, Conservation Year, when wild life and natural resources throughout the world were to receive especial consideration, governing authorities and the public became more conscious of the need for greater care.

The Clean Air Act of 1956 was followed by a second one in 1968 which empowered the Minister of Housing to compel local authorities to issue smoke control orders and imposed further controls over the height of factory chimneys. Claims that these measures had given London a 50 per cent increase of sunshine during an average winter suggested that the legislation had been worth while. At the same time, claims that fish were once again swimming in the Thames as it flowed through London implied that a £40m scheme to purify the river was also proving effective.

The land, where it had been ruined by two centuries of industry, was becoming as much a matter of concern as air and water. One notable project involved the restoration of life to a derelict area on the outskirts of Swansea. Another was the re-establishment of vegetation on the newly levelled mountains of industrial waste which had marred the one-time distressed area on the Cumberland coast.

---

1 First Report of Public Schools Commission under Sir John Newsom, 22.7.68. *Keesing* p. 23057
2 The Direct Grant schools received financial assistance directly from the Ministry of Education on condition that they allocated at least 25 per cent of their places to local authority free-place pupils.
3 Jenkins, Second Reading of Criminal Justice Bill, 12.12.66. *Keesing* p. 22380

40
Britain and the world 1964–70

The ideal of peace remained, throughout the sixties, as elusive as ever. More than half the states of the world were involved in war, international or civil, during the decade, or were preparing for war. The fighting in Vietnam had by the middle of 1970 caused the deaths of 793 000 Vietnamese and American troops, apart from an unknown number of civilians. Conflict between Jews and Arabs on the frontiers of Israel appeared equally interminable. The Nigerian civil war may have resulted in a quarter of a million deaths (the estimates were markedly divergent). At the same time about 700 000 people may have been killed in civil conflict in China, about half a million more may have been massacred in Indonesia, and the tragedies made comparatively little impact outside the countries in which they occurred. Too many of the wars in progress in 1970 were being waged among new nations with arms sold to them by the more advanced industrial nations, including Britain.

RELATIONS WITH WESTERN EUROPE

In these conditions the most favourable claim that could be made was that at least those European peoples who had been at war between 1939 and 1945 had realised that co-operation would have to take the place of conflict. The developments of the fifties continued into the next decade, and after 1964, when Labour attained control in Britain, only one episode, the Russian invasion of Czechoslovakia, seriously interfered with the advance towards closer association in Europe.

Labour's policy was in all essentials a continuation of Conservative policy. Even the American Polaris submarine base in Holy Loch, at the mouth of the Clyde, was retained, despite earlier denunciations from the Left. The enthusiastically welcomed state visit by the Queen and the Duke of Edinburgh to

Germany in May, 1965, symbolised the close relationship which had developed between Britain and Germany. Britain's partners in EFTA were, it was true, affronted by the 15 per cent tariff surcharge which Harold Wilson's government raised

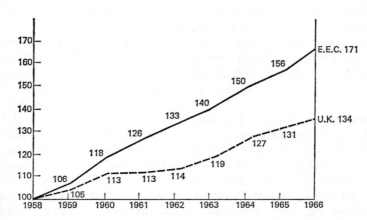

Increase in industrial production in the European Economic Community and in Britain. 1958:100. *Source*: Based on a diagram published by the European Community Information Service.

	1950–70	*1965–70*	
E.E.C.			
Belgium	3·84	5·68	
France	5·64	7·84	
Germany	4·72	6·28	
Italy	6·88	4·78	(6·43 from first quarter 1965 to second quarter 1969)
Netherlands	5·0	7·76	
United Kingdom	2·6	3·44	
Others			
Norway	4·4	3·64	
Sweden	4·88	7·08	
U.S.A.	3·16	1·56	
Canada	3·2	3·0	

Average annual rates of growth of productivity in manufacturing. Source: O.E.C.D. (*The Times*, 1 April 1971)

against their exports as much as against exports from other countries; yet once it had been removed, EFTA was able to go ahead and almost to complete the elimination of tariffs on trade between the seven member countries by the end of 1966, three years earlier than had been originally planned. At the same time, though, even while intra-EFTA trade was growing, the feeling that the association could never effectively rival the Common Market was gaining strength; and consequently, in 1967, after consultation with EFTA partners and after a tour of the Common Market countries' capitals by Harold Wilson and George Brown, Britain once again applied for membership of the E.E.C. Once again, although Conservative support for the application was made clear, a section of the Labour Party, inspired by Douglas Jay and Emanuel Shinwell, opposed it. The main problems were once more seen to be the future of Commonwealth trade with Britain and the reconciliation of E.E.C. and British agricultural policies. And yet again General de Gaulle doubted whether Britain was suited to membership of the E.E.C., while Couve de Murville refused to make concessions on such stumbling blocks as New Zealand's trade outlets and issued ominous forecasts of the undesired consequences for the E.E.C. if Britain, and some of the other EFTA countries, joined. The representatives of West Germany, the Benelux group and Italy rejected the French arguments, but they were powerless to prevent the collapse of negotiations for a second time, and Britain was obliged to postpone again its application until de Gaulle had ceased to be in a position to dictate. Britain did, nonetheless, continue to co-operate with E.E.C. countries in a number of specialised fields: with France, for example, over the production of Concorde aircraft; with Euratom, as well as with Austria, Switzerland and the Scandinavian countries, over research into high temperature nuclear reactors; with Germany and Holland over the production of enriched uranium by processes cheaper than those hitherto employed; and with France, Germany, the Netherlands, Italy (and Australia) over the integration, in 1970, of container-ship operations between Europe and Australia, the division of the revenues, and the establishment of marketing organisations in each country.

Membership of the Council of Europe enabled British delegates to maintain another link with the Continent. Although the

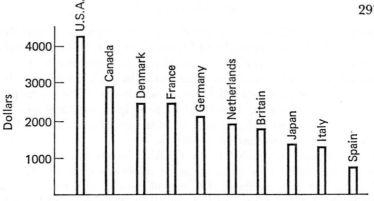

Gross National Product per head, 1968. *Source*: *The Economist*

Council had never developed, as its instigators had hoped, into a European parliament with real international authority, it had at least survived and had encouraged international co-operation on economic, social, cultural, scientific, legal and administrative issues not specifically covered by other organisations. Its Consultative Assembly, enlarged by the addition during the fifties of representatives of Italy, Switzerland, Austria, Malta and Cyprus, became a useful forum for discussion by European M.P.s of such issues as Britain's entry into the E.E.C. Among its positive achievements was the production of a charter for the prevention of water pollution in 1968 and a European pharmacopoeia to standardise the contents of drugs in 1969. Some early enthusiasts, Maurice Edelman and Lord Gladwyn, for example, were still attending its meetings in 1970.

Britain was able also to co-operate with the countries of the Continent as a member of NATO. When in 1966 Michael Stewart declared in the Commons that 'we should stand four-square by NATO'[1] he was expressing an attitude which was consistently expounded in defence White Papers. Until 1968, however, three factors existed which tended to diminish the importance of the organisation or to restrict Britain's contribution. In the first place, the threat from Russia, which had originally provoked the creation of NATO, appeared no longer to be significant. The Communist thaw in Europe, combined with the consistently deteriorating relations between Russia and China, seemed to have deprived NATO of its principal *raison d'être*. In the second place, General de Gaulle decided that membership of NATO limited French sovereign rights and that France should accordingly withdraw from it in 1966. He would not consent that his country 'should efface its personality within international organisations constructed in such a way that the United States can exercise, from within or without, a preponderant influence, to which, in principle, we have only to conform.'[2] He would not accept 'this sort of national abdication'. 'The subordination which is described as integration, which is provided by NATO and which hands over our destiny to foreign authorities will end as far as we are concerned.' The French attitude, by itself, did not, of course, affect the British attitude. A third factor in the situation, though, could not be easily disregarded. With its persistent balance of payments problems, Britain's foreign currency reserves proved quite inadequate for large numbers of troops to be stationed overseas without serious embarrassment. By 1967 it had become necessary for agreements to be made whereby Germany should purchase nearly £50m worth of British military equipment and other goods while the United States spent about £20m more on British goods or facilities for troops; the two countries together providing about seven-eighths of the foreign exchange required to keep British forces in Germany. It was also agreed that 5000 British troops should be withdrawn from the Continent early in 1968.

RELATIONS WITH THE SOVIET UNION

The extent to which British relations with Russia had eased was suggested not only by a visit of the Soviet Prime Minister, Kosygin, to London, and visits of British leaders to Moscow, but by an agreement signed in January, 1968, for Anglo-Soviet co-operation on a wide range of technological issues: in addition to provisions for the exchange of information on the technological aspects of various branches of engineering and transport, the agreement also covered computers, scientific instruments, teaching machines, industrial pollution and microbiological methods of protein production. Unfortunately, the new confidence symbolised by these arrangements did not survive the summer. What would happen, asked Reginald Maudling in the Commons in July, if the Soviet government were to 'impose its will on the Czech people?'[3] The anxiety was quite justified. The Czechs, inspired by Alexander Dubcek, had been introducing their own more liberal form of Communism, and in August, 1968, Russian forces, with troops from other neighbouring Communist countries, invaded to crush the contagion. It was estimated that by the end of the month Czechoslovakia was occupied by 600 000 foreign troops. Gradually, over the next year, the influence of the reformers was broken and their concessions were withdrawn. The Czechs acted with courage and dignity, but confronted with infinitely greater force than they could command themselves, they were as helpless as they had been in 1938 and 1947.

The Russian action was condemned by the United Nations, by the British representative, Lord Caradon, among others. Another condemnation was drawn up by the Security Council, only to provoke the one hundred and fifth Russian veto since the Council was inaugurated. The protests of the British government could not have been more blunt: the action taken by the Soviet government and certain of its allies, declared the British note, was 'a flagrant violation of the United Nations Charter and of all accepted standards of international behaviour . . . in sharp conflict with the often repeated statements by the Soviet government about non-interference with the sovereign rights of independent states. This is a tragedy for . . . the whole world. It is a serious blow to the efforts which so many countries have been making to improve relations between East and West.'[4] No voice of dissent was heard in Britain. The General Council of the T.U.C. came 'to the conclusion that it would no longer be useful to pursue current contacts with the Trade Union movement of the Soviet Union,'[5] and even the British Communist party agreed that military intervention in Czechoslovakia was 'completely unjustified'. The Russians, however, remained unmoved by universal denunciation, and the tendency towards a more relaxed relationship between them and the West was accordingly interrupted.

The anxiety created by these developments found expression in the British White Paper on Defence, published in February, 1969. The need to contain Russian ambitions was now seen to be as vital as it had been two decades previously. Not merely had events in Czechoslovakia demonstrated that the Soviet government was 'prepared to invade an independent state against the wishes of its government and people if it runs no

serious military risks'.[6] Russian warships and aircraft had also
been active during 1968 in the Mediterranean, the Indian Ocean
and international waters round Britain itself. Russia was still
expanding its forces. Its defence estimates for 1968–9 had
increased by 6 per cent, while its scientific estimates, largely
concerned with military expenditure, had gone up by 14 per
cent. The Warsaw Pact countries (the Soviet Union, Poland,
East Germany, Hungary, Czechoslovakia, Rumania, Bulgaria
and Albania) were spending nearly twice the proportion of their
Gross National Product on defence than the NATO countries
were spending. And all this was taking place at a time when the
political instability of Eastern Europe and of the Middle East
was liable at any moment to erupt and to provoke the intervention of other powers. At last it was clear that NATO was,
after all, serving an essential defensive purpose and that, despite
the defection of France in 1966, its strength would have to be
maintained. The White Paper emphasised not only the part that
Britain could play within a NATO framework but the extent
to which its forces had been committed to this international
organisation. Britain was 'the only European power with a role
and military capabilities which cover the three main NATO
fronts from the Arctic to the Caucasus on land, sea and air . . .
We contribute the only European nuclear forces to the integrated military organisation of the alliance.' The Royal Navy
was 'the strongest Western navy in Europe and virtually all of it
is committed to NATO. The British Army of the Rhine and
R.A.F. Germany are a standing guarantee of our involvement.
. . . Most of our forces based in the U.K. are formally committed to NATO.'[7] These forces would be deployed more widely
in Europe in the future, particularly in the Mediterranean; and
the scope of staff talks between the representatives of the
European members of the organisation would be even further
extended in 1969 than they had been during the previous year.
Despite the economies that the government had been constrained to accept and the gradual withdrawal from bases East
of Suez, the defence estimates for 1969–70 still amounted to
£2266m.

PLANS FOR WITHDRAWAL FROM THE EAST

As the situation in Europe became apparently more insecure,

and as the British difficulties in paying for world wide commitments became insurmountable, the determination of Labour (and Liberal) politicians to accelerate withdrawal of British forces from the Far and Middle East gathered momentum. In July, 1967, a White Paper predicted that the forces would be brought back to Europe from Malaysia and Singapore by the mid-seventies. In January, 1968, it was announced that no British troops would remain in these bases, or in the Persian Gulf, after 1971. In December, 1968, the naval dockyard at Singapore was handed over to the government of Singapore, and plans were announced for the transfer to this government and to that of Malaysia of land and equipment worth nearly £20m, for which payment was not being sought. It appeared as if Britain's history as an imperial power East of Suez was being brought generously but very hurriedly to its conclusion.

However, the withdrawal was not planned without protest. The Prime Ministers of Australia and New Zealand expressed regret that Britain should be abandoning a historic role. Conservatives in the Commons doubted the government's wisdom in removing an element of stability from an unstable world in which Britain's long-term interests (the steady flow of Gulf oil in particular) remained substantial. Sir Alec Douglas-Home stressed the potential danger represented by Chinese ideological and imperial ardour; and Reginald Maudling later pledged his party to halt the run-down in the East if Britain's friends and allies wished its forces to stay. Even the Labour government preserved loopholes in its plans which might have served later as excuses for amending its policies. In 1966 Harold Wilson had indicated the folly of leaving power vacuums in Africa or India for unfriendly powers to fill and had claimed that, as a leading member of the United Nations, Britain should be prepared to take part in its peace-keeping activities in the East. The defence White Paper of February, 1968, declared that Britain would remain a member of SEATO and CENTO. It would continue to support a garrison in Hong Kong. British officers would remain as advisers in the states of the Persian Gulf, at the request of the rulers. The possibility of the participation of British troops in operations outside Europe would not be ruled out. When the general election of 1970 brought the Conservatives back to office Britain still had a foothold, albeit an uncertain one, in some of the outposts of its almost forgotten Empire.

The British were well aware by the end of the sixties that they could no longer claim to exercise a dominating part in world affairs. Their situation was fairly recognised by a Committee on Overseas Representation which described Britain in July, 1969, as 'a major power of the second order'. The Committee believed that 'in this role she has much to offer the world as well as much to gain from it; and that her international future will be as distinguished as her past.' She could not, however, afford all the overseas services which she had provided hitherto. She should be presented to the world 'as a trading partner with a great culture and democratic tradition rather than as a world power of the first order.'[8] This analysis may have been disappointing. It was less disturbing, though, than the forecast, also issued in 1969, by Herman Kahn, of the American Hudson Institute, who predicted on the evidence of recent growth rates that by 1980 the G.N.P. of Britain would be no more than $200000m and might be as little as $80000m, while the G.N.P. of Germany and France would be between $200000m and $300000m and that of Japan between $300000m and $600000m.

BRITAIN AS A SCAPEGOAT

As Britain's comparative wealth declined and as its part in world affairs contracted, the attacks on its integrity multiplied. Denunciations of its imperialism, in particular, arose throughout Africa and Asia when only the most unimportant vestiges of Empire survived. While Russia, which had absorbed the Baltic states and much of Poland, Germany and Rumania in the 1940s, remained generally uncondemned for its retention of these territories, Britain continued to be an object of reproach. At the twenty-first session of the United Nations in New York, in 1966, it was strongly criticised for failure to implement earlier resolutions that it should surrender authority in Aden; its efforts to do so in exceptionally harassing conditions were not appreciated by delegates who had realised that it was now an easy victim. A general election, conducted on the 'one man one vote' principle, was demanded for Fiji, to which, furthermore, independence was to be granted at an early date. Britain was to end its 'repressive action' in Oman (where a long-standing association and a treaty of friendship signed in 1951 had involved it in a grant of military aid to the Sultan) and all U.N. member states were called upon to render all possible assistance to the Omani people 'in their struggle to attain freedom and independence'.[9] On other occasions Britain had become the victim of bitter recriminations in a number of African states, particularly in Zambia and Tanzania, for its failure to end the Rhodesian independence movement. Even while accepting a British undertaking to offset to the extent of £7m damage to the Zambian economy resulting from sanctions against Rhodesia (in addition to £16m to cover the first six years of independence) President Kaunda accused Britain in 1966 of 'connivance with the conspirators in Rhodesia'[10] and threatened to propose formally that Britain should be expelled from the Commonwealth.

The moves initiated in Spain, Argentina and Guatemala for the annexation of Gibraltar, the Falkland Islands and British Honduras were in line with these attacks. They had in common a marked disregard for the wishes of the inhabitants of the three territories and for Britain's essentially liberal intentions. They had no clear effects, though they were embarrassing, leaving Britain too frequently to oppose or ignore United Nations resolutions passed by substantial majorities.

Other symptoms of hostility emerged in the Far East. When, in May, 1967, riots broke out in Hong Kong following disputes at an artificial flower factory, the Chinese Communist authorities took the opportunity to inspire attacks on British diplomatic offices in Peking, Shanghai and Canton, and to subject British representatives to insults and indignities. The Hong Kong government was denounced for having attempted to 'exclude the great influence of China's Great Proletarian Cultural Revolution',[11] a movement which had 'dealt a telling blow to imperialism, modern revisionism and world reaction, completely shattered their dream of counter-revolutionary, capitalist restoration in China, and greatly encouraged the liberation struggles of the oppressed peoples and nations of the whole world.' On other occasions British subjects were gaoled by the Chinese for long periods on trivial pretexts. No effective retaliation could be exercised against a country which, in June, 1967, broke the 'nuclear monopoly of U.S. imperialism and Soviet revisionism', and, rejoicing in a 'fresh great victory of Mao Tse-tung's thought',[12] exploded its first hydrogen bomb.

Equally embarrassing was the attitude of some of the Arab

countries. After the Six Days' War of 1967, when dramatic Israeli victories deprived Egypt, Jordan and Syria of territory, Harold Wilson found it necessary to complain of 'the deliberate spreading by the United Arab Republic of entirely false accusations that British and American aircraft had taken part in the fighting on the side of Israel'.[13] 'Malicious inventions' though these were, they nonetheless prompted attacks on British embassies and consulates and on British Council premises in Arab countries, the closure by Egypt of the Suez Canal, the interference with oil supplies to Britain from the Middle East, and the suspension by some of the Arab countries of diplomatic relations with Britain. The British government could not disregard these gestures. George Brown described the severance of relations as 'the most foolish possible action these governments could take', and added that 'this has been put to them as forcibly as possible.'[14] The significance of such endeavours to put Britain at fault was, however, too evident. Britain had become a scapegoat for aggrieved governments all over the world.

In 1970 the Arab governments of the Sudan and Libya were among several (those of Ceylon, Tanzania, Uganda and Zambia were others) which followed the examples set earlier by Iran, Egypt and Zanzibar by nationalising foreign companies and banks. Whereas these measures were not directed particularly against the British, concerns which the British had created were inevitably the largest group to be affected.

GROUNDS FOR HOPE

Yet, in spite of all the symptoms of declining prestige in the world, there may have been, in the late sixties, a number of factors in Britain's position which could, after all, arouse hope or satisfaction. The first of these, the survival of at least some of the essential qualities of the Commonwealth in some of its member countries, is considered elsewhere (see Chapter 42). The second was the prospect of an enlarged European Community once General de Gaulle had withdrawn from his position of dictatorial influence in April, 1969. Britain, whether ruled by Labour or by a Conservative government, was prepared to persist in its endeavours to become part of the Community, and so were those of its EFTA partners who did not value their neutrality above all other factors. EFTA had, indeed, been stimulated by the removal of tariffs in 1966 to expand its internal trade substantially in 1967, but once this first impetus had been spent it was found, in 1968, that the total trade of the EFTA countries with the Common Market countries grew at a much more rapid pace than the trade amongst themselves. British exports to EFTA actually declined by 1·5 per cent in 1968, while its exports to the Common Market rose by 7·9 per cent. Hence the attraction that the E.E.C. continued to exert, and the hope, at least in government circles, that a third attempt at entry might succeed and, in time, exercise all the stimulating effects on the British economy that had been envisaged in the early sixties. Relations with the Common Market countries, apart at times from France, had remained close throughout the decade.

A third factor strengthening Britain's position was the continuing close relationship with the United States. It was true that American failure either to end the Vietnamese war or to avoid the demoralisation and cruelty inseparable from war provoked passionate criticism and demonstrations, leading on one occasion, in March, 1968, to serious disorder in Grosvenor Square in London. Officially, the complexity of the issue generally inspired a discreetly non-committal attitude, though George Brown did not hesitate to praise the stand that America was taking in resisting aggression in Vietnam and the violation of the international agreement that had divided the country.

Finally, an incalculable potential advantage arose from the increasing use of the English language. By 1970 it was estimated that 267m people spoke English as their first language, while another 240m spoke it as a second language. Only Chinese was spoken by a greater number, and this was divided into half a dozen very different dialects. English, in 1970, was the official language of twenty-nine countries and one of the official languages of fifteen others. The claim could be made that 70 per cent of the world's mail was in English, as were 60 per cent of radio programmes and half the world's scientific studies. That the British were not unaware of the possible benefits of these facts was suggested by the increasing encouragement given to the teaching and information services of the British Council in forty countries. This was a sphere in which the Committee on

Overseas Representation specifically did not recommend economies.

---

[1] Michael Stewart, House of Commons, 8.3.66, *Keesing* p. 21607
[2] De Gaulle, Press conference, 9.9.65. *Keesing* p. 21604
[3] Reginald Maudling, Debate of Defence Policy, 25.7.68. *Keesing* p. 22866
[4] British Government statement, 21.8.68. *Keesing* p. 22995
[5] T.U.C. General Council statement. *Keesing* p. 22967
[6] Cmnd. 3927, 20.2.69
[7] Cmnd. 3927
[8] *Report of Committee on Overseas Representation*, Cmnd. 4107
[9] U.N. 20.12.66, *Keesing*, p. 21870
[10] Kaunda, broadcast 24.5.66. *Keesing* p. 21509
[11] Statement from Chinese Government, handed to British chargé d'affaires, D. C. Hopson, 15.5.67. *Keesing* p. 22140
[12] New China News Agency, 17.6.67. *Keesing* p. 22122
[13] H. Wilson in House of Commons, 5.6.67. *Keesing* p. 22115
[14] G. Brown in House of Commons, 5.6.67. *Keesing* p. 22115

41

The last years of the Empire

To the end the dismantlement of the Empire proved to be a process which taxed all the diplomatic skills of the British authorities. It brought them neither the approbation of a world in which the ideal of empire was out of fashion and which continued to regard Britain as an imperialist country, nor the satisfaction of observing the development of stable rule in every one of the countries which had been liberated. The consolations had to be, as so often, that virtue was its own reward and that self-government was a blessing even though it might have been poor government.

By 1964 most of the major problems of Empire had already been disposed of. Two, however, continued to erupt, at frequent intervals, during the years of Labour administration: Rhodesia and Aden.

RHODESIA

Rhodesia had occupied a curious position in the Empire since 1923. With a considerable white population (221 500 in 1961) and an African population (3 610 000) which was smaller than that of Zambia and Malawi and much smaller than that of Tanzania, Kenya and Uganda, it had been almost self-governing, almost a dominion, for about forty years before the other countries gained independence. But British governments had always reserved the right to interfere if they suspected that Rhodesian legislation was likely to discriminate against African inhabitants, and it was on account of a fear that Rhodesia was potentially a second South Africa with its obsession about apartheid that, after the collapse of the Central African Federation, it was denied the independence that was granted to apparently less highly developed countries. Such a situation was unacceptable to the white government in Salisbury. The Labour government at Westminster was accordingly confronted in its early months with the claim that Rhodesia should be treated in the same way as the other African colonies. The position was never entirely clear cut. Ian Smith, the Prime Minister, gained the unanimous support of an *indaba* attended by more than 600 chiefs and headmen, yet when representatives of the British government visited Rhodesia in February, 1965, they met, in addition to the satisfied chiefs, a demonstration of 5000 Africans demanding 'one man one vote' and heard assertions that thousands of others, including the nationalist leader, Joshua Nkomo, were in prison for political reasons.

After an overwhelming victory in May, 1965, for Ian Smith's Rhodesian Front in elections which the great majority of the 11 000 African voters boycotted, Rhodesia became a matter for discussion in a special committee of the United Nations, in the Security Council and at a Commonwealth conference in London. Its future was also considered in a series of discussions both in Salisbury and London. These discussions were all abortive, but they at least enabled the British government to formulate the principles on which it would insist. 'Unimpeded progress to majority rule . . . would have to be maintained and guaranteed.'[1] Guarantees against 'retrogressive amendment of the constitution' would have to be accepted. There should be 'immediate improvement in the political status of the African population' and 'progress towards ending racial discrimination'. And any basis proposed for independence should be 'acceptable to the people of Rhodesia as a whole'. Ian Smith would commit himself to little but acceptance of the fact that the number of African voters would automatically increase under the terms of the 1961 constitution of Rhodesia. At this stage the general Rhodesian view was that the rift between Britain and Rhodesia was not really great. When, however, Garfield Todd, a Liberal ex-premier of Southern Rhodesia was restricted for a year to his farm 250 miles from Salisbury on the grounds that he had associated with the unlawful Zimbabwe African People's Union, it became harder for the British government to accept this view. The rift certainly appeared deep to Harold Wilson and Arthur Bottomley, Secretary for Commonwealth Relations, when they visited Rhodesia in October, 1965. No agreement was reached on the means of giving effect to any of the principles on which the British were insisting. Wilson felt no confidence that the chiefs who had backed Ian Smith were representative of African opinion or that the ideal of majority rule would ever be adopted in Rhodesia.

THE INEFFECTIVENESS OF SANCTIONS

On 11th November, 1965, Ian Smith announced what came to be thought of as U.D.I., a unilateral declaration of independence. His broadcast was followed by the assumption by the Rhodesian government of wide powers, such as authority to censor the Press and radio, to impose rationing and to regulate imports and exports. It was also followed by a proclamation by Sir Humphrey Gibbs, the Governor, that the ministry no longer existed and that the people of Rhodesia should do nothing to assist it. In London Harold Wilson, with the support of Conservatives and Liberals, condemned the Rhodesian gesture as rebellion against the Crown, affirmed that moves to carry it out would be treasonable, and issued the first of a long series of measures designed to bring about the collapse of the now illegal Smith regime. The British assumption was that if the Rhodesian economy became unworkable the government would be unable to retain control of the country. Accordingly, Rhodesia was to be deprived of British supplies of capital, arms and other aid, and stage by stage its trade outlets in Britain were to be cut off. Before the end of 1965 embargoes had been placed on the import into Britain of Rhodesian minerals, and in January, 1966, almost all the limited remaining Rhodesian trade with Britain was ended. By this time, in addition, books, periodicals and medicines were the only important exports which could still be sent from Britain to Rhodesia. The outlawry of the rebels spread. By March, 1966, sixty countries had informed the United Nations that they had declined to recognise the government in Salisbury and had severed trade relations. And, as economic sanctions were extended, Britain took steps to prevent shipments of oil from reaching its beleaguered dependency by way of Beira, sending naval and air forces to exercise surveillance over the approaches to the port. 'We are confident,' said Arthur Bottomley, in February, 1966, 'that whatever petrol is getting in . . . is not enough to enable the economy to survive.'[2]

Yet it soon became clear that sanctions were not going to be immediately effective after all. During the first four months of determined British measures, Rhodesian retail prices rose only 1 per cent, unemployment not at all. Trade with South Africa and Portuguese Mozambique did not come to an end, neither country agreeing to participate in a policy of voluntary sanctions. By the end of the summer of 1966 the most that could be claimed was that Rhodesia was having some difficulty in disposing of its tobacco crop and was experiencing some decline in foreign trade and in railway revenues. Its economy was plainly not fundamentally threatened. Moreover, Ian Smith continued to enjoy the support of the chiefs. 'We wish to state quite clearly,' they announced, 'that we support the government of Rhodesia and we do not support the claim by the British Prime Minister that he has continuing responsibility and authority for and over our people. . . .'[3] The situation did not substantially alter during 1967. The contraction of the markets for tobacco and sugar merely encouraged agricultural diversification, while the restriction of other trade outlets only had the effect of expanding the South African entrepôt trade in Rhodesian goods. No new open opposition to the regime in Salisbury was developing. Even one of the new African countries, Malawi, was becoming reluctant to suffer damage as a result of the imposition of further sanctions on Rhodesia.

The British government did not end its endeavours to gain Rhodesian acceptance of the principles on which it expected independence to be based. Twice, in December, 1966, and October, 1968, Harold Wilson and Ian Smith met for prolonged discussions on board vessels off Gibraltar, and at different times Herbert Bowden (Commonwealth Secretary), Lord Alport, Sir Alec Douglas-Home and George Thomson (Minister Without Portfolio) visited Rhodesia in the hope of evolving a solution to the deadlock. Their journeys were quite ineffective. Ian Smith emphasised that the principle of 'one man one vote' would not be accepted in his lifetime, and compromise therefore appeared to be out of the question. It might indeed have been suspected that Britain was suffering more seriously from the dispute than Rhodesia. In imposing sanctions on trade Britain was not merely refusing to accept Rhodesian goods; it was also denying itself an outlet for its own products at a time when its balance of payments was a crucial issue. In order to offset the disadvantages arising from the fact that Zambia's only rail communication with East African ports lay through Rhodesia, it was obliged to offer Zambia compensation amounting altogether to more than £20m. It gained little but opprobrium from all the Commonwealth countries of East Africa, apart from Malawi, for its refusal to countenance the use of armed force against Rhodesia. Simon Kapwepwe, Foreign Minister of Zambia, denounced a British 'sell-out to the white settler regime'[4] and damned Britain's endeavours 'to placate Black Africa with patronising handouts of an exhibitionist nature.' A Tanzanian representative on the Trusteeship Committee of the United Nations accused the British of 'diabolical behaviour' in talking with 'the white racist rebels'.[5] The Commonwealth Conference in London in 1966 provided another forum for frank denunciation of this kind. The reluctance of the British to resort to war was no doubt realistic and sensible, but in the eyes of many of the newly independent states of Africa and Asia employment of pacific measures was merely an additional symptom of failure. Even the Crown was involved in the failure when the royal pardon for three condemned African murderers was ignored by the Rhodesian authorities.

From one other quarter came condemnation of the Labour government of a quite different kind. To the Marquis of Salisbury, almost the hereditary elder statesman of the Conservative party, Ian Smith was 'a man of outstanding rectitude and honesty,' and British policy represented only a 'supine repudiation of our own kith and kin, who have alone made Rhodesia what it is, under pressure from a hostile junta of semi-civilised states whose motives are wholly political and not moral. . . .'[6] Many less articulate Englishmen quietly agreed.

In such a manner another two years passed. In April, 1970, when Ian Smith's Rhodesian Front won a landslide election victory, securing all fifty European seats in the Salisbury parliament, it was evident that his position had been in no way shaken. No Rhodesian party supported the British ideal that there should be 'no independence before majority rule'. Economic sanctions, at least up to this time, had failed. The country remained stable, with its crime rate low and falling, and its economy remained resilient.

ADEN

The advance of Aden towards independence created entirely

different problems, as disagreeable in their way as those of Rhodesia to the British government even though they did not linger on into the seventies and threaten to plague Britain indefinitely.

The Conservative government, at a time when Duncan Sandys had been Colonial Secretary, had committed Britain to granting independence to Aden and Southern Arabia in 1968. The success of this policy had depended, however, on two conditions: firstly, that a viable federation could be established, including Aden itself and the twenty-three protected sultanates which surrounded the colony and extended Eastwards along the southern shores of Arabia; and secondly, that a British military base should be retained in Aden as the result of a defence agreement with the new South Arabian government after the attainment of independence. However, long before 1968 it had become clear that these conditions would not be fulfilled. Despite having British support, the federal government established in 1962 could not effectively assert its authority, over Aden in particular, in face of nationalist hostility. Terrorism increased. The Speaker of the Aden State Legislative Council, Sir Arthur Charles, was among the Arab and European victims in 1965. The Chief Minister of Aden, Abdul Qawee Mackawee, consistently criticised the Federation and the British, refused to take action against the terrorists or even to condemn them, and was dismissed, along with the Council of Ministers, in September, 1956, only six months after his appointment. The British High Commissioner assumed direct rule.

Meanwhile, a succession of incidents was taking place on the frontier between federal territory and Yemen. In the U.N. Security Council the British representative affirmed that the Sana'a radio was constantly inciting the inhabitants of the Federation to armed revolt. When the British retaliated with a bombing raid on a Yemeni fort, Yemeni spokesmen in the Security Council charged Britain with constant acts of aggression against peaceful citizens with the purposes of destroying the republican regime in Sana'a and of perpetuating its own occupation of Southern Arabia. A feature of these frontier disturbances was a campaign, perhaps the last in British colonial history, which took place intermittently during 1964 and 1965 in the Jebel Radfan.

In 1966 the Labour government confirmed the British intention of leaving Aden in 1968. At the same time it abandoned the idea of maintaining forces there after independence and invited United Nations assistance during the period of transition to independence. The United Nations responded by sending a fact-finding mission to Aden; but its arrival coincided with a general strike and a renewed outbreak of violence, and it left after only five days, bitterly denouncing the colonialism of a power which had done all that was in the circumstances possible to co-operate. Had the mission remained it would perhaps have realised that the basic problem was not unyielding British imperialism but the determination of the Arabs to end the authority of the federal government combined with their complete inability to agree among themselves on who should inherit it.

When in May, 1967, Sir Humphrey Trevelyan became High Commissioner, the principal Arab groups, the Front for the Liberation of the Occupied South Yemen and the National Liberation Front, were virtually at war with each other. Originally FLOSY had been the stronger of these, but its initial readiness to negotiate with the British had inspired the deadly antagonsim of the less representative but more dangerous N.L.F. The leaders of both groups had withdrawn into exile in Egypt, where the N.L.F. was accepted as the one on which the greater reliance could be placed. Since clearly no stable government could be established in South Arabia without the support of one or both, Trevelyan appealed for their co-operation. He failed to secure it. Nor could he prevent the seizure by the N.L.F. of control in all the sultanates outside Aden itself. With the abdication or flight of the rulers the whole Federation had collapsed by September, 1967, and the High Commissioner had been obliged to declare his willingness to recognise the nationalist forces and to negotiate with them for the formation of a new government in South Arabia. Soon afterwards, in London, George Brown, now Foreign Secretary, determined to employ the tactics that had obliged the Indians to face reality in 1948: he announced on 2nd November that Aden's independence would be accelerated and that instead of being granted, as originally planned, in January, 1968, it would be imposed by the end of November. British forces would be withdrawn during the next four weeks. An original offer of naval and air support for the new government would be rescinded.

On the recommendation of the High Command of the South Arabian Armed Forces, sovereignty was bequeathed to the N.L.F., and on 30th November, 1967, the People's Republic of the South Yemen was proclaimed, with control over Aden, over the former sultanates, and also, in view of the people's wishes, over Perim, Kamaran and Socotra Islands. The British troops, their dependants and equipment had left without incident.

THE REMAINING DEPENDENCIES

Neither Rhodesia nor Aden represented success for Britain Fortunately, Empire brought its minor consolations in the sixties. The grant of independence within the Commonwealth to Bechuanaland (Botswana) and to Basutoland (Lesotho) in September and October, 1966, was attended with no crisis. Mauritius also became an independent member of the Commonwealth, in March, 1968, Swaziland in September, 1968, and no hostility marred the celebrations. British Honduras was confronted with a demand for annexation by Guatemala but refused to abandon its right to sovereignty and independence. Two colonial territories, Gibraltar and the Falkland Islands, also threatened with annexation by a much larger neighbour, actually expressed an overwhelming anxiety to remain British.

Spanish pressure on Gibraltar began in 1965 with the creation of difficulties over the passage of traffic across the frontier. In 1967 restrictions were imposed on all but pedestrians. In 1968 the frontier was closed altogether, except for permanent residents and the 5000 Spaniards who held work permits in Gibraltar. For others, only the Algeciras ferry was left. Even these concessions were withdrawn in June, 1969. In December, 1967, the United Nations had interfered, passing by 101 votes to nil (with 14 abstentions) a motion regretting 'the delay in the process of decolonisation' of Gibraltar. However, the people of Gibraltar remained unmoved. As the Prime Minister, Sir Joshua Hassan, indicated to the Trusteeship Committee of the United Nations, they already enjoyed a full measure of self government, their various political parties functioned quite freely, and they wished to retain their association with Britain. A referendum held in September, 1967, amply confirmed the last point: 44 voters sought Spanish sovereignty, 12 138 the continued sovereignty of Britain.

In the same way the inhabitants of the Falkland Islands, which had remained under British rule since 1833, made clear their desire to maintain this constitutional position when the Argentine government laid claim to possession of the islands.

---

[1] Statement by the Commonwealth Relations Office, 9.10.56. *Keesing* p. 21025
[2] Arthur Bottomley, 9.2.66. *Keesing* p. 21417
[3] Meeting at Salisbury, 2.11.66. *Keesing* p. 21699
[4] Security Council debate, 9.12.66. *Keesing* p. 21834
[5] C. Y. Monga, U.N. General Assembly, 22.10.66. *Keesing* p. 21833
[6] House of Lords, 12.11.65. *Keesing* p. 21129

42

The Commonwealth in the 1960s

As Empire turned into Commonwealth and as the number of its independent countries increased, the more insistent became the doubts about the value of the association and the speculation about its future. Could the new Asian and African countries, with their predominantly coloured populations, feel the same sympathy with traditional British ideals that the white dominions were expected to feel? Could the essentials of parliamentary democracy ever effectively operate in comparatively backward countries which had not already known centuries of free speech, toleration of dissent, and government by representatives of opposing parties? Could Law rule? Could countries without viable economies ever preserve their independence? Was it not likely that geographical factors would lead even the older dominions to find that their links were to a greater extent with South East Asia or with the United States or with African neighbours than with Britain and the other members of the Commonwealth? Would new countries exulting in recently acquired independence wish for any further collaboration with a former ruling power whose strength and influence were clearly declining? A blunt and unsettling American view of Britain and the Commonwealth was expressed in September, 1962, by Dean Acheson, sometime Secretary of State: 'Great Britain has lost an Empire and has not yet found a role,' he declared. 'The attempt to play a separate power role . . . based on being head of a "Commonwealth" which has no political structure or unity or strength, and enjoys a fragile and precarious economic relationship by means of the sterling area and preferences in the British market—this role is about played out.'[1] Macmillan, on Britain's behalf, might respond with vigour, but the fear that Acheson might have been right was not easily eradicable.

SOUTH AFRICA

Yet the issue which did more than any other in the late fifties and early sixties to shake the Commonwealth was not a market relationship, nor was it one raised by the emergence of newly independent Asian and African countries. It was in fact the South African policy of apartheid. A deliberate endeavour had been made since 1948 to segregate black and white inhabitants and to encourage separate development in separate regions of the Union. Theoretically, apartheid imposed no ceiling on the advancement of either ethnic group and was sought as much by the blacks as by the whites. In practice, so it appeared in Britain, serious limitations were entailed on the freedom of the former. A conviction of white superiority might have been a long established feature of Boer history. It was, though, not a doctrine which found favour among the more liberal exponents of British policy, as Harold Macmillan made clear beyond doubt in a speech delivered in 1960 before the House of Assembly in Cape Town. In phrases which were widely repeated he indicated that 'the wind of change'[2] was blowing through the African continent. The nationalism that had first developed in the Boer Republics was now, inevitably, affecting other parts of Africa; and this must, in the British view, bring in its train 'the opportunity to have an increasing share in political power and responsibility'. Macmillan appreciated the problems confronting South Africa and expressed his anxiety to give support and encouragement, but at the same time left no doubt that for the British government, at least, apartheid was not acceptable. 'I hope you won't mind my saying frankly that there are some aspects of your policies which make it impossible for us [to support and encourage] without being false to our own deep convictions about the political destinies of free men.'

The Cape Town speech may have stimulated nationalism outside the Union, and, despite Macmillan's warnings, the wind of change may elsewhere have turned rapidly into 'a howling tempest'. Inside South Africa, however, it did nothing to divert a government to which apartheid was an unalterable article of faith. Rather than withdraw from its policy of segregation, Dr Verwoerd's country withdrew from the Commonwealth, in May, 1961. This was not a solution desired by Macmillan. However, the occasion for the break was not one on which compromise was possible and publicly the Prime Minister was constrained to condemn apartheid forthrightly as 'threatening to damage the concept of the Commonwealth as a multi-racial association', having 'grave external effects' in the world outside South Africa, and deliberately transposing 'what we regard as wrong into right'.[3] South African refusal to accept diplomatic representatives from non-European members of the Commonwealth was especially regretted by the British government.

ABANDONMENT OF BRITISH IDEALS: WAR IN NIGERIA

In the years that followed, quite different violations of British political ideals occurred in other Commonwealth countries. Although there was a tendency in Britain to reserve the more bitter condemnations for white transgressors of the traditional code and to turn a blind eye to many of the short-comings of the newly emancipated and less experienced coloured governments, the misdemeanours of Dr Nkrumah's administration in Ghana were too flagrant to escape notice. The stages by which opponents of the regime were muzzled, the imprisonment of some (including Dr Danquah) and the expulsion of others, and the dismissal of a Chief Justice all evoked condemnation in Britain. The failure of the constitutional concept of government and the elimination of a responsible, freely tolerated opposition in one African country after another, and in Pakistan, was saddening to those who had worked for decades to further an understanding of democratic methods in the British dependencies. And yet it was perhaps true that, without British experience, opposition in new countries tended to become indistinguishable from conspiracy and sedition. Julius Nyerere may have been justified when he claimed that Tanganyika was neither wealthy enough nor sufficiently developed to be able to afford the luxury of opposition parties.

The history of Nigeria in the sixties symbolised more regrettably than any other example the complete failure of British inspiration and the collapse of British hopes that stable, prosperous and united countries were being created. In Nigeria the unity, particularly, was imaginary. Elections merely intensified linguistic and tribal differences and weakened a sense of loyalty to a single country to such an extent that an alliance in power of northern and south-western (Yoruba) politicians could be assured, in 1964, only by electoral manipulation. Corruption of this sort was especially resented among the younger, educated classes, and it provoked towards the end of 1965, a popular rising in the West, and the murder, in January, 1966, of the Prime Minister, Sir Abubakar Tafawa Balewa, and the Northern leader, the Sardauna of Sokoto. When a new regime under General Ironsi endeavoured to impose unitary government and provoked the fear among the northern Hausa that the better-qualified Ibo would extend their influence over the whole country, Ironsi was also murdered (July, 1966). Furthermore, about 30 000 Ibos were massacred, and two million others who had left their homeland fled back to the South-east. When in May, 1967, a new attempt to find a solution to the problem of Nigerian government was made by Colonel Gowon and a federation of twelve states was decreed, the South-East, adopting the name Biafra, seceded; and in July, 1967, a war of independence broke out which neither Commonwealth, United Nations nor African influence could stop.

Nigeria's tragedy made an inescapable impact on Britain. To the British, in 1960, Nigeria had seemed to be a model African state. About £400m had been invested in the new country by British concerns when the war began. The oil fields of the Eastern and Mid-Western regions were being developed by B.P.-Shell. About a third of Nigeria's trade remained with Britain, in face of the competition of the E.E.C. and Japan. The Federal army, in 1967, still had some British advisers. At the same time it was possible neither to disregard the massacres which had preceded the war nor to condemn a people, the Biafrans, who were fighting for independence against a stronger opponent and suffering appallingly for their cause. Divided sympathies resulted in endeavours to help, in different ways, both sides. Officially the British government provided about a fifth of the Nigerian government's purchases of rifles and ammunition, though they refused to provide bombs and left Gowon's government to buy its military aircraft elsewhere, particularly in Russia. They were criticised at home, sometimes passionately, but could at least argue that if they had not supplied the federal forces the field would have been left open entirely for intervention by Communist countries. They might also have claimed that the triumph of Biafra might have resulted in the fragmentation of a viable federation at a time when very small states without exceptional resources had only limited hopes of successful economic development. However, neither government nor people in Britain could disregard the plight of the Biafrans. Landlocked from the start, progressively confined to a smaller and smaller territory during the two and a half years of the war, they starved. Supplies were flown to an airstrip at Uli from Fernando Po and Sao Tomé, principally by the Red Cross and Joint Church Aid; but lack of experience among the relief workers, language difficulties, and the view of the federal authorities that if the rebels were fed the war could only be prolonged made this operation a difficult, at times a hazardous one. When in January, 1970, the Biafran resistance collapsed and the Ibo commander, General Ojukwu, fled, the feeling that an insupportable burden had been removed was universal. For Nigeria the war had been a catastrophe. It had been little less than this for the ideal of a united and effective Commonwealth.

RIFTS IN THE COMMONWEALTH . . .

South Africa, Ghana and Nigeria, in different ways, appeared to have focussed the failure of Commonwealth ideals. The failure of Commonwealth countries in the early sixties to agree among themselves were also symptoms of breakdown. Strained relations developed between Ghana and Nigeria. Endeavours to establish a federation of Tanganyika, Kenya and Uganda came to nothing, and all that emerged from discussions was a union of Tanganyika and Zanzibar (in 1964). More serious were the hostile relations between Pakistan and India, where, even after the settlement of disputes over the use of the water of the Punjab rivers, the animosity caused by rival claims to Kashmir continued to fester. Not merely did India obtain no sympathy from Pakistan when Ladakh and Assam were invaded by Communist Chinese in 1962; Pakistan was encouraged to develop closer relations with China and to look with suspicion on the Western world when it sent help to India. In August, 1965, the two dominions resorted to war over possession of the Rann of Cutch.

Very different reasons for anxiety affected the older members of the Commonwealth. During the negotiations in 1962 for British membership of the European Economic Community it was hard to dispel fears, particularly in Australia, that Britain was prepared to sacrifice Commonwealth trading interests for trade with Europe. Inevitably, the negotiations drew attention to the fact that trade between Britain and the Commonwealth was declining while trade with Europe was rapidly increasing. In 1958 the average monthly value of exports to the sterling area (the Commonwealth, with Burma, Ireland, Iceland, Jordan, Libya and seven Trucial States) and to Canada was $383m. In 1961 it was still $383m. In 1961 42 per cent of all British exports went to the Commonwealth; five years earlier the figure had been 48 per cent, and eight years later it had declined to 21 per cent. A marked decline was observed in the late 1950s in the proportion of imports taken from Britain by Australia, New Zealand, India and Pakistan. Whereas in 1958 Australian exports to Britain had been twice as great as those to Japan, by 1966 exports to Japan exceeded those to Britain. Facts of this kind prompted commentators to suggest that imperial preference no longer met the essential needs of most Commonwealth countries and should be increasingly replaced by regional agreements with other countries of the Far East, of North America or of Africa.

... COUNTERBALANCED BY CO-OPERATION AND ASSISTANCE

And yet such newly independent colonial territories as Kenya and Malawi, Malta and Guyana, Botswana and Barbados were all anxious to remain members of this apparently weakening Commonwealth. Eighteen countries were represented at the Prime Ministers' conference in 1964. By 1967 the Commonwealth contained twenty-six members. Britain had been harshly criticised by some of them, by Zambia and Tanzania for example, over the Rhodesian problem; but apart from South Africa, none had opted out. To provide a certain degree of cohesion a Secretary General (Arnold Smith, formerly Canadian Assistant Under Secretary of State for External Affairs) was appointed in 1965 to arrange meetings of officials, to serve Commonwealth ministerial conferences, and to disseminate information, especially on economic and social problems, to member countries. The Commonwealth Foundation was set up in 1966 to encourage professional interchanges between

Commonwealth countries. Older associations survived, despite all the changes that had occurred. The Royal Commonwealth Society, for almost a century, had promoted knowledge and understanding of Commonwealth peoples. The Commonwealth Press Union, founded in 1909, had worked for the maintenance of Press freedom, the improvement of reporting facilities and the training of journalists. The Commonwealth Parliamentary Association had held regular conferences in various capitals since 1911. The Federation of Commonwealth Chambers of Commerce, founded in 1911, had promoted trade between its members and between them and the rest of the world, and had assisted in the provision of technical and commercial training.

The educated classes of Britain's former dependencies still spoke English, and at the very time when Commonwealth unity appeared to be weakening the facilities for educational co-operation were entering a new, hopeful phase. A conference at Oxford in 1959 evolved a plan which would allow 1000 Commonwealth students of exceptional promise to study in countries other than their own. By 1964 this figure had been exceeded. By 1966 506 of these students were in Britain, which was in addition providing 100 medical bursaries and 550 bursaries for prospective teachers. A similar scheme for teachers was being operated by Canada, Australia, India and New Zealand. At the same time, British teachers were being encouraged to work in Commonwealth countries. Particular consideration was given to the propagation of a knowledge of British technology and the English language. British financial aid continued to be significant. During the year 1964–5 Britain spent about £13m on assistance for Commonwealth educational schemes. About £4m of this sum was allotted to the educational work of the British Council. In 1964 it was arranged that about £5m a year should be spent during the next five years on the higher education of teachers and technicians in the Commonwealth. Other advanced Commonwealth countries were also providing increasing aid.

A Commonwealth Air Transport Council was established in 1945 and a Commonwealth Economic Consultative Council in 1958. By an agreement made in 1948 Commonwealth telegraph cable and radio networks were developed co-operatively on the advice of the Telecommunications Board in London. Regular conferences were being held to consider broadcasting training

facilities and the interchange of programmes between Commonwealth countries. Scientific conferences were being held every
two years after 1958. Agricultural Bureaus were distributing
information on various branches of agriculture. Britain, Canada,
Australia, India and Pakistan were co-operating over the
development of nuclear power for peaceful purposes. There had
been some interchange of doctors and nurses, and although this
tended to involved a brain drain from the under-developed
countries to Britain (in 1966 17000 overseas Commonwealth
doctors were listed in the British Medical Register) the older
countries at least were aware of the need to encourage medical
personnel to work in less advanced regions and to increase
training opportunities for people from these regions.

So membership of the Commonwealth could still, in the
1960s, bring to the smaller and less affluent countries facilities,
assistance and information which could not have been obtained
otherwise without expense too great for them to contemplate.
The contacts, though undramatic, were important. The
Commonwealth allowed regular meetings of ministers and
professional representatives of very different peoples, some
wealthy and others under-developed, some giving their support
to the policies of the West and others unaligned. As Duncan
Sandys, the Secretary of State for Commonwealth Relations,
said when South Africa withdrew from the Commonwealth, its
role was 'not to build a block of racially homogeneous nations.'
It was 'rather to build a bridge between peoples of all races and
creeds.'[4]

At least theoretically, British legal and parliamentary ideals
had been inherited by the new countries, and some had made
an endeavour to perpetuate them.

Inter-Commonwealth trade remained significant in spite of
the apparent decline which had been publicised at the time of
Britain's first negotiations for enrolment in the European
Economic Community. In 1962 the value of British exports to
the Commonwealth was £1200m, while exports to the six
countries of the E.E.C., though rising quickly, were worth only
£781m. The purchases, per head, of British goods in Canada
were valued at £10 a year, in Australia at £22, in New Zealand
at £44, whereas purchases in West Germany were valued at
only £4, and purchases in the United States at only £1 18s 6d.
(£1·92½). In 1960 38·5 per cent of all British imports came from

Commonwealth countries. Nearly half of these received preferential treatment. Eighty per cent entered Britain duty free. Of the older dominions, Canada sent 17·5 per cent of its exports to Britain, Australia 26 per cent, and New Zealand 53 per cent (including nearly 90 per cent of its wool, meat and dairy produce). Exports from the newly independent countries to Britain varied in 1960 from Malaya's 13 per cent to Nigeria's 48·5 per cent and Sierra Leone's 83 per cent.

British investments in Commonwealth countries remained substantial. During the 1960s the annual flow of private capital leaving Britain for the Commonwealth averaged about £200m. At the end of 1964 the Board of Trade estimated that investment by British companies in the Commonwealth (excluding oil, insurance and banking) amounted to about £2350m, the largest investments being in Canada, Australia, India and Malaysia. Loans floated by Commonwealth governments or companies on the London capital market were a further important source of capital, averaging several million pounds a year.

British aid to the under-developed countries was another factor which might have been expected to hold the Commonwealth together. By 1969 £1697m had been paid in overseas aid since the war, to Commonwealth countries; and nearly half of this aid had been in the form of grants for which repayment was not expected. Aid was increasing rapidly: in 1955 it had amounted to £76·6m, most of the money going to the colonies and independent countries of the Commonwealth. In 1962 it was £160·1m, in 1965 £205m. By 1970 total official and private aid amounted to almost £400m, 0·85 per cent of the British Gross National Product. This was an approximately average figure for Western donor nations: the United States provided a smaller proportion of its G.N.P. (though the total was substantial), France and Germany more than 1 per cent. Such aid represented only about 20 per cent of the capital invested in the developing countries (the rest was generated inside these countries) but it may nonetheless, according to Reginald Prentice, the Labour Minister responsible for overseas development, have made all the difference between progress and stagnation.

Some of the British aid was administered by the Colonial (later Commonwealth) Development Corporation which had been set up in 1948 to increase the productive capacity and trade of the colonies. By the end of 1965 the cost of its commitments had amounted to £135m and it was assisting 134 projects, mostly in Africa. In 1966 it was announced that about half of Britain's total aid should be interest free. In 1969 91 per cent of its loans were entered into on such terms.

The cynical view of generosity on this scale was that without it the under-developed parts of the world might turn for help to the Communist countries instead and might in the end adopt Communist ideologies. There were other motives, however. Financial aid was designed to allow backward countries to develop their economies and thereby to enlarge their opportunities to trade with the rest of the world. By 1970 it was believed that Britain was obtaining about £3 worth of export orders for each £2 spent on assistance to these countries. Every country that was involved was enriched. Furthermore, and above all, the belief had become established in the West that a division into prosperous and poor nations was morally wrong and that countries like Britain had an obligation to grant facilities to the poverty-stricken to improve their own standards of living. The conscience of the rich had been stirred.

A few examples of British assistance will illustrate the character of the aid programme. India, between the end of the war and 1969, received altogether £345·1m in loans from Britain and £10·7m in grants. Some of the money was spent on the construction of steelworks, the development of coal mines, electrical plant and river steamer services, the training of engineers, administrators and doctors, and the purchase of capital goods abroad which would allow the further development of resources. Aid was also reaching India from Australia, New Zealand and Canada, as well as from Japan and the United States. Meanwhile, Pakistan received loans from Britain amounting to £91·3m and grants of £8·8m. Malaysia, between 1945 and 1969, received £97·9m in grants and £37·5m in loans; and in 1968 additional British aid amounting to £75m, together with land and fixed assets, was offered to it and to Singapore to offset the effects of the withdrawal of British forces from their territories. Nigeria, between 1945 and 1969, received £62·5m in grants and £46·4m in loans. Grants to Kenya amounted to £96m, loans to £78·5m, to Malawi £54·9m and £23·8m, to Malta £80·4m and £15·2m. The aid to British Honduras in one year, 1962, was earmarked for hurricane relief, the building of a capital city and airport improvements.[5]

Britain was a participant in the Colombo Plan, evolved in 1950 at a Commonwealth Prime Ministers' conference to supply help to the countries of South-east Asia. It also took part in the Special Commonwealth African Assistance Plan (introduced after the Commonwealth Prime Ministers' meeting in 1960), in the Aid India and Aid Pakistan Consortia, and in the Indus Basin Development project. The last of these, to which Britain contributed nearly £26m, was an impressive civil engineering scheme designed to divide the waters of the Punjab between India and Pakistan.

The Commonwealth was not a military alliance, despite the combined struggles of the white dominions and India during the world wars. Many newly independent Commonwealth countries made it clear that they wished to remain unaligned in the case of further confrontation between the Communist world and the West. However, Canada joined Britain in NATO; Australia, New Zealand and Pakistan were members of SEATO, Pakistan of CENTO. And the neutrality of the Commonwealth countries which gained their independence later did not preclude their acceptance from Britain of military help in time of need. In 1964 and 1965 British forces assisted Malaysia to resist Indonesian infiltration over the borders of Sarawak and Sabah. Other forces were available when local upheavals occurred in Tanganyika in 1964 and infection from this source was feared in Kenya and Uganda. Cyprus, after independence, required help in curbing its communal animosities, and British forces were among those on whom the United Nations Secretary-General called. In 1970 suggestions were being put forward for co-operative defence arrangements in the Far East between Britain, Australia, New Zealand, Malaysia and Singapore.

---

[1] Speech at U.S. Military Academy, West Point, 1962
[2] Speech in Cape Town House of Assembly, 3.2.60. *Keesing* p. 17269
[3] House of Commons, 22.3.61. *Keesing* p. 18021
[4] House of Commons, 16.3.61. *Keesing* p. 18023
[5] For statistics relating to Commonwealth see *The Commonwealth in Brief*, prepared for British Information Services by Central Office of Information

43

Northern Ireland

For more than two decades after the war Northern Ireland made only a limited impact on British politics. Twelve representatives continued to take seats in the Westminster Parliament, generally as Ulster Unionists; but local concerns remained the responsibliity of the Prime Minister and other ministers of Northern Ireland and of the Northern Ireland Parliament at Stormont, on the outskirts of Belfast. Only a small number of issues were of national significance: an unemployment rate consistently higher than the rate in other parts of Britain, involving usually between 30000 and 40000 workers; endeavours to attract new industry (and tourists) to the region; demonstrations, at general elections, of the strength of the Sinn Fein movement in Fermanagh and Tyrone; and the decision, regretted in Derry, to establish a new university at Coleraine.

In October, 1968, however, disturbances in Derry marked the beginning of a period of trouble which very forcibly drew the attention of the rest of Britain to the problems of the province.

Superficially, the riots were caused by the traditional hostility between Protestants and Catholics. Predominantly Catholic members of a Civil Rights movement collided with the Protestant supporters of two extremists, the Rev. Ian Paisley and Ronald Bunting. The performance was repeated in January, 1969, when Civil Rights demonstrators disregarded the appeals of the Northern Ireland government to abandon a march from Belfast to Derry and Protestant Loyal Citizens of Ulster called on 'all those who value their heritage to take every possible action within the law to hinder and harass' them. After clashes in Antrim and Randalstown Bunting's followers went on to attack the marchers at Burntollet Bridge and along the final ten miles of the road to Derry. In March, 1969, Paisley and Bunting were gaoled after riots in Armagh; but this did not avail to quieten their supporters, who were involved a month later in

327

disturbances in Lurgan and Derry. Communal disorders continued throughout the year to disturb the peace in Belfast. By
August, 1969, maintenance of order had proved beyond the
powers of the Royal Ulster Constabulary, and it had become
necessary to station British troops in Belfast and Derry. Their
presence, unfortunately, did not prevent renewed conflict in
1970, with destruction of property and deaths on the streets of
Belfast.

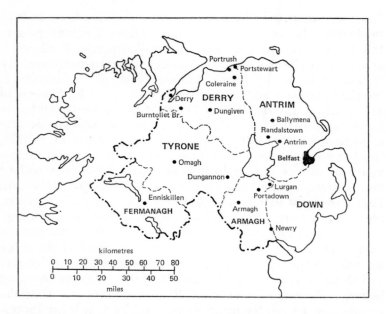

Northern Ireland. Population (1961 Census) 1 425 000 (Belfast
416 000), Roman Catholics 34·9%, Presbyterians 29%, Church
of Ireland 24·2%, Methodists 5%, others 6·9%. Northern
Ireland House of Commons 1965: Antrim (7 members):
Ulster Unionists 7; Armagh (4): U. 3, Nationalist 1; Belfast
(16): U. 11, N.I. Labour 2, Republican Lab. 2, National
Democrat 1; Down (8): U. 6, N. 2; Derry City (1): U. 1;
Derry County (4): U. 2, N. 2; Fermanagh (3); U. 2, N. 1;
Queen's University (4): U. 2, Liberal 1, N. 1; Tyrone (5):
U. 2, N. 3.

Party representation at Stormont after the 1962 election was
identical, except in Belfast, which was represented by 9 Ulster
Unionists and 7 Labour members of different kinds.

Associated with religious antagonism were a number of social and political issues which caused particular resentment among the Catholic minority in Northern Ireland. These issues were listed, in September, 1969, in the report of a Commission headed by Lord Cameron, a Senator of The College of Justice in Scotland. Three problems in particular, the Commission concluded, had provoked the Civil Rights movement to take action: discrimination over housing, the manipulation of local council elections, and the employment of a Special Ulster Constabulary. Catholics suspected that certain councils, notably those of Derry and Dungannon, had discriminated in favour of Protestants when allocating houses. They feared, with good reason, that Protestants and Unionists had been favoured when local government appointments were made, and that local government boundaries had been defined in such a way as to deny Catholics the influence in local affairs which their numbers would have justified. They disliked a Special Constabulary which appeared to be a para-military and partisan force recruited exclusively from the Protestant community. On the other hand, the Protestants undoubtedly feared an increase in Catholic numbers and powers which might threaten not only the Ulster Unionists' position in the government but also their valued association with Britain. Catholic sympathies were regarded as likely to rest with the Republic of Ireland.

The Commission stressed the fact that ever since a Northern Ireland Parliament had been established in 1921 the Unionists had been continuously in office and that no opposition could envisage the day when it could provide an alternative government. The results were evident: 'a party in power which can never in foreseeable circumstances be turned out of office tends to be complacent and insensitive to criticism or acceptance of any need for change or reform', while an opposition which 'can never become a government tends to lose a sense of responsibility.' Undoubtedly there were honourable people on both sides in Ulster. Terence O'Neill, the Prime Minister, was sincerely anxious to ensure the social and political equality of both religious communities. The Catholic Nationalist party, though committed to a United Ireland, was responsibly led by Edward McAteer. The Cameron Commission was impressed by the number of well-educated and moderate members of the Civil Rights movement who sought immediate reforms rather than an alteration of the constitutional position of Northern Ireland. At the same time, there were extremists on both wings who were adversely criticised. Apart from Paisley and Bunting, the ex-Minister of Home Affairs, William Craig, invited condemnation. So did subversive left wing and revolutionary elements who had joined the Civil Rights movement to further their own ends and 'were ready to exploit grievances in order to provoke and ferment . . . disorder and violence'.

'The local hooligan element' had played a significant part in creating turmoil, and on occasions gangs of juveniles had been numbered among them. Hooliganism was, of course, long established in Ireland (and not unknown in other parts of Britain). The involvement of schoolchildren was a less usual feature of British politics, though. The Commission hinted at one reason for it when it commented on the 'segregated education, insisted upon by the Roman Catholic Church', which was as least partly responsible for 'initiating and maintaining division and difference among the young'.[1]

During this period of upheaval the complexity of Northern Irish politics had become very plain to an English public which had hitherto tended to ignore developments at Stormont or to assume that the position of the Unionists was unshakeable. A general election in Northern Ireland in February, 1969, illustrated the political fragmentation of the six counties. The Unionist party had suffered a common fate of a party which had enjoyed uninterrupted office: it had divided into a majority group, which supported Terence O'Neill, and a substantial minority who contested his leadership. Of the 35 returned in 1969, 12 fell into the latter category. In addition, 3 Independent O'Neill Unionists were elected. The Paisley faction, calling itself Protestant Unionist, complicated the issue even further. The principal opposition group was the Nationalist party, Catholic and committed to a United Ireland. It won 6 seats. The Northern Ireland Labour party, composed of supporters of the association of Britain and Northern Ireland, and connected with British Labour, gained 2. The Catholic Republican Labour party, which sought an all-Ireland republic, also won 2. Two smaller factions, along with the Protestant Unionists, remained unrepresented after the election, though candidates from two of these small parties were later returned to the Westminister Parliament.

O'Neill at first won votes of confidence at a number of Unionist meetings, but by April, 1969, after proposing the introduction of universal suffrage in local government elections, his position weakened. Therefore, in the hope that the essential reforms could be more easily carried out by a new leader who was sincerely committed to them but was 'unhampered by personal hostilities',[2] he resigned, and James Chichester-Clark became premier in his place. No other substantial change took place in the Cabinet.

Nor was it easy to see that, by the summer of 1970, any substantial change had taken place in Northern Irish politics and public order either. Despite all the good will that existed in responsible circles, Ulster seemed to have little ability to escape from the worst divisions that its history had produced.

---

[1] *Cameron Commission Report*, 12.9.69
[2] Statement to Unionist Party, 28.4.69. *Keesing* p. 23373

44

The fortunes of the
Labour party 1967–70

The ominous local government election results which followed
the general election of 1966 ushered in three years of disaster
for Labour at the polls. The persistent failure of the government
to find an answer to their economic problems appeared to be
reflected in the decline in their popularity. Only when the
balance of payments had at last turned in Britain's favour did the
party, with astonishing suddenness, at last regain lost ground.

WANING POPULARITY

In April, 1967, the second elections to the Greater London
Council took place. Labour, which had gained 64 seats out of
100 in 1964, was routed. It saved only 18. Its leader, Sir William
Fiske, was among those defeated. Since the 9·4 per cent of the
votes cast for Liberals brought them no representation, Conservatives won the other 82 seats. The reversal of fortunes
seemed all the greater since the L.C.C. and G.L.C. had been
controlled by Labour since 1934. Now they held only six
boroughs. The party's losses elsewhere were almost equally
significant: a net loss of 385 seats in the County Council
elections in April, of 596 seats in the English and Welsh borough
elections in May, and comparable losses in Scotland. The
Liberals and Independents gained some seats in England and
Wales, and the Scottish Nationalists won 69 Scottish seats; but
it was to the Conservative party that the really massive gains
accrued. Conservatives had begun to win the boroughs, quite
apart from London. Liverpool, Manchester, Nottingham, Bradford, Leicester and Bristol were among those which fell to them
in 1967. The trend was maintained in 1968: 559 net Conservative gains and 551 net Labour losses in the English and Welsh

boroughs, apart from London; 749 Conservative gains and 747 Labour losses in the London Boroughs, of which Labour now held only 4 out of 32; further Nationalist successes, principally at Labour's expense, in Scotland. The 1969 results brought no consolation. Conservatives made another 616 net borough gains in England, Wales and Scotland, and Labour suffered another 646 net losses. Labour regained Sheffield and Aberdeen, but the only other city of more than 250000 people of which they retained the allegiance was Stoke-on-Trent. In England and Wales only 22 boroughs altogether were still controlled by Labour, nearly all of them in Northern England and South Wales. The urban districts revealed a similar trend.

Parliamentary by-elections during these years proved no more encouraging for the government. A succession of borough constituencies which had been regarded as impregnable strongholds were lost to Conservatives. Carmarthen went to a Welsh Nationalist, Hamilton to a Scottish Nationalist, Birmingham Ladywood to a Liberal. Any Labour seat where the general election majority had been less than 10000 had to be thought of as marginal.

At intervals in 1966, 1967 and 1968 ministerial resignations were announced. Christopher Mayhew, Minister of Defence for the Navy, was the first to leave. Frank Cousins, Margaret Herbison and the Earl of Longford followed him, all in protest against measures that they found unacceptable. In March, 1968, George Brown, the ebullient Foreign Secretary and Deputy Leader of the Labour Party, resigned because he despaired of the manner in which government decisions were reached and believed that the failure of members of the Cabinet to communicate adequately with each other was leading to a mood of cynicism in the country. Ray Gunter, the Minister of Power (and previously of Labour), resigned in June, 1968. Originally a Trade Unionist, he was increasingly disturbed at the actions of a Cabinet 'overweighted with intellectuals who cannot understand what ordinary people think'. He complained of the lack of 'true comradeship at the top' and feared that the Labour movement was drifting into 'terrible danger'.[1] There would have been many others in 1968 who would have echoed Gunter's forebodings.

As it became increasingly clear that a general election would be held in 1970 the Conservatives, led since 1965 by Edward

Heath, inevitably took advantage of Labour's difficulties. By selecting their statistical evidence they were able to present a telling case. Iain Macleod, in the Commons, contrasted the last five years of Conservative government with the five full years of Labour: production increase during the first period of 23 per cent, during the second of 13 per cent; annual average growth 3·8 per cent and 2·2 per cent during the two periods; average annual unemployment 423600 and 474300; annual increase of savings, 14·7 per cent a year and 0·5 per cent; average price increases 2·6 per cent and 4·1 per cent; tax reductions under a Conservative government of £500m, and additions under Labour of £3100m, net overseas debt reduction under the Conservatives of £360m and net increase 1965–9 of £1650m. Macleod spoke of 'Wilson's Law'—'the more definite the promise the more certain the breach'[2]—and although such condemnation may have been a political convention as an election approached, it was a condemnation which Conservatives found easy to substantiate.

They were supported immediately before the election by claims made on television and in *The Times* by the Earl of Cromer, Governor of the Bank of England until July, 1966. The Earl indicated that whereas, despite all the apparent economic weaknesses existing in 1964, Labour's inherited short-term overseas borrowings in support of the balance of payments deficit had amounted to less than $200m, such borrowing had later reached a peak of $8000m and it amounted still, in March, 1970, to nearly $4000m. Since these debts had to be repaid in foreign currency earned by other sectors of the community, they would undoubtedly remain a heavy burden 'for some years to come'. Overseas borrowings by local authorities, nationalised industries and private enterprise would also, in the long term, prove to be burdens. Thus, Labour rejoicing over the health of the economy was really premature.

FRUSTRATED HOPES

Fortunately for Labour, many of the arguments used in the debates on the economy were too technical to influence a majority of the electorate. More easily comprehensible were the current balance of payments figures, from August, 1969, to April, 1970, which suggested not merely that government measures had been effective but that the balance in Britain's favour would transpire to be twice as large as, in more hopeful moments, Roy Jenkins, the Chancellor, had predicted. In this dramatically changed situation support began to flow back to Labour with remarkable rapidity. Perhaps the electorate was also influenced by the fact that notwithstanding the alleged crises its visible wealth at the end of the sixties, whether reckoned in terms of the number of its cars, refrigerators, television sets, vacuum cleaners, broiler chickens or golf balls, was greater than its wealth in 1960. Whatever the reasons for the change of attitude may have been, the evidence of local elections encouraged Labour to believe that despite all its misfortunes during the previous three years it could still win a general election. The evidence of the opinion polls during May and early June, 1970, showed that they would certainly do so. One opinion poll even predicted a 12 per cent lead for Labour over the Conservatives. Only a single poll, on a single occasion, gave the Conservatives some slight ground for hope. So the campaign could be pursued along customary lines, with wide publicity for the mutual recriminations of the leaders of the two large parties and for the utterances of Enoch Powell, in the confidence that the outcome was, after all, in no doubt.

Yet the pollsters were extraordinarily inaccurate. Labour, so exultant before the voting, found itself losing seat after seat, and the Conservatives were returned with 46·4 per cent of the poll (13 106 965 votes), with a majority over Labour of 43 and a clear majority over all others of 31. Three hundred and thirty seats were now in Conservative hands, and Labour, with 43·0 per cent of the poll and 12 141 676 votes, retained only 287. Among Labour victims was the Chief Secretary to the Treasury, John Diamond. Jennie Lee, who as Minister for the Arts had won only gratitude, was defeated. And, most surprisingly, George Brown, still Deputy Leader of the Labour party notwithstanding his resignation from the government, lost at Belper.

For the Liberals, led now by Jeremy Thorpe, the election represented a calamity. They could still attract 2 109 218 votes; yet 7 of their 13 seats, including Orpington, were lost. The party, which had such limited financial resources compared with Conservative and Labour parties, was obliged to surrender to the Treasury £27 300 in lost deposits.

The Western Isles returned a Scottish Nationalist. A Republican Labour member was returned again for Belfast West.

Mid-Ulster and Fermanagh and Tyrone were won by Independent Unit candidates, one of whom had been sentenced to prison for riotous behaviour in Derry. A Protestant Unionist, the Rev. Ian Paisley, who had figured prominently in the disturbances in Northern Ireland during the previous two years, was returned for Antrim North. The official Labour candidate was defeated at Merthyr Tydfil by S. O. Davies, aged eighty-three, who had declined to stand down and now came back to Westminster as an Independent Labour member. Otherwise the two main parties were able to retain their domination of parliamentary life.

---

[1] TV interview, 2.7.68. *Keesing* p. 22775
[2] *The Times*, 15.4.70

PART FIVE

45

The Permissive Society and its opponents

The sums spent on education rose continually. Unemployment, until the late sixties, remained low. The social services provided security. Incomes rising faster than prices enabled citizens to enjoy more real wealth, more widely distributed, than ever before. At the same time crime rose continually. The rate of illegitimacy grew. Diseases and social problems associated with the more widespread abandonment of traditional restraints provided new reasons for anxiety. By the end of the sixties grounds existed for supposing that a more liberal society was also a more disorderly society.

The idea that the reform of the delinquent was more important than punishment gathered strength after the war. This merciful approach gained the support both of the Conservative Home Secretary, R. A. Butler, and of a Labour successor, Roy Jenkins. A Home Office Research Unit was established for criminological research, and a chair of criminology came into existence at Cambridge. Corporal punishment was abolished in prisons in 1948, the death penalty was suspended for an experimental five years in 1965 and was subsequently ended permanently. Experiments with open prisons and suspended sentences were initiated. Yet the spirit of reform appeared to have little influence on the less law-abiding elements of British society. Whereas in 1939 304000 indictable crimes, the more serious, were known to the police, the number in 1969 was almost 1489000. The situation did not deteriorate at a uniform rate, and occasionally (in 1954, for instance) the number was lower than during the previous year. However, from the late fifties onward the annual increase of indictable crime was depressing: a 43 per cent increase between 1958 and 1962, approximately 9 per cent increases in 1963, 1964, 1968 and 1969. Between 1938 and 1964 crimes committed by young people under 17 more than doubled, while those committed by members of the 17-to-21 age group multiplied threefold. By the mid-sixties about half those found guilty of indictable offences were under 21. Boys and young men continued to be the principal villains, but crime among females also tended to rise sharply during the sixties. Larceny remained the commonest crime but a rapid increase occurred in crimes of violence. The increase in traffic offences and such other non-indictable offences as drunkenness, disorderly behaviour and malicious damage paralleled the rise in indictable crimes. The hooliganism of teenage gangs at coastal resorts during holiday week ends caused increasing anxiety in the late sixties, and even the universities, the London School of Economics in particular, were affected by the restiveness of some of the students, though far less seriously than some American, French and Japanese universities.

In the sphere of domestic relationships the most significant development was, no doubt, the introduction of the contraceptive pill. Its use certainly coincided with a marked decline in the number of live births, from 18·5 per thousand in 1964 to 16·3 per thousand in 1969, a change which could only be welcomed at a time when the world was becoming seriously worried about the ultimate consequences of the population explosion. It did not, however, reduce either the number of illegitimate births or (at least by 1970) the demand for abortions. Illegitimacy in England and Wales rose rapidly after 1956, when the proportion of live births to unmarried parents was 4·8 per cent (slightly higher than the proportion of the mid-thirties), until in 1964 it reached 7·2 per cent. Only after 1967 did some levelling off become noticeable. The figures for Scotland and Northern Ireland were not so high in the sixties, but they were increasing in both countries. A quarter of the babies born to mothers under the age of 20 were illegitimate.

In 1969 54000 legal abortions were performed, the first full year in which the Abortion Act operated. A large number of others were carried out without record, and it was assumed that in Britain there were, for each 100 births, between 10 and 20 abortions. Uncertain though the statistics were, these figures were probably very low compared with the figures for many other European countries. The lowest estimate for France was 50 abortions for each 100 live births; for Italy 70, for West

Germany 100, for Belgium and Austria 150. Estimates for Belgium and Germany rose as high as 300. It was expected that with the more widespread use of contraceptives the numbers would fall. In Britain, at least, evidence was lacking at the end of the sixties that the total number of abortions being performed was rising.

Sexual negligence was also reflected in the increasing incidence of venereal diseases after the mid-fifties. Weakness, or daring, or a spirit of revolt against society were reflected in an increase of drug-taking, possibly not lastingly serious if the drug were only cannabis, but tragic if from this the addict went on to heroin. Gambling, organised openly in betting shops, increased. The traditional bastion of resistance to developments of this kind, the Church, continued to lose ground, not rapidly, it was true, but steadily and with few indications in post-war Britain that the trend would be reversed. The number of children under 14 attending Sunday School classes was, per 1000, 218 in 1939 and 133 in 1960. The total number on the Church of England electoral roll was 3423000 in 1940 and 2692000 in 1964. Although the proportion of Easter Day communicants in each 1000 of the population did not alter appreciably between 1940 and the early sixties, the proportion of candidates for confirmation declined, and so, very gradually, did the number who were married in Anglican churches. Endeavours were made to modernise the image of the Church in the hope of attracting young people who were thought to be hostile to tradition services; moves towards the closer association of the various denominations gathered strength; and a few, like Bishop Robinson of Woolwich (whose book, *Honest to God*, aroused great attention when it was published in 1963), boldly advocated a radical reinterpretation of doctrines. But faith played an insignificant part in the calculations of a majority. Only the Catholic Church in Britain appeared to maintain its strength, yet even here symptoms of rebellion were obtruding themselves towards the end of the sixties—among priests who doubted the virtues of celibacy in particular.

A social frailty, the consequences of which continued to gain ground, was cigarette smoking. Medical research since the war had associated this beyond doubt with respiratory diseases, but the conclusions had had no revolutionary effect on the nation's habits. Each year, therefore, a greater number of people died of cancer of the lung: about 35000 a year by the late sixties. Mortality from chronic bronchitis and coronary thrombosis, which were also associated with smoking, was equally high. The Ministry of Health's report on the health of the nation in 1969, compiled by its Chief Medical Officer, Sir George Godber, estimated that about 100000 premature deaths in Britain from lung cancer, bronchitis and ischaemic heart disease together were connected with smoking. It was clear that a substantial majority of the 38·6m working days lost in industry as a result of bronchitis in 1969 could be attributed to the same addiction. Yet the average British adult continued to smoke some 2830 cigarettes a year.

46

Transport

The total number of licensed road vehicles in Britain in 1938 had been 3094000. By 1969 the number had risen to 14753000. The number of private cars had gone up during this period from 1944000 to 11228000, the number of goods vehicles from 497000 to 1640000. The car had become the most obvious symptom of the increasing wealth of the industrialised countries, the most indispensable possession to those who had experienced its advantages, an essential factor in town and country planning and in domestic architecture, an obsession on which annual family expenditure increased faster than expenditure on anything else.

Before the war the British had not built long stretches of road of the German Autobahn type and had found consolation in the belief that at least their minor roads were better than those of the Continent. Now it became a matter of urgency to construct motorways to serve fast, long-distance traffic. The first of these, the Preston by-pass, was opened in December, 1958. The first stages of the M1 between London and Yorkshire were opened in 1959, and by 1969 622 miles of roads of this kind had been constructed. The Forth road bridge was opened in 1964, the Tay road bridge and the Severn bridge, designed by Sir Gilbert Roberts, in 1966. Total government expenditure on the construction and maintenance of roads soared from £98·5m in 1953 to £536m in 1968. On major improvements and new construction alone expenditure rose between these years from £8·4m to £332m. Unfortunately, outlay could never quite keep pace with the serious problems which the transport revolution entailed. Each summer brought traffic jams miles in length as travellers converged on the coast. Town councils were obliged to build multi-storey car parks. Parking meters became necessary to reduce the number of vehicles at the sides of busy town streets. The truth revealed in the *Buchanan Report* (1963) that

341

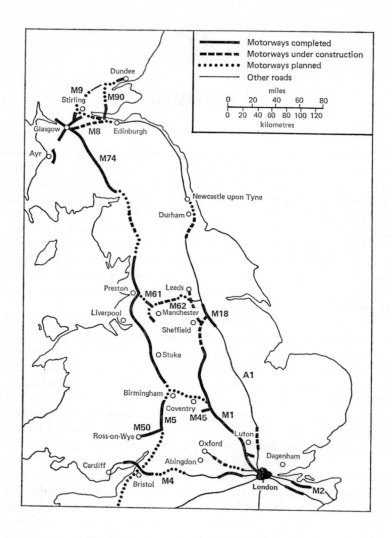

Motorways, April 1967. *Source*: Based on maps published in
The Times and in *Britain: an Official Handbook*

urban traffic problems were created largely by purely urban and
not by long-distance traffic compelled planners to realise that
by-passes were not sufficient and that traffic in future might

have to move through the towns on different levels. Plans for the construction of concentric ring roads round London aroused protests from the many householders whose homes would be destroyed or made almost uninhabitable as a result. Despite the imposition of speed limits, the introduction of an increasing number of one-way streets and campaigns against drinking and

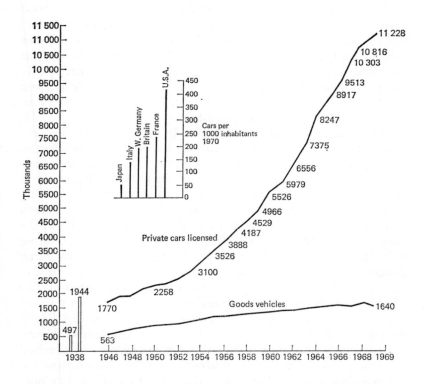

Licensed road vehicles. Total number of licensed road vehicles (including private cars, public passenger vehicles, goods vehicles and agricultural vehicles)

1938	3 094 000
1946	3 113 000
1954	5 775 000
1960	9 384 000
1969	14 753 000

Source: (upper diagram) *The Economist*. Main graph based on figures in the *Annual Abstract of Statistics*

driving, fatal accidents appeared to be inescapable. The car industries which had brought employment and wealth to such such towns as Dagenham, Luton and Coventry had also brought troubled labour relations and, during the late sixties in partic- ular, an increasing spate of strikes. Apparently these were prob- lems that had to be lived with for the sake of the advantages that road transport brought.

Transport by air also increased remarkably. In 1938 219000 passengers had travelled on British airlines. In 1969 13222000 did so. This development reflected especially the rising number who travelled abroad for holidays of brief duration. It was paralleled by the rising amount of freight and mail carried by plane. It brought about the growth of the aircraft industry as a factor too important for governments to leave altogether in private hands. An Airports Authority Act, passed in 1965, provided for the establishment of a body to manage the four international airports at Heathrow, Gatwick, Prestwick and Stansted. The Act was based on a report of the Parliamentary Select Committee on Estimates and on a White Paper, both published in 1961, and aroused no party controversy. Increasing hostility developed, however, to some other aspects of air travel. Throughout the sixties the noise of planes in the vicinity of the airports and beneath the flight routes provoked mounting criticism which intensified as predictions of the approaching inadequacy of Heathrow and Gatwick obliged the authorities to seek a site for a third major airport to serve London. The choice of Stansted evoked such articulate complaint that the idea had to be abandoned. Foulness (Essex), Nuthampstead (Hert- fordshire), Thurleigh (Bedfordshire) and Wing (Buckingham- shire) were thereupon considered. Strong objections were raised to each, and in 1970 examination of the problem was entrusted to a Commission under Mr Justice Roskill. The most widely held view was that however expensive necessary land reclamation at Foulness might be, the sea approaches and the small human population made it the least offensive site.

RAILWAYS

As an increasingly affluent population travelled by car or plane and as manufacturers found it increasingly easy to despatch their goods by road rather than rail, the railways declined. They

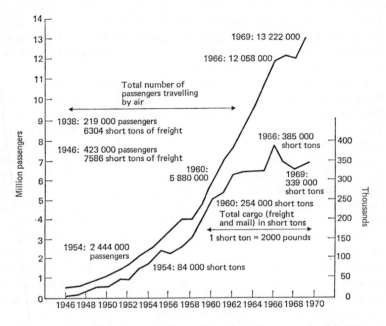

Air travel and transport. *Source*: Based on figures provided in
the *Annual Abstract of Statistics*

paid their way until 1952. Thereafter competition proved too
strong. During the fifteen years before the production in 1963
of Dr Beeching's report on the railways no fewer than 1850
stations had been forced to close, and manpower on the railways
had been reduced by nearly 27 per cent. Modernisation undertaken since 1955 (the electrification of the Kent coast lines, for
example) had not availed to reverse the trend. By 1961 the
railways' deficit was £86 900 000. Half the surviving lines
carried only 4 per cent of the passenger miles. Half the stations
produced only 2 per cent of receipts from passengers. Twenty-
six per cent of the passenger receipts were taken by only thirty
four stations—less than one per cent of the total number. It was
questioned whether the railways met as much as 10 per cent of
the demand for public transport in rural districts, where most
trains carried less than a busload of passengers. The demand for
freight carriage was no greater. The railways had been adapted

in the first place for the transport of goods over short distances. They were no longer valuable for this purpose. Even the once profitable carriage of coal was likely to decrease as an increasing proportion of coal was used for electricity, not needing to be transported over great distances.

The Beeching Plan recommended the closure of about one-third of the route mileage (about 5000 miles) and 2128 stations that had not already been closed. Most of the railways in North Cornwall and Devon were doomed. So were the cross-country routes in Somerset, Dorset, Hampshire and Sussex, branch lines serving small seaside towns, all the lines in central Wales apart from that from Shrewsbury to Aberystwyth and Pwllheli. In the Midlands and North England only the main lines between the larger cities were to be retained, in South Scotland only the main lines between Glasgow and Edinburgh and England. In central Scotland only the main lines and those from Glasgow to Oban and Mallaig were to survive. Inverness was to be the northernmost railhead. Where more than one route to a place existed only one was to remain. In order to introduce the maximum efficiency into the transport of freight the report advocated the creation of 'liner trains' to link the main centres of population and industry and to carry goods in specially designed containers brought to the depots in specially designed vehicles.

The debate that followed was between those who believed, as Beeching did, that the railways were essentially commercial undertakings which ought to show a commercial profit or go out of business, and those who regarded the network as a social service which should exist even if it showed no profit and had to be subsidised by the government. In practice the enormous size of the continuing deficits ($£135m$ in 1966) weakened the case of the latter, and closures continued steadily over the next few years, combined where possible (London to Birmingham, Manchester and Liverpool, for example) with modernisation such as the introduction of electrified services. After a period of stubborn resistance by railwaymen liner trains were also accepted. The idea of railways as a social service was not, indeed, entirely overlooked: a revised plan brought out by the Labour government in 1966 (when Barbara Castle was Minister of Transport) agreed that a certain number of unprofitable lines should be retained where alternative means of transport would be impracticable or excessively costly. Among the lines reprieved

were those from Inverness to Wick and Thurso, Llandudno to
Blaenau Ffestiniog, Ayr to Stranraer, and Middlesbrough to
Whitby. At the same time some which Beeching would have
saved were now threatened with closure: Fort William to
Mallaig, Norwich to Cromer, Cambridge to Bedford, and
Aberdovey to Pwllheli. A considerable number of other lines,
especially in South Wales, the Birmingham region, Derby and
Nottingham, South Lancashire and West Yorkshire and central
Scotland, were to be kept only for the transport of freight.

The fate of the railways was, of course, one faced by lines in
all the advanced countries of the West. Universally the experience was that only the fast inter-city expresses and the commuter
services round the principal towns could pay their way. For the
social effects of closure the British authorities had no need to
have looked further than the West of Ireland, where most of the
winding lines serving outlying communities on the Atlantic sea-
board had quietly died. Road transport had effectively superseded the trains. Few people studied these precedents, perhaps
because few had at the time raised any vigorous and noticeable
protest.

The total number of steam and motor vessels on the United
Kingdom register in 1938 had been 13 229. Newly built boats
had not been able to keep pace with war-time losses, and in 1946
the country had 12 581. From 1947 the number steadily increased until in 1969 it had risen to 21 647.

47

Agriculture

The war-time need to increase supplies of home-produced food, the challenge of a constantly rising population, the realisation that Britain could no longer depend on cheap imported food, and scientific developments all combined to bring about an agricultural revolution comparable in importance to that of the eighteenth century. Modernisation, expanding output and the prosperity of the farmers went hand in hand.

An Agriculture Act of 1947 presented a five-year plan which aimed at a 20 per cent increase in output by 1952 (or an output 50 per cent above the pre-war level). To ensure stable incomes for farmers the government guaranteed the prices of agricultural produce and provided for an annual review of such changes in market demand, farming efficiency or the national economic situation as might have affected agriculture. Thereafter, government grants became available for ploughing up grassland and improving stretches of marginal land which had previously been unproductive, for drainage or provision of a water supply, for the improvement of cottages, the purchase of fertilisers or the construction of silos. Grants could also be obtained to help the elimination of the traditional nuisances, rabbits and wood pigeons, and a new one, the coypu, which had begun to undermine the banks of rivers in East Anglia and was rapidly multiplying. At the same time acreage payments were made for potatoes and rye, and subsidies were promised for hill farmers depending on sheep and cattle. Deficiency payments were made to farmers whose products were marketed at artificially low prices. In 1957 another Agriculture Act assured farmers that the guaranteed prices introduced ten years earlier would not be steeply reduced and provided for grants for the modernisation of equipment. In 1964 the government adopted powers to introduce minimum import prices for agricultural products which might have undermined the prices of home-produced commodities and have involved the payment of excessive subsidies to British farmers who had been obliged to lower their prices in order to compete. The realisation of the economic advantages of large-scale undertakings lay behind yet another Agriculture Act in 1966, which allowed the government to make further grants of 50 per cent of the costs involved in amalgamating small farms, or to buy up holdings outright in order to amalgamate them. This Act also established a Meat and Livestock Commission to assist the breeding, marketing and distribution of animals, and a Central Council for Agricultural and Horticultural Co-operation.

The development of a flourishing agriculture required a substantial outlay. Between 1960 and 1965 the average annual cost of government support for agriculture was £290m. But the results were impressive. In only six years, between 1949 and 1955, farmers were able to install machinery worth £300m. Whereas in 1939 there had been 55 000 tractors on the land, by 1961 there were 481 000, one to every thirty-six acres of arable land. There was thereafter no need for any appreciable increase in the number in use. The number of pick-up balers and milking machines increased on a comparable scale until the middle sixties. In 1956, 33 000 combine harvesters were in use, in 1968 60 000. The introduction of these new mechanical aids to farming combined with the production of new pesticides, increased quantities of fertilisers and experiments with improved plant varieties to bring about a parallel expansion of the output of arable crops. While between 1936 and 1938 the average acre had produced only 17·8 cwt of wheat, the average annual yield during the decade 1959 to 1968 was 31·0 cwt, and in such favourable years as 1962 and 1969 it could rise to between 34 and 35 cwt. Whereas before the war home-grown wheat and the flour made from it had constituted only 23 per cent of the total supply needed, by the middle sixties they were providing 47 per cent of requirements. The average harvest between 1936 and 1938 had been 1 651 000 tons. In 1965 the harvest yielded 4 105 000 tons. Developments of an equally significant character were recorded for other cereals and arable crops. For oats the pre-war yield had been 16·2 cwt an acre, and the average during the decade 1959 to 1968 was 23·4 cwt an acre. For barley the figures for these two periods were 16·4 cwt an acre and 28·0 cwt. The area sown with oats declined during the sixties, so the total yield also decreased. However, the increase in the total barley crop was spectacular: the average pre-war harvest had amounted to 765000 tons, the total in 1960 was 4241000 tons, and by 1967 it had risen to 9069000 tons. Another crop which was grown on an increasing scale was sugar beet. In the three years before the war average output was 415000 tons, and the average yield of each acre was 24·8 cwt, but between 1959 and 1968 output never fell below 5254000 tons and in two years (1960 and 1968) exceeded 7m tons. The yield from each acre increased even more remarkably than did the yield of cereals, approximately doubling over a quarter of a century. Potato yields also increased, though to a less dramatic degree.

Animal farming developed in a similar way. Thanks partly to the eradication of bovine tuberculosis and partly to the practice of artificial insemination, which ensured that by the mid-sixties about two-thirds of the calves born in England and Wales were the offspring of the finest bulls, the milk yield in 1964 amounted to 2499m gallons, whereas the average for the years 1936 to 1938 had been only 1556m gallons. Not merely did the total number of British cattle increase during and after the war, from 8578000 before the war to 12151000 in 1968; the milk yield of the cows also increased, in the 1950s by nearly 20 per cent. Beef and veal production was raised between the late thirties and 1964 from 578000 tons to 793000 tons. Meanwhile, the total population of British sheep and pigs rose, though neither evenly nor substantially during the sixties. Pre-war supplies of mutton and lamb amounted to an average of 195000 tons, while in 1964 the figure was 248000 tons. Pork and bacon from British farms increased during the same period from 368000 tons to 807000 tons. More revolutionary still was the approach to poultry farming. Whereas during the years immediately before the war British hens had produced an annual average of 545m dozen eggs, their achievement in 1964 was 1219m dozen. Between 1936 and 1938 only 71 per cent of the eggs eaten in Britain had been home produced; by the sixties only about 2 per cent were being imported. At the same time mass production of broiler chickens resulted in the sale of about 140m birds for the table in 1961, and 180m in 1965, though the changes were brought about by methods of breeding and rearing which evoked strong criticism from those who deplored the apparent inhumanity of the large-scale commercial farming of the twentieth century.

For the farmers themselves the situation was brighter, at least during the fifties and the early and middle sixties, than it had been for a century. Farming income in 1938 had been £64m. In 1946 it was £190m. By 1950 it had been raised to £302m, by 1965 to £475·5m. Even after payment of taxes it had more than trebled in money terms. In terms of purchasing power it had doubled in a decade. Moreover, this income was distributed among a labour force which, as a result of more efficient methods and an increasing use of machinery, was steadily diminishing. In 1938 599000 workers were employed in agriculture and horticulture. By 1968 the number had declined to 396000. The National Farmers' Union was able to expand its organisation and to improve its status. The agricultural workers' status improved correspondingly: immediately after 1945 wage rates on the land rose faster than in any other industry. Only at the end of the sixties did some serious discontent develop, more especially among those whose farms were purely arable and were worst affected if the harvest were comparatively poor. Imperial Chemical Industry's service records, from a cross-section of 333 farms, indicated that between 1958 and 1968 'fixed' costs rose by 60 per cent while income from products sold at the 'farm gate' rose by only 8 per cent, and that whereas in a good year the gap would be largely covered by increased output, in a bad one farmers were liable to suffer a diminution of their incomes. Others, in Shropshire and neighbouring counties, suffered early in 1968 from an exceptionally disastrous outbreak of foot and mouth disease among their animals. Compensation was paid by the government, but the money could not at once recreate fine herds that had been slaughtered.

An increasingly large number of the professional middle classes began to find occupations on the land as engineers, accountants or marketing officials. At the same time, the traditional domination of the Landed Gentry weakened still further: whereas in 1937 about two-thirds of those listed by *Burke* acquired at least some of their income from land, by 1952 only half did so. Death duties continued to break up the big estates. Between 1938 and 1950, on estates of £100000, they were increased from 20 per cent to 50 per cent, and on estates of £1m they rose from 50 per cent to 80 per cent. As estates subject to these high duties were broken up an increasing number of tenant farmers bought the holdings that they were already occupying, so that by the 1960s about half the farms of Britain were owned by their occupiers. Their holdings varied in size. About 42000 were classified as large 'commercial' farm businesses, and these produced about half the total farm output. Small 'commercial' farms numbering 66000, were providing a reasonable living for their occupiers. Many—112000—were really too small to permit a prosperous livelihood, and it was amongst these that governments encouraged amalgamation. The occupiers of about 230000 other holdings had an additional source of livelihood, and for them farming was only a part-time activity.

One landowner, the Forestry Commission, steadily increased its acreage, until in 1968 it possessed 2897000. Much of the land on which it planted its comparatively fast-growing and profitable conifers was mountainous and of very limited value, even for sheep. It was criticised by those who preferred bare slopes, though in fact it was providing employment, scenic variety, and well-engineered tracks through the newly planted woodlands on the hills of Wales, and in the Highlands and Islands, where an under-employed population had been declining. By 1968 almost two-thirds of Britain's forests were the responsibility of the Commission.

48

Industry and science after 1945

As in the eighteenth century, revolutionary developments in agriculture were accompanied by dramatic industrial advances. Scientific inventiveness and the rapid technological change associated with it produced significant alterations in the pattern of British industry after the war. Some idea of these changes can be gained from consideration of the relative importance before and after the war of Britain's varied exports. In some spheres, it was true, the situation did not differ very substantially. Iron and steel, which had composed 8·6 per cent of British manufactured exports during the years 1935 to 1938, still composed 7·2 per cent in 1960. Metal manufactures, 6·1 per cent of manufactured exports between 1935 and 1938, accounted for 5·2 per cent in 1960. In other spheres, however, notable changes occurred. Both before and after the war non-electrical machinery headed the list of exports, but whereas in the years immediately before the war it had accounted for 12·1 per cent of exported goods, it had risen by 1960 to 23·7 per cent. Chemicals, 8·5 per cent before the war, had risen by 1960 to 10·5 per cent. Exports of electrical machinery and apparatus went up during this period from 4·9 per cent of the total to 7·8 per cent. Vehicles and aircraft rose from 7·7 per cent to 17·5 per cent. Nor was 1960 a peak year, since the expanding industries continued to expand during the sixties. Ignoring international comparisons, and considering the successes of these industries in terms of the income that they brought in, the achievements appeared impressive, even allowing for the fact that goods were about three times as costly in 1960 as they had been before the war. For example, non-electrical machinery sales earned on an average £42m a year between 1935 and 1938; and in 1960, when such sales represented almost double the proportion of total British manufactured exports, they earned £683m; in 1968 nearly £1269m was received for them.

Petroleum and such petroleum products as plastics were becoming far more important. Exports were ten times greater in 1960 than they had been in 1947. Other industries which developed after the war and already by 1955 provided 3 per cent of Britain's manufactured exports included electronic apparatus, combine harvesters, diesel locomotives, detergents, nylon clothes, antibiotics and sulphonamide drugs. Markets abroad were rapidly expanding for articles as varied as oil drilling and refining equipment, fluorescent lamps, radar and navigational equipment, transistors, foam-rubber articles and coffee powder. Office machinery, washing machines and refrigerators were among the longer established symbols of scientific invention to find increase sales overseas.

COAL AND COTTON IN DECLINE

At the same time the traditional bases of British industry, coal and cotton, declined calamitously. Coal, which formed 9 per cent of Britain's total exports in 1938, formed only 1 per cent in 1957; and by 1970 imported supplies were found necessary. Cotton exports, 10 per cent of the total in 1938, had fallen to 3 per cent by 1957 after a brief post-war boom, and the decline continued throughout the sixties. The causes and results of such misfortunes require closer examination.

Coal consumption and exports had amounted in 1938 to 224m tons. In the last year of the war the total had fallen to 188m tons. Then, for a decade, the industry recovered, and in the early fifties its sales were about the same as they had been in 1938. In the late fifties, however, decline set in, and consumption thereafter steadily contracted: to 193m tons in 1964 and to little more than 167m tons in 1968. It was true that the electricity industry continued to increase its purchases of coal, and purchases by the gas industry only slowly diminished. Domestic users however, turned increasingly to other fuels, and the metal industries turned rapidly away from the direct use of coal. The railways were using only a quarter of the coal in the mid-sixties that they had used in the early fifties, and by the end of the sixties their consumption was negligible.

An industry which had employed 1 100 000 men in 1913, 782 000 in 1938 and 724 000 in 1948, employed fewer than 392 000 in 1968. During the decade 1959 to 1968, 506 pits were

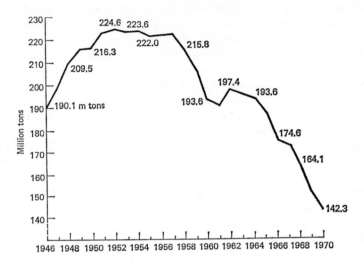

Coal output 1946–70. Highest annual output 1913: 287·4m tons. *Source*: Based on figures compiled by the *London and Cambridge Economic Service*

closed. Modernisation and strenuous efforts by the Chairman of the Coal Board, Lord Robens, to maintain the importance of the industry could not avert the competition of oil, nuclear power and methane gas in a period when many pits had been worked out or had become unprofitable.

The cotton industry flourished in the years immediately after the war. Its exports in 1949 were three times as great as those of 1938. In 1951 they were four times as great. The number of workers employed in the industry rose from 287000 in 1946 to 370000 in 1951. Then came decline. In the early fifties German, Indian and Japanese competition increased, costs rose and the number employed was reduced, by 1956, to 285000. By 1957 cotton had already fallen from second position among British exports to ninth position. By the mid-sixties the situation was far worse. Cotton could not now compete with man-made fibres, many of which had been invented or pioneered in Britain: rayon, for example, developed by Cross, Bevan and Beadle in 1892, and terylene, invented by Whinfield and Dixon in 1941 and produced on a large scale by Imperial Chemical

Industries after 1955. While British production of man-made fibres soared from 472m lb in 1955 to 882m lb in 1965, the cotton mills closed down. In 1951 there were 1750 mills and finishing works in North-west England. One thousand had closed by 1966. Output in the Lancashire area during these fifteen years was practically halved, and the labour force was reduced from 314000 to 123000. In response to protests and demands for government intervention world import quotas were negotiated, and the Conservatives made available £30m to promote modernisation; but the decline showed no sign in 1968 of reversal. Companies, small and large alike, suffered substantial reductions in their earnings from cotton. Well over 700 former cotton mills in the North-west were being used for other industrial purposes, and employees were turning instead to chemicals, plastics, paper and printing, engineering, or the food and drink trades.

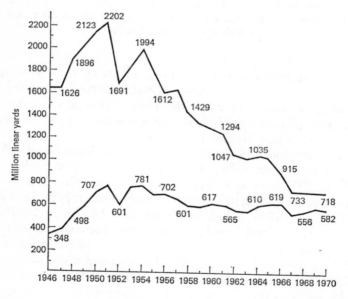

Output of cotton goods (upper graph) and output of man-made fibres and mixtures (lower graph). *Source*: Based on figures compiled by the London and Cambridge Economic Service

TECHNOLOGICAL DEVELOPMENTS AND EXPANDING INDUSTRIES

For the new and developing industries the outlook was far more encouraging than it was for the coal and cotton industries. The technological inventions of the mid twentieth century were no less impressive than had been the inventions which had in the eighteenth century brought about the remarkable development of cotton, iron and pottery; and they affected a much wider range of industries. Even where industries were declining they were not technically backward. For example, experts from many other countries came to Britain to study techniques of remote control and automation in the coal industry. The mine at Bevercotes, Nottinghamshire, was the first in the world to be fully controlled by machinery. Mechanically mined coal was fed into non-stop, automatically unloading wagons for delivery to West Burton Power Station. No miners worked at the coal face, and the 700 men employed represented only about a quarter of the number who would have been required for a pit only partially mechanised. It was possible to introduce many comparable improvements in other mines. By 1969 93 per cent of Britain's coal was both cut and loaded on to a conveyor by machine, compared with only 26 per cent in 1957. Productivity rose in the decade ending in 1968 by 58 per cent. At the same time declining receipts were being counterbalanced by technological revolution on the railways. The railway research centre at Derby established an international reputation for new techniques which would allow communication with, and control of trains from lineside control centres, at far lower costs than those required for newly developed continental methods. It also designed light alloy coaches, which would cut weight by 75 per cent, and a 'roll control' suspension system which enabled trains to round bends at high speeds and promised a major advance in passenger comfort much more cheaply attained than with the use of older 'pendulum' systems.

Developing industries, in an age of rapidly changing technology, were well served. Britain took an early lead after the war in the production of civil aircraft. The initial development of jet aircraft engines was a British achievement. The first radial flow gas turbine to fly was made, to Sir Frank Whittle's design, at Rugby. The first axial flow gas turbine was made by Metropolitan Vickers at Manchester. By 1967 about half the turbine powered civil aircraft in the western world, the United States included, were equipped with Rolls Royce engines. Britain was then also taking a lead in the construction of vertical take-off aircraft and in a new blind landing system. By the late sixties about a third of the money being spent in Britain on research was being devoted to the aircraft industry.

The hovercraft, developed by an electronics engineer, C. S. Cockerell, in the late fifties, was based on the principle that boats, trains, indeed everything, could move on a cushion of air. In the first place, a limited hovercraft service for passengers was introduced between Portsmouth and the Isle of Wight, and the first Channel crossing was made on 25 July, 1959. The success of the venture was not immediately assured; but by 1967 the great potential value of the hover principle had been realised, and four S.R.N. 4s were being manufactured at Cowes to carry, at 70 knots, 609 passengers, or 254 passengers and 30 cars, or 50 tons of freight. A hovercraft cross-Channel service was inaugurated from Pegwell Bay in 1968. Meanwhile, the British Hovercraft Corporation was developing increasingly complex rubber skirts, with multiple fingers at the margins, to facilitate the removal of very heavy objects, such as pylons, over rough ground using a minimum of pumping power, or even over farm land without damage to crops. Studies were being made of the value of hovercraft in moving buildings, in supporting badly burnt hospital patients on a cushion of air, and in moving pottery on a hovering moving belt supported by hot gas which which baked the ware. Enquiries from the Continent showed that an idea had been evolved which had aroused a very widespread interest.

A new type of bicycle was designed, and at first manufactured by Alex Moulton.

Other industries to which British inventiveness made a notable contribution during the sixties included steel, zinc, ammonia production and glass. At pilot plants at Millom, Cumberland, and Irlam, Lancashire, the British Iron and Steel Research Association, working on ideas pioneered in Switzerland and Austria, developed the steel spray process by which droplets of iron falling less than six feet through jets of oxygen and powdered lime were made into steel at a rate of up to 30 tons an hour. Expensive and cumbrous hearth furnaces and converters were shown to be unnecessary, as were the costly processes by which iron had to be heated and cooled during its conversion to steel. Continuous production of steel by automated methods became an important new prospect. So did building with a novel type of steel structure which promised to save about 25 per cent of the weight of single storey frames.

The Imperial Smelting Corporation's new process allowing both lead and zinc ores to be smelted in the same blast furnace was an equally revolutionary development. The £15m plant opened at Avonmouth in May, 1968, represented the climax of twenty years' research and enabled Britain to preserve an industry which was threatened by the prohibitively high cost of the older electrolytic process of manufacture. The new process allowed zinc production on a hitherto unprecedented scale, with great savings of costs. Output of zinc was expected to rise to 120000 tons a year, effectively doubling Imperial Smelting Corporation's annual capacity in Britain. Output of lead (which no longer needed to be separated from zinc before smelting) was expected to be 80000 tons a year. It was also anticipated that substantial quantities of cadmium and copper would be recovered from the process. Sulphuric acid, the largest single by-product, could be converted at Avonmouth into phosphoric acid and made into fertilisers. Licensing of the process to overseas zinc manufacturers was expected to bring in between £1m and £1½m in royalties each year.

The Imperial Chemical Industry's steam naphtha process for the manufacture of ammonia completely changed the outlook for British exporters of nitrogenous fertilisers and for users at home of industrial ammonia. It more than doubled the thermal efficiency of manufactured ammonia, reduced man-hours for production of a ton of ammonia from 11·6 to 0·3, lowered the consumption of electric power to one-sixth of what it had previously been, and lowered the capital costs of plant to one-quarter of the costs of older, coal-using plants. It made I.C.I. the world's largest producer of ammonia, and converted a bill of £28m in foreign currency to an expected profit of about £35m a year.

Traditional methods of making plate glass were entirely changed by the introduction of the float glass process, originally invented by two Americans but developed over a period of seven years at Pilkington's and first manufactured commercially in 1959.

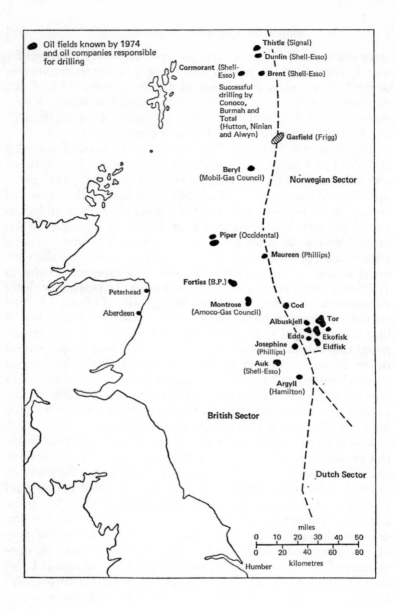

Oil fields known by 1974 and oil companies responsible for drilling

Thistle (Signal)

Dunlin (Shell-Esso)

Cormorant (Shell-Esso)

Brent (Shell-Esso)

Successful drilling by Conoco, Burmah and Total (Hutton, Ninian and Alwyn)

Gasfield (Frigg)

Beryl (Mobil-Gas Council)

Norwegian Sector

Piper (Occidental)

Maureen (Phillips)

Forties (B.P.)

Peterhead

Montrose (Amoco-Gas Council)

Cod

Aberdeen

Albuskjell

Tor

Edda

Ekofisk

Eldfisk

Josephine (Phillips)

Auk (Shell-Esso)

Argyll (Hamilton)

British Sector

Dutch Sector

miles
0 10 20 30 40 50

0 20 40 60 80
kilometres

Humber

While these major changes in leading industries were taking place comparable developments were occurring in the sources of power. The decision to drill for natural gas under the North Sea had proved to have been justified by December, 1965, when

North Sea Oil. Main developments during the 1960s. 1962, gas field found near Groningen, Holland. Interest in further drilling aroused. 1963, traces of oil found off Kimmeridge, Dorset. 1964, Continental Shelf Act vested mineral rights in the Crown. Continental Shelf convention signed. 1965, first British gas strike off Humber. 1969, December, first successful drilling for oil, east of Peterhead, by Amoco of Indiana. Oil found to be low in sulphur content and easily refined. *Source*: Based on map published in the *Illustrated London News*

commercial quantities of methane were found. Further discoveries during 1966 and 1967 some forty miles from the Norfolk coast encouraged the Gas Council to turn from town gas to methane. Although the gas was expected to last only between twenty and twenty-five years, it was hoped, according to a government White Paper on Fuel Policy (1967), that it would eventually save £100m a year on imported fuel. Some benefit had also come to Britain from foreign investment in the exploration for gas. The National Research Development Corporation assisted the production of appropriate new burners. In 1970 oil was also discovered beneath the North Sea and exploration was continuing in the British zone of the sea. Meanwhile, the electricity industry was revolutionised both by the development in Scotland of hydro-electric power and by the adaptation of atomic energy to the creation of power (see page 365).

On the land the continuing decline in the number of farm workers stimulated the evolution of labour-saving machinery. A potentially valuable development of the sixties was the production by the National Institute of Agricultural Engineering at Silsoe, Bedfordshire, of a vegetable harvester capable of collecting everything from carrots and beetroots to lettuces and leeks. Pioneer work was also done on the automatic control of temperatures and ventilation in tomato greenhouses, on the control of carbon dioxide (used advantageously to obtain higher yields per acre), on an instrument which could automatically control the moisture content of grain leaving drying machines, and on a X-ray scanner which could distinguish between harvested potatoes and stones and could separate them.

Most of these industrial and scientific advances were of essentially British origin. The nation also made its contribution to and benefited from developing industries, the growth of which was initiated elsewhere; and some reference should be made at least to those producing drugs, computers, petro-chemicals and plastics.

Although Britain spent far less on pharmaceutical research than the United States, investigations carried out in the country were still significant. In 1965, for example, Government and non-industrial research of this kind was estimated to have cost £25m. The National Research Development Corporation endeavoured to ensure that discoveries should become commercially worth while by bringing together university researchers and industry. For instance, a preparation from waste juice extracted from sisal plants which could be used in the manufacture of cortisone was backed by the Corporation after first being evolved by the Medical Research Council. Semi-synthetic penicillins were discovered by Beechams, with the help of Professor E. B. Chain.

The collaboration of International Computers and Tabulators, English Electric, Plessey and government representatives (together known after 1967 as International Computers Ltd) created the largest company of its kind outside the United States and greatly extended the scope of a new applied science of great potential value. Stocks and shares, bank accounts, typesetting, anything in fact which required the storage of complicated and detailed information rapidly became amenable to treatment in computers. The British Ship Research Association was active in the late sixties in developing computers which could decide whether a rough design deserved further consideration and then could produce a detailed design, eliminating the work of large numbers of draughtsmen. Other computers were being used to control the routing of oil tankers, to control passengers' bookings made in different parts of the world, to take over much of the work of ships' engineers by keeping constant watch on the functioning of machinery and to keep accounts and check wages. A National Computing Centre was established in Manchester to provide information about computer programmes, an Electronics and Computer Division was created as a branch of the Ministry of Technology, and computer programming developed as a new professional career.

Petroleum became increasingly important not merely because of its obvious uses as a fuel but also because it provided British shipyards with the work of tanker construction (nearly half the gross merchant tonnage built between 1952 and 1960) and stimulated the development of oil refining (in which Britain occupied fourth place in the world by 1960). Petro-chemicals, not manufactured outside the United States before Shell set up a plant at Stanlow, Cheshire, in 1942 to make synthetic liquid detergent, had become a British industry worth more than £120m by 1962, making goods valued at about £500m from only about 2 per cent of the petroleum which was being converted into fuels and lubricants. Polystyrene, polyethylene, detergents, fungicides and synthetic rubber were among the products of this industry. Their development was phenomenal: in 1945 10000 tons of petro-chemical substances were manufactured in Britain; by 1959 the total had soared to 710000 tons, and Britain had become the leading producer in Europe. Whereas in 1962 the largest plants in operation for the production of ethylene (the key initial product for most petro-chemical developments) were able to turn out no more than 50000 tons a year, by 1968 I.C.I. was operating on Teesside an ethylene plant which was designed to produce up to 450000 tons a year.

After the United States and Germany, Britain had become, by the late sixties, the largest world producer of plastics.

GOVERNMENT ASSISTANCE FOR INDUSTRY

The technological revolution was on so remarkable a scale that government aid and encouragement were indispensable. The principle was certainly not a novel one. The amount of assistance given, however, had risen to a level which would have been unimaginable half a century earlier. Before 1914 the government's annual expenditure on research had been little more than £600000; and private industry had spent less than £1m. By 1958–9 £478m was being spent on research (2·3 per cent of the country's Gross National Product) and 72 per cent of this sum was being provided by the government. It was true that about three-quarters of government expenditure was allotted to defence research. Sometimes, however, this had an impact on work of civil importance: money spent on research into flight, radar and atomic power, for example, had a clear value in a civil sphere as well. Almost two-thirds of government defence research was sub-contracted to private industry, research associations and universities.

The government-sponsored organisation with the widest ramifications was the Department of Scientific and Industrial Research. Founded in 1916 to encourage the application of science to industry, the D.S.I.R. had evoked an immediate response from a variety of industries, and by 1960 was responsible for research into such subjects as aero-dynamics, engineering and metallurgy, chemicals, building, roads, forestry, pests and radio. Its work was taken over in 1965 by the Science Research Council, the Natural Environment Research Council and the Ministry of Technology. The Medical Research Council (established 1920), the Agricultural Research Council (1931) and The Nature Conservancy (1949) were other government-sponsored organisations. The most important of the post-war organisations was the National Research Development Corporation, set up by the Development of Inventions Act 1948, to advance the cause of potentially useful inventions which private industry was unwilling or unable to sponsor. The Corporation was at first empowered to borrow up to £5m from the government. By 1967 this amount had been raised to £25m. Between 1948 and 1967 about 15 000 inventions, submitted for the most part by government departments and universities, were examined, and patent licences were issued for about 900. Among the inventions for the development of which aid was provided were the hovercraft, the computers for the control and construction of ships, the harvester for vegetables, and such drugs as cephalosporin antibiotics and triiodothyronine (for the treatment of thyroid deficiency). 'Dracone' flexible oil barges and fuel cells for the storage of energy, research into improved types of trains, vehicles for sea-bed exploration and microelectronics were also assisted. In 1968 the N.R.D.C. announced that it was prepared to give substantial backing to a new process for making fertiliser from all kinds of household waste, which was to be shredded, blended with nitrogen, phosphorus and potassium, and sold to farmers and gardeners. The Corporation made a profit at last in 1969, when £1½m of its income represented foreign currency royalties.

The N.R.D.C. and the other organisations backed by the government were not the only sources of money for the develop-

of industry. Between 1945 and 1961 the Industrial and Commercial Finance Corporation had made available about £74m to about 1000 smaller and medium-sized businesses which could not effectively seek a public issue of capital. During the same period the Finance Corporation for Industry made loans of more than £200m to the steel, chemical, oil, textile, shipping and engineering industries. The Distribution of Industry Act 1945 empowered the government to help firms establishing factories in the Distressed Areas of the thirties (North-east England, West Cumberland, South Wales and Central Scotland) and these provisions were extended during the next eight years to South Lancashire, Merseyside, the Highlands of Scotland and North-east Lancashire. Another Act, passed in 1958, reaffirmed government powers and permitted loans or grants to be made to industrialists who were prepared to take their factories to many other regions suffering from high unemployment rates, including the whole of Wales and Scotland. The Local Employment Act 1960 consolidated and extended still further the earlier measures.

For certain very costly undertakings direct government assistance was indispensable. One of these, a sphere of scientific and industrial advance to which the British contribution was impressive, was the use for non-military purposes of atomic energy. Control of developments was assumed in 1954 by the Atomic Energy Authority. Its essential purpose was the production of electricity, and it collaborated closely with the Central Electricity Generating Board. The government, which was responsible for providing most of the money, sanctioned the expenditure of as much as £40m on each atomic power station. By 1970 thirteen, of various types, had come into being. Already by 1965 8 per cent of Britain's electricity was generated in nuclear power stations, as much as was produced by nuclear means in the rest of the world; and it was hoped that as the construction programme proceeded 12 per cent would be derived from such stations by 1980. Research centres were established at Harwell, Winfrith Heath, Culham and Aldermaston, the last being concerned primarily with nuclear weapons and defence. A further programme was announced in 1969 for additional power stations, nuclear, coal fired and oil fired, involving the expenditure of more than £400m.

Atomic energy was not the only rapidly developing, 'sophisti-

Nuclear power and methane gas, 1967. *Source*: Based on a map published in *Britain: an Official Handbook*

cated' industry requiring state aid. Government subsidies were also particularly necessary for the aircraft industry, partly because the development of new types of plane was so enormously expensive that private concerns could not have met the costs and partly because a high proportion of the research undertaken by the industry was connected with national defence and was, indeed, carried out in government research establishments. The Ministry of Supply spent more than £4m on the development of the Comet, almost £5m on Viscounts, and almost £6m on Britannias. If these substantial sums were to be spent effectively they clearly could not be distributed among a number of scattered firms, and in 1957 the government accepted a recommendation by the Select Committee on Estimates that the industry should be concentrated into a smaller number of larger concerns. Some preliminary mergers took place in 1959. For example, Vickers and English Electric agreed to co-operate over the production of a new military aircraft, the TSR 2. After the creation in 1959 of a separate Ministry of Aviation, with Duncan Sandys as the Minister, the concentration of the industry continued until only three main groups were left: British Aircraft Corporation, which merged Vickers, Bristol and English Electric; Hawker Siddeley, De Havilland, Blackburn and Folland; and Bristol and Westland helicopters and Fairey. Only Short and Harland, of Northern Ireland, and Handley Page survived as independent concerns. Even reorganisation on this scale was not considered to be entirely satisfactory. By the early sixties collaboration with continental firms was being suggested. When the decision was taken in 1967 to develop Concord aircraft, designed to transport their passengers faster than the speed of sound, it was arranged that the British Aircraft Corporation and the French Sud-Aviation should together contribute 10 per cent of the costs, leaving the British and French governments to provide the other 90 per cent. Estimated costs continually rose, to £730m by the end of 1969 and to £825m six months later.

From time to time other industries, besides atomic energy and aircraft, received direct aid from the government. Imperial Chemical Industries were helped in 1953 in developing a new process for the production of titanium. In 1960 it was announced that the government would assist Cunard with up to £18m to replace the Queen Mary. Also in 1960 they agreed to lend up to £70m to Richard Thomas and Baldwin for the establishment of a new steel strip mill at Newport (Monmouthshire) while £50m was lent to Colvilles for the development of existing works at Ravenscraig, in Scotland. The decision to expand the steel industry in these places was itself one taken by the Cabinet. Scotland again received assistance when a group of ship-building firms which had combined in 1967 as Upper Clyde Shipbuilders were saved from collapse, at least temporarily, by the financial backing of the government.

The amalgamation of different firms in the aircraft and ship-building industries was symptomatic of a realisation that, however undesirable monopoly might be, the fragmentation of an industry into an excessive number of small firms was equally to be avoided at a time when large sums needed to be spent on research, expansion and marketing. To help amalgamation and the adoption of new methods the Industrial Reorganisation Corporation was established in 1967. Within little more than a year this had put about £50m into business reorganisation and had embarked upon negotiations with a further 400 companies over rationalisation (which tended to mean mergers) and development projects. Its activities have been considered in Chapter 38.

American capital was an increasingly important factor in British industry. Investments worth £2020m in 1968 represented nearly one-fifth of America's manufacturing investment outside the United States and about 12 per cent of all investment in Britain by the end of the sixties. Nearly 30 per cent of the British computer market was controlled by an American company. Nearly 60 per cent of the British car industry's output was in the hands of American firms: General Motors-Vauxhall, Chrysler-Rootes and Ford. Of the ten leading companies supplying the National Health Service, six were American. Americans had massive shares in a wide variety of foodstuffs, rubber tyres, petrol, soaps, colour films, vacuum cleaners and shoe-making machinery. These developments had begun as early as 1856, but the really phenomenal expansion occurred only after 1950. It inspired misgivings as its scope increased in the sixties, but it was in fact almost entirely beneficial, bringing work to the Development Areas (particularly to Northern Ireland and Scotland), raising thereby the British standard of living and stimulating modernisation and technological invention. It reduced Britain's import bill and increased its exports, accounting by 1968 for nearly 18 per cent of its exported manufactured goods. It preserved some companies from collapse.

The British were also investing overseas. By 1970 they had invested £568m in the United States and were receiving in return an income of £86m. They had also invested £605m in in the Common Market countries, from which the yield in 1968 was £65m. Banking and insurance facilities abroad, as well as the factories established by leading British firms, contributed to these dividends. E.E.C. investment in Britain amounted only to £256m.

Apart from the dividends received from foreign countries and the proceeds of sales abroad of industrial products, annual income from overseas sales of inventions patented in Britain amounted by 1968 to about £60m. Chemical processes earned a substantial part of the total. For example, I.C.I., was gaining about £13m a year from the sale of its inventions.

INDUSTRIAL WEAKNESSES

However, despite all the achievements of the technologists in industry and British expansion in certain spheres, critics were forceful in stressing the weaknesses which bedevilled Britain's industrial system. Its overseas sales of the products of developing industries may have been impressive. The decline in its share of total world exports was not. Complaints of excessive British costs, failure to meet promised delivery dates and insufficient attention to local market requirements and after-sales service were too frequently heard. Further weaknesses were emphasised by William W. Allen,[1] an American consultant with years of experience of British industry. He indicated in 1964 that the production of a ton of steel, which in America required the work of one man, required in Britain the work of three. Aluminium production revealed a discrepancy almost as serious. Maintenance engineering in the chemical industries which could be done in the United States by one man generally required about four in Britain. Yet Britain was not technologically backward. House building in Britain was condemned for taking three to six times as long as in the U.S.A. The construction of flats or offices was taking two to three times as long. Ship building could have been undertaken with 40 per cent fewer men if labour and management alike had not practised an inefficient limitation on the type of work done by each class of worker. Allen concluded that virtually every employee in British industry was under-employed, and that with greater efficiency wages could have been higher and hours shorter. An average of 12–14 per cent a year overtime pay should have been quite unnecessary. As others had pointed out, overtime was a hangover from days when workers were chronically and systematically underpaid; by the sixties its main *raison d'être* had disappeared and it was merely leading to deliberate slow working during normal hours in order that higher rates could be earned at other times.

The harm done by the custom among trade unionists of restricting certain operations to members of certain unions and refusing to allow others to perform them was constantly stressed, both in surveys conducted by individual writers and in government reports such as those produced by the Royal Commission on Trade Unions and Employers' Associations and by the Prices and Incomes Board. These restrictive practices dated from a period of prolonged unemployment when workmen were essentially concerned to preserve each others' jobs. By the sixties they had the effect of guaranteeing that some men should be idle for a large part of their paid time waiting for others (frequently members of another union) to complete the work, which they were not permitted to do themselves. They were particularly prevalent in the printing industry, ship-building and the docks. The remarkable results achieved as a result of productivity bargains between management and workers in a number of firms (Tube Investments Ltd and the Transport and General Workers' Union reached such an agreement in 1968; so did the management of the Fawley oil refinery and the British Petroleum Chemicals complex at Grangemouth, Stirling) demonstrated the value of eliminating restrictive practices and/or overtime pay. Unfortunately, effective bargains had not so far been made on a really wide scale. Generally the efforts of governments, employers' organisations and the Trade Union Congress had had only a negligible impact. In many industries workers' associations were developing independently of Trade Union influence. Gulfs between the leaders and those who preferred not to be led were often increasing. Most strikes were unofficial, begun in defiance of the advice of union authorities. There might be a rapid growth, following American example, of management consultancy; business schools might be established in London and Manchester, and an increasing number of business courses might be offered by the universities old and new; organisation and methods surveys might be carried out. Yet the revolutionary attitudes which many industries needed remained elusive.

SCIENTIFIC ADVANCES

If the pre-eminence of a country's scientists may be judged by the number of Nobel laureates among them, the British could with some justification have been satisfied during the twenty-five years which followed the war. In Physics, Chemistry and Medicine alike distinction was generously recognised. During the first post-war decade honours were bestowed particularly on physicists. The recipients were, or had been, associated with a number of British universities, though all of them had at some stage in their careers undertaken research, either as students or teachers, at Cambridge. Much of their important work had, of course, been done before 1939, but it was during or after the war that the full impact of the new discoveries was felt.

In 1947 the Nobel Physics prize was awarded to Sir Edward Appleton, whose researches into electro-magnetic waves and the characteristics of the ionosphere had been of great practical value to the development of both radio and radar. The 1948 prize went to Professor P. M. S. Blackett, of Manchester University, for his development of an instrument, the cloud chamber, which could be used for the accumulation of data on cosmic radiation. This invention greatly stimulated the study of radio astronomy. Professor C. F. Powell, of Bristol University, received the 1950 Nobel prize for his work in evolving a photographic method for the study of nuclear processes and for experiments which led to the discovery of new forms of matter known as heavy mesons. In 1951 prizes were awarded to Sir John Cockcroft and to an Irishman, Professor Ernest Walton, of Trinity College, Dublin, who had extended Rutherford's study of the atomic nucleus by producing high energy particles by artificial means. Cockcroft, after holding a professorship at Cambridge, had become Director of the atomic energy research establishment at Harwell in 1946.

Professor Max Born, a German who had left his country for Cambridge in 1933, had been appointed to a professorship at Edinburgh in 1936 and had become a British citizen in 1939, was rewarded with the 1954 Nobel prize for his statistical studies of wave functions, which threw light on the behaviour of electrons and other small particles.

British chemists were even more successful than the physicists. In 1947 the award for Chemistry was bestowed on Sir Robert Robinson, Waynflete Professor at Oxford from 1930 to 1955 and an outstanding contributor to many aspects of research in organic Chemistry: anthocyanin pigments, aromatic compounds, the electronic theory of chemical reactions, explosives and medicines. Dr A. J. P. Martin and Dr Richard Synge, who received Nobel prizes in 1952, discovered a method, known as paper chromotography, for separating the substances of a mixture by letting them flow over paper. This method was used by Frederick Sanger for separating fragments from insulin. Sanger was himself honoured in 1958 for the development of a method of determining the sequence of the amino-acids which form various types of protein. Meanwhile, in 1956, another Chemistry Nobel prize had been awarded jointly to Sir Cyril Hinshelwood, Dr Lee's Professor of Chemistry at Oxford, and the Russian scientist, Nikolai Semenov, for work on chemical kinetics, the speeds with which chemical reactions or changes take place. The 1957 prize was awarded to Sir Alexander (later Lord) Todd, Professor of Organic Chemistry at Cambridge, for the discovery of methods of synthesizing the nucleotides forming an essential part of the cells dictating the nature of life. Dr J. C. Kendrew and Dr Max Perutz shared the 1962 Nobel prize for work on the structure of the molecule of the protein myoglobin, which enables muscle tissue to store oxygen. Professor Dorothy Hodgkin received the 1962 prize for studies in the sphere of crystallography which made it possible for the chemical structure of any substance to be determined solely by X-ray analysis. In 1967 Professor R. G. W. Norrish and Professor G. Porter were honoured for their discovery that a process known as flash photolysis permits the examination of chemical reactions which take only a few millionths of a second to complete. Professor D. H. R. Barton became a Nobel laureate in 1969 for the discovery and elucidation of rules governing the shapes of molecules.

Nobel prizes for medicine were awarded in 1945 to Sir Alexander Fleming, Sir Howard (later Lord) Florey and Dr Ernst Chain for their discovery of penicillin and its remarkable curative effects. Florey was an Australian who had become Professor of Pathology at Oxford, Chain a German who had settled in Britain in 1933, when the Nazis gained control of his country. Another German exile, who received the 1954 prize, was Dr (later Sir) Hans Krebs, a biochemist distinguished particularly for his researches into the metabolism of carbohydrates. During the early sixties further awards were made to Sir Peter Medawar, Alan Hodgkin and Professor Andrew Huxley, Francis Crick and Maurice Wilkins. Medawar, with an Australian colleague, Sir Macfarlane Burnet, helped to advance the surgical transplantation of various anatomical organs by the discovery that it was possible for a body to acquire a tolerance towards foreign material if it were exposed to it at a very early stage. Hodgkin and Huxley discovered the electro-chemical origins of nervous impulses. Dr Crick, Dr Wilkins and James Watson, an American, had found, in 1953, the structure of a substance called deoxyribonucleic acid (DNA), the nuclei of the cells of which living matter is composed. Wilkins (of King's College, London) and an assistant, Rosalind Franklin, had after long investigation obtained fine X-ray diffraction pictures of DNA. Crick and Watson, at Cambridge, used these pictures and chemical evidence about the constitution and behaviour of DNA and realised that there were two intertwined chains of chemical units, linked together in certain ways, and that the ways in which these chemicals were strung along the chains and linked determined the nature of the life which developed and the hereditary qualities which were passed on. The discovery was acclaimed as the most important single scientific discovery of the twentieth century. From it developed an explosion of research in the biochemical field which within a few years transformed knowledge of the life processes.

British astronomers also earned acclaim. The work at Jodrell Bank (Cheshire), directed by Sir Bernard Lovell, of tracking the satellites that were circulating in space, was significant. The Isaac Newton telescope at Hurstmonceux (Sussex) was the largest in the world apart from three in the United States.

---

[1] W. W. Allen, *Sunday Times*, 1.3.64

49
The arts

The historian of recent political and economic developments can never be quite certain that the issues which he considers will be regarded still as important after the lapse of a century. It is generally much harder to decide what is significant than to determine what happened. Even more true is this of developments in literature, music, art or the theatre. One can be sure only that tastes will change and that although a few writers and composers will survive the changes, the majority will be familiar only to students of their particular art. The survivors, moreover, may be the beneficiaries of favourable publicity (a television performance, perhaps, or a collected paper-back reprint) or some comparable accident rather than of real merit. Clearly, then, it would be foolhardy to pretend that any condensed survey of the artistic scene in the fifties and sixties could do more than refer to some of the practitioners who in their time gained knighthoods or notoriety, without claiming that these will necessarily be the ones whose works will live.

If any generalisation can be made, it must be that the twenty-five years after the war constituted a period of experiment in which conventions and long-established standards were cheerfully abandoned for the sake of originality. *Avant-garde* music turned into an almost completely new art. Much mid-century painting and sculpture sacrificed any attempt to represent the scenes or objects that ordinary persons thought they saw. Dramatists experimented with the portrayal of simple characters behaving irrationally. No limitation applied any longer to the subject matter or methods of presentation of the novel. Architecture, under the influence of land shortage and new materials, evolved an even more markedly original style than the other arts.

However, in most spheres traditional forces survived and co-existed with the forces of novelty and experiment. For these not even the World War was a watershed.

374

MUSIC

Endeavours to demonstrate the development of characteristic-ally English features of English music (apart from works based on folk melodies) have never been very convincing. Composers have generally pursued their individual lines, not consciously national ones. Even though many have shared the same teachers at the Royal Schools of Music or elsewhere, they have rarely formed a recognisable school of their own. The common features have perhaps been purely negative ones. After 1945, for example, Britain had no outstanding composer whose efforts were con-centrated on solo instrumental works (apart, perhaps, from Franz Reizenstein, a pianist-composer of German origin) and the repertoire of soloists continued, as always, to comprise predominantly the achievements of continental musicians. British composers were less forward than their continental contemporaries in indulging in the more extreme experiments which resulted in compositions without noticeable melody, harmony, rhythm, tonality or obvious recurrent themes. It may have been significant that the leading experimenters of an older generation composing in post-war Britain were of continental origin: Egon Wellesz, a Viennese, Roberto Gerhard, a Catalan and Matyas Seiber, a Hungarian. It was left to a French con-ductor and composer, Pierre Boulez, to introduce to the British public many of the more remarkable manifestations of the *avant-garde*. Novelty arrived in the end, but only several decades later than it arrived in Vienna.

These factors do not imply a lack of vigour in post-war British music. On the contrary, the opportunities which attracted foreign composers, conductors and executants in large numbers also enabled British artists to earn high reputations, even outside their own country, and allowed a wide range of new works to obtain first performances. London developed into one of the world's busiest musical centres. Annual festivals of music, with or without accompanying drama, films or exhibitions of various art forms, proliferated until, by the end of the sixties, it was possible to list more than fifty. Especially good opportunities for performances of works by living British composers were provided at Aldeburgh, Cheltenham, Bath and Newcastle. Camden, Cardiff, York and Dartington. Some of the universities became increasingly lively centres of composition: Birmingham,

Cardiff, Newcastle, Oxford, Southampton and York in particular were active during the sixties. So were the Royal Academy of Music and the Royal College of Music. Composers like John Joubert, Alun Hoddinott, Kenneth Leighton and Wilfrid Mellers were able to pursue their creative work while holding academic positions. Meanwhile, the B.B.C. acted as a patron, relaying, from 1948 onwards, on its Third or Music Programme, constant music of an infinite variety and providing a hearing for new works and employment for British orchestras, national and regional. The Arts Council gave generous financial backing to British opera and all kinds of other musical projects. New concert halls, notably the Royal Festival Hall (opened 1951) and the Queen Elizabeth Hall in London (1967), the Colston Hall, Bristol (1951), the Fairfield Halls, Croydon (1962) and the Northern College of Music halls in Manchester (begun 1969), ensured that concerts should take place in modern buildings, incorporating up-to-date accoustical and engineering skills. Music rapidly became a subject of increased importance in the schools. Audiences became accustomed to applauding the most unusual noises. In such circumstances such limitations as may have affected the art seemed insignificant.

No date in Britain's twentieth-century musical development could be described as crucial. Each generation produced its composers, each one overlapped with the next, no change was sudden and dramatic. During the early post-war years Ralph Vaughan Williams (1872–1958) was still composing major works of an original character. Sir Arnold Bax lived until 1953, John Ireland until 1962 and Sir George Dyson until 1964. Sir Arthur Bliss, Herbert Howells and Gordon Jacob, all born before 1900, were still alive in 1970. Havergal Brian, indeed, composed the great majority of his thirty-two symphonies after the war, though he was already 68 when it ended.

The first decade of the twentieth century saw the birth of most of the composers whose reputations were already made before the war and were consolidated during the twenty-five years which followed it: Alan Bush, Edmund Rubbra, Sir William Walton, Lennox Berkeley, Alan Rawsthorne, Sir Michael Tippett, William Alwyn, Benjamin Frankel, William Wordsworth and the Polish musician, Andrzej Panufnik, who settled in England in 1954. Between them they added after 1945 a considerable body of symphonies, concertos for various instruments and orchestra, choral works and chamber music to the British repertoire. Bush, Berkeley, Walton and Tippett added operas. Several of them, Walton, Rawsthorne, Frankel and Alwyn in particular, found opportunities in writing for films or ballet. All composed in an idiom which was at least recognisable. Rubbra, for example, a pupil of Holst, was indebted to the polyphonic techniques of the sixteenth and seventeenth centuries. Tippett, complex and revolutionary though his long works sounded, was interested in the madrigals of this earlier period and in Beethoven's and Purcell's music as well as that of Hindemith and Stravinsky. Bush owed something to Northumbrian folk song. All experimented with harmonies and orchestration of individual, original character; but they did not abandon altogether the ideas of melody, rhythm and tonality which had traditionally been the essential features of western music. Nor did the slightly younger Benjamin Britten (born in 1913) who was widely supposed to be the most successful of them all. Britten's music was entirely individual but it did not turn its back on tradition. It consisted of cantatas and song cycles, concertos, chamber music, an enterprising variety of pieces falling into none of these broad categories, and, above all, a succession of operas of exceptional significance, starting in 1945 with *Peter Grimes*. Britten was also among those responsible for the inauguration in 1948 of the Aldeburgh Festival.

A new generation of composers whose names became familiar during the fifties and sixties included Peter Racine Fricker, Geoffrey Bush, Malcolm Arnold, Robert Simpson, Iain Hamilton and Anthony Milner, all of whom were in their twenties in 1945. Fricker and Hamilton concentrated on large-scale instrumental works and Milner on religious choral music. Arnold's orchestral compositions were more light-hearted and probably, as a result, more popular. Bush's music, which included one-act operas, was also comparatively simple, with a direct appeal to listeners. Simpson's symphonies owed something to the inspiration of Sibelius and Nielsen.

Among the leading figures of an even younger generation were Malcolm Williamson, Peter Maxwell Davies and Richard Rodney Bennett.

Increasingly, after 1945, the effects of the twelve note and serial technique began to spread to Britain. This was based on an assumption that there was no eternal virtue in a traditional system of keys or in major and minor scales and chords and that musical works could instead by based upon a series of the twelve different notes of an octave arranged in such a way that conventional tonality disappeared. The idea was taken up by Elisabeth Lutyens and Humphrey Searle among the older composers and by a group of younger *avant-garde* experimenters born in the early thirties. Experiments were also undertaken in England from 1968 in electronic music, in which computers and tape recorders played an essential role. Only the passage of decades could determine the survival value of works of this kind, of course. It was certainly true that the works of some earlier, continental twelve-note composers remained in the repertoire of British orchestras; yet it may have been significant that the three operas written by Searle between 1958 and 1968 received their first stage performances not in Britain but in Germany; and the more bold of critics did begin to wonder when music stopped and noise began. It was inescapably true that few people's musical education had accustomed them to works of a quite revolutionary character, whether produced by Britons or by the continental composers who had settled in England. The musicians who obtained mass support were, after all, not the serious composers who have been mentioned here but the exponents of 'skiffle', Rock 'n Roll and Pop.

'Skiffle' was the characteristic popular music of the early fifties: an essentially amateur, home-made variety of jazz, performed on an assortment of improvised instruments like washboards. Since it was not commercialised its powers of survival were limited, and by the late fifties it was being superseded by Rock 'n' Roll, which added to it elements of American hill-billy and White South 'Country and Western' popular music and was vigorously plugged by commercial interests, by recording and film companies, by radio disc jockeys and (because of its association with jive and the 'twist') by dance hall managers. To a number of young singers Rock 'n' Roll brought both fame and wealth. So did Pop, which enjoyed such fabulous success in the sixties, when groups like The Beatles, Rolling Stones, Cream and Pink Floyd were in their turn publicised by the record companies and other media. The simple, lively tunes of Pop, often lacking variety but emphasising the easily appreciated themes of youth, love and sex, made an immediate appeal to teenagers who enjoyed noise and derived emotional satisfaction from the mass hero-worship with which it was connected. Various groups employed different instruments, but the electronically amplified guitar, drum, bass, organ and piano provided most frequently the accompaniment to the singer, and recording techniques helped to create the requisite sound. Careers in such an atmosphere tended to be meteoric and brief; and the average life of each 'single' was only six to eight weeks. Yet, as an essential factor in the lives of of many young people who may not have enjoyed as much money as was sometimes supposed but certainly had more to spend than had their counterparts in earlier generations, Pop undoubtedly made an impact.

BALLET

The young English ballet companies had inevitably been seriously affected by the war. Dancers had been conscripted or had left for America, companies had been broken up and international links had been suspended. Yet even during these years important new ballets had been created, and after 1945 the art was to share very fully the vitality characteristic of British music and theatre. With the reopening of Covent Garden in 1946 and the establishment of the Sadler's Wells Opera Ballet Company full scope could once again be given to the inventiveness of the country's leading choreographers, Ninette de Valois and Frederick Ashton. Ninette de Valois excelled as an exponent of the dramatic narrative ballet: *Job*, *Checkmate* and *Don Quixote*, danced respectively to the music of Vaughan Williams, Arthur Bliss and Roberto Gerhard. Frederick Ashton was primarily a creator of moods and of abstract movement unconnected with any theme other than the musical one. His wartime *Dante Sonata* (with music by Liszt) was essentially a ballet of this kind, and so were many of his post-war productions, from *Symphonic Variations* (César Franck) in 1946 to *The Two Pigeons* (Messager) in 1961 and *Enigma Variations* (Elgar) in 1968; though he could also treat effectively such tales as *Cinderella* (Prokofiev), *Ondine* (Henze) and *La Fille Mal gardée* (with music by Hérold, arranged by John Lanchbery, and décor by Osbert Lancaster).

A substantial output, concern for both beauty and humour and interest in all aspects of production enabled Ashton to earn fame far beyond the London stage. However, many other choreographers also contributed to the growing importance of British ballet. Robert Helpmann incorporated comment on the contemporary scene in such ballets as *Miracle in the Gorbals* (Bliss) and *Adam Zero*. Kenneth MacMillan explored the underlying passions, tensions, desires and frustrations of society and individuals. He used twentieth-century music, by Stravinsky, Seiber, Frank Martin, Prokofiev, Mahler and Shostakovich, but his choreography was based fundamentally on the classical styles. John Cranko, experimenting with a variety of styles, combined story-telling and mood, comedy and philosophical reflections on human psychology and society. His *Pineapple Poll*, which embraced the arts of Sullivan and Lancaster, became particularly popular. Benjamin Britten provided music for *The Prince of the Pagodas*.

The cosmopolitan links that ballet stimulated rapidly revived after the war. World-wide tours were undertaken by British companies and visits to Britain were made by companies from Russia, America, Denmark and other countries. Cranko, a South African, left Britain in 1961 to direct, with notable effect, the Stuttgart ballet. Antony Tudor, having made a significant impact on London ballet in the thirties, spent much time in America, Sweden and Australia before returning to Britain in the late sixties. Jack Carter worked in Holland and Sweden before his appointment as choreographer to London's Festival Ballet. MacMillan temporarily left the Royal Ballet in 1966 to work in Berlin. The reputations of such individual dancers as Margot Fonteyn and Beryl Grey, David Blair and the Russian émigré, Rudolf Nureyev, were international.

The activities of the Western Theatre Ballet, first in Bristol and from 1969 in Glasgow, ensured that London should not monopolise talents. The company was directed by Peter Darrell.

Stage design developed less significantly than either choreography in Britain or design in some foreign countries, partly because insufficient money was available for elaborate scenery or for the conversion of nineteenth century stages. Increasingly, though, painters like John Piper were prepared to employ their artistry in the theatre; and an agreement with the Arts Council in 1968 to subsidise the Royal Festival Ballet was an encouragement to an art which, within little more than a generation, had established itself in Britain and had gained a deserved celebrity by its variety and high standards.

TELEVISION AND RADIO IN BRITAIN

In 1939 only some 20000 pioneers in the London region possessed television sets. Even in 1950 only about 340000 licences were issued. The costs of development were too great to be met in the years of post-war austerity. By 1970, though, licences were issued for about 16m sets. Within a quarter of a century social life had probably been altered more by this invention than by any other single factor. The value of television as a medium of enlightenment and entertainment was incalculable. Increasingly other arts, the film and theatre in particular, came to depend on it. It had became an essential feature of education in the widest sense, a sphere of remarkable technoloigcal advance and a means of escape in lives which might otherwise have been empty.

A landmark in the post-war history of television in Britain was the coronation in 1953 of Queen Elizabeth, watched by an estimated 23m people at home and by very large numbers abroad, and proving beyond all doubt the potentialities of the medium. Another landmark was the Television Act of 1954, which allowed the first Independent Television programme to break the B.B.C. monopoly in September, 1955. Thereafter improvements were rapid. During the late fifties quality of reception was improved and screens increased in size. During the early sixties the invention of an efficient method of videorecording made it possible for 'instant playbacks' of news items and sporting events to be prepared. In 1962 the first live transatlantic transmission was made with a space satellite, Telstar, used as a relay station. The B.B.C. introduced its second channel in 1964, and in 1967 this became the first colour service in Europe. Other services turned to colour in 1969. European viewers had been able to see live colour pictures of the Mexico Olympic Games, transmitted by a more sophisticated space satellite system, in 1968. In 1970 they saw colour pictures from the moon.

Reference is made on other pages to the impact of the medium on drama and the film. A further artistic genre which was entirely dependent on television and which also deserves mention was the episodic series involving the same characters. The scope was infinite. *Z-Cars* and *That was the Week, That Was* began in 1962. The virtues of B.B.C.2 were finally established with *The Forsyte Saga* in 1967. *Coronation Street, Till Death Us do Part, Steptoe and Son,* were among other series which ministered particularly to the British love of domestic comedy (and of other people's misfortunes). Increasingly, History was called upon to provide themes for scholarly and dramatic treatment. A new form of employment had been created for a large number of scholars, writers, actors and engineers.

In competition with television, sound radio found itself threatened. It responded by widening its scope and improving its transmission. By 1967 the B.B.C. was broadcasting on four channels designed to serve all tastes. The audience which was stirred by such Pop music as had been provided between 1964 and 1967 by floating 'pirate' stations could now turn instead to Radio 1. At the other extreme Radio 3, the successor of the Third and Music Programmes, broadcast concerts of serious classical and contemporary music. The long-established Light Programme and Home Service continued under other names, Radios 2 and 4. V.H.F., first introduced in 1955, provided almost the whole of Britain with a choice of three services by the late sixties and made stereophonic broadcasting possible. Meanwhile, the B.B.C. was perpetuating the reputation that it had gained by broadcasting to occupied Europe during the war by transmitting overseas about 700 hours of programmes each week in 40 languages. The factual impartiality of its news bulletins had survived even pressure to adopt a propagandist attitude during the Suez war in 1956.

The Directors-General of the B.B.C. between 1944 and 1969 were Sir William Haley, Lieut.-General Sir Ian Jacob and Sir Hugh Carleton Greene.

DRAMA

Television, more than any other single factor apart from the private car, altered the pattern of social life during the fifties and sixties. It superseded the political meeting. It threatened to destroy the cinema, one of the principal forms of relaxation before the war. It reduced the importance of radio. Fortunately, though, it did not destroy drama. Indeed, by publicising the works of many new playwrights it helped their reputations,

provided them with a novel and stimulating medium and may
well have contributed to the creation of as active and enterprising a theatre as any in Britain since the early seventeenth
century. Writers seized their opportunity and produced, for a
variety of stage, a variety of play which defies generalisation.

For a decade after the war most of the dominant authors were
those who had already made names for themselves before 1939.
Terence Rattigan, Noel Coward, N. C. Hunter and Emlyn
Williams were all adept at writing plays which dramatised a
story, entertained and did not normally go out of their way to
affront the susceptibilities of the essentially middle-class
clientele of the West End theatres. The light comedies and
thrillers of writers like William Douglas-Home, Anthony
Kimmins, Peter Ustinov and Agatha Christie gave pleasure to
their audiences without arousing the anxiety or bewilderment
evoked by translations of some of the plays of continental
dramatists, such as Ugo Betti, Jean Anouilh, Brecht, Ionesco, or
the Dublin born Parisian, Samuel Beckett, whose *Waiting for
Godot* was the perplexing sensation of 1953. Audiences in Britain,
as Somerset Maugham had discovered much earlier, disliked
the irrational and inexplicable on the stage, and they were consequently not confronted with it.

At the same time, the theatre did not stagnate. Experiments
with new plays or foreign ones were made in little theatres which
came into being and frequently closed down after a few years;
and particular interest was aroused by a revival of plays in
verse. The verse play was not entirely a post-war phenomenon:
T. S. Eliot's success with *Murder in the Cathedral* was achieved in
1935 and his reputation was merely confirmed by the three
verse plays that he wrote in the 1950s. After the war, though, he
was joined by Christopher Fry, whose exuberant and witty
plays, *The Lady's not for Burning* and *Venus Observed* among
them, aroused considerable attention in the late forties and
fifties.

However, the verse play, perhaps because it demanded from
its audience too great an effort of the intellect, did not after all
become the dominant form of drama. For those who sought new
departures it was superseded after 1956 by a great wave of
plays which may sometimes have contained a full share of
fantasy but were, nonetheless, from the point of view of speech,
thoroughly realistic. Dramatic form was employed to cover a

much wider range of social types than had been customary in West End productions: the humble masses of working class cities, the young, disorganised and drifting, the poor. The writers, as individual as any other group of creative artists, were not bound together by common aims or styles, but they did each have something novel to offer to their public: symbolism, absurdity, a disturbing realism, the spectacle of ordinary people behaving with characteristic unreason. These playwrights were encouraged by experimental London theatres like the Royal Court and Joan Littlewood's Theatre Workshop, by some provincial theatres, even on occasions by the established theatres of the West End. Money was made available by the Arts Council: £76 193 in the 1952–3 season, £252 144 in that of 1961–2. The publicity accorded by televised performances was valuable.

Critics agreed that the precursor of the new wave was John Osborne's *Look Back in Anger*, produced at the Royal Court Theatre in May, 1956, after rejection by West End managements. This portrayal of a young working-class graduate exercising his talent for invective on his socially superior and patient wife in an attic apartment of a Midland town was followed by a play, *The Entertainer*, in which the principal character was a broken down music-hall comedian. The rebel Luther and the seedy solicitor of *Inadmissible Evidence* were the dominating figures of some of Osborne's later plays.

Osborne's success opened the way for an upsurge of dramatic vitality. Success bred success. Arnold Wesker, whose Jewish family had emigrated from East Europe to London's East End, earned a reputation with socially realistic plays in which the biographical background was significant: *Chicken Soup with Barley, Roots, I'm talking about Jerusalem, Chips with Everything*, were all produced between 1958 and 1962. Harold Pinter, another East Ender of Jewish ancestry, turned to the theatre of the partly absurd, writing in *The Caretaker* (1961), *The Birthday Party* and a number of shorter plays about pathetic characters, many of limited intelligence and negligible achievements, conversing in ordinary speech of nothing in particular, failing to communicate with each other, and threatening the petty routines of those into whose drab environments they intruded. Other writers, all born between 1923 and 1932, who generally depicted more realistic or probable situations, included Alun

Owen, Peter Terson, Henry Livings, John Mortimer and Clive Exton. Owen and Terson set some of their plays in Liverpool and the Vale of Evesham respectively. To Livings the comedy of existence provided themes. Exton, writing especially for television, was more pessimistic, satirical and symbolic. Mortimer championed the lonely and unsuccessful in a run-down middle-class world. At least their characters spoke a language which was comprehensible to their audiences and sometimes conveyed a social message which was recognisably valid. N. F. Simpson, on the other hand, turned to the theatre of the entirely absurd, which some found difficult to accept.

Inevitably, a number of dramatists emerged who clearly fitted into no particular category. John Whiting (1917–63) turned to the Napoleonic wars for *A Penny for a Song*, to the 1620s for *The Devils*. Giles Cooper (1918–66) wrote a number of original, macabre and effective plays for radio, such as *Unman, Wittering and Zigo*, *Happy Family* and *The Return of General Forefinger*. John Arden (b. 1930) experimented with a mixture of prose, verse and ballad, and in plays like *Armstrong's Last Goodnight* and *The Workhouse Donkey* made considerable demands on his audiences by presenting his characters as puzzling mixtures of unpredictably good and bad qualities and by the intricacy of the plots in which they were involved. History provided the themes for the most outstanding plays of Peter Shaffer (b. 1926), author of *The Royal Hunt of the Sun*, and of Robert Bolt (b. 1924), whose *A Man for All Seasons* depicted in chronicle form and contemporary language the heroism of Sir Thomas More.

So Britain reached the end of the sixties with a drama of unusual variety and originality, written to please audiences, or viewers, of very different types. Playwrights, a majority of whom could not hope for a living from the theatre, were able to turn to other media, apart from the stage. How many of their products had the qualities required for survival was, of course, an imponderable subject on which critics pronounced different verdicts according to their tastes and expectations; and it is not the task of the historian to prophesy. However, two questions might be asked. First, was the writing of plays a task which could be pursued successfully over a long period by anyone other than a very rare author? A high proportion of the plays that earned greatest praise were written during the decade

beginning in 1956 by dramatists in their late twenties or thirties
who achieved their most notable successes with their earlier
works. Secondly, how many plays written by British authors
would a later generation find as gripping, searching and memorable as *The Strong are Lonely* by the Austrian Fritz Hochwälder,
The Queen and the Rebels by the Italian Ugo Betti, *Mother Courage*
by the German Berthold Brecht, or *Monserrat* by the Algerian
Emmanuel Roblès, all of which were performed or broadcast
for the first time in Britain after the war? Were not most British
authors reluctant to confront the tragic side of life, too hesitant
to dramatise themes of really profound and permanent significance?

FILMS

Judged by the number of cinemas remaining open and the
number of patrons, the film industry suffered. In 1950 4584
cinemas existed in Britain and nearly 1380m admissions were
reported. By 1969 the number of cinemas had declined to 1581
and admissions to about 220m. Yet these figures did not imply
deterioration in all respects. As a form of art the film generally
flourished; and as the number of television licences rose towards
16m in the late 1960s more films, not fewer, were in fact
watched. American companies worked in Britain, British
directors in America. British films were made in France, Spain,
Italy. Small, independent film units were financed by the
British Film Institute, and large cinemas which were no longer
commercially viable were reshaped into three or four small ones,
providing the big towns with a greater variety of programme.
The number of books on the film multiplied.

During the war the cinema had served a valuable purpose,
providing entertainment for a mass audience and dramatising
service and civilian life in many fine films. Actors and playwrights with established reputations turned to it. Its fame spread
overseas during the first post-war decade, when themes were
found both in older works such as *Hamlet*, *Oliver Twist* and
Great Expectations and in recent novels such as Graham Greene's
The Fallen Idol and *The Third Man*. The Ealing Studios, with
Sir Michael Balcon as producer and T. E. B. Clarke as script
writer, humorously portrayed the individuality and eccentrici-
ties of English life and earned widespread acclaim both at home

and abroad. *The Lavender Hill Mob, Passport to Pimlico, Whisky Galore* and *Kind Hearts and Coronets* were among the best products of this phase.

The 1950s saw the emergence of a 'free cinema' movement which criticised the tendency for British films to be essentially middle class and Southern English in character, living on the myths of the past and avoiding many of the real social and human issues. Dissatisfaction led to the development of a new wave in the cinema parallel to that which the late fifties brought to the stage. An adaptation in 1959 of John Braine's *Room at the Top* stimulated the trend by depicting the social rise of a young man of humble origin from a drab Northern industrial town. *Saturday Night and Sunday Morning* (1961), based on Alan Sillitoe's novel, exposed the dreariness of factory work. Osborne's *Look Back in Anger*, Shelagh Delaney's play *A Taste of Honey*, David Storey's *This Sporting Life*, Sillitoe's *The Loneliness of the Long Distance Runner* and Stan Barstow's *A Kind of Loving* were also adapted for the screen. Such films dealt with issues previously banned or regarded as too thorny, like abortion or homosexuality, and they attempted, for a change, to portray honestly a working-class environment, with the boredom, frustration and coarse language of harsh reality. Key figures in these developments were Lindsay Anderson, Tony Richardson, John Schlesinger, Czech-born Karel Reisz and American Joseph Losey.

An important, though not a new feature of the post-war film was its association with the other arts. Many works, apart from those referred to, were based on successful novels or plays. Authors like Pinter, whose reputations had been made in the theatre, adapted themselves to script-writing for the screen. Artists who had served an apprenticeship in television turned to film-directing. The cinema was linked with ballet when *The Red Shoes* was produced in 1947, with Pop when the Beatles starred in *A Hard Day's Night* in 1964. And at all times serious composers readily provided music for films, some of it of sufficient value to justify concert performance as well.

FICTION

From time to time prophets had foretold that the novel would die. By the end of the sixties, though, all the statistical evidence was against so gloomy a prediction. The number of new works of fiction published each year in Britain remained remarkably constant: in 1935 it had been 2405; in 1958 it was 2421, in 1968 2282. In addition, each year saw the publication of a steady number of reprints and new editions: generally between 1500 and 2000. A medium which was capable of such infinite variety of subject matter and of such varying length clearly could not easily be destroyed. Equally clearly, it continued after the war to attract such a very large number of practitioners that no simple generalisations about its character could give universal satisfaction. Critics were agreed in selecting for comment a limited number of exceptionally successful writers, most of whom had found the opportunity to write a considerable number of volumes, to have had them published in paperback editions, perhaps to have had some adapted as film scripts; but beyond this the choice tended to be very personal, and commendation was earned by a large number of authors whose restricted output appealed particularly to reviewers of differing tastes. It chanced, moreover, that many novels which were generally ignored by the critics nonetheless became best sellers among a public whose tastes were perhaps less exalted.

The war was no more a watershed in the history of fiction than it was in most of the other arts. Indeed, more ambitious experiments had probably been undertaken before 1939 by such authors as James Joyce than were tried after 1945. No post-war year was as significant in the development of the novel as 1956 was in the history of British drama. Inevitably, post-war Britain inherited a large number of important (or popular) novelists whose varying styles had already been developed and who continued to make their contributions to the reading matter of an established public: Joyce Cary, Compton Mackenzie and P. G. Wodehouse, for example; Ivy Compton-Burnett, Agatha Christie, Elizabeth Bowen, J. B. Priestley, Aldous Huxley, C. S. Forester, and Richard Hughes. All these had been born between 1881 and 1900 and had built up secure reputations before 1939 as writers of many types of fiction, from light-hearted nonsense and detective stories to sombre family chronicles and the novel of ideas. Their styles had been as varied as their themes. The search for originality was compulsive, and necessarily so if fiction were to maintain its vigour.

After 1945 a number of rather younger writers turned to the

production of a series of books portraying the same characters at different stages of their careers. Anthony Powell, whose *Music of Time* began in 1951 with *A Question of Upbringing*, dealt particularly with a galaxy of shrewdly observed upper middle-class figures, business men, writers, the newly successful. C. P. Snow published the first of his sequence, *Strangers and Brothers*, in 1940, adding to it at intervals throughout the next thirty years and concentrating especially on the academic, administrative and managerial society with which he was familiar. Lawrence Durrell developed a view of fiction as presenting 'layers of reality', generally rejecting any chronological, narrative approach, and examining, in his *The Alexandria Quartet*, the art of novel writing and the nature of love in an amoral, cosmopolitan city. Evelyn Waugh, in a trilogy on the experiences of a Catholic war-time officer, as in many other novels, contrived to invent memorable comic actors in an apparently disordered and farcical world and yet at the same time increasingly to convey a serious message beneath the satire. In another trilogy L. P. Hartley described the middle-class scene between the wars and the relationship of a brother and sister, Eustace and Hilda, through childhood and adult life.

A genre which was important since, at its best, it combined serious scholarship with imaginative fiction, was the historical novel. In the post-war world this seemed especially to attract women writers. H. F. M. Prescott turned to the 1530s for *The Man on a Donkey*. Mary Renault wrote a series of novels on the Theseus legend. Stephanie Plowman vividly described the last years of Czarist Russia and the Revolution. Georgette Heyer's popular romances generally took the Regency period as their setting, Margaret Irwin concentrated after the war on the life of Elizabeth I, while Jean Plaidy ranged from fifteenth century Rome to the French Revolution in search of themes. Less frequently men also turned to history for their backgrounds. Henry Treece wrote particularly for children. Rex Warner chose classical subjects. Events in Britain and Germany in 1923 played an essential part in *The Fox in the Attic*, by Richard Hughes. L. P. Hartley's sensitive account of the relationship of a boy with his contemporaries and elders, *The Go-between*, portrayed also the relations of gentry and village in 1900.

An exotic scene, colourful, squalid or backward, had always brought an original and arresting element to fiction. Before the war Joyce Cary had made good use of his knowledge of West Africa. After 1945, with improved facilities for rapid travel, geography was added to history as a factor in a large number of novels. Lawrence Durrell set his fictional characters in Corfu and Cyprus as well as in Alexandria. Some of Anthony Burgess's outrageously inventive novels were set in Malaya, where the author was an education officer in the Colonial Service. John Masters exploited his knowledge of India, Nevil Shute's later novels had the Far East and Australia as their background, Ian Fleming set his best-selling suspense novels in various countries from Japan to the Caribbean. Graham Greene, whose reputation had already been assured before the war, confirmed his significance as a novelist with works of even more varied settings than those called into service by his contemporaries: Mexico, Vienna, West Africa, Cuba, Vietnam and the Congo. Greene was interesting for his skill in making the thriller into a serious literary form, for his technique of introducing into his writing 'shots' characteristic of the film, and for the Catholic philosophy which underlay some of his books.

Fantasy might lead in any direction, particularly, perhaps, towards oblivion. One long work published in the fifties evoked unusual interest, however: J. R. R. Tolkien's *The Lord of the Rings*. This combination of myth and romance, with its remarkable diversity of characters and scenes, comic and serious, made a wide appeal to those who sought an imaginary world which could still have some relevance to the human condition. Another imaginary world, depicted in another lengthy trilogy, was Mervyn Peake's account of Titus Groan. John Wyndham's contributions to science fiction, beginning in 1951 with *The Day of the Triffids*, quickly became popular. William Golding, while peopling his novels with human beings, nonetheless produced a number of symbolical fables in which an improbable situation exposed serious moral issues. The first of these books, *The Lord of the Flies*, was published in 1954. Two other pieces of symbolism which had by then become very celebrated were George Orwell's contrasting condemnations of dictatorship, *Animal Farm* and *Nineteen Eighty-Four*. A later novel which made a particular impression by its combination of satire and fantasy was Nigel Dennis's *Cards of Identity*.

Yet another feature of the fifties was the emergence of several novelists, all born in the early twenties, whose works seemed entertainingly to symbolise a repudiation of conventional values. John Wain and Kingsley Amis enjoyed immediate success with *Hurry on Down* and *Lucky Jim*. *Room at the Top*, by John Braine, concerned a young man who was not prepared to allow scruples to impede his worldly progress. Four slightly younger writers whose inside knowledge of working-class life enabled them to publish books which were regarded as widening the scope of the novel (and, incidentally, of the film) were Alan Sillitoe, David Storey, Keith Waterhouse and Stan Barstow. Three women writers whose different varieties of originality drew attention to their novels were Elizabeth Taylor, Muriel Spark and Iris Murdoch. Angus Wilson examined the impact on a number of liberal and distinguished characters of forces of cruelty and harshness in their worlds. Patrick White, a Londoner, educated in England, gained a Nobel prize for novels written in Australia. Henry Green, Nicholas Monsarrat, H. E. Bates, William Cooper, John Fowles, Michael Frayn. . . . Each reader's list would no doubt be different.

There was one limitation. British authors, without the personal experiences that the Continent had suffered from Nazism and Communism at their most evil, could not easily base their works on the most fearful of twentieth century tragedies. Otherwise their field was almost unbounded; their achievement was varied and notable.

It was estimated, in 1963, that there were working in Britain between 45 000 and 50 000 authors, apart from those who were writing technical or educational books. Only about 6500 or 7000 were full-time professional writers, and of these only a small proportion (13 per cent was suggested) derived more than £1500 a year from their craft.[1] More books were sold, particularly when the production of paperbacks became general: but expenses increased and profits declined, and the commercial lending libraries began rapidly to disappear. Fortunately for the writers, new occupations developed or increased in number and allowed them to pursue their interests while earning a regular income from some more routine avocation. As the B.B.C. served as a patron of musicians, so did university teaching, journalism, broadcasting or publishing help to support imaginative writers as well as scholars following their own specialised lines. Others had pursued careers as schoolmasters or civil servants until literary success had enabled them to concentrate on writing.

There was one sphere where a slump in sales was especially marked: verse. A little known poet could hope to sell only about 300 copies of a volume, however good the poems may have been. Yet publication figures did not alter substantially during the post-war years, and opportunities for the appearance of individual poems were offered by the Press and the weekly journals; and when a reputation had been established by a poet of the stature of T. S. Eliot (1888–1965), W. H. Auden (1907–73), Louis MacNeice (1907–63), Dylan Thomas (1914–53) or John Betjeman (1906) the public was prepared to buy collected editions. Betjeman, in particular, became known for verse which was readily comprehensible and, thanks to its witty juxtaposition of unexpected ideas, entertaining.

Other poets were helped by the appearance of their writings in anthologies, some of which were studied in schools. In this way writers like Vernon Watkins (1906–67), Roy Fuller (1912), R. S. Thomas (1913), Philip Larkin and Donald Davie (both born in 1922), Thom Gunn (1929) and Jon Silkin (1930) reached at least some sort of public. A further group had some success in the late sixties with more easily understandable verse which was designed to be read to an audience.

ARCHITECTURE

The continuity characteristic of literature and music was not revealed so obviously in architecture. Post-war building was quite distinctive. It was affected not only by new techniques but by a shortage of materials, of skilled labour and, increasingly, of land. In response to developing social needs it found expression in schools and university buildings, power stations and office blocks, and new towns or large-scale extensions of old ones. With the abandonment of the pre-war limitation on height to 100 feet (nine or ten storeys) office blocks could rise to thirty storeys or more. With the end of inter-war restrictions on the number of new houses per acre architects could plan estates on which private gardens no longer figured and life in flats became increasingly normal. Functionalism could be carried to an extreme since neither money nor time allowed the emphasis on the needless decoration which characterised buildings of earlier periods. Distinction lay instead in bulk, height, and the grouping of skyscrapers. Britain was not, of course, unique. Similar tendencies were to be found, indeed, in all westernised countries. An outlet for the experiments of a considerable number of architects was provided in 1951 by the Festival of Britain, on London's South Bank, under the direction of Hugh Casson. A Dome of Discovery and pavilions devoted to such features of life as transport, power and production, the countryside, sea and ships suggested to the great number of visitors the potentialities of architecture when combined with engineering and technological skill. The buildings, apart from Robert Matthew's Royal Festival Hall, were dismantled, but the recollection of bold originality may have lingered.

More permanent than the Festival were the 100 new schools of Hertfordshire, designed by C. H. Aslin and W. A. Henderson during the decade after the war. Prefabricated and standardised parts were essential features of these schools, since they saved both material and labour and could be adapted to varying requirements and local topography. Glass and flat roofs were characteristic. Such methods were followed elsewhere, and in 1957 a 'Consortium of Local Authorities Special Programme' came into being with the aim of extending the construction of prefabricated schools at low cost by a small labour force. As the Welfare State extended its scope, so did expectations, and except in times of crisis school building all over Britain absorbed an appreciable proportion of rates and taxes. Much architectural experiment was lavished, meanwhile, on the construction of the new universities or the extension of the old. Basil Spence designed extensions at Durham, Exeter, Liverpool, Newcastle, Nottingham and Southampton. His buildings for the University of Sussex were precursors of the modern structures at the other new universities of the 1960s. At Oxford and Cambridge expanding numbers of undergraduates made necessary the addition to long undisturbed colleges of new rooms in experimental styles which on occasions harmonised with their environment and were nearly always original and individual. These were the symbols of the period. Earlier symbols, the churches, were on the other hand finding it hard to avoid conversion to museums, concert halls, dwellings or ruins. Few new ones were built. Two, though, were outstanding: Coventry Cathedral, rebuilt on its bombed foundations between 1954 and 1962 to the design of Basil Spence, and Liverpool Catholic Cathedral, of which the architect was Frederick Gibberd.

Symbols as important as the educational buildings and, because of their isolation, even more striking, were the power stations. Whereas the best-known of the pre-war power stations, at Battersea, had been predominantly of brick, those devoted to nuclear energy made greater use of such light materials as glass, aluminium and asbestos. Some were condemned as objectionably obtrusive in fine surroundings (Trawsfynydd, for example, had its critics) but most were established in bleak environments and were designed with care by such architects as Frank Farmer, Bernard Dark and Frederick Gibberd, who did what was possible to integrate the buildings into the geographical background. Similar endeavours were made with many of the new factories. Where it was possible to start from scratch factories could be grouped with serious consideration of their visual effect: the new town factory areas at Stevenage, Hemel Hempstead, Crawley and East Kilbride were among the best.

Some endeavour was made also to consider the impact of the office skyscrapers which dominated the centres of an ever-increasing number of British towns as land values continued to soar and made ground space ever more precious. The Vickers Building with thirty-four storeys, the highest in London, was given a curved façade by its architects, Ronald Ward and Partners. The London Hilton Hotel was built with a Y-shaped ground plan. Tower blocks were sometimes designed to rise from lower blocks of only two or three storeys. Very many, though, were open to the criticism that they were merely rectangles of concrete and glass, lacking in individuality, and tributes more to engineering skill than to architectural ingenuity. Standing in isolation tower blocks could seem disproportionately intrusive. Where they could be grouped in considerable numbers, of varying heights, they sometimes developed a certain monstrous beauty, as they did in Croydon.

Towers were also built to replace houses in the decayed areas of old towns. During the decade after the war new housing estates were built in various parts of London (the L.C.C. estate at Roehampton, the Spa Green Flats at Finsbury, the Golden Lane estate in the City of London, for example) and all were characterised by buildings of up to twelve storeys and by serious attempts to fit them to their environments. Grass and trees were planted, modern heating methods were introduced, windows were better designed. And, often, unexpected social problems were created for those living in the high flats. Outside London height was less necessary, but there could be no return to the extravagant use of land for the houses built between the wars. The new and enlarged towns abandoned the idea of the garden city and replaced it by terrace housing grouped around rectangular communal gardens, each unit providing its limited number of occupants with adequate but never over-generous space. Monuments to Victorian affluence, large families and servants were, where they were in the way, destroyed. The new precincts became at the same time architectural and social experiments.

PAINTING AND SCULPTURE

Art seemed now to be firmly committed to the subjective, personal vision of invented or imagined shapes. Painters retained their individuality. One development did not follow another logically, and no generalisation about the works produced would be valid. There seemed nothing in common between the paintings of Stanley Spencer (1891–1959) on the one hand, and the abstract designs of rectangles and curved lines by Ben Nicholson (born 1894) or the sinister, disturbing distortions of Francis Bacon (b. 1910) on the other. Graham Sutherland and John Piper (both born in 1903) combined reality with visions of their own. Others concentrated on purely abstract or surrealist works which may have conveyed a message to some who viewed them and undoubtedly left others deeply perplexed. Perhaps those who achieved the greatest success with the non-expert public were those whose works were clearly neither camera studies nor unrecognisable as human or natural subjects: L. S. Lowry (b. 1887), for example, with his scenes of crowds in drab industrial cities, or, from another generation, John Bratby (b. 1928), who brought a combination of expressionism and realism to domestic scenes.

Sculptors, like painters, sought to convey an idea by nonnaturalistic means, either by carving stone into shapes that hinted at reality instead of reproducing it or by associating various metal pieces which might have evoked some thought in the mind of the beholder. Much sculpture expressed the tortured spirit that was believed to be characteristic of the age. Henry Moore, Barbara Hepworth, and Reg Butler were leading exponents of the two styles.

HISTORY

The necessarily restricted and subjective résumé of the arts since 1945 could profitably end with a reference to writing on History. A subject which embraced or impinged upon so many others had become too significant to be ignored. Studied, alone or with associated subjects, at almost every British university, it steadily replaced classical languages for the student of the so-called humanities. It provided the themes of approximately 220 new books each year during the 1950s and of a rapidly increasing number during the next decade: the annual average 1966-70 was 1045. With new editions, translations, and biographies and memoirs, the grand total of 775 in 1950 (628 of them new books) rose to 2549 in 1968 (of which 1767 were new).

It probably did more than most academic studies to influence the political and social attitudes of those who read it. Controlled by governments with Nazi or Communist political philosophies, its facts carefully selected to illuminate the virtues of totalitarian or 'classless' societies and to denigrate the actions of governments or individuals of opposing views, it could be a potent factor in forming prejudices of the required kind. In the hands of writers who regarded facts, on both sides of an argument, as sacred, it could provide a valuable lesson to a democratic society which had to recognise that one side or one individual rarely possessed a monopoly of wisdom. British historians strove to place scholarship above indoctrination. They acknowledged that complete impartiality was difficult to attain, that facts and characters were open to varying interpretations and that the selection of material might unintentionally convey a bias to a reader. Yet not even historians of Marxist sympathies could allow an emphasis on economic factors to involve an unscrupulous manipulation of the facts. Standards of impartiality set by such series as the Oxford Histories of England and the New Cambridge Modern Histories were high. Standards of research which in a generation enormously increased knowledge of the Dark Ages in Britain were as notable as the scholarship which so greatly enhanced an understanding of the economic and social history of later centuries or spheres of study like the histories of Russia, Germany and Africa, which had previously been followed by only a limited number of British writers. An increasing tendency to study developments in Britain as features of European or global developments also characterised British post-war historical writing.

The study was neither confined to nor designed merely for scholars. Biographers and well-informed popularisers wrote for a public which was also provided with a high proportion of articles on historical themes in successful weekly periodicals or the colour supplements of the week-end Press. The large number of English language histories or translations from the English on the shelves of German bookshops in the fifties and sixties suggested that these were not designed purely for an insular public; and the histories which the Germans wrote themselves as the period of Nazism receded suggested that respect for impartiality had triumphed in other countries apart from Britain. This was encouraging. A common regard for the facts and a general Western endeavour to eliminate, as far as possible, the more outrageous forms of bias may have been small factors in bringing the Western world together. They were, nonetheless, indispensable if Europe were not to revert to the barbarism which threatened its destruction during the decade before 1945.

---

[1] Estimates by Richard Findlater, quoted by J. W. Saunders, *Profession of English Letters*, p. 227, Routledge and Kegan Paul Ltd (1964)

Index

399